GEORGE W
Legacy of
Leadership

A. WARD BURIAN

New York

GEORGE WASHINGTON'S
Legacy of Leadership

by A. Ward Burian
© 2007 A. Ward Burian. All rights reserved.

Published by:

MORGAN · JAMES
THE ENTREPRENEURIAL PUBLISHER ™
www.morganjamespublishing.com

Morgan James Publishing, LLC
1225 Franklin Ave. Ste 325
Garden City, NY 11530-1693
Toll Free 800-485-4943
www.MorganJamesPublishing.com

Librarty of Congress Cataloging-in-Publication Data

Burian, A. Ward
George Washington's Legacy of Leadership
p. cm.
Includes index
ISBN: 978-1-60037-161-5 (paperback)
History/Biography
Library of Congress Control Number: 2007921604

Interior Design by:
Bonnie Bushman
bbushman@bresnan.net

*Houdon's 1785 sculpture considered
to be the most accurate likeness of
George Washington.
Photograph by Mark Gulezian.
Courtesy of the
Mount Vernon Ladies Association.*

Dedication

To the memory of George Washington whose courage and vision forged the foundation of the American Republic. His personal virtues and leadership skills represent timeless qualities that should serve as inspirations for those who cherish freedom and democracy.

Every noble work is at first impossible.

—Thomas Carlyle (1795–1881)
Scottish philosopher

Acknowledgments

Some assistance is helpful in the creation of most books, and, while this one was a solitary effort, I would like to thank several people who made its publication possible:

First, David Hancock, the founder of Morgan James Publishing, was the first "outsider" to read the manuscript and believed it was of sufficient value for publication.

Second, Bridget Reddick did the editing, and her eagle eye and computer skills were most helpful.

My special thanks to Gerald Kahler, formerly of Williamsburg and a most ardent Washington scholar, whose extensive library was of great assistance.

The Swem Library and the Omohundro Institute of Early American History and Culture at the College of William and Mary provided excellent sources for material.

The silhouette of George Washington is taken from Mark Gulezian's photo of Houdon's famous sculpture done in 1785. My thanks go to Dawn Bonner and Shandel Johnson at the Mount Vernon Ladies Association for extending permission to use this photograph.

Finally, encouragement from friends and my wife, Martha, who appreciated my deep admiration of George Washington and provided the impetus for completing this work.

Contents

Preface

$\mathcal{T}$he purpose of this book is to bring George Washington back into the life of all Americans—young and old as well as long-established or newly created citizens. If we know the incredible story of how one man changed the course of history, we will know most everything about the critical events that surrounded the Revolutionary War and the founding of the United States. This is not meant to be a scholarly work filled with new research and insights. Hundreds of biographers from as early as David Humphreys and John Marshall in 1801 to David Hackett Fischer and Joseph J. Ellis in 2004 have given us ample research about Washington's life. I have attempted to study a good cross-section of some of our past and present historians and have concentrated on Washington's major contributions to the cause for freedom. I have tried to bring out more of the recent scholarship on Washington, revealed within the past ten years, that has given us much better insight into Washington's character and motivations as well as his early political experience. I have conveyed his life in strict chronological order so we can see how Washington developed from a relatively obscure farmer's son and loyal British subject into an American revolutionary and then into the leader of a new nation and the most famous man on earth. We will then study his character and learn what enabled him to achieve such extraordinary success. We will see how the renunciation of his military and then his political power caused his adversary, King George III, to call him the greatest man in the world. By learning about Washington's motivations and policies, we can discover his comprehensive and visionary leadership. We will see why Henry Lee in his eulogy to Congress referred to Washington as "first in war, first in peace, and first in the hearts of his countrymen." To Americans and foreigners of that time, George Washington symbolized the United States. He represented something new and special. He was someone to admire and be proud of. For over one hundred and fifty years after his death, Americans remembered him with reverence and honored him. Sadly, that changed in the 1960s and 1970s, and for most of the past fifty years our high schools and colleges have relegated him to mere footnotes in their declining emphasis on history. However, within the past ten years there has been a renewed interest in Washington. Ironically, this book was started before the 2004 release of David Hackett Fischer's *Washington's Crossing,* Joseph Ellis's *His Excellency: George Washington* and Bruce Chadwick's *George Washington's War.* Each work treats Washington with a different emphasis, and each brings out new facts and information resulting from ongoing research. With this biography, it is my intention to keep the current renaissance in Washington alive and to give the reader the scope of his entire life in an easy-to-read format so one may appreciate the enormity of his many contributions to the birth of the American nation. In the Appendix, I have added a table showing the genealogy of George Washington, which also shows the generational inheritance of Mount Vernon.

For those who wish to learn more about our Founding Father I have included a brief description of the major educational monuments and sites that are available to the public.

Williamsburg, Virginia

A. Ward Burian

Introduction

A nation reveals itself not only by the men it produces but also by the men it honors, the men it remembers.

—John F. Kennedy
President of the United States of America

The search for George Washington, the man, continues, and the more we learn about his extraordinary life the more our admiration of him grows. He has been described as "the Founding Father," "the Indispensable Man," "Best of Men," "a Great and Good Man," "Patriarch," "the Father of His Country," "the First of Men" and so many more epithets that he has assumed a mystical personage beyond our grasp. Here was a man who had no formal education and no early political influence or great family wealth, and yet through natural leadership skills, determination and a grand vision he achieved so much more than most people know or comprehend. In fact, his life defined the spirit of the new American nation with its sense of fairness, loyalty, work ethic, fierce independence and optimism for the future. Washington was not perfect in every personal or professional sense, but he was a perfectionist who inspired confidence in those around him. He trusted his advisors and associates and treated them with respect in spite of some detractors who tried to undermine him.

Washington was slow to anger, and he worked all his life to control his emotions. On rare occasions he lost his temper in Congress, at Cabinet meetings and on the battlefield. His colleague, Gouverneur Morris, reported that Washington had violent passions and had to learn self-control. Such moments were betrayed by stony silence, but those around him knew what he was thinking. As his responsibilities grew, he was keenly aware that his opinions were closely listened to and were very influential. For this reason he tried diligently to conceal these lest he stifle open discussions or reach a premature conclusion. As a result, many have thought of him as aloof and cold. However, his warmth and kindness can be seen in his early life with his brother, with his step-children, with some of his military aides and officers, upon his farewells and in his retirement years.[1] Considering the stress he endured with his awesome responsibilities, it is no wonder he acquired a serious countenance. But when these pressures were relieved just after his military and then political retirements, his more genial and sensitive nature emerged.

The emergence of George Washington at such a critical moment in history could be seen as Providential in much the same way as John Winthrop was regarded in the leadership of the Massachusetts Bay Colony in the 1600s. Washington's early life was uncertain upon his father's premature death leaving George with very little education or preparation for a career. His guidance by a half-brother, his survival from smallpox and other life-threatening illnesses, his narrow military escapes, his early rejections for a commission by the British army and the despair of the Continental Army were enough to defeat even the bravest and most experienced of men. But George Washington surmounted all the obstacles in his path and emerged as one of the greatest

1   Richard Brookhiser, Founding Father, Rediscovering George Washington (New York: Simon & Schuster, Inc., 1996) 5-6. Copyright by Richard Brookhiser. Reprinted with permission of The Free Press, a Division of Simon & Schuster Adult Publishing Group. All rights reserved.

leaders in all of history. He did this with the self-developed skills of controlled ambition, restraint, listening, observing, faith, compassion, civility and discipline. He had strong beliefs and convictions about his goals and followed them throughout his life. He has left us 135,000 individual letters, documents, speeches and diary notes—more material than any of the forty-three presidents in our history.[2] Perhaps his greatest gift to America was his vision of what this nation could become and his untiring efforts to accomplish that vision. He was a legend from the age of twenty-seven following his exploits in the French and Indian War, and he was considered the "Father of His Country" following the Revolutionary War long before he was president. During his final hours we can only hope that he sensed some satisfaction for his lifetime of sacrifices to his country when he uttered his final words on December 14, 1799—"'tis well."

---

2   Frank E. Grizzard, Jr., *George Washington: A Biographical Companion* (Santa Barbara: California, 2002) 361.

CHAPTER 1
Family Background

Aspire to the Heavens.

—The Washington Family Motto

To more fully understand George Washington, one should learn about his ancestors and in particular his great-grandfather, John Washington, who was the first Washington to arrive in America. The Washington family can be traced back to eleventh-century England, and their history is one of educated and civic-minded people who were loyal to their king, church and country. Oddly enough, it was the life of Lawrence Washington and his son, John, in the mid-1600s that changed the future course of England, America and the world. The Reverend Lawrence Washington was born in 1602 into a family that had a six hundred-year history in England. The Washingtons had achieved a highly respectable "county Family" position and were staunch royalists. Relatives included knighted courtiers, pages to the court of James I, descendents of King Edward III, and the Churchills.[1] In 1616, their ancestral home, Sulgrave Manor, in Northhamptonshire was sold. Lawrence's uncle and great-uncle were graduated from Oxford University where Lawrence attended Brasenose College

---

1   Willard Sterne Randall, *George Washington: A Life* (New York: Henry Holt & Co., 1997) 8.

and was graduated in 1623. At the age of twenty-four he was elected Lector of Brasenose, and at twenty-nine he was one of two university proctors appointed by Archbishop of Canterbury William Laud who was also Chancellor of Oxford and the agent of King Charles I who was active in the suppression of Puritanism.[2] Lawrence was appointed the vicar of Purleigh Parish in Essex in 1633 just having married Amphyllis, the daughter and co-heiress of John Twigden. Their son, John, was born in 1633 either in Spratton, Northhamptonshire, or at his mother's home in Tring, Hertfordshire. The Washington's close association with royalty is evidenced by their receiving a petition from Charles I for nine-year-old John to be admitted to the highly regarded Charterhouse School in London for "schollers." However, that all changed with the outbreak of the English Civil War in 1642 when Charles was deposed. John was then educated at a lesser school and by his tutor father. Later records in Virginia reveal that John was well versed in Latin and apparently received a sound classical education from his father. Lawrence was branded a "Malignant Royalist," and consequently in 1643 he was removed from his comfortable position at Purleigh where his house and possessions were confiscated by the Roundheads. Approximately twenty-eight hundred clerics were removed from their positions by the Puritans. The distraught family was then sheltered by Lawrence's Aunt Margaret, wife of Sir Edwin Sandys.[3] As treasurer of the Virginia Company and one of the earliest investors in the tobacco trade, the Sandys connection may have helped young John, who had moved to London to be apprenticed to a merchant. It is more likely that his mother's brother-in-law, William Roades, who managed an estate in Virginia for the Verney family, assisted John.[4] John

---

2   Willard Sterne Randall, *George Washington: A Life* (New York: Henry Holt & Co., 1997) 9.
3   Ibid., 10.
4   Chares Arthur Hoppin, *The Washington Ancestry* (Greenfield, Ohio: Published privately for Edward Lee McClain, 1932) vol. 1, 146.

was employed in a counting house in the London ports where business was booming with the country's maritime expansion. As England competed with France, Holland and Spain for new markets and trading routes, many opportunities for profitable trading became available to strong, smart and adventuresome young men. Lawrence had been appointed to another smaller parish and became impoverished for the rest of his life. It is likely that John remained in London after his early schooling to find a career for himself owing to his family's difficult situation. John was essentially on his own, and, after several years of apprenticeship, he decided to use his small inheritance and good contacts to seek a career in overseas commerce and particularly in the export of tobacco from America to England. When his father died in 1652, John was out of the country and unable to attend the funeral. He also could not participate in the handling of the estate because he was under the legal age of twenty-one. He must have become a qualified navigator in the years 1650 to 1654, because in 1654 he sailed as second mate on Captain Edward Prescott's cargo ship *Sarah,* which plied between England and Barbados and possibly Virginia. John returned to England in 1654 to administer his recently deceased mother's estate. In 1656, Prescott asked John to meet him in Dantzic, Poland, and they then sailed to Copenhagen, Denmark, where he negotiated contracts for overseas cargoes.[5] Prescott was not affiliated with any of the large London or Glasgow traders, but he seems to have owned several smaller trading ships to engage in a market that was open to all entrepreneurs. These included the *Hannah, Sarah* and *Sea Horse of London.* Prescott offered Washington a partnership in one of the cargoes, and John used his inheritance to invest in the cargo on the *Sea Horse,* which he was to sail to Virginia

---

5   Chares Arthur Hoppin, *The Washington Ancestry* (Greenfield, Ohio: Published privately for Edward Lee McClain, 1932) vol. 1, 145.

by way of the Azores and Barbados. After he offloaded goods he was to return to London with a cargo of Virginia tobacco. He successfully reached his destination on the Potomac River in late 1656 or early 1657 near Pope's Creek, about thirty miles south of Alexandria. After the ship was loaded, it blew aground in a storm in the river with the total loss of the tobacco and most of his personal effects. John was able to re-float and rescue the ship, but Prescott refused to pay him his share of the delivered goods because he blamed John for the damages that he sustained. After losing his investment, John was left with nothing. Prescott again sailed to Virginia in 1658 with John's brother, Lawrence, but he never settled his accounts with John who had filed a lawsuit against him. According to Nathaniel Pope, Prescott was a difficult man to deal with, and, as a justice of the Westmorland court, Pope tried to intercede in the Washington-Prescott dispute. Prescott was even accused of hanging a woman for witchcraft on his 1658 voyage to Virginia, and even though Lawrence was witness to it, John considered the case too weak to pursue. Upon his arrival in the winter of 1656–57, John met Nathaniel Pope almost immediately; it is likely that Pope was a customer of Prescott. Pope had settled in that region about twenty-five years earlier and became a successful tobacco planter and a member of the Maryland Assembly.[6] He was elderly and took a quick liking to Washington, who had the unusual credentials of being an Oxford don's son, a navigator and someone who knew the tobacco trade. John and Nathaniel developed a close relationship, and to help him get started Nathaniel loaned him £80 in gold and the possibility of a bequest of seven hundred acres on the water. In December of 1658, John married Nathaniel's daughter Ann. Their wedding present from her father was a seven hundred-acre estate on Mattox Creek where their son Lawrence was born in

---

6   Randall, 11.

1659. Ann also gave birth to two children who died in infancy as well as to John and Ann, who survived their parents. Shortly after the marriage, Nathaniel Pope appointed John to administer all his family's lands, which marked the beginning of a life of land acquisitions by John and eventually by his grandson, Augustine, and his great-grandson, George.

As John settled into Westmorland County, he served as an officer in the Virginia militia and as a member of the House of Burgesses. By 1662, he was appointed a judge, became a vestryman of the local Anglican Church and later rose to Major in the Virginia militia. He was tall, strong, athletic and greatly respected by the community. His military, civil and judicial appointments were based on merit and abilities and not on political favors. He was known to be bold, straight-forward, level-headed and determined. Throughout the 1660s and 1670s, John acquired by gift, purchase and grant approximately nine thousand acres of land close to the Potomac River. He has been criticized for "insider trading" through a practice of surveying land just before its unfulfilled patent was scheduled to expire. If the original patent did expire, he supposedly filed a patent for himself and other partners. In 1666, after he took a seat in the Colonial Assembly and became a member of the House of Burgesses, Washington broached the subject of Indian occupation on his land in northern Westmorland County. Contrary to some historians' accounts, he did not take forcible measures to remove the Nanzatico Indians. Instead, he respected the Burgesses' order to reoccupy his land only when the Indians deserted it. Local Indian tribes reportedly gave him the name "Conotocarious" which translates to "town taker," and this gave rise to the myth that he savagely eliminated the Indian occupants. Historian Charles Arthur Hoppin ascribes the myth to Moncure Conway who described Washington's fierceness with the

Indians in his 1892 book *Barons of the Rappahannock*. Conway alleged that Washington was "rebuked" by Governor Berkeley for his behavior. In fact, Conway is discredited because he confused Indiantown on the Appomattox River near Petersburg with Appomattox Creek (also referred to as Mattox Creek). The latter was in Westmorland County where John and Ann first settled following her father's wedding gift.

In 1662, John Washington was appointed a justice of the court, and his reputation for being level-headed and loyal to the government is noted by historian and Washington family biographer Charles Hoppin. Washington was held in the highest regard by Governor Berkeley, and it is unlikely that he would disobey the English policy of peaceful relations with the Native American Indian tribes in the 1660s or in 1676 with Bacon's Rebellion. In 1667, John erected a fort at Levy Point on the Yeocomico River near the Potomac to protect vitally needed shipping in that area. By 1669, John was concurrently a justice of Westmorland County, a member of the House of Burgesses and Lieutenant Colonel of the Virginia military. He was one of the two chief men of the county responsible for arms and ammunition for the people and for organizing them into companies and training and commanding them. In 1672, he was named president of the Court of Westmorland. He was close to the most illustrious governor of Virginia, Sir William Berkeley, who relied on only three men: Major John Washington, Colonel Nicholas Spencer and Major Issac Allerton.

In 1675, the English discovered a plot by New England Indians to destroy them, and this event led to the opening of King Philip's War. In Maryland Nathaniel Bacon asked Governor Berkeley for permission to war against the Indian tribes. When permission was denied, Bacon proceeded to take matters into his own hands, and his killing of Indians in Maryland prompted more killings in Virginia. Berkeley appointed John Washington to deal with the growing hostilities. He was given a free hand to fight them or negotiate with them, and on his shoulders rested war or peace. The British were extremely sensitive to maintaining a good relationship with the Native Americans, and Washington and Allerton (a Harvard graduate), as the newly appointed Indian Commissioners, were well aware of that policy. When they arrived in Maryland the Indians had just emerged from their fort to allegedly negotiate with the local Marylanders, who promptly massacred five of their representatives. Maryland Major Trueman tried to pass the blame to Washington and Allerton, but after an official investigation ordered by Berkeley, they were exonerated, and the Maryland Assembly later impeached Trueman for the murders. In 1676, Berkeley pardoned Bacon for his traitorous acts, which history has labeled Bacon's Rebellion. Immediately thereafter, Bacon proceeded to Jamestown where he turned against the government, broke into the House of Burgesses and proclaimed himself the supreme head of the military and the civil government. He raided the properties of the government officials and tried to overturn Washington's authority. He recognized the importance of Washington's position but was unsuccessful because of Washington's loyalty to Berkeley who was then in hiding for his life. In September of 1676, Governor Berkeley returned to Jamestown which then provoked Bacon to burn the capital as well as the first church built in America. Bacon fell ill and died on October 1, 1676. His estate was forfeited to the king. Berkeley returned to England where he died on July 13, 1677. Historians have suggested that the dissensions and conflicts among the whites actually saved Virginia from a devastating war with the Indians. Both races were engaged in a struggle for survival and dominance on the continent, which was not settled until the conclusion of the French and Indian War in 1763, almost one hundred years later. John Washington actually sustained losses to his estate as a result of the 1670s conflict, but he never made a claim against the county or colony other than reimbursement for his expenses in suppressing the rebellion.

In 1669, John Washington and Nicholas Spencer surveyed five thousand acres along the Potomac River about thirty miles north of Pope's Creek. The tract was located between Little Hunting Creek on the north and Dogue Creek to the south. Five years later they received a grant for the land from the Proprietor of the Northern Neck, Lord Thomas Culpeper of Leeds Castle, Kent, England, who owned five million acres in northern Virginia that encompassed the grant to Washington and Spencer. The five-year delay was attributed to Lord Culpeper waiting for an official charter on the Northern Neck which he finally obtained in 1673. His daughter and heiress, Catherine, married Thomas, the Fifth Lord Fairfax, which brought Fairfax the five million acres in Virginia. Catherine's son, Thomas, the Sixth Lord Fairfax, came to Virginia in 1734 where he built Belvoir Manor. In 1743, John's first great-grandson and George's older half-brother, Lawrence, married Ann Fairfax which union introduced young George to the new world of aristocratic society and one of his most influential mentors, Colonel William Fairfax who was Anne's father and the cousin and land agent of Lord Thomas Fairfax.

The five thousand acres on the Potomac were granted jointly and equally in 1674 to Lieutenant Nicholas Spencer and John Washington. We do not know when they petitioned for the grant or if it was influenced by Charles II in recognition of past loyalties to the crown and the losses sustained by John's parents under the Roundheads. The grant was subject to the usual quit-rent, which in this instance was two shillings annually per one hundred acres. The grantees were required to "plant (usually a minimum of one acre) and Seat (build a house) the sd. Lands, or cause the Same to be planted or Seated within the tenure of three years next ensuing the date hereof." If these conditions were not met, the grant would become null and void.

Very little else is known about John Washington owing in part to the loss of his personal letters and diaries. These were possibly lost with the sinking of the *Sea Horse* or with the fire that destroyed George's Pope's Creek birthplace, Wakefield, in 1779. John was unquestionably one of the leading citizens of Virginia and enjoyed an outstanding reputation. It is also recorded that he personally arranged and paid for the emigration of sixty-three white indentured servants from England to start a new life in America. He obtained the "Head Rights" of fifty acres for each servant he brought over and indentured them for five to seven years in the clearing and cultivating of his land.[7] Many of these men went on to build their own farms, plant tobacco and prosper, realizing the American dream of self-sufficiency and personal independence. John apparently inherited the Washington characteristics for leadership, eminent citizenship and a sense of loyalty to church and state. Many of these traits were evident in his father's mother, Margaret Butler Washington, who was known for her noble and royal ancestry. After his first wife, Ann Pope, died in 1668, John married widower Anne Brodhurst Brett, who bore no children by him. After her death he married Frances (Gerrard) Speke-Payton-Appleton who also bore him no children. John died in 1677 at the age of forty-four leaving his half-interest in the five thousand Little Hunting Creek acres to his son Lawrence.

---

7   Randall, 12.

John Washington had prepared his will on September 21, 1675, four days preceding his confrontation with the Indians in Maryland and in obvious anticipation of a possible conflict with them.[8] The inventory called for in the will has never been found, but it was valued at £377. The original will was found among George Washington's private papers and was sold at auction in 1891 for $700, but it is now inaccessible in private hands. However, a copy of the original was made in 1891. John's estate was divided equally among his wife and their three children; Lawrence, John and Ann. The Washingtons did not practice primogeniture, but Lawrence did receive most of the land as well as a share in the water mill. Lawrence married Mildred Warner, the daughter of the late Speaker of the House of Burgesses and a member of the governor's council. Lawrence became a member of the House of Burgesses and a sheriff of Westmorland County. He died at age thirty-seven.

It is interesting that Lawrence's will does not mention any improvements (house) on the Little Hunting Creek land. In 1690, the five thousand acres were split evenly between Lawrence and the widow of Nicholas Spencer. Because Lawrence acquired the western portion, considered more valuable, he paid Madame Spencer £2,500. The surveyor, George Brent, showed small crude houses on each portion of the divided land with a house on the Little Hunting Creek piece located about 1.5 miles north of the present mansion. In 1698, Lawrence bequeathed his twenty-five hundred acres to his daughter Mildred. There is no record showing whether he erected another house or improved the property in any way during his lifetime. Mildred and her husband, Roger Gregory, released the property to her brother Augustine Washington in 1726 for the consideration of £180. Upon Augustine's death in 1743, his son Lawrence (by his first wife, Jane Butler) inherited

8   Hoppin, 205-207.

Little Hunting Creek. Lawrence built a mansion house there for his bride, Ann Fairfax, whom he married that same year. It was Lawrence who renamed the estate "Mount Vernon" in honor of his British commander, Admiral Edward Vernon, with whom he served in the military campaign against the Spanish in Cartagena, Columbia. Mount Vernon was later inherited by Lawrence's half-brother, George, and it remained in the Washington family until 1858 when it was sold to the Mount Vernon Ladies' Association by John A. Washington, Jr., for $200,000.

The most remarkable aspects of John Washington's life were the civil and military responsibilities he assumed at a young age after arriving in America with almost nothing. He had inherited virtuous qualities, a love for acquiring land and a strong sense of loyalty to his government and country. He was considered a fair-minded person who cherished the importance of maintaining an honest reputation. He was courageous and determined and achieved much during his relatively brief forty-four years. It is a startling testimony to the significance of genes that so many attributes of John Washington were almost identical to those of his great-grandson, George, one hundred years later, especially as George reportedly knew very little about his great-grandfather or his ancestors. Examination of John Washington puts the life of George Washington into perspective; the virtues, stamina and abilities that George possessed did not suddenly emerge from nowhere. John's unusual gifts flowed through the veins of the Washington family, and he and his great-grandson demonstrated the power of such a noble inheritance.

John's male descendants were to inherit his traits for the love of land acquisition, physical strength, civic and military responsibilities and relatively short lives. John's grandson, Augustine Washington, was born in 1694 and grew to be over six feet tall and was known for his unusual strength. He married Jane Butler in 1715, who bore him four children, one of whom was Lawrence, born in 1718. Shortly after Jane's death in 1729, Augustine married Mary Ball, who gave birth to George, Samuel, John Augustine, Charles and Elizabeth. George was born at Pope's Creek Farm. When he was three years old, he and the family moved to Little Hunting Creek on the Potomac River, where they stayed for three years before moving to Ferry Farm near Fredericksburg. George was eleven when his father died in 1743 leaving the Little Hunting Creek property to Lawrence, the Ferry Farm property to George and the Pope's Creek property to, "Austin", George's other half-brother. Augustine Washington had moved his family to Ferry Farm in 1738, not too distant from Fredericksburg, where he could be close to his six iron furnaces. George was fortunate to have a surrogate father in his half-brother Lawrence who all but adopted him. Lawrence was fourteen years older than George, and, even though he only lived to his thirty-fourth year, he proved to play a critical role in the development and life of George Washington.

George's two half brothers, Lawrence and Austin, were educated in England, but George was tutored at home because of insufficient funds for a formal education following his father's death in 1743. Some say that his mother did not put a high priority on education or merely wanted her son to be close at hand to work on the farm considering she was widowed and required help. George did not spend much time with his father who was busy with his farms, mines and the furnace on his property. He sent George to a school in Fredericksburg in anticipation of further advanced learning at the Appleby School in England where he and George's two older half brothers were educated. In his teens, George studied Seneca's *Dialogues* and, copied from a London magazine, "Rules of Civility And Decent Behavior in Company and Conversation" which allegedly was written by Ignatius Loyola around 1550 for educating young Italian aristocrats who were about to serve as court pages. Many historians believe Washington closely followed these rules at least until he gained self confidence as an adult. The book contains 110 maxims that became the framework of George's character and served as guiding principles for much of his life. Most of the maxims have to do with proper manners and hygiene, but some are directed at character and virtue. Many of them are apparent in Washington's developing life and his relationships with his superiors, generals and advisors. Rule number one: "Every action done in Company, ought to be with Some Sign of Respect, to those that are Present." Washington seems to have learned this rule well as it had to do with "reputation" which was one of his highest concerns. Rule number nineteen: "Let your Countenance be pleasant but in Serious Matters Somewhat grave." This very much describes Washington's appearance during his public life. Another rule he followed when he spoke of Providence or the Creator was number 108: "When you Speak of God or his Attributes, let it be Seriously & with Reverence." His very limited schooling consisted of some tutoring in mathematics, composition, geography and deportment. Some historians believe Washington merely wrote the "Rules of Civility" in his copybook as a writing exercise after seeing their reproduction in a London magazine and that their influence on George has been exaggerated. This is based on the fact that they are located in the back of his book. Others believe that the young teenager Washington studied and used the maxims in order to fit into the new social life that his half-brother Lawrence had introduced him to at Belvoir, the home of the aristocratic Fairfax family. Historian Richard Brookhiser notes that rules number forty-five and 105 advise against anger especially among strangers, and rule number twenty-three suggests pity for even the criminal, and rule number thirty-six teaches to treat people of "low degree" with courtesy. Rule number forty-four could have applied to John Jay when he returned from London with his disappointing treaty because it instructs one not to blame someone for not succeeding if they did the best they could. Another rule which Washington practiced was to accept honor only reluctantly and with modesty. In many ways the "Rules" comply with the polite civility of eighteenth-century Whig culture and were the mark of aristocratic behavior in Virginia.[9]

Through his brother's connections, George could have been enrolled as a midshipman in the Royal Navy at the age of fourteen, but his mother intervened and prevented him from joining. Also, she may have been influenced by her brother who lived in England, Joseph Ball, who advised that George did not have adequate "interest" (patronage) that was necessary for success in the Royal Navy. Mary Ball Washington was a strong-willed, domineering mother who probably instilled a deep sense of discipline in young George. Her son was anxious to gain his independence from her, and without a father by age eleven, he soon found himself idolizing his brother Lawrence and seeing first-hand the lifestyle of the aristocratic Fairfax family into which Lawrence had married. Lawrence's wife, Anne, was the daughter of Colonel William Fairfax, and George became a close friend of her brother George William Fairfax and his wife, Sally. Between the ages of eleven and sixteen, George Washington's view of life was enlarged far beyond that of a Virginia planter. He became enraptured with the elegance, grace, education and wealth of the Fairfax family and their aristocratic friends and neighbors. These included such prominent families on the Northern Neck

9   Brookhiser, 128.

as the Lees, Carters, Marshalls and Custises. Through their intermarriages and social exchanges, they also influenced young George. Their shared values of self-discipline, reason and restraint served as models for George. As historian David Hackett Fischer points out, these families practiced the relatively new philosophy of "moral striving through virtuous action and right conduct." They felt it was their duty to lead others and combine power with responsibility and liberty with discipline. Honor and reputation were of the utmost importance, and from this early age Washington lived his entire life upholding his reputation and fearing dishonor. A significant aspect of this code of conduct was courage. Courage was expected in physical danger and suffering, but it was also necessary in moral stamina, strength and endurance.[10] Colonel William Fairfax admired the young teenager's reserve, strength and intelligence, and he reportedly recommended surveying as a career for him. Young George was inclined to the exactness of numbers, and this, combined with his love of the outdoors were suitable interests which further led him to the field of surveying. In effect, George Washington had two surrogate fathers who were mentors in his early years, his half brother Lawrence and Lawrence's father-in-law, Colonel William Fairfax. After receiving his license from the College of William and Mary at the age of seventeen, George became the Surveyor of Culpepper County, Virginia, and was soon hired by his best friend's father, Colonel Fairfax, to survey the Fairfax land in the Ohio River Valley.[11] This experience brought him familiarity with the wilderness of western Virginia and the ability to gauge distances, both of which were to serve him well in the future war. Perhaps even more importantly, he was now able to earn a living

---

10   David Hackett Fischer, *Washington's Crossing* (New York: Oxford University Press, 2004) 13. By permission of Oxford University Press, Inc.
11   Richard Norton Smith, *Patriarch* (New York: Houghton Mifflin & Co., 1993) 6.

and find the independence he craved from Ferry Farm and his domineering mother.

George spent less and less time with his mother, and their relationship grew to be strained and formal for the rest of their lives. Mary Ball Washington has been described as a "tough, opinionated, selfish, overly protective and possessive woman... quiet, aloof, imperious and very strong."[12] In spite of this, George and his brothers always provided for her comfort and care by sending her an annuity and funds for her living expenses. Neither Lawrence nor George ever invited Mary to Mount Vernon. Later in her life she asked to live there but Washington declined on the grounds that the visitors and busyness of the place would upset her. Mary Washington stayed at Ferry Farm until 1771, at which time George and his siblings moved her to a house on one of George's lots in Fredericksburg, which remains as a museum today. She negotiated an annual payment from George, who then sold Ferry Farm, which he had inherited upon his father's death in 1743. However, he rarely wrote to his mother. Their relationship grew steadily worse over the years. She did not agree with her son's politics and remained a Loyalist all her life. Washington believed she was avaricious, and during the war Washington was informed by Benjamin Harrison, who was Speaker of the Virginia House of Delegates, that his mother claimed to be destitute and accordingly requested a pension from the state. A mortified Washington wrote to Harrison that she was well cared for by him and his brothers. Later, when Washington's brothers—Charles, Sam and Jack—all predeceased him, he was left to see that she was looked after and protected from a community that had little regard for British sympathizers. When he was first elected President, Washington visited his mother in

12 John E. Ferling, *The First of Men: A Life of George Washington* (Knoxville, Tennessee: University of Tennessee Press, 1988) 6.

Fredericksburg before leaving for his inauguration in New York. She was eighty-one, and with his new responsibilities he had a premonition that this was to be his last time with her. In her youth she was a fine horsewoman, but by the time of Washington's last visit she traveled all over town by walking and did not even own a carriage. Reportedly, she did not bother to receive him and his companions and did not even invite them into her house. She remained in her garden while George bid her his last farewell. She died of breast cancer six months later.[13]

Lawrence was appointed adjutant general of the Virginia militia and was elected to the House of Burgesses in Williamsburg. In 1743, he married Anne, daughter of Colonel William Fairfax, owner of Belvoir, a plantation next to Mount Vernon. The Colonel was a member of the Virginia governor's council and a distant cousin of Thomas Lord Fairfax in England, who owned more than five million acres of land in the Northern Neck between the Potomac and Rappahannock Rivers. Because of George's many visits to his brother he came to develop a close relationship with the Fairfax family. This had a strong influence on George and no doubt led to his growing interest in land ownership. At the age of sixteen, George was asked to survey the Fairfax land in the Shenandoah Valley, and the following year he obtained his surveyor license at the College of William & Mary. In the next few years as an appraiser and surveyor he earned sufficient funds to purchase over fourteen hundred acres before he turned twenty-one.[14]

George's work as a surveyor and his excellent relationship with the Fairfax family marked a critical and formative period in George's life because it gave him several important building

13 Willard Sterne Randall, *George Washington: A Life* (New York: Henry Holt & Co., 1997) 440.
14 John R. Alden, *George Washington, A Biography* (Louisiana State University Press: 1984) 4-9. Reprinted by permission of LSU Press. Copyright 1984 by LSU Press.

blocks for his future: 1) it introduced him to the landed aristocracy of Virginia to which he aspired, 2) it gained him intimate knowledge of western Virginia, 3) it provided contacts in very high places in the British government at Williamsburg, and 4) it offered him the opportunity to associate with refined and well educated aristocrats and learn proper manners and behavior.

The Fairfax family, as well as Lawrence, saw life's highest goal as duty to one's country. They took inspiration from leaders of the Roman Republic who exhibited courage and high principles. One in particular was the Roman General Cincinnatus who in 458 B.C. defeated the invading Aequis and Volsii tribes and then declined becoming a dictator in favor of returning to his farm as an ordinary citizen. His life is portrayed in Joseph Addison's play *Cato*, which was performed often at Belvoir where young George frequently visited. The themes of liberty, virtue and honor had to influence George, and this is underscored by his having the play performed at Valley Forge in 1778 during the darkest days of the war. In 1744, Lawrence was elected to the House of Burgesses in Williamsburg representing Fairfax County. He was reelected in 1748, and the sixteen-year-old George moved into Mount Vernon, where he was introduced to politics at that time as another avenue toward honor and social status. This is evidenced by his saving of his brother's election poll.[15] All of these aspects came together when George was at a very young age and proceeded to become the building blocks of George's ambitious behavior and illustrious career.

In 1751, Lawrence was suffering from tuberculosis and George accompanied him to Barbados for some rest and possible cure. This was George's only trip outside the American colonies during his entire life. George contracted smallpox and recovered

---

15   Paul K. Longmore, *The Invention of George Washington* (Charlottesville: University Press of Virginia, 1999) 15.

after a month's recuperation. He thereby became immune from the future smallpox epidemics that pervaded Philadelphia in the 1790s and prompted him to have his family and troops inoculated during the war, an unusual, visionary and daring decision. Lawrence failed to improve and moved on to Bermuda while George returned to Virginia where he presented letters from the West Indies to the newly appointed Governor of Virginia, Robert Dinwiddie. This initial meeting between them proved to be a critical event as George made a very favorable impression upon the Governor.[16]

Upon Lawrence's death in July 1752, George applied for the vacated position of Adjutant General of the Virginia Militia, which was responsible for maintaining some basic skills among the militiamen. He gained the position because of his knowledge of the Ohio territory as well as through the strong recommendation of the influential Colonel Fairfax. He was to train the militia in martial skills that he himself did not possess. Nonetheless, he assured Governor Dinwiddie that he would fit himself for the office and was given a salary of £100 per annum.[17]

Upon the death of George's father, Augustine Washington, in 1743, the farm at Little Hunting Creek was inherited by Lawrence who promptly renamed it Mount Vernon and built the "Mansion House" for his new bride. The plantation consisted of 2,126 acres of land which later grew to eight thousand acres. Upon Lawrence's untimely death from tuberculosis in 1752, Mount Vernon passed to his widow, Anne Fairfax Washington, who was remarried within six months to George Lee, the uncle of "Light Horse" Harry Lee. When her only surviving child by Lawrence died suddenly in 1754 at age four, Mount Vernon was left to Anne

---

16   James Thomas Flexner, *Washington, The Indispensable Man* (New York: Little Brown & Co., 1974 [originally published 1969]) 6-9.

17   Thomas Fleming, *Liberty! The American Revolution* (New York: Viking Penguin, 1997) 30-34.

for life before it was to pass on to George. She was living with her new husband at Westmoreland, so she leased it to George who was the ultimate beneficiary for his life under Lawrence's will. With Anne's early death in 1761, Mount Vernon legally passed to George Washington. (After the death of George's wife, Martha, in 1802, Mount Vernon was willed to Bushrod Washington who was the son of George's favorite brother, John Augustine. Mount Vernon and five hundred acres of the eight thousand total were eventually sold by Washington's great-grandnephew.[18])

It should be noted that during his earlier visits with the Fairfax family at Belvoir, George developed a friendship with Lawrence's brother-in-law, George William Fairfax and his wife Sally. However, in later years when the threat of war loomed the Fairfax family moved to England. There is some evidence of a romantic relationship between George Washington and Sally Fairfax. In a letter written by him to Sally on September 12, 1758, Washington does profess his love for her, but they both realized nothing could become of it.[19] Another letter written from George to Sally just before his marriage to Martha and still another letter written to her in London in his retirement suggest mutual admiration, but historians conclude there never was a sexual relationship. Sally did serve as a social tutor to the teenager George and nursed his sickness in 1757, but his stoic nature and perhaps his principles would not allow his true feelings for Sally to dominate his emotions. In 1773, Sally and George William moved to England and never returned because of the Fairfax loyalty to the Crown. In what was undoubtedly a nostalgic moment, his last letter to her in May 1798, openly states how the happiest years of his life were spent at Belvoir and Mount Vernon with the Fairfaxes, and he

18   Grizzard, 228.
19   Ferling, 55.

unabashedly asked Sally to return to Virginia to be his neighbor once again. She, of course, did not return to America.[20]

---

20   Flexner, 19-35.

CHAPTER 2

Early Military Experience: 1754–1759

Courage is rightly esteemed the first of human qualities
because it is the quality which guarantees all others.

—Winston Churchill, British Prime Minister

The Ohio Expedition

From the 1680s, England and France were battling each other over the North American territories in Newfoundland, Nova Scotia, eastern America and the Caribbean. Their conflicts were seldom settled, and with the large migration of English settlers moving over the Alleghenies into the Ohio River Valley, the French were sufficiently concerned to send troops in 1753 to oust them. Virginians believed that close to five hundred thousand acres of that area were included in their 1609 charter from King James I. This was of particular concern to the Ohio Company who hoped to gain estates and commerce in the Ohio Valley. Investors in the Ohio Company included Governor Dinwiddie, Lawrence Washington, several Lees, a Carter and George Mason. When Washington learned of the impending problem he went to Williamsburg in 1753 to volunteer his services. Governor Dinwiddie remembered Washington from his first visit in 1752 and also from his appointment as Adjutant General of the Virginia militia. Although Dinwiddie did not know much about Washington, he must have been impressed with his confidence in requesting such a difficult assignment. He sent Washington to advise the French at Fort Le Boeuf that they were infringing on British land in the Ohio River territory. Washington's exchanges with the French were most cordial and upon his return he presented Dinwiddie with the "Journal" of his experience which was later printed in American newspapers and in London. Dinwiddie prompted Washington to publish his "Journal", and from that moment on the name of Washington became recognized in America and Europe. At the age of twenty-two George Washington started on his way to notoriety. The diplomatic effort initiated by Dinwiddie was refused by the French, and immediately thereafter Dinwiddie appointed Washington as Lieutenant Colonel and authorized him to take 140 men to turn back the French infringement. This led to a confrontation with the French under Captain de Contrecoeur near Fort Duquense (present day Pittsburgh), and while Washington did not realize it at the time, it marked the true beginning of the French and Indian War. There is much controversy on the exchange of gunfire that left ten Frenchmen and their commander, Jumonville, dead who were supposedly sent to deliberate with Washington and not engage in hostilities. The French then sent four hundred men and overpowered the British and Virginians at Washington's Fort Necessity, but because France and England were not officially at war they allowed Washington and his men to retreat. In spite of the international furor raised by the French, Dinwiddie was pleased with Washington and promoted him to the rank of Colonel and commander of the Virginia regiment. Ultimately, the blame for the defeat was placed on the second in command, Lieutenant George Muse, who resigned in disgrace. Upon Washington's return to Williamsburg, Burgesses declined to raise more taxes to pay for the unpopular war which then led to Dinwiddie's conversion of the Virginia Regiment to independent companies and ultimately to Washington's resignation in spite of retaining his good reputation. However, it is important to note that this experience introduced young Washington to wilderness warfare and just as importantly to the practice of writing journals. To this day, he remains the most prolific writer of all the presidents of the United States, and this was done without the benefit of receiving a formal education.[1]

The French and Indian War Expeditions

The first and best victory is to conquer self

—Aristotle, Philosopher

Washington had little desire at that time in becoming a planter, and he lacked the resources to develop Mount Vernon into a viable plantation. Instead, he missed the military life and believed he could achieve more recognition and prestige in the service of Virginia. Soldiering provided a faster path toward becoming someone of importance in society. Nonetheless, he leased Mount Vernon from his brother's widow, Anne, and started to restore the house and fields until the following spring of 1755. When he learned of the arrival of the thirty-five-year veteran, British General Edward Braddock, who was sent by London to remove the French from the Ohio territory, he turned his attention back to the military.

---

1   Flexner, 20-31.

Under the sixty-year old General Braddock, Washington served as a volunteer aide because he was unable to gain a suitable rank in the British army. He was interested in British training and desperately wanted the experience writing to his brother, "I have now a good opportunity and shall not neglect it, of forming an acquaintance which may be serviceable hereafter, if I shall find it worth while to push my Fortune in the Military line."[2] Braddock became impressed with Washington and later in the field promised him a future position in the regular army at the campaign's end, but he was soon killed and could not fulfill the promise.

Braddock did not adopt Washington's suggestions for single-file wilderness warfare and suffered a disastrous defeat while Washington barely escaped with his life. He reportedly had two horses killed from beneath him and his uniform was riddled with bullet holes. About two-thirds of the British and Anglo-American troops were slaughtered, but Washington survived the nightmare and experienced his first test of warfare. Washington also learned something that Braddock did not comprehend, namely: the European style of warfare did not work in the American frontier. Long baggage trains, slow movement, rows of open field artillery and the lack of independent decision-making with fighting in forests at close quarters were not effective methods to defeat a stealthy and agile foe who knew their territory. In spite of the disastrous defeat, the legend of Washington's bravery and indestructibility was born. Even the highly respected Reverend Samuel Davies said of him, "I may point out to the Public, that heroic youth Col. Washington, who I cannot but hope Providence has hitherto preserved in so signal a Manner for some important Service to his Country."[3] During the campaign, Washington

---

2   Joseph J. Ellis, *His Excellency: George Washington* (New York: Alfred A. Knopf, 2004) 33.
3   Ibid., 39

26

came to know Thomas Gage, Horatio Gates and Charles Lee, all of whom he was to meet again in the Revolutionary War. He borrowed their military manuals and probably studied the science of warfare for the first time.[4] Upon his return Washington soon discovered that his bravery was recognized in the reports of surviving British officers. After the horrible defeat of the Braddock Campaign, Governor Dinwiddie remodeled the Virginia military with a centrally commanded army. His choice for a commander was George Washington, but Washington would only accept the post if he was given the kinds of authority he deemed necessary, particularly the naming of officers. Negotiations between the two men proved difficult, but Washington compromised and was named commander of Virginia's army in the fall of 1755 at the age of twenty-three. His mother objected to his returning to the army, but he replied that he had to do it to retain his "honor." In fact, Washington commented to his brother that he would serve if he could "gain by it."[5] He then sought a royal commission in the British Army and traveled to Boston with an appointment to see Massachusetts Governor William Shirley in February 1756. He was received politely but in spite of his being in charge of all the British military in North America, Washington was informed that the Governor did not have the authority to grant his request. Although disappointed, Washington returned to Williamsburg and enlisted the support of Governor Dinwiddie for his proper place in the British military. When London sent over British officers to recruit American colonists, relations between Dinwiddie and Washington deteriorated. Washington still returned to fight the Indians in the western Virginia territory but suffered many hardships and felt he was being treated in an "ambiguous and uncertain way" by Dinwiddie. He was not

4   Ferling, 33.
5   George Washington Papers at the Library of Congress,
    <www.memory.loc.gov/ammen/mgwquery.html>.

permitted to go on the offensive but was relegated to defensive tactics. Washington's regiment was severely criticized in the *Virginia Gazette*, which infuriated the Colonel, and the entire regiment threatened to resign. Washington rose to the occasion by offering to speak with the Governor on their behalf, but on the way he was ordered to move his headquarters to Fort Cumberland in Maryland. He later returned to Dinwiddie to pursue his case for a royal commission and prepared a report for the chief aide of the commanding British General, John Campbell, the Earl of Loudoun. The report condemned both the House of Burgesses and Dinwiddie for lack of support during his three years defending the western frontier. He met with Loudoun in Philadelphia, but in spite of being "very much pleased with the accounts you [Washington] have given him", Loudoun and Dinwiddie reduced the importance of Washington's command.[6] Loudoun was a wealthy and experienced soldier who treated Washington poorly and dismissed him after little discussion. Washington was dismayed but followed orders and knew if he resigned in a pique his military career would be finished. He tried to build an army with very few recruits and supplies, but he was able to stabilize the Indian menace by the end of 1757. Dinwiddie later wrote to Washington accusing him of ingratitude. Washington was stunned by his rebuke and was unable to secure another meeting with Dinwiddie to discuss the matter. It was a sad ending to their relationship considering that Dinwiddie was the one who supported Washington for years and was partly responsible for his growing fame and popularity. As author John Alden states, "Washington had not yet learned that remorseless telling of the truth is a vicious virtue, or a virtuous vice."[7]

---

6   Alden, 58.
7   Ibid., 61.

In 1758, the thirty-year Scot veteran, Brigadier General John Forbes, was sent with seven thousand men to retake Fort Duquense. In late 1757 and early 1758, Washington became dangerously ill and lost all hope of becoming a regular in the British army. He recovered in the spring and was asked to join Forbes as a colonel in the Virginia militia. Forbes acknowledged and followed Washington's advice on forest-fighting techniques, but ultimately he rejected Washington's advice on the best route to the Ohio. Even though Forbes politely listened to Washington before rejecting his advice, he did not expect Washington's criticisms that followed. This was undoubtedly due to Washington's first-hand experience with the Braddock disaster and his deep concern for a repetition of that infamous campaign. He saw similar tactics and typical British superiority, and tried to prevent another catastrophe. Also, at this time relations between France and England were growing complex and interfered with hostilities in the campaign. In spite of Washington's concerns, the British navy blocked the French supply routes, and the recapture of Fort Duquense was achieved following its abandonment and destruction by the French. Forbes proceeded to rebuild the fort and renamed it "Fort Pitt" in honor of the dominant figure in the British cabinet, Prime Minister William Pitt. Believing the frontier now safe, Washington resigned and returned to Mount Vernon.

From his war experiences from 1753 to 1758, Washington emerged as a hero who had exhibited bravery, confidence and the respect of his subordinates and superiors. He was seemingly impervious to bullets and was entrusted with responsibilities well beyond his abilities. Although he claimed to be fighting for patriotism, he also was calculating his own advancement. While he was ambitious, he did have a personal magnetism that inspired others to his leadership.[8] At times he was brash, impolitic, over-confident and mistaken. But his energy, discipline and strict attention to detail, particularly of the supplies for his men, were attributes that served him well. His reputation is best described by his officers' farewell remarks: "In our earliest infancy, you took us under your tuition, trained us in the practice of that discipline which alone can constitute good troops... Your steady adherence to impartial justice, your quick discernment and invariable regard to merit—wisely intended to inculcate those genuine sentiments of true honor and passion for glory, from which the greatest military achievements have been derived—first heightened our natural emulation, and our desire to excel." Washington was twenty-six years old![9] It is fascinating that from defeat under Braddock and then the successful campaign under Forbes young Washington emerges as hero in spite of his less than distinctive service. His first-hand experience in wilderness warfare was invaluable, and he used it to good purpose in coming years. He also learned the necessity and advantages of fighting in a defensive manner. He copied the Indian methods of ambush and their hit-and-run tactics. He also saw the ineffectiveness of the British army in dealing with this type of fighting. Most importantly, he learned from his mistakes. Figuratively, the foundation of the future monument was established, and several stones were already in place.

---

8   Ferling, 58.
9   GW Papers at the Library of Congress.

CHAPTER 3

Early Political Experience: 1759–1775

Washington's biographers have misunderstood his ambitions and development during these years. He remained active in provincial politics and attentive to colonial-imperial relations. He continued to develop his skills and style as a leader... he underwent a transformation not so much of personal character as of political perspective.

—Paul K. Longmore
The Invention of George Washington[1]

*I*t should be noted that when Washington resigned as commander of the Virginia forces in 1758, the Seven Years' War (as the British called it) went on for another five years. The final outcome was a resounding British defeat of the French culminating with the conquest of Canada. However, the British military and Parliament soon forgot about Washington's efforts, and he in turn no longer sought a career in the British army. While the House of Burgesses praised his contributions and leadership, British leaders failed to reward his services to the Crown. Yet, he remained a loyal British subject and turned

---

1   Longmore, 56.

from soldiering to building a domestic life with his new bride and family which he soon moved into Mount Vernon.[2] He was aware of his popularity and attempted to seek a position in the House of Burgesses in Williamsburg. He lost his first effort in 1755 from Fairfax County, but three years later he was elected to represent Frederick County which he served for seven years. He was then elected from Fairfax County in 1765 and again in 1769. He served on the vestry of his Anglican Church and attended services regularly. At that time, vestrymen were responsible for community affairs such as ministering to the poor and to those in need of help. They also hired and appointed the church ministers unlike the Anglican churches in England where such positions were made by the local bishop. Washington was appointed to serve as Justice of the Peace in 1770 and as part of the gentry tended to the poor, lent money and executed wills for widows and orphans. He was a businessman, land speculator, planter, farmer and politician and was known to be honest and shrewd.[3] During this sixteen-year period Washington concentrated on the enlargement of Mount Vernon and the planting and propagation of its crops. The one-story house was remodeled to include a second story in 1759 and in 1774 and 1776 two wings were added together with a pediment over the center and a cupola. The management of plantation life agreed with him, and he was always experimenting with new ways to improve the crops through fertilizers and irrigation. Mount Vernon became self-sufficient with its exports of tobacco and foodstuffs, and Washington was able to increase his wealth. By 1766 he no longer grew tobacco with his major crops being wheat and corn. In fact, he discovered that tobacco depleted the soil so he abandoned it. He continued to diversify and actually constructed a weaving mill which he later

---

2   Alden, 71.
3   Ibid., 81.

automated.[4] He also started to abandon the age-old practice of dealing through "factors" in England for the purchase and sale of his goods and machinery. Instead, he dealt with local merchants and became independent of foreigners who he believed were not representing his best interests. We then see a slight shift in his attitude of being a bit more American than British. In his leisure time he bred horses, fox-hunted and gambled to some small extent. He designed the additions to Mount Vernon as well as gardens and landscaping. Between 1768 and 1775 he entertained about two thousand guests. Both he and Martha considered the house lonely without guests, and yet they also desired their privacy between visitors. He gladly dispensed his advice when sought and never refused suppliants who were deserving of help. He was kind toward his slaves and would never consider separating family members. He clothed and fed them and treated them as part of his extended family, and he often referred to them as his "family." No slave was sold without their consent, and with only two exceptions, none had the desire to leave Mount Vernon.[5]

Ever since Washington's first ventures as a surveyor in the western lands of Virginia, he was enamored with the acquisition of land. He expected wilderness land to appreciate fivefold over a twenty-year period. He believed it was the most likely vehicle for attaining wealth, and no doubt he was influenced by the vast tracts of land owned by his first client, Colonel Fairfax. As soon as he earned his first fees at the age of eighteen in 1750, he bought his first piece of land. It was a 450-acre tract in the Shenandoah Valley. This was followed by a thousand-acre purchase near the current boundary of West Virginia and Virginia.[6] The frontier military assignments also had their financial rewards in that the participants were awarded the purchase of large tracts of land at

---

4   Flexner, 49.
5   Ibid., 54.
6   Ferling, 14.

very little cost. The bounty awards of 1754 and 1762 to officer veterans of the French and Indian War were particularly important to Washington. These initial options were eventually exercised after the Proclamation of 1763 which set the boundaries for colonial settlement of the western lands. In that year he invested in the Mississippi Company which applied to the Crown for four thousand square miles between the Wabash and Mississippi rivers. He later employed a frontiersman, William Crawford, to find good land for him in western Pennsylvania. Later, he also hired an agent to find good land in West Florida.[7] Washington believed that fortunes would be made by securing as much land as possible and then waiting for it to appreciate as the colonies expanded westward. Opportunities occurred after treaties with the native tribes were reached in 1767. As reward for his first excursion on behalf of Governor Dinwiddie in 1754, Washington acquired 20,147 acres of the allotted two hundred thousand-acre bounty. There has been some criticism of his purchase because the original proclamation suggested that the bounty should be restricted only to the enlisted men, but this was later clarified by Governor Botetourt in 1770. Washington selected land along the river bottom which was superior to other tracts. He defended his purchase based on his considerable efforts and adequate notices to other qualified officers. His next purchase was made under the 1763 bounty which was awarded to those who served until the conclusion of the war with the French. Washington received his colonel's share of five thousand acres, and he purchased some additional acres all of which represented some compensation for the personal losses he sustained because of his military service. Lastly, he purchased land vouchers from fur traders bringing his total to thirty-five thousand acres of western lands at little cost. However, there was a serious problem with securing title to

---

7   GW Papers at the Library of Congress.

such land because the British government had no comprehensive policy over the western lands. Some treaties with the Indians were recognized and others were not. The government could not even determine the western boundary of Pennsylvania.[8] London was also considering the creation of a new colony to be carved from western Virginia, but nothing came of it. Washington never realized his anticipated riches from these lands, but later they proved useful to America when he started to bind Virginia together by promoting the Potomac River as a major commercial part of the country. His vision of a larger and more commercial country started to take shape and was another aspect of Washington's ability to see beyond provincial boundaries.[9]

His Marriage and New Life

These are the things which once possessed

Will make a life that's truly blessed;

A good estate on healthy soil

Not got by vice, nor yet by toil;

Round a warm fire, a pleasant joke,

With chimney ever free from smoke:

A strength entire, a sparkling bowl,

A quiet wife, a quiet soul.

—"True Happiness," poet unknown
Recorded by George Washington[10]

---

8   GW Papers at the Library of Congress.
9   Robert E. Jones, *George Washington: Ordinary Man, Extraordinary Leader* (New York, Fordham University Press, 2002) 29-31.
10 Smith, 7.

Upon returning to Mount Vernon in 1758, Washington was a far different man than the younger messenger of Governor Dinwiddie in 1753. His military travels and heroics brought him recognition by politicians and businessmen. He gained access to important men, and he had acquired self confidence. He realized that his goal of obtaining a commission in the British army was not possible, and he started to think more of the powers that wealth and social standing could bring. He was well known locally and in the northeastern colonies from Williamsburg to Philadelphia, New York and Boston. He was no longer dependent on his brother or the Fairfax family. He assessed his strengths and weaknesses. He learned from the well educated British officers with whom he served. He learned from the polished businessmen and politicians he encountered. He worked to correct his lesser qualities like his temper and pomposity. He lacked some social graces and was insecure about his poor education. He overcame these shortcomings with virtue, toughness, strength and maturity. He combined a natural affability with courage and determination. Not everyone was impressed. Certainly Loudoun and later Dinwiddie were not among his admirers. He played to those in powerful positions and elicited their approbation. He tended to be serious without humor and assumed a remoteness that left him with few close relationships other than George William Fairfax and his father, Colonel William Fairfax, his brothers (particularly John), and his brother-law, Burwell Bassett. However, Washington had an instinctive ability to elicit confidence from his subordinates and his superiors. He was forthright, direct and honest, and those around him were infected with his sense of right and determination. It was a remarkable trait considering he was only twenty-six years old.[11] He was about to enter a new chapter in his life with his approaching marriage to Martha Dandridge Custis.

---

11 Ferling, 60.

Before going on the Forbes campaign, Washington became engaged to Martha who was the widow of Daniel Parke Custis with two young children, Martha Parke Custis (Patsy) age two and John Parke Custis (Jacky) age four. Martha was less than a year older than George and barely five feet tall. She was the great-granddaughter of Rowland Jones who was the first pastor of the Bruton Parish Church in Williamsburg, Virginia. She came from a modest family but married well and inherited a large tract of eighteen thousand acres and an estimated estate valued at £30,000.[12] Upon their marriage on January 6, 1759, only eight months after their first meeting, George became the custodian of her children and her estate as well, thereby making him part of the landed aristocracy. In spite of some portraits showing their marriage in St. Peter's Anglican Church, records indicate they were married at the Dandridge home on the Pamunkey River in New Kent County. The house had been built by her first husband's father, and ironically it was named "White House." Years later the President's Palace in Washington, D.C. was renamed "The White House" in honor of Martha Washington. Martha's gentle charm and warm nature were qualities that appealed to George especially in contrast to his stern and distant mother. There are some indications that the marriage initially was not a smooth one. George later reported that his marriage was "most conducive to happiness."[13] George soon discovered that being a stepfather required a different type of fathering from that of a parent, but reportedly he was "generous and attentive" to them while Martha remained overly possessive and indulgent. Jacky proved to be uneducable in spite of George's efforts for his schooling. At the age of twelve, Patsy was diagnosed with epilepsy, and she died quite suddenly in 1773 at the age of sixteen from one of

---

12   Ellis, 60.
13   GW Papers at the Library of Congress.

her seizures. Martha was devastated and took consolation by becoming even more protective of Jacky and retreating to her room for daily prayer. Martha and George were well matched, and their childless marriage did not interfere with their happiness.[14] In fact, some historians believe that Washington's paternal instincts were later directed toward his officers and soldiers as can be seen in his future relations with Nathanael Greene, Marquis de LaFayette and Alexander Hamilton. His future title as the "Father of His Country" also suggests that he viewed the new Republic as a father would his children by guiding and protecting them and finally leaving them to manage for themselves.

House of Burgesses and the Road to War

The ear of the leader must ring with the voices of the people.

—Woodrow Wilson
President of the United States of America

When at Williamsburg, Washington spent a good deal of time with sophisticated Virginians. He attended the theater, danced at assemblies, drank tea and played cards. He was not regarded as an intellectual but instead was considered thoughtful and deliberate.[15] His habit was to speak briefly and to the point. This was similar to Franklin and Jefferson who also were not gifted public speakers. When Washington entered the military his five years of service were intended to serve his country by defending the King's Virginia properties and at the same time striving to acquire recognition and his just rewards. While he did gain the approbation of his American peers, he failed to attain the status of a regular British officer or receive the recognition

---

14   Alden, 82.
15   Ibid., 83.

of his British superiors. By the time of his resignation from the military in December 1758, he had become suspect of British justice and their treatment of him and his Virginia militia. Although he harbored a personal grievance, it sowed the seeds of greater discontent with Britain's attitude of superiority toward the colonies and no genuine interest in their economic well-being. Most biographers claim that Washington was not a particularly active or noteworthy politician when he entered the House of Burgesses in February 1759, but recent research by Paul Longmore reveals a totally different picture. Because protracted wars with France and Spain had cost Britain a total of £137 million Parliament invoked increasing measures to seek revenues from the colonies. It was precisely at this time from 1759 to 1774 that Washington was serving in the House. Records show that Washington was intimately involved in colonial-imperial relations, and he responded with personal and official statements on most of these matters. As a junior delegate from Frederick County, he initially concentrated on the defense of these more vulnerable lands giving advice on troop strength and pay. After all, he was still in the army when he was elected and was chosen because of his knowledge of that area and his good military reputation. But as Britain began its series of trading restrictions, taxes and duties, Washington took an increasing interest in political issues. His first assignment was as a member the Committee on Propositions and Grievances responsible for issues of business and government. His initial objective of entering politics was to gain personal honor through recognition for civic leadership. However, as England tightened its commercial grip on the colonies, Washington began to understand the far-reaching implications of their economic and political acts. He saw American freedoms and its self-governing institutions become suppressed and sometimes eliminated. He saw grievances expressed to Parliament and the King totally ignored. He witnessed the dissolution of his own position as a Burgess. Washington was dutiful in attending the Assembly sessions from 1759 to 1762, and his opinions and advice on military matters regarding the frontier and Indian issues were eagerly sought by his colleagues. He spent his first four years studying the workings of the House. He took his apprenticeship seriously, and, contrary to popular belief, he did not go into politics reluctantly as a path to social status. This is evidenced by his strenuous campaign for re-election in 1761. He was even accused by his adversary of exerting undo influence on the sheriff who was managing the election polling procedure. Historian Paul Longmore suggests that the election of 1761 marks the beginning of the myth of Washington cast as "reluctant politician."[16]

During his fifteen-year service in the House, Washington took part in the debates on most of the new acts of Parliament:

1759—The London Board of Trade ordered the colonies to pay outstanding debts in sterling. War debts and the scarcity of hard money forced Burgesses to issue paper currency as legal tender which amounted to £440,000 during the war. The colonies needed a medium of exchange so it ignored the Crown's order.

1763—The Proclamation of 1763 drew a north-south boundary line from the Great Lakes to the Gulf and the Appalachians to the Mississippi River prohibiting colonial settlers and speculators and voided all prior contracts of sale and deeds. Washington protested and organized a reversal of this several years later when Parliament allowed English investors into the territory.

1763—The Lords of Trade in London reprimanded Burgesses for continuing the issuance of paper currency.

---

16   Longmore, 67.

Washington commented that the issue would "set the whole country in flames."[17]

1764—Parliament passed the Currency Act which prohibited issuance of paper bills as legal tender thereby ignoring the plight of colonial debtors to repay English creditors.

1764—The Plantation Act or Sugar Act increased customs revenues and protected British commerce with the colonies from foreign competition. Washington called it a tax and warned that it would force Americans to reduce imports and hurt British manufacturers and creditors. Washington adopted a calm, self-assured manner and suppressed any emotional response. He correctly predicted repeal of the Sugar and Stamp acts.

1765—The Stamp Act required all legal documents, pamphlets, newspapers, etc. to contain official tax stamps in order to pay for British troops stationed in the colonies. Fairfax County led the movement to resist the Act. With Virginia's Stamp Act Resolves, the royal governor dissolved the Assembly and called for new elections. Fairfax delegate George Johnston resigned for ill health, and Washington filled the vacancy by getting elected in Fairfax. Washington called the Stamp Act an "unconstitutional method of taxation… a direful attack upon their Liberties…an act of Oppression."[18]

1766—Washington was named to the powerful Committee of Privileges and Elections, which supervised admissions to House membership.

1766—Parliament passed the Declaratory Act, which asserted its authority to raise revenues in the colonies.

---

17 GW Papers at the Library of Congress.
18 Ibid.

1767—Parliament passed the Townshend Duties, which placed taxes on tea, paper, glass and lead and forced the colonies to maintain a Board of Customs Commissioner for North America and to support British military defense and royally appointed civil officials.

1767—Parliament suspended the New York Assembly for not adequately supplying the regular British army stationed there.

1768—Colonial militants in Boston, New York and Philadelphia adopted non-importation associations, and they urged other colonies to do the same.

1769—Washington was assigned to the newly created Committee for Religion, which was designed to deal with the alarming decline in public virtue.

1769—Washington condemned the measures and wrote that Britain was deprecating American freedoms. He was the first politician to raise the issue of possible armed resistance but stated that it should be avoided. He suggested that the non-importation of British goods would spur the colonies to build more manufacturing and economic self-determination. He consulted with his neighbor, George Mason, who then drafted a Virginia non-importation association.

1769—The Crown sent Lord Botetourt as the new Governor of Virginia to quell the protests and opposition to the Townsend Duties by the House of Burgesses.

1769—Parliament threatened protestors in Massachusetts with transportation to London to be tried there for treason as traitors. They ordered General Gage to take a regiment to Boston to control the protests there.

1769—The House of Burgesses passed four resolves: 1) they had the sole right to impose taxes, 2) Virginians had the privilege to petition their Sovereign for redress of grievances, 3) all trials for criminals should take place in Virginia, and 4) they assured King George III of their loyalty to the Crown.

1770—Parliament repealed most of the Townshend duties but retained the tax on tea. The measure was designed to allow the failing East India Company to revive by gaining a virtual monopoly on the enormous tea trade and drove colonial competitors out of business by undercutting their prices.

1770—The Boston Massacre leaves five Americans killed and six wounded by British soldiers which further encourages colonial resistance led by the Sons of Liberty.

1773—Parliament passed the Quebec Act, which annexed part of western Pennsylvania above the Ohio River and east of the Mississippi River to the Province of Quebec. It was intended for fur trade with the Indians but proved to be a menace to settlers in the surrounding area.

1774—Parliament passed the Boston Port Bill closing Boston's port commerce until reparations were paid for destruction of the tea from the December 1773 "Tea Party."

1774—Governor Dunmore dissolved Burgesses for introducing non-importation measures.

1774—Parliament altered the Massachusetts charter by reducing the authority of the Lower House and appointing some of its own delegates.

1774—Parliament protected its agents from criminal trials in Massachusetts and ordered them to be transferred to England under the pretense of not being fairly tried in the colony.

1774—Parliament passed the Quartering Act, which allowed their soldiers to be lodged in private homes in areas of unrest.

By the summer of 1769, Washington had become one of the leading politicians in Virginia. He knew he was not a political expert on the legal aspects of the British Constitution, but he did state that the taxes were "repugnant to every principle of natural justice" before "abler heads than my own" convinced him that these measures violated the rights Americans had inherited from Britain.[19] Washington had left for home just before the assembly responded with their Virginia Resolves. During the period of 1765 to 1770, Washington became increasingly concerned with his financial condition and the British acts that seemed to undermine his economic independence. Like many Virginia planters, Washington used an agent in London to sell his tobacco and buy his machinery and goods. Following his marriage to Martha and the increased size of his needs, he continued with the Custis family agency of Cary & Company. In spite of Cary's good reputation, Washington believed he was not protecting the family's best interests because he seemed to sell at the bottom of the market and the problem was compounded by receiving costly and inferior goods. By 1763, with his expansion of Mount Vernon, Washington had spent an estimated two to three million dollars and found he had exhausted his funds. He was surprised to then learn from Cary that he was in debt for £1,800 and was incurring a 5 percent interest charge. This was exactly the pattern of other American colonists that eventually put them into bankruptcy which was abhorred by Washington. More importantly, the system left many planters dependent on others far away, and being a man who wished to control his own destiny and remain independent, Washington felt trapped into the

---

19   GW Papers at the Library of Congress.

consignment system.[20] The situation grew worse in late 1765 with the imposition of the Stamp Act, but oddly enough Washington did not get involved in the debates other than to declare the Act as an attack on American liberties. He then took measures to become more independent by abandoning tobacco, growing wheat for the domestic market, building a mill to produce flour and building a ship for commercial fishing. During this time, Washington also devoted considerable time and energy to improve navigation on the Potomac River, a project that remained one of his principal objectives throughout his life. He had purchased large tracts of land in the western part of the colonies and firmly believed that the future lay in western migration and development. However, with the conclusion of the French and Indian War in 1763, Britain declared that an enormous section of America from the Great Lakes to the Gulf of Mexico and the Appalachians to the Mississippi was to become a reservation for the Native American Indians and was not available to British-Americans. To Washington and many other investors as well as settlers already there, the British Proclamation represented a determined plot to control the colonists and confine them to the eastern seaboard. In 1765, the Mississippi Land Company requested a grant for 2.5 million acres in the Ohio River Valley, but Parliament turned them down on the pretext that it would violate the recent treaty with the Indians. Five years later, Parliament approved a similar request from some English investors thereby indicating to Washington just how negative the British were toward the colonists. Washington could not accept the Proclamation of 1763 and felt it was unenforceable and defied all sense of fairness and rationale. He also saw a broader sinister plot by Britain in a race with the colonists to control the rest of the continent to the Mississippi. He believed that the western lands represented the

---

20   Ellis, 88.

future growth of America and that the British were making every effort to prevent that growth. The quest for land divided British and American interests and set them on a separate course.

It is important to note that during the 1760s and early 1770s, the economy in America was flourishing. From farming in Pennsylvania and Virginia to trade along the coast and shipbuilding in New England as well as iron works in the middle Atlantic region, Americans were exporting and importing a significant amount of goods albeit under increasing control by and through English intermediaries. In its first one hundred and fifty years, America had developed its own economy and government and was looked upon by Britain as a great source of wealth. The French and Indian War was seen as an encroachment upon that source which the British needed to defend against at considerable cost. Parliament levied taxes to pay for those efforts, but the American colonists regarded these measures with increasing concern for their economic and political freedoms, which they felt they had earned over the years with little or no help from the British. The Sugar Act and the Stamp Act and then the Townshend Act in the 1760s were seen as never-ending efforts by Britain to milk the colonies dry. By April 1769, Washington was deeply involved in colonial politics and wrote in a letter to his friend and neighbor, George Mason, that he believed the British acts were deliberate and a threat to American freedom: "At a time when our Lordly Masters in Great Britain will be satisfied with nothing less than the depravation of American freedom, it seems highly necessary that something should be done to avert the stroke and maintain the liberty which we have derived from our Ancestors."[21] As historian John Ferling notes, it is interesting that at this early stage Washington expressed the belief that petitions to London were ineffectual, and yet he was still clinging to the philosophy

21   GW Papers at the Library of Congress.

that use of arms should be the last resort and that war might be averted. None of the Founding Fathers had thought in terms of possible war until five years later at the First Continental Congress.[22] When Mason drafted a response calling for an anti-importation agreement, which Washington tried to introduce into the House of Burgesses in May 1769, Governor Botetourt dissolved the House for considering anti-Crown resolutions.[23] The assembly then met illegally at the Raleigh Tavern in Williamsburg to draw up an embargo plan primarily on taxed goods. An indication of the continued peaceful relations between the Burgesses and the Crown was the party they attended at the Governor's Palace that same evening honoring the queen's birthday. On March 5, 1770, Parliament rescinded the Townsend Duties on all goods except tea. Relative calm in the colonies prevailed for the next three years, and there was no apparent threat to the union with Great Britain. However, for the prior twenty years England had steadily increased its control over the economy of the colonies and particularly that of Virginia. Taxation, the banning of paper money as legal tender, talk of changes to colonial charters and even dictating the terms for selling lands at public auction, were all efforts to exercise control over the colonies. These measures threatened to undermine and perhaps deprive the Virginia gentry of their livelihood, social position and their perceived liberties. Considering Washington's new-found political position in the House of Burgesses and his history of dealing with British military superiors who looked down on colonials without royal commissions, it is not surprising that this very independent man regarded these events as a personal affront.[24] Washington was still not greatly alarmed over British efforts to subjugate the colonies until it was learned that the East

22 Ferling, 92-93.
23 Jones, 33.
24 GW Papers at the Library of Congress.

India Company was exempt from remitting the duty it extracted from the colonies, thereby giving it a virtual monopoly and forcing colonial tea companies out of business. Also, the tax on tea was retained to preserve the Crown's right to tax the colonies whenever it wished. The colonists reacted strongly and refused the imported tea, but in Boston the resistance by the Sons of Liberty led to their dumping of the tea overboard in the notorious Boston Tea Party in December 1773. At the same time radicals in Charleston, South Carolina, confiscated the newly arrived tea, and in Philadelphia and New York British merchant ships turned back to England when greeted by the angry colonials. London became alarmed when the news reached them in January. When no restitution was offered by the participants, an incensed Parliament responded with passage of the Intolerable (Coercive) Acts in 1774, of which The Port Act closed the port of Boston and other acts enforced stricter controls in all the colonies. The economy of Boston came to a halt, but to the surprise of Parliament all the colonies supported Massachusetts by sending food, goods and necessities to them. With Washington in attendance, Burgesses set aside June 1 as a day of fasting and prayer for the people of Boston. Matters started to change when Massachusetts wrote to Burgesses requesting their support of a boycott on English goods, adding that Philadelphia and Annapolis had already agreed to support them. Washington left Williamsburg to attend some meetings in Alexandria to learn their reactions to events and was elected by them to head an emergency governing body for Fairfax County. Washington met with his political mentor, George Mason, and it is generally agreed that together they wrote the "Fairfax Resolves," which called for Virginia's non-importation of British goods and was adopted on July 18, 1774, in Alexandria with Washington as chairman of the meeting.

They formally challenged the unconstitutional acts of Parliament. These specifically arose out of the harsh British measures taken in Boston following the Tea Party in December 1773, but they were really a general protest against the loss of the colonies' rights under the British Constitution in the matters of taxation, British military forces within their borders and control of judicial powers and commerce. The Resolves called for the colonies to form an association to protest the British actions and violations of their fundamental rights, and it called for a meeting of a Continental Congress to approve a complete boycott of British imports. The Resolves contained an implied threat of further action and called for a "general congress for the preservation of our lives, liberties and fortunes."[25] These measures had strict orders to resort to force if necessary to enforce the blockade. Committees were formed to report violations and publish the names of those colonists who did not abide by it. Naturally, this enraged London, but the situation had reached a point where Virginia's rights and British power came to a head. In August at Williamsburg, the Burgesses called for a general meeting of all the colonies scheduled for September in Philadelphia. By then Washington had spent sufficient time with George Mason to have learned much more about political and constitutional matters from a man who was considered an expert. Washington was among seven delegates sent to represent Virginia.[26] Upon reflection, it was logical for Washington to be chosen as one of the delegates because of his reputation for integrity, honesty, personal independence, wealth and his new-found political leadership. Also, he was the only delegate with military experience, which must have influenced the assembly considering the recent British occupation of Boston. It could be said that

---

25 GW Papers at the Library of Congress, Series 5
26 Jones, 36.

Washington and Mason were the first to declare America's independence, but we must keep in mind that the mood of most delegates was one of loyalty to England and the hope for redress of their complaints. Most of the delegates believed their problems with England originated from corrupt politicians in Parliament, and they were very explicit in their loyalty to King George. At the First Continental Congress in 1774 most delegates were hopeful of reconciliation with England through intercession by King George over a corrupt Parliament. Pennsylvania Assembly Speaker Joseph Galloway was a strong supporter of American rights, but he advocated a plan to share colonial self-governance with a new Grand Council with a Crown-appointed president. Legislation would be shared with Parliament and the colonies, but the Parliament would be the final arbiter. Moderates favored the plan while militants opposed it on the grounds that it would inevitably lead to the same corruption that infected the British Parliament. In London, Benjamin Franklin rejected it saying, "When I consider the extreme corruption prevalent among all orders of men in this old rotten state, and the glorious public virtue so predominant in our rising country I cannot but apprehend more mischief than benefit from a closer union."[27] Support for the moderates waned in spite of the fact that very few militants wanted an outright break with England. Even the most militant in Philadelphia, Sam Adams, was not optimistic about colony-wide support for the defense of Massachusetts. The vast majority of delegates pledged their loyalty to the king and implored him to address the crimes of his ministers and protect his American colonists. The Fairfax Resolves reasoned that the colonial governments had always acted in concert with Parliament for the good of Great Britain and the colonies. Now, Parliament was usurping provincial government and reducing Americans to

---

27 GW Papers at the Library of Congress.

"slavery." The colonists insisted they were not planning to set up independent states, but were merely petitioning the king for redress of their grievances based on one hundred and fifty years of precedent. When Washington debated these issues with other delegates in Philadelphia, he observed that he saw no indication of a Parliament willing to address their petitions. He believed that Parliament had overreacted to the Tea Party with their several coercive measures. He firmly believed that the best and only effective response was to impose their own economic sanctions on England by restricting imports. He did not support suspension of all trade because it would hurt American exports and their own economic interests. The Congress adopted an economic plan very similar to the Fairfax Resolves and also adopted measures to promote greater domestic manufacturing and self-sufficiency. They created a Continental Association that not only instituted economic measures but also allowed committees to establish military forces in case armed resistance became necessary.[28] Fairfax County was the first to establish such a militia even though their convention in August 1774 had not authorized a militia. Congress reaffirmed their allegiance to the king, but at the same time gave Parliament until August 1775 to address their plight and repeal the Coercive Acts. If there was no resolution by then, the colonies would then ban all exports to England. However, before leaving Philadelphia, Washington ordered a book entitled *A Military Treatise on the Appointments of the Army*, thereby indicating his growing suspicion of an impending war.

At this juncture in his life, George Washington must have taken stock of himself. He was master of a growing plantation, owned thousands of acres, was a respected member of the House of Burgesses and had accumulated furnishings, horses, slaves and indentured servants, and yet he did not enjoy the same sense

28   Longmore, 74.

of purpose he possessed while in the Virginia military. His first portrait was painted by Charles Wilson Peale in 1772, and it is most revealing that he chose to pose in his uniform rather than simply as an aristocratic planter. As the colonies came together in 1774 to address a common threat, Washington seems to have gravitated towards a new purpose by affixing his strong personal independence to that of the colonies' desire to be free from the growing interference and domination of Parliament. Washington arrived in Philadelphia in late August 1774 together with Patrick Henry and Edmund Pendleton. The Virginians soon met with delegates from New England and learned first-hand of their difficulties with the Crown. The city of twenty-five thousand inhabitants was slightly larger than New York and 50 percent bigger than Boston. Its twelve-by-twenty-five blocks contained six thousand houses, and the noisy and crowded city smelled of smoke and manure during its long, hot summer. Washington met with the former governor, Richard Penn, as well as influential men such as Thomas Mifflin, John Dickinson and Joseph Reed. Congress agreed to boycott England until the Tea Act and the Coercive (Intolerable) Acts were repealed. The only dispute was whether to impose a non-export measure, but with crops waiting to be harvested the South prevailed with just a ban on English imports. The delegates also agreed to meet the following year if there was no progress with Great Britain.

While the First Continental Congress was meeting in the fall of 1774, Fairfax County in Virginia, considered one of the most radical areas in the colonies, was organizing their own militia. This was done despite the conciliatory mood of the Congress toward Great Britain. It was also done because the colonists saw in Boston with the quartering of British troops that armed intervention was possible elsewhere, and by taking the initiative they might influence other colonies to do the same. When Governor Dunmore continued to ignore the House of Burgesses, Fairfax County elected Washington as its delegate to the Virginia Convention in Richmond in March 1775. Virginia called the convention in their new capital of Richmond and directed the colony to prepare for its defense. It was at that convention that Patrick Henry gave his stirring speech calling for "liberty or death," which marked the turning point in Virginia from political debates to military action. Events occurred rapidly throughout the spring that would inevitably lead to war. The militia elected George Washington as their commander—not surprising considering his experience and reputation and that he was their political representative. As the militia began to drill under Washington's supervision, he also used them to enforce the economic boycott in Virginia. He was to supervise Virginia's military and was then overwhelmingly reelected to the Second Continental Congress. It is also important to remember that the initial excuse of Parliament for levying taxes on the colonies was to pay for the costs of the Seven Year's War and maintaining defenses of the frontier from Indian attacks. Some colonists argued to the British that an indigenous militia could do the job and at the same time relieve the British of such expenses. Upon the failure of the First Congress to resolve their differences with the Crown (in spite of some sympathy from Parliament), a Second Continental Congress was scheduled for May 1775. During that spring Washington was busy with sorting out his land development at the Great Kanawha River. He soon learned that Governor Dunmore was revoking the land grants that were awarded from service in the French and Indian War because the surveyor, William Crawford, was not properly certified. Washington was dismayed at the prospect of losing twenty-three thousand acres, so he conferred with Dunmore. Only days after their meeting, Washington expressed the belief that war with England was possible. In late April, Governor Dunmore seized the gunpowder stored in the magazine at Williamsburg, and local militia marched on the Governor's Palace to demand its return. Immediately, another messenger arrived at Mount Vernon with news of the conflict that occurred ten days earlier between the colonists and British troops in Lexington and Concord. Washington realized that war was inevitable, so before he left for the Second Congress he instructed his cousin, Lund Washington, to manage the estate until his expected return by Christmas. On May 3, 1775, he left to attend the Congress as a Virginia delegate, and when he arrived he was so disturbed by the Boston situation that he reportedly offered to personally equip and lead a thousand-man force to expel the British from the city. He also brought along his uniform and sword obviously thinking about a possible armed conflict. At the First Continental Congress the delegates expressed their rights as Anglo-Americans under the British Constitution. They regarded themselves as loyal Englishmen and continued to appeal to the King for redress of Parliament's acts. During the following months, the mood of the colonists changed dramatically as they learned of the King's indifference to a more sympathetic Parliament. The conservative delegates still wanted to petition the King, but by this time they were in the minority. As the New York and New England colonies asked Congress for supplies and direction regarding their militia, pressure was building for answers. Congress created two committees to study the situation and appointed Washington to chair them. This is quite revealing considering that Washington had not even served on one committee in the First Congress. By early June, Massachusetts asked Congress to have all the various New England troops put under the command of one national army. The question was who would be nominated for commander in chief. There were several alternatives such as the present commander in Massachusetts, General Artemas Ward, or the wealthy, eager candidate from Massachusetts, John Hancock, or Charles Lee who was a London-born Virginian and had been a professional British soldier. Realizing that the southern colonies would have to join the northern colonies, and that their support was vital, John Adams had become sufficiently impressed with the Virginia delegate, George Washington. He also nominated Washington to be commander in chief because of his military experience from twenty years prior in the French and Indian War and also because he regarded him as one who resented the economic controls being forced on the colonies. Most historians have believed that Washington was a compromise candidate for the commander in chief position, but historian Paul Longmore has used more recent research that reveals Washington as the only real choice for the post. As Congress deliberated the need for a new Continental Army in May 1775, Washington was heading two military committees and advising New York on defensive preparations in the event of an anticipated attack by the British. The delegates had heard of the King's rejection of their previous petition and that Parliament was preparing to send more troops. Moderates won a request for one more plea to the King, but sentiment was rapidly shifting to the militants. Meanwhile, Washington was arranging for an inter-colonial system for supplies and ammunition. In early June, Congress voted to borrow £6,000 to purchase gunpowder for the "Continental Army."[29] They then voted to recruit ten companies of soldiers from Pennsylvania, Maryland and Virginia to serve in a Continental Army under a chief officer in Boston. Washington was then asked to chair another committee

---

29 Longmore, 162.

to draft the rules and regulations for the new army. Washington attended the Congress in the military uniform he had designed and worn in the French and Indian War and apparently made a striking impression on the delegates. Artemas Ward did not have widespread support in Massachusetts even though they had the largest fighting force and called for another thirteen thousand men. Also, southerners were concerned that after expelling the British, the New Englanders might attempt to conquer the other colonies. This gives us a better idea of the extent of regional rivalries and jealousies. Charles Lee was only briefly considered, but his English birth together with his reputation as an eccentric went against him. A critical issue was the need for unity especially after the moderates were forced out of the picture. By this time, most delegates knew Washington and came to admire his upright character and his willingness to leave a comfortable home-life and put his fortune and reputation on the line. When he offered to take the position without pay he said, "As to pay, I beg leave to Assure the Congress that as no pecuniary consideration could have tempted me to have accepted this Arduous employment at the expense of my domestik ease and happiness I do not wish to make any profit from it: I will keep an exact Account of my expenses; those I doubt not they will discharge & that is all I desire."[30] John Adams was awed by this gesture, and Congress then realized he represented the kind of deep personal commitment that was necessary to the cause. One must assume that Washington harbored some desire to be selected as commander, but it could be argued that he merely wanted to be an officer in the Continental Army. When Adams overruled the New England delegation and presented his name on June 14, 1775, Washington quickly left the room careful not to hear or impede any debate on his nomination. Adams was smart enough to realize that a Virginian was critical

---

30   GW Papers at the Library of Congress.

to bringing the south into the conflict. It was the largest and wealthiest colony, and Washington was its leading citizen. Also, we must remember that Washington had been a celebrity for close to twenty years and was generally regarded as a serious, calm, brave, modest and thoughtful person. Historian Joseph Ellis tells us that when Washington arrived in Philadelphia in his custom-built coach, he was greeted by five hundred riders who escorted him into the city. Another indication of his growing stature was his appointment to chair the four committees on military preparedness. During the First Congress he had no committee assignments. A good indication of Washington's diplomatic skill was his choice of Edmund Pendleton to help him draft his acceptance speech and his will. Pendleton had not been in favor of Washington, and certainly there were many other lawyers available. But, he reached out to his adversary in an effort to gain his support. Another extraordinary event was his decline to accept a salary as a matter of honor so as not to be seen as profiting from the new position.[31] His acceptance of the position was with sincerity: "if some unlucky event should happen unfavorable to my reputation, I beg it remembered by every gentleman in the room, that I this day declare... that I do not think myself equal to the command I am honored with."[32] Congress felt comfortable with Washington's disinterest in power and his desire to unify the very independent colonies. It granted Washington full power and authority to do whatever was in the best interests of the colonies, and it is to his everlasting credit that he used this power in a positive way for the public good. His reputation was everything to him, and he must have been held in very high regard in order for Congress to offer him such sweeping authority. The real irony of his appointment was that there was still no army to command.

---

31   Ferling, 115.
32   GW Papers at the Library of Congress.

We must remember that the colonies were quite independent entities and were competitive and jealous of each other. It was a momentous and extraordinary decision for New Englanders to offer such power to a Virginian. After Washington's appointment, Congress had to struggle with appointing his generals. John Adams reported that these discussions were the most "tortuous he had yet experienced as a congressman."[33] After Congress soothed Artemas Ward with the first major generalship, Washington used his influence to gain positions for Charles Lee and Horatio Gates, and then the final ten appointments were made in an effort to appease most of the New Englanders. Congress also allowed Washington to select two adjutants, and after days of thinking about how much confidence he would need in such positions of trust, he choose two highly intelligent and well educated men who were nine years his junior, Thomas Mifflin and Joseph Reed. Immediately thereafter as he was preparing to leave for Boston, Washington was told of the "great victory" of the colonists at Bunker Hill.

We should take a moment to analyze the impact of these fast-moving events on Washington. As we have seen, Washington did not have good relationships with the British military under Braddock, Forbes or Loudoun. He must have harbored deep resentment when he failed on two occasions to gain a British army commission. We know that he felt cheated by the economic bias of the consignment system. He saw other Virginia planters being drowned in eternal debt to British merchants, and he himself briefly fell into its clutches. His independent spirit compelled him to become far less economically dependent on England, and he hoped his action would influence other Virginians to follow suit. The British Proclamation of 1763 denying his rights to western lands was infuriating to him. The Stamp Act was a

---

33 Ferling, 116.

minor event, but the Townsend Duties seemed to get his attention. His corroborations with George Mason educated him on a less personal and more legal plain, so when the Intolerable Acts were passed and English troops occupied Boston, Washington must have concluded the worst. Certainly by May 1775, before he left for the Second Continental Congress in Philadelphia when he packed his uniform, war must have been obvious to him. Keep in mind that he and Congress still had no knowledge of events in Lexington and Concord. It is safe to conclude that in the spring of 1775, Washington no longer considered himself to be a British subject. Instead, possibly just before his appointment and definitely with his appointment, he was transformed into an American revolutionary patriot.

The appointment of Washington as commander in chief marked the turning point in his life as well as for the future of the emerging American nation. We can ask the eternal question about most great men in history of whether the man makes the times, or do the times make the man. Is it Providence, fate, luck or skills that brought Washington to his new position? Hopefully, we have already touched on enough of these points to come to a reasonable conclusion, but a quick review is in order. He was born into a family that worked hard, achieved a comfortable living, honored public service and provided a decent education. His father's early death left George without a mentor, but his half-brother's marriage into a very wealthy family was fortuitous and filled that void. However, it was George's ambition that led him to develop those early relationships and showed us how observant and quick he was to learn. His skills as a surveyor were sufficient to earn a living, but they also brought him to the western lands which proved so critical in his future life. His brother's untimely death and his widow's remarriage soon followed by their child's demise left George as master of Mount Vernon before he turned thirty. His efforts to resume his brother's position in the Virginia militia and volunteer for service in the French and Indian War were events under his control, but the timing in his young life was sheer luck. His miraculous escapes from death in war and smallpox and other serious illnesses were just that. His failed efforts to gain a British army commission were cases of bad luck which transpired into future opportunities. His own marriage into landed aristocracy was most helpful especially in his acquisition of land and improvements to his social and political standing which increased his interest in personal rights and British wrongs. He had the bearing, stamina and looks of a military officer along with the ambition, toughness, tenacity, and determination that people often admire. Finally, he had the ability to judge men and situations with remarkable accuracy. In summary, George Washington's character and skills were in concert with events in history that presented him with a unique opportunity to become the most powerful and effective leader of his time. Even though he had no control of the fate that created many of these events, he did have the drive and discipline to turn these events into a successful outcome. But from the very beginning, Washington had no illusions of victory and knew that he was up against the greatest army and navy on earth. He had no idea of how weak and ill-prepared the colonists were. Yet, he was the first to put his life and property on the line knowing that the failure could bring him shame and a horrible death. In pledging his life, fortune and sacred honor and commanding the American army Washington risked being captured and sent to England where he would have been executed and drawn and quartered in the most grueling death ever devised by the mind of man. His was a deadly serious commitment, so it is not surprising that he wore a serious countenance while bearing the unimaginable weight of the destiny of his country.

As late as November 1775, moderate Americans were still harboring thoughts of reconciliation. British-Americans had a long history of devotion to the monarchy, and they had celebrated King George III as a "Patriot King" who was revered and beloved. Even Washington referred to the British army as the "ministerial troops." He carefully avoided the term "King's Troops." In November when Washington and Congress learned of the King's October address to Parliament accusing colonists of open revolt and the need to put down the rebellion, all hopes of the conciliationists died. The King accused them of trying to establish an independent empire, and was ordering massive numbers of British troops and foreign mercenaries to defeat them. To most Americans, the King had abdicated his responsibilities to them, and the attitude of reverence switched to one of hostility. The King was then regarded as a tyrant, and the entire system of monarchial rule was challenged. Thomas Paine picked up on the sense of revulsion in his publication *Common Sense*, in which he called the King a tyrant. This new attitude greatly influenced most Americans, and even Washington changed his enemy's name to the "King's troops." Past crimes attributed to Parliament were then blamed on the King. Americans were urged to place their dependence on their local governments and not the Crown. Statues, signs and any replicas of George III were destroyed. The result in the colonies was a void in traditional monarchial leadership, but that void was rapidly being filled by another George. Washington led Americans to repudiate the entire concept of kingship and to create a republican system based on individual talents. As Paul Longmore states, "This was the utopian idea they fought for, believing them selves the vanguard of a worldwide republican revolutionary movement. Americans fought, they asserted, not simply for their own liberty, but for the liberty of all mankind."[34]

There has always been a question of Washington's military skills and whether he relied solely on his earlier frontier experiences under Braddock and then Forbes. Critics maintain that he knew nothing of real military strategy or tactics, but this is belied by a search of his own library now kept in the Library of Congress. In spite of the fact that military books were few, expensive and difficult to find, Washington owned a number of technical military works composed by British and French officers who were considered authorities in their field. In 1756, just after his disastrous episode under Braddock, Washington ordered from London Bland's *Military Discipline*, the most popular military handbook of the time in England. Its text was followed by Marlborough and his contemporaries and is considered an excellent treatment of the art of war. On July 29, 1757 he urged his officers "to devote some part of your leisure hours to study of your profession, a knowledge in which cannot be attained without application; nor any merit or applause to be achieved without a certain knowledge thereof."[35] He also read *Essai sur l'Art de la Guerre* by Count Turpin de Crisse, which was used extensively by the French. Washington was frequently asked by his own officers for recommended reading, and he suggested five books that he was familiar with: the newest edition of Bland's *Military Discipline*; Count Turpin's *Essai* (also extolled by General Forbes and General Wolfe); *Military Instructions for Officers* by Roger Stevenson; *The Partisan* (a treatise on small war) and *Manoeuvres, or Practical Observations on the Art of War* by William Young. Washington also owned Simes's *Military Guide*

---

34 Longmore, 206.
35 GW Papers at the Library of Congress .

and two others by Simes. One of his favorite books was Guibert's *Essai General de Tactique*, also favored by Napoleon.[36]

Washington knew he was up against the strongest army in the world, and it is no wonder that he studied as much as possible, never being one to take his duties lightly. There were thousands of Tory sympathizers in the colonies with reportedly only a minority of the population in favor of a break with England. On top of this, Britain had total command of the seas until the French entered in the spring of 1778. However, by the summer of 1776, the British had amassed an army of thirty-six thousand men which included nine thousand Hessians. It is important to note that during the course of the war, Britain hired a total of 29,867 German soldiers which meant Washington was facing two of the best-trained armies in the world.[37] The Hessians were the most expensive mercenaries in Europe, but the unpopularity of the war in England forced the Parliament to hire outside forces. Offsetting this was the disadvantage of the great distance across the Atlantic that made it more difficult and more expensive for the British to send troops and supplies. Washington must have been well aware of these factors, even if the Congress was not. After the British left Boston, he probably thought reconciliation was possible, but after the losses of Long Island and Manhattan, he knew it was going to be a war of attrition and maneuver and hopefully time was on his side. His greatest challenge was to keep an army in the field and train them into a disciplined fighting force. He was not convinced that an inspired militia of short-term volunteers could defeat a veteran British army, but he needed time and men to train a professional American force. Being a man of action, Washington as well as leaders in Congress and

---

36 Oliver L. Spaulding, "The Military Studies of George Washington," *American Historical Review*, vol. 29, no. 4 (July 1924).

37 Stanley Weintraub, *General Washington's Christmas Farewell* (New York: Penguin Group, Inc., 2004) 29.

some military aides wanted a major confrontation in the open field. However, certain trusted generals like Greene and Knox convinced Washington that he was at a distinct disadvantage and risked an early and total defeat. The war was fought in four major areas; New England, Upstate New York, The Middle Atlantic New Jersey area and the South. After retaking Boston in the first nine months of his command, Washington spent most of the war in the hundred-mile segment between New York and Philadelphia. While at Valley Forge, Washington came to realize what his strategy should be. Historically, military success was determined by gaining victories in a series of battles which meant the taking of enemy land. However, by the spring of 1778, Britain occupied New York and Philadelphia and controlled the entire coast. Yet, the Continental Army was still intact, and the American Revolution was very much alive. In effect, while Washington and his army remained a fighting force it meant Britain could not win the conflict. Washington knew that time and distance were his allies, and if he could protract the war his chances of success in wearing down the British could prevail particularly as this was an unpopular war in England. When France recognized the new nation of the United States in May 1778, and agreed to supply arms and men, the odds for American success increased dramatically and raised the stakes to an unanticipated level for the British.[38]

---

38 Joseph J. Ellis, *Founding Brothers* (New York: Random House, 2000) 130.

CHAPTER 4

Commander in Chief of the American Military: 1775–1783

By the rude bridge that arched the flood,

Their flag to April's breeze unfurled

Here once the embattled farmers stood

And fired the shot heard round the world.

—Ralph Waldo Emerson, American Poet

When Washington and his entourage reached Cambridge on July 2, 1775, they learned that the American "victory" was actually a loss of Bunker (Breed's) Hill. It was a moral victory because the Americans under General Artemus Ward left a thousand British soldiers dead or wounded, or 42 percent of General William Howe's army.[1] It was such a great shock to Howe that it influenced his military tactics for the rest of the war. He soon succeeded General Thomas Gage as commander of the British troops in North America, but Bunker Hill and the siege of Boston converted Howe into a much more conservative general, which accounts for his later delays and lack of aggression in several

1   Ferling, 121.

key battles that could have altered the war in his favor. Once he
was settled, Washington was inundated with administrative work,
internal squabbles among the officers, inadequate supplies and
the task of organizing an army from untrained militiamen. Many
officers were upset with their new rank and had their political
friends implore Washington on their behalf. Supplies of tents,
clothing and ammunition were far less than had been reported,
and there were only fourteen thousand available soldiers instead
of the twenty thousand he had been told. In the words of historian
John Ferling, "Washington soon learned that every problem, no
matter how big or how small, inevitably was passed on until it
stopped at his desk."[2] Washington's organizational skills swung
into action. He enforced the Articles of War he had composed
for Congress while waiting for his appointment in Philadelphia.
Drunkards, swearers, thieves, slackers and deserters were
severely punished by flogging or humiliation. Hygiene and
cleanliness were demanded. Dignity, deportment and discipline
were required. He weeded out inept and corrupt officers and
then delegated his remaining officers to teach their regiments.
He ordered that everyone attend church services and expected
the chaplains to see that it was done. He designed colored
cockades and shoulder stripes to denote rank and invited each
day's adjutant and officers of the day to dine with him thereby
giving them a sense of importance and giving Washington first-
hand information from the ranks.[3] Washington understood the
importance of information about his own army as well as that of
his opponents. He discovered there were only six thousand British
soldiers and not the original estimate of twelve thousand. He also
learned that Gage was sufficiently impressed with the colonials
at Bunker Hill that he decided to wait for reinforcements from

2   Ferling, 124.
3   Ibid., 127.

England before waging another battle. This gave Washington the time he needed to train his men and plan his strategy. From July through the fall, Washington concentrated on building an army knowing that the British were not very likely to go on the offensive. During the summer and fall Washington wrote to Congress about the severe supply and ammunition shortcomings of the army and the prospect of not getting re-enlistments. In September, Washington wrote that conditions were so bad that he was compelled to conclude that unless the shortages could be resolved, the army would have to disband. Finally, this blunt message got their attention, and after sending supplies and money, they sent a committee of Benjamin Harrison, Thomas Lynch and Benjamin Franklin to Cambridge. The meetings with Washington were cordial, but the committee reported that Congress wanted Boston to be attacked by year-end, and they wanted the officers' pay to be cut. Washington was dismayed but used his political skills to overcome both directives. He called his Council of War to discuss these issues, and with their support he rejected the Congressional orders. The committee not only backed off, but they acceded to Washington's request for 25 percent more troops and more clothing and essential supplies. In this first encounter with political pressure, Washington showed his executive talents by establishing his authority at the very beginning leaving no doubt as to who was in charge of the war. He was also given even greater powers to impress local goods and increase disciplinary action.

During the fall Washington started to develop an information network to learn more about British strength in Boston and in Canada. This was particularly important regarding Canada where Washington learned of the weak British defense. Both he and Congress were hopeful that the Canadians would want to shed their British rulers and ally themselves with the American colonies and perhaps even decide to become a fourteenth colony. General Schuyler was commander of the northern army, but in spite of Washington's pleading for him to go on the offense, Schuyler procrastinated on the grounds of inadequate and untrained troops. Washington even considered sending part of his own army to Quebec, but instead he appointed Benedict Arnold to take a thousand men on an alternative 350-mile route to Canada through Maine. He was to coordinate an attack on Montreal and Quebec with Generals Schuyler and Montgomery against General Guy Carleton. Meanwhile, the British sent General John Burgoyne with a large force to defend Canada, and the American effort failed. It was a poorly devised and hopelessly bold campaign based on courage and patriotism against overwhelming odds and brutal weather. It was Washington's first lesson on the need for a trained army and better tactics.

The Siege of Boston: March 1776

The battle for Boston demonstrated Washington's leadership and cunning as well as the pluck, endurance and sheer determination of soldiers like Henry Knox, Benedict Arnold and Ethan Allen. The victory at Boston was really determined earlier in May at Ticonderoga where Allen and Arnold had taken that strategic fort on Lake Champlain without firing a shot or losing a man. Later that year Henry Knox and his troops had the strength and cleverness to haul fifty-nine cannons on forty sleds from the fort three hundred miles across Massachusetts to Boston. The plan and ultimate placement and strategy for the siege were Washington's, and, by acting under cover and against all odds, Washington commanded Dorchester Heights, and his cannon effectively provided control over Boston. The next day "providential" weather prevented General William Howe from attacking the Heights, so he decided to evacuate Boston with his seventy-five hundred men realizing the mortal danger of losing even more men than at Bunker Hill.[4] In analyzing the Battle of Boston, we should examine the situation that faced Washington:

- There was no Continental Army until the beginning of 1776. Washington commanded untried militia from various colonies whose voluntary enlistments expired on December 31, 1775;

- He had no cannon;

- He had no military engineers;

- He had only thirty-six barrels of gunpowder;

- He was very short on munitions;

- His fourteen thousand men fit for duty were living in sod and plank huts;

- Most of his men wore the shirts and vests they had on when they left from home;

- There were no trained sergeants and few experienced officers;

- There were sectional rivalries;

- Their guns were the family firelocks brought from home;

- He had to train an army under the watch of the finest military force in the world;

- He faced constant sickness that reduced his force from sixteen thousand to twelve thousand;

---

4   Fleming, 165.

- He had to contend with "stupidity" and lack of order and control;

- There was an enormous and catastrophic epidemic of smallpox that took a total of one hundred thousand lives in the colonies and incapacitated about a fourth of Washington's army.

In spite of all these obstacles, Washington won the day by:

- Instituting strict discipline and eliminating unsoldierly practices;

- Using court martials, public floggings, and drumming out of camp all those men and officers he considered unfit;

- Forbidding swearing and drunkenness;

- Imposing severe penalties for theft and straggling from camp;

- Requiring daily attendance at church services;

- Insisting on the best possible sanitation;

- Requiring neatness of officers and enlisted men;

- Putting all the militia together in the Continental Army with all enlistments to last until December 31;

- Organized a General Staff to replace the militia system;

- Taking the offensive by planning the siege of Canada led by Benedict Arnold; even though it meant sacrificing 1,050 men for that expedition;

- Acceding to his officers, who voted to wait for a possible reversal of policy by a new Parliament, even though he wanted to attack Boston to end the war with one blow;

- Planning the effort by Henry Knox to secure the fifty-nine cannon from the recently captured Fort Ticonderoga and having them dragged to Boston;

- Using surprise as a major weapon by directing the barricades and cannon on Dorchester Heights and supervising their installation under cover of night;

- Adopting a strategy of mobility and remaining in the field while preserving an army to take advantage of opportunities and defeat the enemy by piecemeal, according to his aide, Alexander Hamilton;[5]

- Inoculating the army, prompted by the smallpox epidemic (while it took two years to become mandatory, some consider it was one of Washington's most critical decisions keeping in mind that the procedure was feared and considered dangerous).

While Washington did demonstrate good organizational skills, it should be noted that his decision to seize the high ground of Dorchester Heights was a true gamble. He realized that General Howe was waiting for reinforcements from England and that may have influenced his decision to build the fortifications as soon as possible. However, if the work had been detected before completion, he probably would have been overrun by superior forces. The execution was stunning to the British and three weeks later, on March 17, 1776, they evacuated Boston leaving Washington with his first great victory even though historians have never regarded it as such. Shortly thereafter in May, the British were repulsed in Charleston by the South Carolina militia and by the North Carolina militia at Moore's Creek Bridge. When the British set fire to Norfolk, they were turned back by the Virginia

---

5   Randall, 292-299.

and North Carolina militia thereby expelling every last British soldier and sailor in the United States. No doubt this euphoric atmosphere influenced those who voted for independence the following July.

The Campaign of 1776: Long Island & New York City

General Nathanael Greene was crushed by his error in recommending that the fort [Fort Washington] be held. He wrote to Henry Knox, "I feel mad, vexed, sick and sorry... this is a most terrible event: its consequences are justly to be dreaded".

George Washington was shattered by the event. He was a witness to the final scenes, looking on helplessly from the Jersey Palisades across the Hudson River... The worst of it was to watch them surrender and see some of them put to the sword. He blamed no one else for what happened, took all the responsibility on his own shoulders, and judged himself more severely than anyone else could judge him... he turned away from his lieutenants, and began to weep.

—David Hackett Fischer
Washington's Crossing[6]

One has to be reminded that the war between England and her colonies actually started more than one year before Congress voted for a Declaration of Independence. Lexington, Concord and Bunker Hill were the catalysts that ignited the issue, but it was not until July 4, 1776, that the colonies officially decided to support the struggle in Massachusetts. This event was not a certainty as all the colonies were quite provincial and conducted business in their separate manner with their distinctive customs, laws, religions, commerce, trade and tariffs. At that time, Philadelphia

---

6   Fischer, 113.

was the largest city and Virginia was by far the largest colony, stretching all the way to the Mississippi River and the Great Lakes. The capital of Virginia, Williamsburg, was the center of political dialogue with Parliament, so it is no wonder that Virginians played a significant role in the events of the day. Many of the colonies had gifted men, but Virginia had more than most with Peyton Randolph, Thomas Jefferson, George Mason, James Madison, James Monroe, Patrick Henry and George Washington. Support by Virginia for the Massachusetts conflict was essential for the success of this bold venture, and they all appreciated that fact and accordingly acted with unanimous decisions following their deliberations.

While New Yorkers were celebrating the Declaration of Independence, one of Britain's largest armadas in history was sailing into New York harbor with fifty-two men-of-war, 427 troop transports and thirty-three thousand seasoned fighting troops. Washington fully expected that the British would attempt to occupy New York considering its strategic location and its large loyalist support. He had sent General Charles Lee to the city in February to assess its defense, and Lee reported that it was indefensible largely because of the surrounding waters which Britain dominated. Washington was inclined to agree, but after his arrival there in April he determined to set up defenses from Brooklyn on Long Island to various places along the Manhattan Island. In May, Washington conferred with Congress in Philadelphia and assured them he could defend New York or at worst inflict heavy enough British casualties to give them pause. He knew the odds were greatly against him, but he still felt that courage and patriotic fervor could win the day. From their headquarters on Staten Island, the British under Generals Howe, Cornwallis and Clinton and fifteen thousand troops together with two brigades of Hessians embarked for Long Island in August. At the last minute Washington had to replace his designated commander, Nathanael Greene, due to sickness, but no one knew the territory as well as Greene. Washington's forces were outnumbered three to one and were outmaneuvered. The Americans realized too late that the British had slipped behind them, and from the Bedford area only 950 men were attempting to hold off seven thousand redcoats. Washington arrived on the scene too late and had to watch from afar as his troops retreated to the American camp at Brooklyn Heights. He had placed too many men in Manhattan at the expense of Long Island, but if he had done otherwise the chances were great for Howe to have first struck the city. Once again, Howe did not press his advantage and waited for the next day to pursue Washington and the probability of annihilating his army. On August 30, under cover of night, Washington directed the evacuation of his troops, and by some unexpected good fortune, or Providence, a heavy fog descended the following morning and allowed him to remove all of his twelve thousand soldiers across the East River without detection by the British.

In mid-September the British landed on Manhattan at Kip's Bay (Murray Hill) and easily overpowered the poor American defenses. Washington had already retreated north to Harlem Heights to command the nine thousand-man line along the Kings Bridge to Harlem. Again, the British did not pursue him until Howe's arrival. This allowed Washington the luxury of regrouping and ordering a surprising counterattack, which gave his soldiers a much needed psychological lift. He then ceased the attack when the British reinforcements appeared. Once more fate, or Providence, intervened when a fire started in lower Manhattan on September 20 and devastated the city. In a letter to his cousin Lund, Washington wrote: "Providence, or some good honest fellow, has done more for us than we were disposed to do for ourselves."[7]

Another month passed before Howe could regroup his forces and attack Washington in White Plains. The British and Hessians sustained heavy losses but did force the Americans to withdraw. Yet again, fortune smiled on Washington with a severe storm that protected his escape from the clutches of General Howe, who then decided to return to New York City at the end of October. The only remaining American force left on Manhattan was Fort Washington on the upper West Side around present day 184th Street. Sadly, one of the Fort's twenty-eight hundred-man garrison was an English-born soldier who betrayed the Americans by selling plans of the Fort and its defenses to the English. Washington wanted the Fort to be abandoned, but he relented under Nathanael Greene's surprising decision to defend it. When the assault came in mid-November 1776, Washington was forced to abandon the Fort and watch in dismay from across the Hudson River as the Hessians under Colonel Johann Rall captured the twenty-eight hundred Americans. The British then crossed the Hudson and repeated their attack with the capture of Fort Lee after it was abandoned by Washington and his troops. The New York campaign was a total and humiliating defeat for Washington with five thousand Americans killed or captured. As he retreated across New Jersey, Washington was pursued by General Cornwallis while both men hoped to gain enlistments along the way. In Newark only thirty men joined Washington while three hundred enlisted with the British. Clearly, Washington's army was in a critical condition, and the vastly superior British were in hot pursuit. By the time Washington's army crossed the Delaware to safety, it had dwindled to five thousand men from

7   GW Papers at the Library of Congress.

an original nineteen thousand the prior month. Desertions were high, and the British had captured most of the cannons abandoned in New York leaving Washington with only eighteen pieces of artillery. Washington informed Continental Congress President John Hancock that the American army was all but finished, and his beliefs in the strengths of patriotic amateur militiamen ended. Washington also realized that the war would be far longer than the short decisive one for which he had hoped.

With Washington all but defeated as he raced in retreat from New York and across New Jersey we should consider his impossible situation:

- His poor strategy for defending Long Island and being outmaneuvered;

- His sending an alternative commander to Nathaneal Greene, one who did not know the terrain;

- His personal late arrival on the scene;

- His risky effort to even try to defend New York knowing its vulnerability;

- His loss of men and material on Long Island;

- His poor defense of Manhattan;

- The total ineffectiveness of militia at Kip's Bay and elsewhere in the city;

- The poor defense of Fort Washington;

- The introduction of veteran Hessian mercenaries;

- The questionable policy of invading Canada with the subsequent loss of vital men and materials;

- The lack of support for arms and men in loyalist New York and New Jersey;

- His lack of a navy and therefore no way of preventing British reinforcements and supplies and their command of American port cities.

In spite of such enormous disadvantages, Washington was able to keep the revolution alive by adopting new techniques and adapting to new circumstances:

- He knew when and how to retreat;

- He employed harassing tactics;

- He took calculated risks especially with his counter-attack at Harlem Heights;

- He took advantage of British mistakes—like their not pursuing him and their generals not heeding their subordinates' advice;

- He used surprise tactics for short-term gains;

- He attacked only when the rewards exceeded the risks;

- He used the power of his convictions to inspire his officers and men;

- He listened to his officers;

- He was visible to the fighting men and built their trust and loyalty;

- He showed concern and caring for his army's needs;

- He was subservient to the Congress;

- He knew his army's strengths and weaknesses;

- He drove himself to do the impossible and expected his troops to do likewise;

- His faith was unshakable;

- He learned from his mistakes.

Trenton and Princeton: December 25, 1776 to January 3, 1777

Had Washington lost the gamble—had his men been repulsed from Trenton and pinned against the river—the continent would have been lost.

—George F. Will
Author and Historian

No single day in history was more decisive for the creation of the United States than Christmas 1776. On that night a ragged army of 2,400 colonials crossed the ice-choked Delaware River from Pennsylvania to New Jersey in the teeth of a nor'easter that lashed their boats and bodies with sleet and snow. After marching all night, they attacked and defeated a garrison of 1,500 Hessian soldiers at Trenton. A week later the Americans withstood a fierce British counterattack in Trenton and then stole away overnight to march fifteen miles by back roads to Princeton, where they defeated British reinforcements rushing to Trenton... These victories saved the American Revolution from collapse. Without them there would have been no United States, at least as we know it.

—James M. McPherson, Editor
Washington's Crossing[8]

As winter set in, the British decided to rest near Trenton before their spring offensive to take Philadelphia, the largest American city and the birthplace of the rebellion. The British under Cornwallis turned over their New Jersey campaign to General James Grant, who garrisoned the British and Hessian troops along a thirty-mile front. Washington was well aware of

---

8   Fischer, ix.

their vulnerability and accordingly made plans to take advantage of the situation. He was determined to redeem his reputation from the defeats in New York, and he considered a surprise attack to attain a much-needed victory and morale-booster. In Trenton, the Hessians were commanded by Colonel Johann Rall, the officer who had slaughtered the Americans on Long Island and as they surrendered at Fort Washington in New York City. He quickly acquired a reputation for pillage, rape and brutality, which influenced many local Jersey farmers to side with the Americans. Previously, they had mostly been loyalists who wanted to protect their property, but they soon formed their own militia and ambushed the Hessians and British scouting parties. Washington was developing skills as a master disinformer and actively used spies to mislead the enemy about his troop's weak condition. He also procured hard and paper currency from Congressman Robert Morris, who had remained in Philadelphia and who borrowed it from the wealthy Quakers who would not support the war effort but who would loan money to Morris. Washington needed such bounty funds to re-enlist those soldiers whose term was about to expire on December 31. He had to act decisively before his army shrank away. Some have called his decision to attack the enemy as foolhardy, but as noted at Dorchester Heights, he was a risk-taker who could sense the rewards of a successful surprise attack. The plan was said to have originated with Benedict Arnold who, with Horatio Gates, left Fort Ticonderoga to reinforce Washington. The planned attack on Trenton called for backup support from the west and south to cut off retreating Hessians and employed veteran reliable officers such as Henry Knox, Nathanael Greene, James Munroe, John Sullivan, John Glover and William Washington. Before marching, Washington addressed his men with a passage from the newly published *The American Crisis* written by Thomas Paine just one week earlier. He ordered his officers to read the following passages to his men:

> These are the times that try men's souls. The summer soldier and the sunshine patriot will, in this crisis, shrink from the service of their country; but he that stands it now, deserves the love and thanks of man and woman. Tyranny, like hell, is not easily conquered; yet we have this consolation with us, that the harder the conflict, the more glorious the triumph.

Of the twenty-four hundred men in camp, only half were fit to fight due to illness. The December 25 trip across the Delaware with supplies, cannon and horses amid a bitter cold and snowy night took fourteen hours. Washington admonished his men to stay close to their officers as they marched ten miles to Trenton. Colonel Rall was alerted but refused to be disturbed after an evening of heavy dining and celebrating. His men were exhausted from having served at their posts non-stop for a week expecting an imminent attack through an informer. When Washington attacked, it was swift and fierce with two hundred Hessian casualties and 948 prisoners. Washington quickly withdrew his forces back across the Delaware when he learned that a fourth Hessian regiment escaped to tell the news to their comrades in Princeton. The Christmas night raid was a daring one that saw the Americans take the offensive for the first time. It was bold and risky, but Washington knew he had to take the initiative and could no longer fight defensively. His troops had gone for forty-eight hours without food and had marched for twenty-five miles, but their victory boosted American morale to a new level. After December 29, half of Washington's volunteer army had gone home. He then made one of his most impassioned pleas directly to the remaining twelve hundred men. When no one agreed to re-enlist, he simply said:

You have done all I asked you to do, and more than could be reasonably expected. But your country is at stake, your wives, your homes and all that you hold dear. You have worn yourselves out with fatigues and hardships, but we know not how to spare you. If you consent to stay only one month longer, you will render that service to the cause of liberty and to your country which you probably never can do under any other circumstance.[9]

By the end of the day twelve hundred men re-enlisted. Meanwhile, Congress was in Baltimore and offered Washington the authority for whatever he needed for the army. He was permitted to raise troops from the states, grant officer appointments, arrest those who did not accept Continental currency as payment for goods and arrest those who proved disloyal. In brief, he was allowed to manage the army in the manner he deemed best.[10]

When Cornwallis learned of the Trenton defeat he immediately rushed to Princeton and prepared to face Washington just outside Trenton. Once again, Washington was reluctant to fight a superior force head-on so he cleverly camouflaged a midnight retreat around the right flank of the British to attack their rear guard in Princeton. The Trenton victory had also brought sixteen hundred recruits, who Washington ordered to join him for the impending Princeton battle. Forward scouts informed Washington that seven thousand Hessians and British troops were marching to Princeton. After they arrived, Cornwallis was advised by his Quartermaster General, William Erskine, to attack immediately, but Cornwallis was so confident of his troop strength that he elected to wait until morning. When morning came on January 2, 1777, Washington's army had vanished. On the following day, the first engagements shattered the Americans, and it was only the new recruits, barely holding onto the line, who gave Washington enough time to regroup his men. He personally led

9   GW Papers at the Library of Congress.
10   Randall, 327.

the counter charge against the British cannons with hat in hand shouting orders to move forward and fire. Raw recruits were actually charging against British veterans, who turned and ran for cover in Princeton's Nassau Hall. When the American cannons started shelling the building, the British surrendered and the Battle of Princeton marked a significant turning point in the war. When Benjamin Franklin informed King Louis XVI of the two American victories, the French sent four shiploads of guns and ammunition to America. The American victories also resulted in a change in British strategy whereby they withdrew their New Jersey forces to New York and abandoned the idea of holding large pieces of land. Instead, they intended to capture the key coastal cities. The majority of Americans lived in the countryside, which now belonged to Washington.[11] By March 1777, Washington had concluded that he needed to change his strategy. He knew his inferior forces could not win an offensive war, so he adopted a "war of posts." Essentially, this was a defensive maneuver that ran counter to Washington's preference for offensive tactics. But the strategy had to change in order for the depleted, outmanned and outgunned army to survive for the long haul. Also, in spite of the Trenton and Princeton victories, general support for the war was waning, and Washington had to reluctantly accept the need to change strategy so he could keep the spark of liberty alive.

The winter campaigns of 1776–77 did not mark the turning point in the war, but they did unveil some interesting aspects of the war. After Princeton, the New Jersey militia continued to attack British and Hessian forces in a series of small battles known as the Forage War. These lasted for twelve weeks and took a heavy toll on the enemy. The British and German armies together totaled 31,600 men in August 1776, and by February 1777, due to deaths, disease, exposure and malnutrition, their numbers had declined

---

11   Randall, 330.

to fourteen thousand.[12] These small battles were instigated and carried out by small units, able to beat larger and better trained enemy forces by engaging in quick, surprise, night, flanking and defensive maneuvers. Like Trenton and Princeton, Washington was at the center of the decisions, but he listened and inspired his men more as a leader than as a demanding commander. More importantly, the new American initiatives had a profound impact on the Europeans who were managing the war from a great distance. Public opinion in England turned against the war as was evidenced by the steady decline in British government bonds from a price of £89 in 1776 to £76 in 1778.[13] The British field commanders, who hoped for conciliation from their leaders, now had to begin to plan for a protracted war. Their success in recruiting American loyalists suddenly failed as more enlistments now turned to the Continental Army. While the British and Germans were losing enthusiasm for the war, Americans were regarding it with greater conviction as a just cause. As historian David Fischer tells us, the British role was to conquer, but the Americans believed they just had to survive to win the contest. To survive, Americans relied on their inner strengths, which included religious faith, freedom, independence and a high degree of literacy and economic well-being. In 1775, more than 70 percent of the northern free male population was literate. Also, agriculture and the general economy were strong.[14]

A key element for Americans was the suspicion of power and the need to have civilian rule over the military. Washington understood this completely and reinforced it with his officers. Both elements improved their direct communication as the war escalated. However, when it came to executing the war, Washington drew the line, and when it became painfully clear

12 Fischer, 366.
13 Ibid., 367.
14 Ibid., 368.

just before Trenton that Congress could not manage the war, they gave Washington total power to do whatever needed to be done. Some Congressmen thought he was granted too much power, and they only accepted the measure because of their growing respect for Washington. However, there were other characteristics that separated the Americans, who temporarily fought out of necessity to achieve a stated purpose, from the Europeans, who regarded war as a career or hobby. Americans fought to win and then get back to their livelihoods. Europeans fought for the sake of fighting or conquest. Americans were always mindful of public opinion and expected their armies to win quickly and without great loss of life. Washington understood this and always tried to plan his battles for maximum gain and minimal casualties. He was faced with this constant challenge, but Trenton and Princeton gave rise to changing tactics. The principal change was taking the initiative, which, in turn, determined the tempo of the war. His surprise attacks for over three months showed that by controlling tempo he could maintain flexibility and opportunity. He also learned that in the face of a larger superior enemy, he could concentrate his forces on one of their weaker or more isolated positions and inflict heavy casualties. His smaller units were quicker than the larger British forces with their extensive baggage trains, cannons and artillery. By quick and speedy initiatives he kept the British and Hessians off balance.[15]

Another important development from the 1776–1777 winter campaign was the decision by Congress to fight a war on a higher humanitarian plane. Led by John Adams, the majority of congressmen believed that Americans should grant their British and German prisoners the kind of human rights that exemplified the ideals they were fighting for. The Americans were shocked at the brutality of their enemies,

---

15 Fischer, 372.

and many witnessed the unmerciful behavior of both the British and the Germans, who practiced a barbaric code of conduct toward their enemies. Washington himself observed the killing and desecration of his troops trying to surrender at Fort Washington. At Princeton, wounded Americans who surrendered were beaten to death and mutilated without quarter. The European code of warfare allowed the victors to grant or withhold "quarter" depending on the circumstances of the particular battle, but the British and Hessians rarely granted it. Prisoners had no rights whatsoever. When they did take American prisoners, they were starved and left to rot in the holes of British ships in New York harbor. Complaints to the British officers were not acknowledged, but their cruelty only stiffened American resolve to act in a more humane manner. Congress formally adopted a policy of humanity, and Washington strictly followed it. One of the great ironies of the war was the treatment of the Hessian captives from Trenton. Many were sent to Lancaster, Pennsylvania, and their diaries record how surprised they were to have been treated so well. These were the same troops who had butchered the surrendering Americans at Fort Washington earlier that year. Of the 13,988 Hessian soldiers who fought in America, 3,194 elected to stay after the war—a good indication of their benevolent treatment. Washington took a personal hand in this policy, claiming that the Germans were "innocent people in this war" and were forced to fight.[16] This policy of human rights was intended to underline the higher values of the American Revolution, and it became a tradition in American warfare ever since. Historian David Fischer is clear to point this out because it runs counter to American debunking by recent scholars who depict America's

---

16   GW Papers at the Library of Congress.

past as a "record of crime and folly." Through his research and scholarship, Professor Fischer puts the record straight.[17]

The Campaign of 1777: Brandywine, Germantown & Philadelphia

Washington set up his winter headquarters in Morristown and spent the next five months rebuilding his army and gaining recruits. Perhaps the most significant aspect of the Trenton and Princeton victories was how they changed British strategy. In London, General John Burgoyne convinced the ministry office that they should divide the colonies along the Hudson River north-south line from New York City clear up to Canada and thereby isolate New England. Sir William Howe, who commanded the British in New York, would move north and meet Burgoyne in Albany to secure the plan. However, neither Burgoyne nor the war offices at Whitehall told Howe about their plan, and meanwhile Howe devised his own strategy for capturing the colonial capital of Philadelphia. In late July 1777 he loaded seventeen thousand troops and all their horses and supplies aboard 267 ships and sailed from New York harbor without Washington knowing their destination. His dilemma was whether to send forces north to support Gates or south to defend Philadelphia. By July 29 he learned that the British were south in spite of several course changes by Admiral Richard Lord Howe (William's brother) to confuse the Americans. Actually, the British did not land at Philadelphia but went ashore about sixty miles to the south in Maryland near present-day Elkton. When the sighting was reported to Washington, he quickly marched his eleven thousand men to Wilmington to confront Howe's army, which had spent five weeks holed up in hot, stinking ships suffering from exhaustion and sickness. Again, Washington skirmished and harassed them

---

17 Fischer, 379.

with his perfected tactics of hit-and-run. He then decided to make a stand at Brandywine Creek. Although he assured Congress he could defend Philadelphia, we do not know for certain if Washington really believed it himself. We can surmise that he felt his primary objective should be to prevent Howe from going to the aid of Burgoyne on the Hudson by pinning him down along the Delaware River, which had been fortified by the Americans. Secondly, Washington wanted to buy time to allow the much needed arms and gunpowder to arrive from France. Thirdly, he did not want the British to move inland where the iron mills, forges and stockpiles of weaponry were stored at Reading. Howe assumed Washington would defend the capital and give him the opportunity to crush the Continental Army, quickly ending the war. At the Brandywine, Howe and Cornwallis used the same outflanking maneuver as they had on Long Island, and even though Washington and other local citizens warned the general in charge, one of Washington's best, John Sullivan of New Hampshire, the British succeeded in driving the Americans back. Yet again, the British rested instead of pressing their advantage and thereby gave Washington time to get to the scene and regroup his men. (This time, Washington had the newly arrived nineteen-year-old Major General Lafayette at his side.) Again, Washington had to go to the rescue of another unit under General Anthony Wayne and personally take charge. While the British did manage to hold the field of battle, the Continental Army stood up to the best British and Hessian troops and kept Howe from his objective of destroying them. This was Washington's first European-style battle, and, while its loss provided more criticism from Congress, it built new confidence in the army. In two weeks, Cornwallis entered Philadelphia and Washington retreated to Reading to rest his battle-weary soldiers. During this time, Congress had moved from Baltimore to Reading to York, 110 miles west of Philadelphia.

With three weeks of rest and nearly five thousand recruits and veterans, Washington was ready to counterattack. He knew that Howe's troops were thinly placed over too wide an area with their main force of eighty-five hundred men in Germantown. He also realized that he had to move very quickly before British defenses were built, and this prompted him to make his greatest gamble. For the first time in the war, he put his entire army into the attack. It was late September, and he was aware of progress near Saratoga against the British. The initial fighting saw the Americans winning the field, and the British actually sounded their retreat. When General Howe saw his top troops in disarray and retreat he rallied them and soon a thick fog settled over the field whereby it was almost impossible to discern the two sides. Virginians and Pennsylvanians were shooting at each other and by morning the Americans were in retreat. In spite of the defeat, Washington won praise from Europe for such a daring and difficult battle. This, together with the Gates and Arnold victory over Burgoyne at Saratoga, proved to be a major turning point in the war because the Americans won the full support of sympathetic France and forced the British to change their strategy. Washington referred to Philadelphia, the Brandywine and Germantown as "defeats not disasters." In fact, he observed that his army did well except for maneuvering under fire, so he was intent on solving that problem with further professional training. Also, Washington was vindicated for dividing his forces between the Hudson and Philadelphia and for having fortified the waterways around Philadelphia and preventing the British from gaining additional troops, supplies and food into the capital. Howe suddenly and surprisingly sent his resignation to London thereby setting the stage for a new British strategy.[18] Let us again analyze Washington's challenges in 1777:

- He was faced with the British in control of Canada and New York City and the fear of seeing New England isolated—he knew he had to reinforce his Northern Army at the expense of losing valuable men and arms in the mid-Atlantic area;

- He did not know where Howe would go when he loaded seventeen thousand troops and supplies in New York harbor;

- He knew he had to defend Philadelphia, the capital and largest seaport in the colonies and the home of Congress;

- He had to neutralize the British navy without a navy of his own;

- He had to fight Howe's seventeen thousand troops with fewer and lesser trained soldiers;

- He knew he had to fight effectively and not lose his army while retreating;

- He could not be in two different places so was forced to delegate command to his officers in the north and at strategic places around Philadelphia;

- His losses in Philadelphia, the Brandywine and at Germantown gained critics in Congress and within his staff;

- His troops had no professional training especially under fire, which cost two battles that should have been won;

---

18   Randall, 340.

- His losses caused Congress to flee to Baltimore then to Reading and finally to York;

- As Congress fled, the Continental currency depreciated so rapidly that it was increasingly more difficult to retain recruits with adequate bounties;

- The depreciating currency led many farmers to deal with the British, who could offer hard currency of the realm, thereby impoverishing Washington's army.

Now, let us see how Washington dealt with these challenges:

- He made the decision to deplete his New Jersey forces and reinforce the Hudson Valley;

- He spent over a year fortifying Philadelphia and the surrounding Delaware River, including massive underwater works to blockade British ships;

- Upon the sighting of Howe off Maryland, he took the initiative to march his eleven thousand men to meet him just south of Philadelphia in an effort to keep him from going inland;

- He personally took command of most battles and by leading and regrouping his men he demonstrated fearless leadership;

- He took the offensive when it was least expected as in Germantown;

- He took risks when he thought the rewards would be even greater;

- He kept his army in the field avoiding a head-on battle;

- He thwarted his enemy's objectives;

- He took advantage of Howe's mistakes of caution and poor pursuit;

- He turned the defeats of the Brandywine and Germantown into positive events by showing sufficient military prowess that led to growing recruits, the aid of French arms and a growing sense of confidence and morale;

- His deeds and the defeat of Burgoyne at Saratoga brought the French into serious discussions about aiding our struggle for independence;

- The British victories came at a very high cost to them in men and materials, and they were forced to change their strategy from controlling large tracts of land to one of consolidation.

- In addition, for whatever reasons, General Howe resigned and returned to England.

Valley Forge: December 19, 1777 to June 19, 1778

Never give in, never give in, never, never, never, never—in nothing great or small, large or petty—never give in except to convictions of honour and good sense. Never yield to force; never yield to the apparently overwhelming might of the enemy. We stood all alone a year ago, and to many countries it seemed that our account was closed, we were finished.

—Prime Minister Winston Churchill
October 29, 1941

Often referred to as "the Crucible of Victory", Valley Forge marked the nadir of the Revolution. It is very much the story of

George Washington's leadership. It was a time and place for soul searching, courage and resolve. It was a common practice for combatants of that era to refrain from conflict during the winter with its unreliable weather and poor roads. Even wives of senior officers joined their husbands with Martha leaving Mount Vernon for seven of the eight winters of the war. This literally was a "recess" during the war and another of those many episodes that some mark as Providential. If General Howe had pursued the Americans, the war would probably have been won by the British soon thereafter. But Howe and his men decided to stay in their comfortable quarters in Philadelphia, believing that with the colonial capital and largest American city in their control, it was only a matter of time before the colonies would submit to defeat. Morale in the American army was low and popular support for the war was declining. Washington needed men, money and supplies, but the Congress did not have the authority to provide these essentials because those decisions were in the hands of the state governments, and they were not willing to raise new taxes or meet their required enlistments.

Valley Forge is most often depicted as a severely difficult time with starvation, bitter cold and a demoralized army. Actually, the privations lasted for only two months until cabins could be constructed and supplies and food distribution could be reorganized by Nathanael Greene. Enlistments were growing, and the soldiers were learning new skills under the recently arrived Baron Friedrich von Steuben. Contrary to popular belief, that winter was unusually mild, which greatly helped in their training. Although von Steuben was a disciplined drillmaster, the troops came to respect and even enjoy learning from him, especially in perfecting their ability to maneuver in ranks instead of their single file methods, which had hindered them in Germantown and Long Island.[19]

The six-month period at Valley Forge was filled with intrigue. It was a time when political and military forces influenced the future course of the war. Although no major battles were fought there, a new American army emerged, and its structural change left its imprint on America's unique interrelationships within the army that survive even to this day. One must keep in mind that Washington was attempting to mold an army from eleven colonies (Georgia and South Carolina had none) with a newly formed Continental Army. It was obvious to him that training and discipline were greatly lacking and had probably cost them the Battle of Germantown. When Baron von Steuben arrived at camp in February 1778, and unofficially assumed the duties of Inspector General, a new military era was born. In effect, Washington introduced a "chain of command" quite different from his British adversaries. Past defeats had shown glaring American weaknesses, but there was no infrastructure in place to deal with the problems. By remaining in Philadelphia, the British allowed enough time for the Americans to reorganize and train their army. Realizing that battles are won or lost by the quality of fighting men, von Steuben was given the responsibility of training the men in the art of war. Unlike the British officers, who did not participate in drills and exercises, von Steuben trained the troops and officers, and when a small contingent was ready they in turn trained other men one regiment at a time. The American officers were responsible for their own men, but when necessary, von Steuben stepped in to retrain those who needed it. Within three months, the American army was transformed into an effective fighting force that would ultimately change the outcome of the war. Although still inferior to their British veteran

19   Flexner, 117-118.

counterparts, their skills at forming lines and moving in unison challenged the British sufficiently enough to make a difference. The composition of the army also changed from the emotionally charged farmers and merchants at Lexington, who volunteered for several months, to younger more rugged men between fifteen and twenty-five years of age who signed up for the long haul because they had little opportunities elsewhere. They included immigrants from Europe, indentured servants, and blacks. They respected Washington, and, even though he was a tough disciplinarian and kept his distance, they had a mutual admiration for each other. Washington recognized their hardships and willingness to tough it out, and his devotion to them earned him their loyalty.

In addition to the newly established training program, the key to success at Valley Forge was Congress's "Committee at Camp," which arrived on January 28, 1778. Only four days after arriving at Valley Forge, Washington wrote a shocking letter to Henry Laurens, President of Congress, in which he said:

> Unless some great and capital change suddenly takes place... this Army must inevitably be reduced to one or another of these three things. Starve, dissolve, or disperse... behold! To my great mortification, I was not only informed, but convinced, that Men were unable to stir on Acct of Provision, and that a dangerous Mutiny begun the Night before, and which with difficulty was suppressed by the spirited exertions of some officers.[20]

The letter got Henry Lauren's attention. The Committee was the idea of Washington, and it served as a vital communications link between the Continental Army and Congress. It consisted of four members of Congress, three members of the Board of War, and both Gouverneur Morris of New York and Charles Carroll of Maryland. Washington's officers were skeptical of the Committee, but within one month, they found them helpful in addressing

---

20 GW Papers at the Library of Congress.

the camp's supply, clothing and food shortages. The Committee also supported changes to the army's organizational structure. Another vital link in their fast-improving communications was provided by Washington's aide, Lt. Colonel John Laurens, the son of Henry Laurens. Also, senior officers developed closer relationships among themselves and with congressmen which further enhanced communications. This was all in sharp contrast to the British, who had a much longer and more complex line of communications involving months of delays across the Atlantic Ocean. With Congress only ninety miles from Valley Forge, communication was relatively quick, and this enabled Congress to solve problems and build rapport with Washington and his officers. Also, John Lauren's correspondence with his father was regarded as personal, and therefore it was not scrutinized as much as official letters and exchanges. The Committee frequently met with Washington and his officers and reported directly back to Congress on recommended changes. One such change was the March 5, 1778 appointment of Nathanael Greene as Quartermaster General. This position was left vacant by General Thomas Mifflin's resignation in July 1777, thereby causing a total lack in the organization of supplies and materials. Another proposal was for a Corps of Engineers with input from the French volunteer, General Duportail. A cavalry organization was adopted on May 27, 1778. The Committee addressed other aspects, like prisoner exchanges, officer fitness, tents, horses, equipment and money. Most importantly, when the Committee ceased in May 1778, the members returned to Congress as strong supporters of the Continental Army and its Commander in chief. Many of the Committee's accomplishments were due to the political savvy and public relations efforts of Henry Laurens. As President of the Continental Congress, he was at the center of all the communications. Much of his information came from his son, John, who had been well educated in the law, mathematics and philosophy at schools in London and Europe. He was fluent in French and had actually fought in the Battles of Brandywine and Germantown. He served as Washington's aide without pay and gained a reputation for loyalty, bravery and intelligence. Henry Laurens used his son's information to protect Washington and his loyal officers from personal attacks by those in Congress and the army who wanted to replace Washington. In a January 12, 1778, letter to Lafayette about certain detractors, Henry Laurens confided:

> In a word, Sir, be not alarmed, I think it is not in the power of any junta to lessen our friend [Washington] without his own consent, I trust his good sense & his knowledge of the World, will guard against so fatal an error. If you desire it Sir, Mr. John Laurens will communicate what I have written in confidence to him, I say in confidence, not because I am afraid of having my sentiments known, I speak them honestly and unreservedly upon every proper occasion but I very much dislike correspondences which may be misunderstood & charged with design to foment dissentions—it is my constant endeavor to reconcile & make peace.[21]

Shortly thereafter, Laurens forwarded an anonymous letter critical of Washington directly to him suggesting it was "stuff... that the hearth was the proper depository for such records." Washington appreciated the support of Henry Laurens, and on January 31, 1778, he wrote to acknowledge it:

> I cannot sufficiently express the obligation I feel to you for your friendship and politeness upon an occasion in which I am so deeply interested. I was not unapprised that a malignant faction had been for sometime forming to my prejudice; which, conscious as I am of having ever done all in my power to answer the important

---

21   Hermann O. Benninghoff, II, *Valley Forge: A Genesis for Command and Control, Continental Army Style* (Gettysburg, Pennsylvania: Thomas Publications, 2001) 77.

purposes of the trust reposed in me, could not but give me some pain on a personal account; but my chief concern arises from an apprehension of the dangerous consequences, which intestine dissentions may produce to the common cause. My Enemies take an ungenerous advantage of me; they know the delicacy of my situation, and that motives of policy deprive me of the defence I might otherwise make against their insidious attacks. They know I cannot combat their insinuations, however injurious, without disclosing secrets, it is of the utmost moment to conceal.[22]

Washington and Henry Laurens formed an "inner circle of influence." Historians are not certain of all its members, but we do know Lafayette, von Steuben, Greene and Knox were included even though they probably never completely appreciated all the efforts made on their behalf by Laurens in Congress. The Baron was promoted to Major General in March 1778, and Lafayette was reassigned to Washington following his expressed concern over the ill-advised Canadian campaign, and General Thomas Conway was reassigned from the Northern Department to Peekskill. All of these moves seem to have been quietly and diplomatically influenced by Henry Laurens. It really was Henry Laurens who facilitated the reorganization of the army's newly created command and control structure. He firmly believed in Washington's leadership. He protected Washington from political attacks and diffused tensions in the military by recommending specific assignments in order to promote greater cooperation. An influential delegate to Congress, Joseph Reed, wrote to Henry Laurens on June 15, 1778:

I cannot but congratulate you, Sir, on the respectable Appearance of our Army & their Improvement in Discipline & every soldierly Quality—On the Extinction of every Spark of Discontent & Faction against the best of Men & the Regularity with which the several Departments seem now to be conducted. To the latter I ascribe

---

22 GW Papers at the Library of Congress.

97

very much of the former, as the Attention & Care of the General being no longer called off from his Command to exercise the Duties of the Staff, his time & Talents are devoted more directly to the military Duty of his Troops, the happy Consequences of which are more & more conspicuous every Day.[23]

However, Valley Forge proved to be the turning point of the conflict in several other important ways. It showed the British that holding major cities like Philadelphia and New York was not sufficient to defeat the enemy, and this had resounding results when they evacuated Philadelphia only to be ambushed and badly hurt at Monmouth. More importantly, it gave Washington the opportunity to train his troops under von Steuben and transform the untrained militia into a competitive disciplined army, which emerged as a fighting force to be reckoned with—soon to be recognized by the British. During this protracted six month recess, Washington also was able to confer daily with his officers on strategies and to communicate with members of Congress who were ninety miles away in the relocated capital at York. Those politicians who had ignored his pleadings for material could travel to Valley Forge and witness just how dire the army situation was.

Other events flowed from this period such as the effort to remove Washington from command due to his poor military record. Known as the "Conway Cabal", it involved a French army Irish émigré, Thomas Conway, who communicated his effort to replace Washington as Commander in Chief with Major General Horatio Gates. When Washington was informed of Conway's letter to Gates and confronted him on it, Conway offered to resign. Washington tried to keep the matter quiet because of the devastating effect it could have had on morale. Conway was still treated with respect, and after being reassigned to Albany, he later

23 Benninghoff, 89.

alienated too many members of Congress, who then accepted his resignation. In spite of being seriously wounded in a duel with Brigadier General John Cadwalader, Conway survived to eventually return to France. Before leaving, he wrote to Washington saying "you are a great and good man... may you long enjoy the love, veneration, and esteem of these states, whose liberties you have asserted by your virtues."[24] Some historians attribute the failed mutiny to Thomas Mifflin, who had been Washington's aide in Cambridge. Mifflin resigned that position because Washington did not assign him to a command post, and as a member of Congress at the time of Valley Forge he supposedly retaliated by trying to thwart Washington's command. He was associated with distributing an anonymous list of Washington's military blunders that was circulated in Congress, but Washington ignored the deed. Instead, he responded in the press with "Whenever the public gets dissatisfied with my services, or a person is found better qualified to answer her expectations, I shall quit the helm... and retire to private life with as much content, as ever the wearied pilgrim felt upon his safe arrival in the Holy Land."[25] The Conway Cabal actually had several positive results. It provided evidence of the power and influence of the "Inner Circle" to which Conway fell victim. It also cleared the air of officer dissension. Finally, the episode gave Washington a stronger position in the army—he was the undisputed Commander in chief with the loyalty and support of Congress and his closest officers. It was the last time his authority was challenged.

It should be noted that Valley Forge also witnessed tensions and intrigue among the officer staff each with differing loyalties and attitudes toward Washington. Generals Henry Knox, Nathaniel Greene, Marquis de Lafayette and Anthony Wayne

---

24 Grizzard, 57.
25 GW Papers at the Library of Congress.

were perhaps the most loyal and trusted aides, and Colonel Hamilton was loyal but was not considered a great admirer. Colonel Aaron Burr, Major General Horatio Gates and General Charles Lee were decidedly dissatisfied with Washington and tried to subvert him behind his back whenever they could in spite of his trust and confidence in them. Most all of them felt betrayed by Congress for lack of support and probably were just as displeased about those political leaders who were enjoying the comforts of their homes and family while soldiers were freezing and starving to death.

In spite of the intrigues and the hardships, most of the eleven thousand men remained steadfastly devoted to Washington because of his constant concern for them and his continuous efforts to obtain clothing and food. His presence was everywhere, and he even designed the log cabins for them. He shared their discomforts before finally retreating to more comfortable quarters realizing his health was critically important for the prosecution of the war. Life at Valley Forge was grim and became a nightmare. Washington wrote, "To see men without clothes to cover their nakedness, without blankets to lie on, without shoes (for the want of which their marches might be traced by the blood from their feet)... and submitting without a murmur, is a proof of patience and obedience which in my opinion can scarce be paralleled."[26]

The Continental Army faced another obstacle in the winter of 1778, and that was the animosity of the civilian population. Farmers and merchants had been paid with a fast-depreciating currency for several years and they finally refused to sell their goods unless they were paid in gold or hard currency. Soldiers who were starving, freezing and dying for the freedom of all Americans were shocked at the lack of support from their fellow

---

26 GW Papers at the Library of Congress.

Americans. Soldiers frequently disobeyed orders by sneaking out from camp to steal food from nearby farms. Additionally, Valley Forge was situated in the heart of southeastern Pennsylvania Quaker communities, which did not support the war for their religious beliefs. In addition, a less visible but equally important problem was the attitude of most rural America that the army was an independent force created and funded by Congress through taxes, a European-type entity separate from the small local communities. Also, the recent American victories at Saratoga, Trenton and Princeton negated the sense of urgency to the army's plight and promoted an attitude of optimism for a speedy conclusion to the war. Washington was caught between uncaring civilians and an ineffective Congress without an administrative branch of government. He could clearly see the need for a governmental chain of command similar to the structure of his newly organized army. Washington took the only alternative—to appeal to each state by pleading directly to their governors and congressmen. The last thing Washington wanted was to declare martial law because he knew that it could have a devastating effect on the civilians and their loyalties to the cause. In spite of every effort by Washington and the Congress to assure the local merchants of the value of Continental currency, they refused to sell goods to the army. Starvation became so pervasive by February 1778 that the Pennsylvania Assembly gave Washington the authority to impress food and supplies from farmers who were unwilling to sell to them. However, he did not confiscate the goods without paying in certificates of credit for future redemption. Other states and finally Congress adopted similar measures and also tried to protect their citizens even though credit was soon discontinued as the food and clothing supplies deteriorated. Some congressmen even criticized Washington for being too noble and for not having invoked martial law sooner. But Washington was adamantly opposed to such measures and did not want to risk the popular support of the people. He wanted civilian law to prevail over military law. He knew that people feared a military dictatorship and that confiscation of personal property was a dangerous step in that direction.[27] When the Pennsylvania Assembly voted to suspend the writ of habeas corpus in order to take clothing from loyalists, Washington refused and replied that "such a procedure, I fear, would not relieve our wants and at the same time would greatly distress the people and embitter their minds... an evil much to be apprehended even by the best and most sensible among us. I have been cautious and wished to avoid as much as possible any act that might [cause] it."[28]

It is important to remember that Washington had to deal with every aspect of military policy from the broadest scope to the smallest details. He had aides and secretaries, but he had no officers to whom he could assign these responsibilities. He dealt with supplies, recruitment, organization, training, discipline, health, strategy and diplomacy. He was responsible for the troops at Valley Forge, Wilmington, Delaware, and Trenton, New Jersey, as well as in the Hudson Valley and in New England. He communicated with the Congress and the Board of War in York, Pennsylvania, and all the governing bodies of the states. He had to cope with his own household details for two months until Martha arrived in February. He succeeded in all these duties while building the confidence and loyalty of his officers and soldiers. One soldier's diary referring to Washington said:

> He has always acted wisely hitherto. His conduct when closely scrutinized is uncensurable. Were his Inferior Generals as skillful as himself, we should have the grandest Choir of Officers ever

---

27 Bruce Chadwick, *George Washington's War* (Naperville, Illinois: Sourcebooks, Inc., 2004) 214-27.
28 GW Papers at the Library of Congress.

God made... His Excellency... is deserving of the greatest encomiums... History will... reflect lasting honor on the Wisdom & prudence of Genl Washington.[29]

Although Washington himself experienced the entire range of human emotions throughout the encampment, he alone had the ability to inspire others and gain their trust in him. It was a time of greatness in his leadership.

By far, the most crucial event of the entire war took place during the time of the Valley Forge encampment: namely, the decision in February by France to recognize the independence of the United States and to officially send officers, troops and a navy to assist the colonies. This news finally reached Washington in early May, and amid much rejoicing, he then realized the war could be won by patiently pursuing his harassing strategy.

Detractors see Washington as an ineffective military leader. With only two victories prior to Valley Forge (Trenton and Princeton), some wanted to see him replaced by Gates for his victory at Saratoga (actually it was Benedict Arnold under Gates who defeated General Burgoyne). Critics fail to mention his skill at recapturing Boston without the loss of a single soldier or in keeping an inexperienced militia in the field against the greatest army on earth. Critics judge him as a military man but fail to realize he was never trained in the art of war but instead was a farmer and politician who volunteered for service. His skills were in leadership and motivation and common sense. He was often advised to have open field head-on battles with the British, but he came to realize it would be disastrous. Instead, he learned from his experience in the French and Indian War and employed harassing and retreating tactics that saved the Continental Army from annihilation in Long Island, Manhattan and Philadelphia.

29   John B. B. Trussell, Jr., *Birthplace of an Army: A Study of the Valley Forge Encampment* (Harrisburg: Pennsylvania Historical and Museum Commission, 1998) 99.

His faith infected his men, and few people today appreciate how he admonished his men to attend church services. While there is some dispute whether he actually knelt to pray in the quiet of the snow-covered woods in Valley Forge as depicted in the famous painting by Arnold Friberg, it is true that he gave general orders for divine services every Sunday.[30]

A little discussed and often overlooked issue that derived from Valley Forge was the profound effect it was to have on Washington and the future course of the Republic. Perhaps even the congressmen observing the camp did not realize what was happening. Namely, Washington was creating a "national" army from portions of many colonies. This was obviously necessary to create an effective fighting force as it became clearly evident that the militia could not stand up to their professional adversaries. Washington came into the war as a Virginian, but if there was any one time that he changed into an "American" it must have been at Valley Forge. Perhaps this experience led him to think in much broader terms about the need for a standing army and the need for a central government to administer the growing complexities of a nation.

The Battle of Monmouth

The British occupation of Philadelphia has often been portrayed as a time of relaxation, comfort and social graces exchanged with loyalists. But it should be noted that the war still surrounded them, and every time they ventured outside the capital, they were ambushed and harassed by American soldiers. Also, local supplies had previously been stripped by Washington and the Delaware River ports were sabotaged thereby preventing supplies being received by the British. To add to their frustrations,

---

30 Peter Marshall & David Manuel, *The Light and the Glory* (Grand Rapids, Michigan: Fleming H. Revell, Inc., 1977) 323.

the British expected disillusioned American civilians to flock to their side and cause the revolution to implode in their favor. However, this did not happen, and when Howe resigned and was replaced by Sir Henry Clinton, the orders from London in June were for him to evacuate Philadelphia and return to New York City. Howe claimed to have requested retirement, but his recall was more likely based on his failure to "locate the strategic center of the rebellion."[31]

Before leaving Philadelphia, both sides exchanged prisoners in the traditional manner, and this brought General Lee back to Washington, who enthusiastically welcomed his return. However, his enthusiasm was short-lived when Lee continued his outspoken criticism of both Washington and the Continental Army. When it was learned that Clinton would not be sailing back to New York but would be marching his ten thousand troops across New Jersey, Washington called a Council of War on June 24, 1778. He believed his thirteen thousand troops could severely damage Clinton and possibly end the war before they could reach New York. General Lee was not in favor of such a move and convinced most of the Council to reject it. Generals Knox, Greene, Wayne and Lafayette wanted to go ahead, but Washington conceded to the Council's wishes. Although he never liked overruling the Council, he then changed his mind and ordered a large detachment to skirmish the rear and flanks of the retreating British especially when he learned of their twelve-mile-long lines. Lee declined the command, but when Washington replaced him with Lafayette, Lee relented and reluctantly accepted the post. He and others on the Council thought it was foolish to take such a risk since they would be fighting in the open field where the British veterans excelled. Again, Washington was in a dilemma because he believed his army had been so well trained that winter that with

31 Ellis, *His Excellency: George Washington*, 205.

slightly more men than the British, the odds for taking that risk were decidedly in his favor. On the night of June 27 Washington ordered Lee to attack the next morning while Washington and Greene would move up to support him if required. Shortly after the initial contact Washington encountered Lee's men in full retreat, and in disbelief he charged to the front where in a fury (allegedly with cursing and swearing) he reprimanded him for not following his orders. He sent Lee to his rear to regroup while he took command. With Greene, Washington arranged defensive ambushes and then organized a charge directly at the advancing British. The Americans employed their newly acquired skills and drove the British veterans back to their refuge from which they later escaped during the night. Monmouth marked a major event in the war because the Continental Army now proved to be capable of effectively fighting the British, who suffered twice the casualties of the Americans. Although successful, Washington believed he was denied a major victory by General Lee's incompetence and insubordination. Washington placed Lee under arrest and ordered a court-martial. Lee was convicted and was later temporarily discharged from the army.[32] Thirty years after the war, documents were found proving that during his captivity in Philadelphia, Lee had turned traitor. He actually presented detailed plans to Howe for the defeat of the Continental Army.[33] Other historians disagree, and believe it was planted by Lee to trick Howe. The Battle of Monmouth caused the British to abandon the colonial capital and the mid-Atlantic region. They were now confined to New York City and were on the defensive facing a more professional American army and their French allies, whose navy equaled that of Great Britain.

---

32 Flexner, 122-124.
33 Randall, 358.

The War in the South: South Carolina and Georgia

The Battle of Monmouth was the last major conflict in the north. Clinton retreated to the loyalist fortress of New York while London developed the new strategy of attacking the relatively weak southern colonies of Georgia and the Carolinas. Contrary to Washington's hopes and expectations, the British elected to double the size of their forces and hold New York while invading the south. Lord Cornwallis intended to sweep north and finally defeat Washington in Virginia. In August 1780 General Gates suffered a resounding defeat at Camden, South Carolina, and with the British in control of Georgia and South Carolina, Cornwallis was preparing his move northward. Realizing the seriousness of the situation, Washington appointed the popular and skilled Nathanael Greene to lead the southern army. Leaving the Hudson in October 1780, he acquired the services of "Light Horse" Harry Lee and his 150 dragoons because he was certain that he would need cavalry units for hit-and-run tactics. Lee would join with Lt. Colonel William Washington who was already in the south. Also, he needed experienced officers and added Colonel Edward Carrington, Colonel William Davie and Colonel Thaddeus Kosciuszko to his staff. At the time of his arrival, the American militia had just defeated the British at King's Mountain in South Carolina, and even though Cornwallis commanded a vastly larger and superior army, they were located in garrisons stretched across Georgia and South Carolina. Cornwallis chose not to enlarge his main force at the expense of the garrisons after seeing their defeat at King's Mountain. Instead, he waited for reinforcements from Virginia, which prompted Greene to split his small army to prevent the British from coming to aid Cornwallis. This was fraught with danger and was the kind of risk that Washington took at Saratoga. Greene justified his decision on the basis that it would force Cornwallis to do the same so he ordered Brigadier Daniel Morgan to encircle him at Winnsboro. While the Americans kept Cornwallis at bay with successful skirmishes, Greene reorganized his troops. The British reinforcements finally arrived in January 1781, and Cornwallis ordered Colonel Banastre Tarleton with his 1,150 veterans to smash Morgan's force at Cowpens. However, Morgan won this little-known but strategic battle, and his army raced to rejoin Greene. In a series of skirmishes and retreats of over two hundred miles, similar to those under Washington, Greene kept Cornwallis and Tarleton at a safe distance until he crossed over the Dan River into Virginia. In March, Greene decided to take a stand at Guilford Court House in North Carolina. With new troops from the Continental Army and local recruits of militia, Greene had forty-two hundred men compared to two thousand British veterans. The battle was so close and fierce that at a desperate moment Cornwallis ordered his gunners to fire grapeshot into the front lines even though it meant killing some of his own men. The technical victory by Cornwallis was extremely costly having lost a quarter of his men, thereby forcing him to retreat to Wilmington and leaving North Carolina to Greene. The more significant result was the decision by Cornwallis to attack Virginia which was the base for American supplies. He believed Greene would follow him, and give him the opportunity to annihilate the Americans and bring the South under British control. Greene did not oblige, and after a brief distracting pursuit, he changed course and headed south where he proceeded to take all the British forts in South Carolina and Georgia except Savannah and Charleston where he left some troops to contain those cities. Greene's moves throughout the South were heralded by Lafayette, Thomas Jefferson, Henry Knox, John Adams and others. His performance justified Washington's confidence in him and showed why he recommended him as his successor as commander in chief if it became necessary. Greene's fame spread to the North as well, and Georgia honored him with the gift of Mulberry Grove plantation near Savannah. Sadly, Greene died from an infection in June 1786, in his forty-fourth year.

In the period between Monmouth and Greene's command in the South, Washington operated out of his Morristown, New Jersey, headquarters and in New England conferences with American and French forces. The British army was confined to New York City, but Washington needed some sea power to oust them from their defensive fortress. The major fighting occurred in upstate New York where Iroquois Indians and Tory marauders savaged many villages murdering innocent men, women and children. Washington decided to put an end to this while he had the opportunity. He placed General John Sullivan in command of four thousand men and together with George Rogers Clark's two hundred frontiersmen, they reclaimed much of the New York and Ohio River areas and actually took Detroit from the British.[34]

Meanwhile, Congress moved back to Philadelphia seemingly unconcerned with the stalemate and precarious position of the war effort. Washington waited for the French fleet, but Admiral d'Estaing decided not to sail to New York where Washington had raised another twelve thousand men. For years Washington dreamed of retaking New York with one major battle that would end the war. He knew this could not be done without naval support, and he hoped that would be provided by the French. So, until the French navy would arrive, he positioned his army from western Connecticut to the Hudson Highlands to northern New Jersey. These sites were designed to keep Clinton in New York, protect New England from along the Hudson River and maneuver

---

34   Fleming, 291-92.

quickly whenever the French fleet arrived. However, instead of sailing to New York, d'Estaing attacked Savannah on September 4, 1779. The Americans under Major General Benjamin Lincoln and Polish cavalryman Casimir Pulaski were beaten back and when d'Estaing sailed away back to the Caribbean, they were forced to retreat to Charleston. When the news reached General Henry Clinton in New York, he thought they had finally found the route to victory, so he immediately set sail for Charleston on December 26, 1779 with eighty-seven hundred veteran troops. Washington and Congress soon realized the war was far from over, and to compound the situation the Continental currency depreciated to where, by 1780, six hundred Continental dollars bought one Spanish silver dollar, and the snowbound army at Morristown suffered far worse conditions than at Valley Forge. In 1776 dollars, a captain was living on $13 a month and a lieutenant on $3.50.[35] It was the worst winter in memory with blizzards and sub-zero temperatures that froze the Hudson River to eighteen feet and thick enough for the British to march across with three thousand-pound cannons. At Charleston, Clinton overwhelmed Lincoln, who was forced to surrender on May 12, 1780 losing fifty-five hundred prisoners to the British.

Being encouraged by the victory at Charleston, the British in New York under the German commander, Wilhelm von Knyphausen, decided to attack Washington at Morristown on June 8, 1780. The Continental Army was in a weakened condition having just prevented the Connecticut brigade from deserting. The near-worthless Continental currency made it impossible to gain recruits. Knyphausen's seven thousand men were beaten back by Washington's thirty-five hundred Continentals, but it was only after retreating to allow Washington time to regroup

---

35   Fleming, 300.

his men. The victory was unheralded, but defeat would have been a disaster.

As the beginning of 1780 approached, Washington reassessed the American situation in broader and more vocal terms. Heretofore, he had considered that time was on his side, but he now reasoned that Britain enjoyed the tremendous advantages of being led by a national entity that could raise substantial forces and vast sums of money through its well established financial system. Its renewed commitment to the war through the south was ample proof of their intentions and abilities. He now envisioned a long, protracted conflict that would require more American financial resources than were available. He had already learned the weaknesses of the state-dominated Continental Congress, but now he recognized their dilemma. One of the principal reasons for fighting the war was their opposition to taxation without representation, especially from a Parliament located far away. It appeared to him that Americans could perceive Congress in the same light if they raised taxes and assumed central governmental powers. However, if victory was to be achieved then it was imperative to have a national body empowered to enact the necessary measures. His appreciation of financial strength must have influenced his future decision as president to place that issue as a top priority in the newly established government. Adding to his dilemma was Washington's belief in civilian authority thereby causing him to leave politics to the politicians and accept their control. In May 1780, he felt compelled to speak out on the issue and told a Virginia delegate,

> Certain I am that unless Congress speaks in a more decisive tone; unless they are vested with powers by the several States competent to the great purposes of War, or assume them as a matter of right... that our Cause is lost. We can no longer

drudge on in the old way. I see one head gradually changing into thirteen… In a word, our measures are not under the influence and direction of one council, but thirteen, each of which is actuated by local views and politics… it will be madness in us, to think of prosecuting the War.[36]

The winter of 1779–80, was even harsher and more desperate than two years prior at Valley Forge. Large numbers of enlistments ended on January 1. The army was reduced to eight thousand men, and of these barely six thousand were fit for duty. By summer, Charleston fell and Gates was routed at Camden in South Carolina. In September, Benedict Arnold's treason was uncovered, and Washington feared it marked the possible start of mutiny and the end of their Cause. In early 1781, over a thousand Pennsylvania soldiers marched on Congress to demand back pay. Within a month another mutiny occurred when New Jersey soldiers marched on Trenton also pressing for unfilled financial promises. The Pennsylvanians were persuaded to desist, but Washington dealt severely with the men from New Jersey and ordered the two leaders to be executed. Washington saw unqualified and apathetic delegates in the Congress and called for more professional leaders. He felt indifference was a greater threat than the British military. By early 1781, with no further help from the French navy, Washington thought the Cause was lost.

Yorktown: October 1783

In May 1781, Washington and his French counterpart, Count de Rochambeau, conferred in Wethersfield, Connecticut, to discuss the upcoming campaign. Because the French officers did not entirely trust Washington's discretion and their respective troops had differing military skills, Rochambeau was not candid

---

36 GW Papers at the Library of Congress.

about French strategies. Also, after the intrigues of the Conway Cabal at Valley Forge, Washington was less open with his own staff and tried to maintain as much secrecy as possible about battle plans. Washington was not told that the French fleet in the West Indies was ordered to sail north in July or August. He continued to press Rochambeau to agree to a combined American and French attack on New York, and they finally both signed off on such a plan. Then, without telling Washington, Rochambeau ordered Admiral de Grasse to sail directly to the Chesapeake where the combined forces would meet him. His objectives were to cut off Cornwallis' shipping facilities and his post at Portsmouth. After returning to his Hudson River quarters, Washington learned from his representative in Paris that the French fleet was heading from the Caribbean to North America, so he began to formulate a contingency plan in case the New York attack appeared vulnerable. Using his disinformation technique, he became more vocal on the New York plan, which served to gain more recruits and prompted Clinton to call back two thousand men from Cornwallis to reinforce New York. With his army weakened, Cornwallis decided not to advance but to fortify his camp at Yorktown. On July 6, 1783, the joint American-French army moved south to within twelve miles of New York City. On August 14, Washington was informed that Admiral de Grasse would not go to New York but instead would go to the Chesapeake with thirty-two hundred soldiers. Washington's long-standing belief in an all-out major attack on New York was abandoned. Rochambeau did not share his convictions and was adamantly opposed to any plan that did not include French naval support. He was aware of the dangerous shoals just outside New York harbor that could maroon the massive French ships, and whether this was his only reason, he nonetheless rejected New

York and directed de Grasse to the Chesapeake. Washington admitted his strong preference for New York, but he deferred to Rochambeau. This would require a march of 450 miles which was fraught with such uncertainties as to whether de Grasse would actually arrive, or would Cornwallis stay in Yorktown or would they be intercepted by British forces. Using disinformation through spies, Washington convinced Clinton that de Grasse was headed for New York, and his combined forces were then able to reach the Delaware River before Clinton became aware of the situation. With only a twelve-mile march to the head of the Chesapeake, Washington and Rochambeau were able to carry out their plan. At the same time a small French fleet from Newport arrived carrying cannons and small ferrying ships to sail down to Yorktown. Washington and Rochambeau arrived at the Tidewater Peninsula on September 15, 1781, sent Lafayette to block any possible escape to the north through Gloucester and effectively sealed Cornwallis in Yorktown. Cornwallis had chosen Yorktown because it would have provided a good deep-water port to evacuate on expected British ships. But by the time Clinton discovered what had happened, it was too late. The British sent Admirals Graves and Hood to attack de Grasse, but after a brief skirmish off Cape Henry they returned to New York leaving de Grasse in control of the Chesapeake. The American and French troops proceeded to build parallel trenches outside the town and systematically bombarded the British positions. Simultaneously, French and American defenses were placed across the York River in Gloucester to block a possible escape by Cornwallis. After the bombardments on Yorktown, the plan worked perfectly, and on October 17, 1781, Cornwallis surrendered his 7,241 troops, 840 seamen, 244 pieces of artillery and thousands of small arms.

Contrary to popular belief, Yorktown did not mark the end of the war. Even Washington wrote that the victory at Yorktown was "an interesting event that may be productive of much good if properly improved, but if it should be the means of relaxation and sink us into supineness and [false] security, it better not have happened."[37] While Washington rejoiced at the decisive victory, he believed it would bring the same kind of reaction from Parliament as they had with the British loss at Saratoga; namely, an even larger military response. Accordingly, he continued to train his army not knowing that he had just won the last major battle of the war.

In reviewing the last major battle in which he was engaged, Washington faced a number of obstacles which others may not have overcome:

- He had to rely on foreign officers and troops and hope they would work as one;
- He had to subordinate his plans and in effect take orders from strangers;
- He was not treated with respect by the French;
- He was intentionally uninformed about his allies' plans;
- He had to maintain complete secrecy and his army's trust in him;
- He had to deceive the enemy;
- He had to lead demoralized men who were ill fed, clothed or paid;
- He had to bring his men to the limits of their endurance with a 450-mile march;

---

37   GW Papers at the Library of Congress.

- He had to take enormous risks by even attempting Yorktown;

- He worked under tremendous pressure.

Washington succeeded because:

- He listened to others;

- He had the loyalty of his men;

- He was patient with the French although they had disappointed him before;

- He used his own sources for information;

- He used deception and disinformation on his enemy;

- He surprised his enemy;

- He remained personally involved with his men;

- He led by example and endured the same hardships as his officers and troops;

- He remained flexible and could change strategy quickly;

- His stamina matched his determination;

- His reputation earned the respect and admiration of the French government;

- He demonstrated compassion and mercy in victory.

The Newburgh Conspiracy: March 15, 1783

During the relatively calm period of late 1782, the army at its headquarters in Newburgh, New York, became restless with the fear that Congress would soon end the war and dismiss them without their promised compensation. The two key issues were back pay that was owing and the half-pay for life pension that Congress had pledged two years prior. Washington was well aware of the growing impatience of his officers, and he repeatedly warned Congress of the dangers of the situation. A written grievance was presented to Congress by Henry Knox. However, this seemingly narrow issue had some very broad implications because the compensation would require a "national" solution to the problem whereby sufficient revenues would have to derive from a new funding source. For years there was speculation that nationalists (Federalists) like Hamilton and Robert Morris may have influenced the officers to threaten civil insurrection to gain their pay, and that they also probably informed Washington of this in order for him to keep his men in line. The likely leaders in this effort were Hamilton, who advised that the Treasury would be empty by June, and Gates, who was deeply in debt. It is also probable that Washington wanted no part of the intrigue surrounding the issue other than to see that responsible people in Congress were trying to solve it. It should be remembered that much of the army and staff had a low opinion of Congress throughout the war for their seemingly unsympathetic support. On March 10, 1783, an aide to General Gates, Major John Armstrong, published a statement calling for a general meeting to vote on resignation en masse if the war continued. Washington apparently deduced that the real instigators were in Philadelphia, and they were using the army for their own purposes. He dealt with the crisis by suggesting that his officers ignore the meeting and issued his own orders to attend an official meeting in four days. At his meeting he commented that the other petition was "unmilitary" and "subversive". He even wondered if Britain had sent a spy to instigate the matter. He asked them to have patience and advised that Congress would resolve their issue. Nothing seemed to move the men, so as a final effort he removed a letter from a sympathetic Virginia delegate to the national legislature,

Joseph Jones, and stumbling with it, he took out his eyeglasses and said: "Gentlemen you must pardon me, I have grown gray in your service and now find myself growing blind."[38] Reportedly, the officers were speechless and some were even reduced to tears. Here was Washington at his finest in the face of a crisis. He knew his men and he knew how to defuse a difficult situation. Who else could have engendered such support but one who had been there from the beginning, suffered along with his men and gained their respect. After the crisis ended, Washington continued to lobby relentlessly for his men, and in the end he achieved an even better package with officers receiving full pay for five years at the war's end.[39]

In recent years more light has been shed on the Newburgh Conspiracy and the intrigue surrounding it. Historian Stuart Leibiger elaborates on the political implications of those events in his 1999 book, *Founding Friendship*. He explains that after Yorktown the Continental army settled into relative calm in Newburgh hopeful of an imminent end to the war. In Philadelphia, two philosophies emerged whereby the moderates focused on ending the war and then improving the Confederation, while the extreme nationalists wanted to strengthen the government before the war ended because they feared when peace came the country would lapse into local factions and reject a strong central government. In either case, the government was derelict in its promised pay and pensions to the military principally because it did not have adequate funds. Congress attempted to pass a 5 percent impost on the states to raise the revenue, but it was defeated in late 1782, much to the dismay of the army officers. Virginia delegate James Madison proposed a settlement for the soldiers through a congressional revenue, but this too did not

---

38   GW Papers at the Library of Congress.
39   Ferling, 312.

pass. The nationalists did not like his plan because it ran counter to their desire for a centralized government with independent revenue powers. They knew time was running out and therefore decided to scare the Congress into taking action. Hamilton, Robert Morris and Gouveneur Morris secretly met with General Horatio Gates and several officers stationed at Newburgh and planned a coup against the government. However, they supposedly apprised Washington so he could control any possible rebellion thereby allowing them the opportunity to convince Congress of the need for the government's revenue power. Washington was not aware of the nationalists' plans and neither was Madison. Instead, they both pressed for meeting the officers' legitimate complaint. They both realized that unless Congress met its obligations it would dissolve and possibly be replaced by a mutiny and military dictatorship. Hamilton then proceeded to spread word that the army would not give up their arms until the pay issue was settled. He also rumored that Washington was becoming unpopular because he was not taking a leading role in the struggle for the army's pay, but he did not disclose his own role in staging the revolt. Madison greatly admired Washington and became alarmed at the situation. He proposed a twenty-five year impost together with a $1.5 million annual requisition from the states. Hamilton and his allies opposed the plan and increased their pressure on Congress for an impost by the Confederation not realizing that if the army tried to pressure the Congress, the states would likely block such a measure. It was then that General Gates called a meeting of the officers in Newburgh and directed Major John Armstrong, Jr., to post an anonymous letter calling for a general meeting and urging that no attention should be paid to any leader [e.g. Washington] who took a moderate stand. When Virginia delegate and long-time friend of Washington, Joseph Jones, told him about the Hamilton plan, Washington told Hamilton that he would have no part of a coup. Washington and Madison wanted to resolve the issue through proper political channels, so he called his own meeting for a few days after Armstrong's. It was there that he expressed his sympathy for the officers and vowed to pursue the issue with Congress. Henry Knox took over the meeting, condemned the anonymous letters and had the officers reaffirm their loyalty and support of Washington and the Congress.[40]

The Treaty of Paris: 1783

In spite of his victory at Yorktown, Washington was very much concerned about the likelihood of Britain's retaliation. He wanted a decisive end to the war, and he still believed that it could be achieved only with a defeat of the British in New York. He sent some of his forces to reinforce Greene, but he felt the need to return to his troops on the Hudson. Rochambeau remained in Yorktown for six months, and while Washington tried to coax him into further campaigns in New York and even in Canada, he resisted and finally received orders to confront the British in the Caribbean. Washington's fears of continued fighting were reinforced in April 1782, when Britain successfully defended French attacks on Jamaica, overcame the French navy and captured Admiral de Grasse. Because Washington did not trust George III or Parliament, he kept the army at full strength. Unfortunately, this raised some concerns about his true intentions and whether he would assume a military dictatorship similar to Cromwell after the English Civil War. The irony of the situation was the colonists' fear of a "standing army" and at the same time knowing that such a centralized "national" army was necessary to win their fight for independence. The issue of local rights versus

---

40 Stuart Leibiger, *Founding Friendship and the Creation of the American Republic* (Charlottesville: University Press of Virginia, 1999) 25-28.

national powers was at the core of the revolution and would permeate decisions on establishing the future government.

On July 10, 1782, America's foreign minister in London, Benjamin Franklin, presented his informal peace proposal to his designated counterpart, Richard Oswald. Franklin included four "necessary" provisions and four "advisable" provisions. The necessary items were:

- A full and complete recognition of America's independence together with the withdrawal of all British troops including those in the western lands;

- Establishing the Mississippi River as the western boundary of the United States and the right to use the river;

- Re-establishing the Great Lakes as the northern boundary; and

- Allowing Americans to secure fishing rights on the Newfoundland Grand Banks.

The four advisable articles included:

- British payment of reparations for their destruction in America;

- An official apology and admission of British guilt;

- A free trade agreement;

- Ceding Canada to the United States.

The British agreed to the necessary points, but they rejected three of the advisable ones. On the question of reparations, they countered that the United States should pay for the property of the loyalists that was lost or seized by the rebels. Franklin responded with a proposal that England should pay for all the seaports and houses they destroyed during the war. Both sides then compromised whereby Congress would ask the individual states to give some compensation to loyalists who did not actively oppose the American war effort. However, negotiations ran into trouble upon the arrival of John Adams and John Jay about the delicate issue of America's previous agreement with the French that France would be a third party to any Anglo-American treaty. Franklin was able to use his considerable influence in Paris to pacify the French, and the only significant change to the preliminary agreement with England was the issue of prewar debts owed by Americans to British merchants. When Adams insisted that such debts should be honored, the provisional Treaty of Paris was in place and finally signed in London on November 30, 1782. However, the issues of British troop withdrawals and outstanding American debts were not fully resolved for another twelve years and proved to be thorny issues for President Washington.

Within six months of Yorktown, there was talk of elevating Washington to the status of king, but he quashed the very idea. He knew there were very few successful attempts throughout history to establish a republic, but he was committed to that course. More than any of the founding fathers, Washington knew the importance of a strong central government, but he knew it had to be by a civil self-appointed process created by the citizens. He knew he had to act decisively to relinquish his unique and powerful position. But he also knew that the current Confederation Congress was too weak to govern effectively because it had retained the one state-one vote system and lacked the resolve to honor its obligations.

By September 1782, amid rumors of peace negotiations, it became clear that Britain wanted to end the war. Just before Christmas, Sir Guy Carleton replaced Clinton as commander in New York, and unbeknown to Washington, the Royal Navy was en route to pick up all the remaining troops in Savannah. In early 1783, Washington learned that Carleton planned to withdraw from Charleston and reduce his forces in New York. On April 9, 1783, Washington and Carleton signed a cease fire. For the following six months Carleton carefully organized the withdrawal of British and German troops as well as American loyalists who lived in New York City and the greater New York-New Jersey area. It was a complicated task that required coordination with London and diplomacy in New York. Neither side wanted reprisals or bloodshed that could easily arise from the bitterness and resentments from an eight-year war. The Treaty of Paris had been signed in London in September, but it did not arrive in New York until November. It then had to be ratified by Congress which was sitting at Annapolis. Carleton faced significant challenges in the logistics of peacefully evacuating hordes of civilians and soldiers. In November, 32,224 American loyalists along with their personal property sailed to Nova Scotia, 1,328 left for Quebec, and 1,458 sailed to the Bahamas. Of the 29,867 Hessian mercenaries employed by the British, five thousand had deserted, 7,754 had died, and half of the remaining 17,317 returned home. Of the thirty-nine thousand British troops, ten thousand had been killed, most of the fifteen thousand prisoners survived leaving a total of approximately twenty-nine thousand to be transported home.[41] For comparison purposes 6,284 Americans were killed in action and ten thousand died of disease. Of the thousands of American prisoners who were held in rotting British vessels in New York harbor, approximately eighty-five hundred died from malnutrition and disease.[42] A total of 120,000 Americans had served during the eight years from a total population of three million.[43] In September 1783 the Treaty was signed, but it was not

---

41 Weintraub, 30.
42 Independence Hall Association in Philadelphia, FAQ, 3, <www.ushistory.org>.
43 Ibid., 9.

until November 25, 1783 that the last British soldier disembarked from New York harbor.[44] Washington then began the process of dismantling his powers. In November he bid farewell to his soldiers in Newburgh, and following a victory march into New York City he then hosted an emotional farewell to his officers at Fraunces' Tavern in downtown New York on November 30, 1783. He quickly left for a triumphal journey to Annapolis where the Congress was meeting. On December 22, 1783, Washington performed one of the most memorable acts in history by voluntarily surrendering his powerful position as Commander in chief and preeminent leader of a nation.

---

44   Ferling, 306-308.

CHAPTER 5

General Washington's Relationships With His Officers

Associate yourself with Men of good Quality if you esteem your own Reputation; for 'tis better to be alone than in bad Company.

—Ignatius Loyola, ca. 1550
Rule 56—*Rules of Civility and Decent Behaviour in Company and Conversation*

George Washington was known for his astute judgment of men with intelligence and character. Early in the war he tended to micromanage the many administrative details as well as the strategic and tactical aspect of the battles. As his responsibilities grew with increasing political considerations and the theater of war enlarged to the north and south, he realized the need for more personal aides. Men such as Alexander Hamilton, Tench Tilghman, John Laurens, Thomas Mifflin, Joseph Reed and David Humphreys were well educated, competent and trusted aides who were assigned extensive authority. Without them, Washington could not have administered the myriad of details that he accomplished. He was not only fighting a war, but he was trying to unite the colonies, and this required extensive correspondence with state and local government officials. He usually asked for their opinions in writing and always wrote personal notes of thanks for their contributions to the war effort. Whether it was pleas for men, supplies, money, ammunition, food or clothing, he depended on civilian support. This was especially critical in late 1776 after the humiliating defeats in New York and the evaporation of his army to twenty-four hundred fighting men before Trenton. His aides were absolutely critical in prosecuting the war, and their quality is attested to by their eventual leadership roles in the future government. Washington had acquired a total of thirty-two aides over the course of the war, and of these there emerged six cabinet officers, four governors, three U.S. senators, two diplomats to Europe, an associate justice of the Supreme Court, a president of the Continental Congress, a delegate to the Constitutional Convention and a Speaker of the House of Representatives.[1] We will study some of these men later, but here we will focus on Washington's military officers.

Nathanael Greene: 1742–1786

Close to ten years his junior, Greene had many similarities to Washington. He was born into a middle class merchant family in Rhode Island and had little formal education. However, he did learn geometry, philosophy, Latin and theology from his tutors, the most notable being the future president of Yale College, Ezra Stiles. Raised as a Quaker, he later left the Society of Friends and took an interest in military studies. He was strong and athletic and enjoyed social activities like dancing. He was not over indulgent and was witty and handsome. Like Washington, he had an intuition about people's character after first meeting them. Because of his popularity he was elected to the colonial legislature of Rhode Island which, in turn, led to his involvement with the

1   Chadwick, 140.

Rhode Island militia known as the Kentish Guards. He seemed to understand the implications of the growing difficulties with Great Britain, and his strong character and sense of duty led him to report to Boston in June 1775 even before the arrival of Washington. Rhode Island had made him commander of their sixteen hundred-man force, which he had stationed around Boston upon his arrival there. When they first met in July, Washington and Greene quickly established a good rapport, and the two men developed a life-long close relationship. Both shared a similar education, a self-taught interest in the military and personal strong convictions about the American cause for independence. He was a quick study, and one of Washington's ablest generals, Henry Knox, said that in a single year Greene had transformed himself "from the rawest, the most untutored being" into the finest general in the Continental Army. It is important to note that Washington held Greene in such high regard that he named him as his successor to be commander in chief if he, Washington, was killed or captured. Also, Greene is credited with having been the first revolutionary leader who called for independence from England and committed his wishes to writing in January 1776. Prior to that time, most all the American military and political leaders believed they were fighting to preserve their freedoms which were being threatened by the invading redcoats. Even Washington himself assured the New York Congress that he would try to reestablish harmony with the mother country.[2] Perhaps fate intervened in the summer of 1776 when Greene became too ill to take a lead role in the disastrous Battle of Long Island. He next fought with Washington in New York where they both decided to defend Forts Washington and Lee on each side of the Hudson River. Both men escaped while the British overran the Americans in what was the worst experience in Greene's career. Those heavy losses taught Greene,

---

2   David McCullough, *1776* (New York: Simon & Schuster, 2005) 54-55.

and Washington as well, to be far more cautious. Their three thousand men were facing General Howe's ten thousand veterans, and it was Greene's greatest mistake to think he could win against such overwhelming odds. As Washington retreated through New Jersey, Greene was at his side and later participated in the defeat of the Hessians at Trenton. Greene was especially proud that Washington was asking for his advice and relying on his judgment.[3] He also fought bravely at Princeton in January 1777 and stayed close to Washington for most of that year. In August 1777, while Washington reviewed the defenses along the Delaware River, he placed Greene in command of the entire army for several days.[4] Following their defeats at the Brandywine and Germantown, Greene was severely criticized by Congress for giving poor advice to Washington. He was regarded as the closest aide to him along with Knox, Lafayette and Joseph Reed. However, Washington strongly defended him and assumed the blame. For the first three months at Valley Forge supply conditions were in total disarray under Thomas Mifflin, and in spite of his reluctance to accept Washington's orders, Greene was appointed Quartermaster General in March 1778 and restored order much to the great relief and thanks of Washington. Greene returned to the field of battle at Monmouth when Washington replaced the retreating General Gates and subsequently played a key role in the American victory there. He was then sent to fight under Sullivan in Rhode Island and finally was given a command in 1780 at Springfield, New Jersey. Like Washington, Greene had a running conflict with Congress, and when they changed procurement procedures, Greene resigned under Congressional pressure only to be retained by Washington's interference and support. Just at this time, Cornwallis was moving inland from

---

3   David McCullough, *1776* (New York: Simon & Schuster, 2005), 115.
4   Grizzard, 139.

Charleston and inflicted a crushing defeat on General Gates at Camden, South Carolina, in August 1780. Reportedly, Gates fled from the battle and was subsequently relieved of his command by Congress thus ending his military career. The new British strategy of defeating the southern colonies was succeeding, so it was critical to stop their advance north. Again, it was Washington's decision to place Greene at the command of the Southern army that proved decisive in the war. Greene moved south in October 1780 first stopping in Philadelphia for supplies and then recruiting "Light Horse" Harry Lee and his 150 dragoons to provide the cavalry he knew was necessary. He also realized the need for experienced officers and picked up Colonel Edward Carrington, Lieutenant Colonel William Washington, cavalryman Colonel William Davie and engineer Thaddeus Kosciuszko. While he remained in Charlotte, North Carolina, to rebuild the defeated Gates army, a small mountaineer militia badly defeated a British force at King's Mountain, South Carolina, and thereby prompted Cornwallis to wait for reinforcements from Virginia before heading back north to defeat Greene. In a daring move, Greene split his smaller inferior army by sending Brigadier General Daniel Morgan to encircle Cornwallis and harass his efforts to gain recruits. At the same time, while other troops also skirmished against British loyalists, Greene used the time to train his own men and in effect forced Cornwallis to split his own army to deal with Morgan. When his reinforcements finally arrived in January 1781, he appointed Colonel Tarleton with his 350 dragoons and eight hundred veterans to crush Morgan. In the Battle of Cowpens, one of the most decisive victories of the war was achieved by Morgan and enraged Cornwallis to pursue him. Upon learning of Morgan's position Greene raced south to guide him north to join his Southern army in their march to Salisbury, North Carolina, where he hoped to meet the pursuing Cornwallis. Greene's reinforcements did not arrive and forced him to retreat across the Yadkin River in North Carolina and then over the Dan River into Virginia with his weary shoeless exhausted army. Like Washington, Greene stayed with his men and kept just out of reach of the advancing British. The two hundred mile retreat was too exhausting for Cornwallis who decided to return for rest at Hillsboro, North Carolina. Greene, again using Washington's strategy of surprise, re-crossed the Dan in February and with Cornwallis falling back to Guilford Court House in March, Greene decided to attack. His odds were much improved with forty-two hundred men to two thousand British veterans. An American victory could have ended the war, but Cornwallis won the two-hour battle with the loss of one-quarter of his men and in such a weakened position that he retreated to Wilmington, North Carolina, to await supplies by sea. Cornwallis expected Greene to retreat to defend Virginia and the capitol at Williamsburg, but once again, Greene surprised him by moving south to recapture all the British posts in South Carolina and Georgia except Savannah and Charleston. He placed some forces outside the two capitals and then moved north. He endured some losses on the way, but in his words, "we fight, get beat, rise, and fight again."[5] By this time, all the South except the two port cities was under American control. Greene was determined to finish off the British Army and attacked at Eutaw Springs, South Carolina, in September 1781. Both sides suffered heavy casualties, but again, Greene gained further control of the South. Greene was aware that a powerful French fleet was heading to the coast, and after Washington and Rochambeau's capture of Cornwallis at Yorktown in October, he was hoping that Admiral de Grasse would then

---

5   George Athan Billias, *George Washington's Generals and Opponents* (New York: First Da Capo Press, 1994) 131.

head to Charleston to help him regain that important city. However, de Grasse was ordered to the West Indies leaving the British in Charleston for another year when they finally evacuated in December 1782. When Greene returned home, he was greeted as a hero throughout the North and South by Congress, the military and especially his home state of Rhode Island. Thomas Jefferson had the highest praise for him, and Georgia gave him Mulberry Grove plantation near Savannah for his great feats. He retired there and developed the orchards and gardens with the same kind of zeal that Washington devoted to Mount Vernon. When he suddenly died in 1786 at age forty-four with considerable debts, Washington offered to provide his namesake, George Washington Greene, with the best education available. In 1791, as President he visited his widow at Mulberry Grove and personally arranged to have Greene's old Revolutionary War bonds indemnified by Congress considering he had used them to pay for his troops' clothing during the war. Nathanael Greene was very much like his mentor in war and peace and should be remembered as the one man Washington had named as his successor during the war.

Horatio Gates: 1728–1806

Perhaps the most controversial and least appreciated officer, Gates stands at the center of the Revolutionary War's three critical episodes. His military career rose from despair in the British army to great heights as the American victor at Saratoga and then to the depths as the loser to Lord Cornwallis in the southern campaign. His lasting reputation is based on his ignominious defeat at Camden, South Carolina, where his loss opened the way for the British advance into Virginia and his hasty two hundred-mile retreat from the battle. His military experience was more extensive than any American officer, including Washington, and these were surpassed by his administrative and organizational skills. In spite of his important contributions, he has been regarded as "the whipping boy... of the Revolution."[6]

Gates was born in England and though not of the privileged class, his parents were able to secure his commission in the British army. He was stationed in Nova Scotia under Governor Edward Cornwallis, ironically the uncle of Charles Lord Cornwallis. His first battlefield experience was under Braddock in the French and Indian War where he first met George Washington. After being badly wounded, he returned to England and attempted to further his military career. Between lack of funds and sponsorship as well as the fact that England was reverting to a peacetime budget, Gates was unable to advance. However, while in America he did become deeply interested in the politics of the colonies and came to sympathize with their cause. In 1772, he wrote to Washington inquiring about the possible purchase of an estate in the western part of Virginia. In 1773, he moved to Traveller's Rest and soon thereafter he accepted an honorary commission as lieutenant colonel in the Virginia militia. When the war broke out in 1775, Gates saw his opportunity to pursue a military career and he quickly accepted a commission as brigadier general and became Washington's assistant in Cambridge. He wrote the American army's first regulations and set up procedures for the recruitment and training of soldiers. His fine work was praised and appreciated by Washington who was then allowed greater time to command the war. His position provided a voice in Washington's war council, and he consistently proposed defensive and cautionary moves. He, like many others, thought there would be a brief conflict due to the economic constraints in England. He opposed

6   George Athan Billias, *George Washington's Generals and Opponents* (New York: First Da Capo Press, 1994), 79.

Washington's plan to directly attack the British in Boston which Washington reluctantly accepted. He also was not in favor of taking Dorchester Heights, but Washington followed his own instincts with that decision. By May 1776, Gates was promoted to major general and was ordered to command the American withdrawal from Canada. He acquired an army in defeat, division, desertion and rampant with sickness. They were faced with annihilation from Guy Carleton's Anglo-Hessian army which was preparing to sail down Lake Champlain. Gates quickly saw the need to build a fleet, and he put Benedict Arnold in charge of the project as commander in the summer of 1776. When General Philip Schuyler claimed that Congress had made him commander of the Northern army, Gates stood aside and accepted their decision and worked under him as commander of the field forces. Within two months, Gates had worked a miracle by turning the troops into an organized and inspired fighting force who held him in the highest esteem. Gates was responsible for the organizing and directing of the fleet and ordered Arnold to use all caution and take no risk. Arnold disobeyed Gates, took the offensive initiatve, and was ultimately defeated by Carleton after a lengthy battle which did cost the British valuable time with the onset of winter. This allowed the Americans to refortify Ticonderoga and force Carleton to abandon his advance and return to Canada for the winter. Although Arnold is usually credited with that event, it was Gates who organized and led the defense and thereby saved the Northern army.

An interesting episode that reveals Gates' loyalty to Washington was when he was urged by the New York Committee on Safety to disobey Washington's orders to join him farther south in New York. The Committee wanted Gates to form an independent army together with General Charles Lee to defend the Hudson Highlands. Gates declined and marched south.[7] After commanding the troops that guarded the Continental Congress in Philadelphia during the winter of 1776-77, Gates was sent back to Ticonderoga in March 1777. Once again, Gates and Schuyler bickered over their respective positions of authority, but with Schuyler's loss of Ticonderoga in July 1777, Congress gave the command to Gates in August. With morale low and the army in disorder Gates had to pick up the pieces and rebuild his troops. He had an almost magical effect on his men, who welcomed his discipline and camaraderie. He achieved this by sharing in their hardships and caring for their well-being. He much admired the militia and saw first-hand how they responded to defend their homeland. Unlike Schuyler, who remained distant and haughty, Gates operated in the trenches with his men and was able to join the New England Yankees with the New Yorkers. He did this as a gray-haired, be-spectacled man of fifty who must have been regarded as a father figure training his "children."[8]

The British maintained their strategy of separating New England from the rest of the colonies by controlling the Hudson and loyalist New York City. Burgoyne's intended invasion of Albany was delayed by minor but time-consuming losses in the Mohawk Valley and at Bennington. Simultaneously, Gates developed a propaganda war claiming that the British were burning down villages and butchering men, women and children. These fears caused more local men to join the American militia, and Gates knew how to forge them into effective soldiers. He used several techniques that few other officers followed. First, he called the militia into action only at the last moment when they were needed. Second, he let them return home immediately when their tour ended. Third, he thanked them. Fourth, it was

---

7   George Athan Billias, *George Washington's Generals and Opponents* (New York: First Da Capo Press, 1994), 89.

8   Grizzard, 127.

fall and most of the crops had to be harvested. As a result, militia outnumbered the regulars in the Northern army.

The First Battle of Saratoga commenced on September 19, 1777, when Burgoyne moved his forces towards Gates' front line. Gates responded with Colonel Daniel Morgan's frontiersmen using their long-range rifles with deadly accuracy in the warfare style of the French and Indian War. Next, Gates used a bayonet charge that held the British back. Gates retreated to his headquarters and left the field to Burgoyne who had lost twice as many men as the Americans. During the next weeks the American sharpshooters picked off the British every night and day until finally Burgoyne went on the offensive on October 7, 1777, starting the Second Battle of Saratoga. When Gates ordered Morgan to begin his attack, Benedict Arnold suddenly appeared on the field even though he had just been relieved of his command following a dispute with Gates. Arnold breached the British key position forcing Burgoyne to retreat. Gates then pursued and encircled the British forcing their surrender. Contrary to what most historians have said, it was Gates who had organized and executed a cautious strategy that wore down the British and kept the main American army safely behind heavy fortifications. The significant outcome of this victory was its world-shaking consequences. The British lost and surrendered fifty-seven hundred men or 20 percent of their entire North American army. With the Hudson River in American control, the British had to abandon their strategy of dividing the colonies. Finally, the victory convinced France to openly support the Americans with ammunition and supplies.

With the euphoria of the greatest American victory, Gates violated protocol by reporting directly to Congress rather than to his commander in chief. Further, Washington criticized Gates for not returning the troops that had been loaned to him for that campaign. These events created a strain in their relationship which was further heightened by the rumors of certain efforts to replace Washington with Gates as commander in chief. General Thomas Conway, who was an Irish-born citizen in the French army and who emigrated to serve in the American army wrote a letter to Gates in which he severely criticized Washington. When the letter reached Henry Laurens he sent it to Washington, who then confronted Conway assuming that both he and Gates were part of a cabal to have him replaced as commander in chief. Historians have differed in their views of whether there was an actual attempt by anyone to execute such a plan, but there is no evidence that Gates was a party to it. Some argue that Washington was overly sensitive to criticism especially considering his string of defeats and the poor condition of his army at Valley Forge when the Conway letter emerged. On top of this, Gates had just been rewarded by a thankful Congress in November 1777, with a new position as president of the Board of War thereby making him technically superior to Washington. Gates then used his position to make military plans without consulting Washington and to engage in petty arguments with him thereby further cooling their relations. In the spring of 1778, Gates was sent to the Hudson Highlands and then to Massachusetts in the fall. He considered himself too old for the Mohawk Valley campaign offered by Washington and after a post in Providence, Rhode Island, he gained a furlough home to Traveller's Rest. In June 1780, Gates accepted a call to command the Southern army just after the British had occupied Charleston and captured fifty-five hundred American soldiers. With their defeat at Saratoga, the British were trying a new strategy to conquer the colonies by invading from the south and driving to take control of Virginia which they regarded as a major stronghold of the Americans. In replacing Benjamin

Lincoln, Gates expressed sympathy for him and fully realized the challenge facing him. Gates soon found himself in quite a different situation than he experienced in the north. His efforts to revitalize the beleaguered troops were not successful due to their undisciplined, untrained and unreliable state. Unlike the northern militia who fought to defend their nearby homes, the Southern army was farther from their hearths and lacked the guerrilla tactics of the Yankees. Gates still relied on the militia, but it was misplaced trust. He also moved out in only two days anxious to prevent Cornwallis from getting his reinforcements to Camden. Gates had three thousand men, but two thousand were militia. Cornwallis had twenty-two hundred seasoned veterans including the brigade of the notorious Banastre Tarleton. Gates could have withdrawn for a more favorable position, but he decided to fight with the approval of his war council. When the British advanced with their bayonet charge, the Americans ran from the battle. Gates tried twice to rally his forces but without success. His use of untrained militia against British veterans was a great mistake, and he thereby brought defeat upon himself. Gates rode for two hundred miles in just three days to reach the safety of Hillsboro, but was deemed a coward for such a blatant withdrawal. As a result, Congress relieved Gates of his command in October 1780 and ordered an inquiry. He was later reinstated in 1782 and was stationed at Washington's headquarters in Newburgh, New York. His relationship with Washington was cordial but superficial, and there is some suspicion that he was later involved with the officers' anarchy there.

After the war, Gates became an outspoken Jeffersonian Republican with decidedly liberal views serving one term in the New York legislature from 1800 to 1801. He died in 1806 at his Rose Hill Farm in New York City. He made many contributions to the American fight for independence with his administrative and disciplinary skills. While liked by his troops, he tended to quarrel with other officers and congressmen and did not have the leadership qualities that were so necessary in holding the army together. In spite of these shortcomings, Gates provided an important role in creating an American army and commanded the victory at Saratoga that marked the turning point in the Revolutionary War.[9]

Henry Knox: 1750–1806

Washington's closest adviser and personal friend, Henry Knox is remembered as the "Father of the American Army Artillery". He fought at Washington's side in every major battle and even served as his Secretary of War during his presidency. Robust at three hundred pounds, he was congenial and always the optimist giving his commander sound advice and studied opinion.

Knox was born in 1750 at Boston, and following his father's untimely death, he was forced to leave school in his early teens to support his mother. Working in a bookstore, he read a great deal to satisfy his intellectual curiosity, and he soon developed an interest in military matters including artillery and engineering. He reportedly was present at the Boston Massacre in March 1770, and tried unsuccessfully to keep the British from firing into the crowd. In 1772, he became a member of the Boston Grenadier Corps, and in June 1775, he was a volunteer at the Battle of Bunker Hill. He served under General Artemus Ward who commanded the militia around Boston. When Washington arrived in July he learned of Knox's knowledge of British military tactics and his expertise in artillery. On the recommendation of John Adams, Washington appointed Knox as a colonel in charge

---

9   Grizzard, 128.

of the Continental army artillery of which there was none at that time. Because of his patriotic beliefs and serious study of military theories, Washington quickly took to Knox, and they were to become life-long friends.

It is unclear whether Washington, Arnold or Knox conceived the idea of retrieving the recently captured artillery at Fort Ticonderoga, but Knox was sent to carry out the task which later enabled Washington to surround the British confined to Boston. For six months while Washington organized an army from his Cambridge headquarters, both the British and Americans stood in their positions possibly waiting for some clarification from London on whether a peaceful solution would be offered by King George and Parliament. There were rumors of such a possibility, and Washington even raised a brand new American "Grand Union" flag showing the Union Jack and the thirteen red and white stripes of the colonies. But when the King's vengeful speech arrived by year-end, the Americans knew that all-out war was inevitable. Within three months from his departure for Ticonderoga, Knox arrived back in Cambridge in early February 1776. He returned with fifty-nine cannons, howitzers and mortars and stores of ammunition, which had been dragged by forty-two ox-driven sledges. It was a stupendous feat that required 120,000 pounds of weapons to be carried over snow and ice down the Hudson and over through the Berkshires and then onto an old Indian path across Massachusetts. While his generals resisted any overt move, Washington decided that the cannons should be placed high above Boston on Dorchester Heights. He and Knox carried this out in a well-executed all night plan that surprised the unsuspecting British and forced General Howe to evacuate Boston rather than risk more English blood. When they finally departed in early March, America had scored its first major victory, and the British had removed all of its troops from the colonies. It was Knox who made the difference, and his heroics served him in good standing for the rest of his life.[10]

After Boston, Washington went on to New York in anticipation of a British invasion. Knox went to prepare the defenses of Connecticut and Rhode Island and then on to join Washington with his 520 men to manage their 120 cannons. He fortified Manhattan and Fort Washington. In early July 1776, Howe arrived with thirty-two thousand troops who were to face twenty thousand largely untrained American militia and regulars. Also, it should be noted that at no time in the entire war did Knox have uniform artillery. He operated with British, French and American pieces that used different types of ammunition from cast-iron shot to grapeshot to canisters which meant they were not interchangeable. With their disastrous defeats on Long Island and Manhattan, Knox was the last American officer to retreat safely to Harlem Heights, having supervised the removal of his artillery. His experience there led Knox to realize how unprepared the Americans were, and he submitted a plan to John Adams for a military academy.

The United States Military Academy at West Point was established in 1802, and its concept and origin can be traced to Henry Knox.

Knox was a thinker, and his insights taught him how artillery could be used most effectively. The Ticonderoga expedition showed how heavy artillery was mobile and could be used in conjunction with foot soldiers. When Washington decided to cross the Delaware on Christmas night in 1776, the movement of cannon was a key element in his surprise attack on the Hessians at Trenton. Knox collaborated with Colonel John Glover's

---

10   Fleming, 152-165.

Marblehead fishermen to supervise the ferrying operation just as they had done in the retreat from Long Island. Around twenty-four hundred men and eighteen artillery pieces were brought across the river which in itself was an unusually large ratio of cannon to men. This was prompted by the weather which could (and did) prevent the muskets from firing. Also, the large supply of cannon was to help the troops' morale. With a sudden snowstorm, the cannon proved to be a decisive factor as they were strategically placed at the head of the enemy camp's street and at the opposite escape side where they dominated the battle and decimated the Hessians. Once again, Knox's artillery won the day. At the Second Battle of Trenton on January 2, 1777, the artillery saved the Americans from the reinforced British. On the next day, January 3, 1777, at the Battle of Princeton, while Knox held the attacking British at bay, Washington was able to rally his men to win another victory. For his services, Knox was promoted to Brigadier General. With the onset of winter, Washington retired to his headquarters at Morristown, New Jersey, and sent Knox to develop a cannon and munitions factory in New England. Knox choose Springfield, Massachusetts, to establish the United States Army arsenal where it still remains to this day.[11]

During the war, American diplomats in Europe were seeking experienced military men, and if Congress gave their blessing it was up to Washington who had to fit them into the right position careful not to disrupt his existing officers. The American Minister to France was Silas Deane who recruited Philippe du Coudray who claimed to have been appointed as the commander in chief of the Continental Artillery. This alarmed Washington who wrote to Congress on May 31, 1777 supporting Knox in such glowing terms that it is worth quoting:

---

11   Billias, 239-248.

General Knox, who deservedly acquired the character of one of the most valuable officers in the service, and who in combating almost innumerable difficulties in the department he fills has placed the artillery upon a footing that does him the greatest honor, he, I am persuaded, would consider himself injured by an appointment superseding his command, and would not think himself at liberty to continue in the service. Should such an event take place in the present state of things, there would be too much reason to apprehend a train of ills, such as might confuse and unhinge this important department.[12]

Knox requested to resign if du Coudray was given the command. A compromise was settled whereby Knox remained as head of the artillery, and, ironically, du Coudray was later accidentally drowned when thrown from his horse.

Knox was with Washington at the Battle of the Brandywine where he tried to check the British advance to Philadelphia. In spite of his retreat, Washington went among the artillerymen and was so impressed with their accuracy that he wrote a glowing letter to Congress relating their performance. He was particularly impressed with their *esprit de corps* and courage in manning their guns while being overrun by the enemy. A short while later at Germantown in early October, Knox encountered his first and perhaps only mistake of the war when he insisted on leveling a British holdout in the Chew House. Rather than advancing with Washington, Knox believed the house containing British soldiers should be leveled, but the structure proved impregnable, and the time lost enabled the British to rally from certain defeat to victory. It was a loss Washington attributed to heavy fog, but it was nonetheless another Continental defeat for Washington that caused considerable dissatisfaction in Congress. Again, with the coming of winter, the army retired to Valley Forge for rest and

---

12   Independence Hall Association.

rehabilitation. Knox organized and erected the forts to defend the Valley Forge encampment and was then sent to Massachusetts to gain men and supplies. Upon his return, he assisted Baron von Steuben with drilling and training troops.

As summer approached, Washington called his war council to decide on an attack of Philadelphia. While some were in favor, Knox was strongly opposed and believed it probably would be abandoned by the British. Almost immediately thereafter on June 18, 1778, the British evacuated Philadelphia and were ordered to defend New York. Washington saw this as a great opportunity to attack the twelve-mile long British lines and choose to overtake them on June 28, 1778 at Monmouth Court House, New Jersey. It was the artillery's mobility going from flank to flank that won the day, and it was Knox's personal leadership, skill and bravery that stood out during this last major battle of the war in the North. For the remainder of 1778 and 1779, Knox trained troops in New Jersey and taught gunnery and tactics in the "academy" he established as the forerunner of West Point. In January 1781, Washington sent Knox throughout the north seeking assistance from everyone of influence to assist in the clothing, feeding and paying of the army which had fallen into a crisis. Upon his return, Knox joined Washington in the siege of Yorktown in October 1781. He issued precise orders for the placement of artillery to be targeted at specific British posts. He recorded each firing and placed observers in order to calculate where shots should be directed. As cannon balls rained down on British fortifications and buildings collapsed, Knox moved his artillery even closer. He then destroyed the British ships at anchor on the York River, and after eight days of relentless pounding, Cornwallis decided to surrender. The French were awed by Knox as were the British, and with Washington's recommendation, Henry Knox was promoted to become the youngest Major General in the Continental Army at the age of thirty-one years.

In 1782, Knox was stationed at West Point. On August 25, 1783 he led the troops down to New York to see the British finally leave the City. On December 4, Knox joined Washington's farewell lunch in Manhattan, and when he shook Washington's hand, the commander in chief reportedly threw his arms around Knox and wept. Washington's last official act in the army designated Knox as the commander in chief to succeed him. It was Knox who conceived the idea of the Society of the Cincinnati in 1783 and served as its first vice president until his death. Knox returned to Boston and was greeted as a hero. He later served as Secretary of War for eleven years under the Confederation government and also in Washington's Cabinet. He wrote plans for a national militia and helped to suppress Shays' Rebellion in 1786-87. He was a strong supporter of the new Constitution and helped to get it ratified in Massachusetts. He assisted with building a strong navy and coastal fortifications. He retired after six years in the Cabinet and spent his remaining days at Montpelier in Thomaston, Maine, with his large family until his death in 1806. His contributions to winning the war and serving his country were enormous. From the Battle of Boston to Yorktown he served Washington faithfully and with the optimism so much admired by Washington. He was Washington's loyal and trusted adviser and a true hero in the American fight for independence.[13]

Charles Lee: 1731–1782

Charles Lee was perhaps the most enigmatic officer of the war. He possessed a complex personality that challenged authorities from his military superiors in England (including King George

---

13   Grizzard, 171.

III) to the American Congress, after he changed his allegiance to the colonies, and Washington himself. He antagonized most everyone he dealt with, and in spite of this, members of Congress took him seriously probably because of his extensive military experience in England, Poland and Spain. He was a compulsive talker who also put his thoughts in writing and seemingly wanted them distributed as widely as possible. He became so critical of Washington that even his friends abandoned him. It has been suggested that Lee would be best understood by a psychiatrist rather than a historian.

Lee was born in England and grew to be a tall, ugly man with slovenly habits and course speech. He was disliked by his mother and rejected by the women he pursued. He never married and was content with the love of his animals. Lee's military career began at age fourteen when he received a commission in his father's regiment. He went on to serve as lieutenant in a regiment sent to America in 1755 to serve under Major General Braddock where he may have met George Washington. He was seriously wounded in the French and Indian War at Ticonderoga. He then fought at the siege of Niagara, then on to Fort Pitt and eventually took part in the attack on Montreal. After returning to England, he served under Brigadier General John Burgoyne in Spain. He became an *aide-de-camp* for the King of Poland and was commissioned a Polish Major General. He then joined the Russian army in its fight with the Turks. Lee was unusual in that he was an intellectual with extensive military combat experience. His formal studies included classical and modern languages and literature as well as military theory and tactics. Having seen other armies he became critical of the British army and doubted their effectiveness especially in the frontier fighting in the French and Indian War. By nature, he doubted and questioned his superiors and the monarchy itself. He admired democracy and knew the writings of Rousseau and the rights of man. Washington was impressed with Lee and insisted that he be appointed to his staff. From the very beginning in Boston in 1775 and 1776 he brought organizational and engineering skills to the fledgling American army. His achievements earned him a command of one of the three divisions in Boston where he faced the British at Bunker Hill and had Greene and Sullivan as his brigadiers. Washington was so pleased with Lee's fortifications that he sent him to Rhode Island and New York to defend against British naval raids. In fact, he was so well regarded that his expertise was wanted in Baltimore, Williamsburg, Norfolk and Charleston, and he obliged them all. He was equally active in extolling the patriot cause up and down the coast and insisted on American loyalty oaths and a clean break with England. In the early days of the struggle, most colonists were quite indecisive about their loyalties, but Lee spoke out strongly for an American declaration of independence in order to awaken them to the cause. He was outspoken in his efforts to gain Patriots and deride Tories. He was hard-driving and offensive to others because of his determination especially in commanding the building of bridges, batteries and trenches. His outstanding work in Charleston was successful in defending the city from British invasion, and even though Colonel William Moultrie, the commander of the fort there, despised Lee he nonetheless gave him credit for his fine work. Congress ordered Lee to New York in August 1776 just as Washington was retreating from his Long Island disaster. Lee was critical of Congress who ordered Washington to hold the two forts on each side of the Hudson, and he told Washington he should not let Congress dictate military strategy. Lee was able to hold off the advancing British and allow Washington to escape to White Plains. When Howe reversed his pursuit and attacked Fort Washington, Washington retreated across the Hudson in November taking only his southern troops and leaving Lee with seventy-five hundred Yankees and "Yorkers" on the east side of the river. This may be due to Washington's low opinion of the New England soldiers and Lee's more favorable confidence in them because they were closer to their homeland and seemed more eager for republican virtues. White Plains and then the collapse of Forts Washington and Lee marked a deteriorating relationship between the two generals. Lee did not agree with defending Fort Washington and risking three thousand men to Howe's ten thousand men. Washington was skeptical but was persuaded by Greene to face the British. When the Americans were captured and then lost Fort Lee on the New Jersey side, Lee was in disbelief and let certain members of Congress know his feelings but was careful not to blame Washington. At the same time, Washington's chief staff officer, Joseph Reed, wrote to Lee hinting at his preference for him instead of the retreating Washington. This suggestion apparently went to Lee's head, and he ceased being a willing subordinate to the commander in chief. Washington urged Lee to join him in New Jersey, but he refused to do so because of alleged sicknesses and the fear of being taken by the British. Lee really thought Washington's orders were unwise, so he disobeyed them and attempted to round up enough militia to retake some of the New Jersey areas previously lost to Howe. Shortly thereafter, on December 13, 1776, Lee was captured in a Basking Ridge bawdy house and remained a prisoner until April 1778 when he was exchanged back to Valley Forge.

Upon his release, Lee proposed his plan to Washington and Congress for fighting a defensive war through guerilla tactics. This was totally in contradiction to von Steuben's training in the traditional European Plan. Lee's supporters were those who distrusted Washington, but they still preferred the open field fighting for which they were being trained. Lee was absent too long to gain sufficient followers, and Washington's authority and methods were more firmly established. Also, Washington had learned about Lee's disloyal letters written to his aide, Joseph Reed. Howe retired to England and was replaced by Sir Henry Clinton in Philadelphia. When London ordered Clinton to evacuate Philadelphia and march to New York in June, Washington called a council of war to determine what action should be taken. Lee and most of the council advised caution, but Knox, Greene, Lafayette, Wayne and Hamilton wanted to prevent the British from reaching New York without a major strike against them. A compromise was reached and Lee was put in command. When he declined, Washington appointed Lafayette to lead an expanded force of five thousand men. Lee then changed his mind and agreed to take the command which commenced on June 28. As the Americans advanced, Clinton anticipated a rearguard action and swung two divisions back toward the Generals Scott and Wayne who apparently were caught in the confusion. Lee could see that he might be trapped and proceeded to take up a defensible position. Just at that moment Washington appeared and after sharp criticism of Lee, he ordered Lafayette to take command. Although the Battle of Monmouth ended as an American victory, it was not well executed and upset Washington, who felt he was deprived of a major opportunity to do serious damage. After the battle, Lee's propensity to air his grievances in writing started the end of his career. In complaining of poor treatment by Washington, he requested a court martial, which was convened in July 1778. The court found Lee guilty of disobeying orders, misbehavior in a shameful retreat and disrespect in his letters to Washington and was sentenced to a one-year suspension. Lee then began to complain to Congress and persisted to the point of antagonizing one of Washington's aides to challenge him in a duel. John Laurens, the son of the president of the Continental Congress, seriously wounded Lee. He later accused Hamilton of perjury at his court martial, but this led to his dismissal from the army in January 1780. He spent the final two years of his life preparing plans for a military colony in the West.

In the early nineteenth century, a document dated March 29, 1777, and written in Lee's hand was found in his family's papers. It was a plan to end the war by the British and could be considered highly treasonous. Because it was so ambitious for Howe's forces, some historians suggest it may have been a trick against Howe. Having been written during his captivity it could be considered an attempt by Lee to save his neck or to strike at Washington who he had just disobeyed. Perhaps, it was his attempt to remain actively involved instead of idly sitting out the great conflict. Whatever the reason, it cast serious doubts on Lee's loyalties and perpetuated his reputation as a conflicted soul. In his book, *Memoirs of a Life*, Alexander Graydon says of Lee, "if he committed a fault it was because he was too respectful of the enemy; and that he was too scientific, too much of a reasoner." George Billias in his *George Washington's Generals and Opponents* believes:

> Lee saw the Revolution as a fight by free men for their natural rights. Lee envisioned a popular war of mass resistance. A war based on military service as an obligation of citizenship. He sought a war that would use the new light-infantry tactics among the military avant-garde of Europe, the same tactics the free men at Lexington and Concord had instinctively employed. But to Washington—a practical man not given to theorizing—this was all madness. He never seriously considered resorting to a war of gorilla bands drawn from the militia. He would have recoiled with

horror from such an idea. Such strategy would change the war for independence into a genuine civil war. It would tear the fabric of American life to pieces. It might even undermine the political process, and throw power to a junta—a committee of public safety with a Lee, not a Washington, as its military member.[14]

Benedict Arnold: 1741–1801

Considered by many historians as the greatest combat general of the war on either side, Benedict Arnold would surely be remembered as one of America's heroes if he had not turned traitor. His valor and leadership at Ticonderoga, Quebec and Saratoga were outstanding feats much admired and openly appreciated by Washington. He was absolutely fearless and tried to be at the center of the action wherever it took place. He was totally obedient to Washington and Washington, in turn, put his complete trust in Arnold. He was sympathetic to Arnold's difficulties and always supported him during his several confrontations with Congress. One can barely imagine Washington's shock when Arnold's treachery was discovered in September 1780. Ever since then, scholars have examined Arnold in an attempt to learn why he did what he did rather than focus on what he did. However, what he tried to do should not be treated lightly. If his plan had succeeded the British would have controlled the Hudson, isolated New England, captured Washington along with Knox, Hamilton, Lafayette and several key officers, and the war for independence would probably have been lost soon thereafter. Arnold presented Washington with one of the most serious crises of the war, and Washington knew its consequences could have been catastrophic.

Born in Norwich, Connecticut, in 1741 into an aristocratic family, Arnold could not complete his schooling due to family

---

14   Bilias, 47.

sickness and declining fortunes. His Yale-graduate cousins gave him an apprenticeship in their prosperous apothecary business, and he later set himself up with his own shop in New Haven. As business progressed he bought ships to trade in Canada, the West Indies and Central America. He lived the life of a gentleman and became an active supporter of the local New Haven radical political group. When Connecticut established a militia composed of New Haven's more important and influential men in the early 1770s, Arnold was chosen as its captain. When hostilities broke out in Lexington, Arnold was quick to march to Cambridge where he sought permission from the Massachusetts Committee of Safety to capture Fort Ticonderoga which was not only strategically located but contained heavy artillery and supplies which were badly needed by the Continental army. Without his knowledge, Connecticut made plans to send other troops to Ticonderoga and commissioned Ethan Allen with his Green Mountain Boys to take the Fort. Allen quickly took command over Arnold who as an experienced seaman was sent to seize control of Lake Champlain. Arnold's achievements were not reported to Massachusetts, thereby furthering his rift with Allen. When Allen finally left, Arnold drew up plans for an invasion of Canada and specified that the Green Mountain Boys should be excluded. Suddenly, Colonel Benjamin Hinman of Connecticut arrived with one thousand men to take command, and in a fit of resentment for having to serve under men of less experience and skills, Arnold resigned. He clearly was caught in an internal rivalry between Connecticut and Massachusetts for the victory at Ticonderoga, and when Massachusetts gave Connecticut control of Lake Champlain, Arnold could see that his authority was undermined. He went to Albany at the suggestion of General Philip Schuyler and wrote letters to Congress about events at

Ticonderoga. He also started his expense accounts, which were not well received by Massachusetts who awarded him only half of the total amount. Arnold then appealed to Congress, who made up the balance.

In the summer of 1775, Congress made plans for the invasion of Canada which comprised a move north from New York along the St. Lawrence River to Quebec and a simultaneous move across Maine to Quebec. Washington proposed Arnold for the Maine campaign, and he accomplished a daring feat of marching one thousand men and supplies through forests and rivers, constructing four hundred-pound boats and suffering from cold, exhaustion, sickness and desertions. His men were driven to eat "boiled moccasins and a gruel of shaving soap".[15] He finally reached the St. Lawrence with six hundred men. After dealing with blizzards, delays, and treason, he was joined by General Montgomery and his three hundred men. Meanwhile, British reinforcements reached Quebec. Against all odds, they decided to attack, but with Montgomery killed and Arnold shot in the leg, they were forced to retreat. Arnold was praised by Washington and Congress, which promoted him to brigadier general. General David Wooster was sent to relieve him, and once again Arnold was humiliated by being reduced to a lieutenant's role. Back at Montreal to recuperate, Arnold held off two British attacks and successfully evacuated his beleaguered troops after being ordered by Congress to seize all the needed supplies from local merchants. In mid-1776, Arnold became involved with charges of plundering the Montreal merchants for his own gain, and after heated exchanges and threats, the case was sent to Congress where the Board of War exonerated Arnold in May 1777.

---

15 Bilias, 171.

The new commander of the Northern army, General Horatio Gates, recognized the imminent British threat from the north down through Lake Champlain. He placed Arnold in charge of the construction of a flotilla of ships, and once completed, he was put in its command. Gates instructed him to retire if a stronger British fleet appeared, but when it did, Arnold chose to engage Carleton's superior forces. Although severely crippled, Arnold silently moved his ships past the British at night and eventually reached safety at Crown Point and then Ticonderoga. Arnold was criticized for losing the fleet, but his actions delayed Carleton from pursuing Ticonderoga as the onset of winter prompted him to retire to Canada. With Washington's troops being badly defeated on Long Island and New York and Gates on the defensive in the north, Carleton's fateful decision cost the British a probable victory of the war.

In February 1777, Congress promoted five brigadier generals to major generals, but passed over Arnold, who had seniority over them. He was not the only one passed by, but his exclusion upset Washington especially because he had not even been consulted by Congress. Arnold believed he had enemies in Philadelphia and was allowed to go there to argue his case. Fate intervened when the British suddenly raided Danbury prompting Arnold to defer his trip, raise some militia and harass the British withdrawal. His quick and heroic action caused Congress to promote him to major general in May, but it did not restore his seniority. Even with Washington's and John Adam's strong support, Congress would not act, so Arnold resigned his commission in July. Again, fate played its hand. As Burgoyne captured Ticonderoga, Washington recommended that Arnold go to the assistance of General Schuyler. Arnold immediately suspended his resignation and went north. Congress still voted not to restore his seniority, and

Arnold was again deeply hurt by their actions against him. Their motives were probably the result of being challenged by Arnold and dealing with prior difficulties on expenses and promotions.

Arnold's problems became Washington's problems, and the effects of these problems were far-reaching. One of Washington's first aides in 1775 was Joseph Reed, and when he later became president of the Supreme Executive Council of Pennsylvania he and his Whig radicals became strong opponents of the increasing power of the military over local domestic life. Even though Reed came to power through moderate men, he switched parties into a new Radical Whig segment, which openly attacked in print the more Republican older leaders like Robert Morris and Silas Deane. Washington had appointed Arnold as military governor of Philadelphia, and with his sense of discipline he became the symbol of strong government, and he thereby became the object of the radicals' attacks. The attacks seemed undeserved to Greene and Washington, but when Reed learned of certain Arnold deeds, the radicals exploded and began a major offensive against him. Specifically, Arnold was accused of using publicly owned wagons for hauling possessions of his bride (Peggy Shippen) and issuing a passport to help a friend's daughter (Hannah Levy) to join her family in Tory New York City. When Reed's council summoned him to testify, Arnold tersely remarked that he was only answerable to Congress, which so infuriated the council members that they asked Congress for his removal and an investigation. In doing this, Reed put himself into a box over the issue of federal versus state authority. If Pennsylvania had to go before the Congress, then their local authority would be subservient. If they did not provide evidence against Arnold, they knew Arnold would be acquitted. However, in frustration they threatened to withhold essential Pennsylvania troops and their vital Conestoga wagons, which they knew were essential to Washington. Meanwhile, Arnold's thankful friends in New York State offered to give him forty thousand acres near Lake Champlain so he could establish a settlement there for those men who served with him. When learning of this, Reed was outraged and immediately filed formal charges against Arnold. Further, the Pennsylvania Council stated as long as Arnold stayed in Philadelphia they would no longer pay their share of the army costs and would not call out their militia unless absolutely necessary. Arnold then sought the aid of Washington who was sympathetic to him and advised a court-martial to clear his name. Arnold abandoned his plans to relocate to New York State and returned to Philadelphia to face their criminal charges. Every state except Pennsylvania voted in Congress to refer the charges to a committee, which soon acquitted him of six charges and recommended a court-martial for the remaining military matters. However, the issues became so controversial with regard to states' rights and their impact on the war effort that Congress decided to turn the matter over to Washington, who quickly set a court-martial date. Once again, another burden was placed on Washington. When Reed learned that Congress was about to dismiss all charges against Arnold, he threatened to have Pennsylvania leave the Union. Washington then wrote Arnold that he was postponing his trial, and this delay so upset Arnold that he wrote a revealing letter to Washington that some interpret as his "farewell" marking perhaps the moment he decided to take a different course. Dated May 5, 1779, Arnold wrote:

> Having made every sacrifice of fortune and blood and become a cripple in the service of my country, I did not expect to meet the ungrateful returns I have received from my countrymen; but as Congress have stamped ingratitude as a current coin, I must take it. I wish, your Excellency, for your long and eminent services,

may not be paid in the same coin. I have nothing left but the little reputation I have gained in the army. Delay in the present case is worse than death.[16]

Arnold had been denied promotion three times. He was court-martialed twice. He had not been paid for the three and a half years he served in Canada. His expense accounts were to be examined yet again, and on top of this the Continental currency of one dollar in 1777 had depreciated to less than two cents by 1779.[17] It appears that Arnold finally succumbed to all these insults and pressures in May 1779, even though it was not until September 1780, that his treason was uncovered.

In December 1779, Arnold was exonerated of all charges in a court-martial, and he was only mildly reprimanded by Washington for his use of military wagons and issuing a pass for a known Tory. However, Arnold was still bitter for not having been completely cleared of all the charges. During 1779 and 1780, there was little field action in the North. In July 1780, Clinton abandoned his planned attack on the French stronghold in Rhode Island and returned his remaining Long Island and New Jersey troops to New York City. Washington tried to entice the British to fight outside the City with the hope of a simultaneous French naval attack, but Clinton did not oblige him. The old problems of inadequate food, supplies and men plagued the Continental Army, and Washington was hard pressed to maintain a sufficiently manned and trained army. With General Benjamin Lincoln a prisoner in Charleston and General Greene off to South Carolina, he also needed experienced officers in the North, and therefore he appointed Arnold to an important field command. When Arnold was advised of his new post in August 1780, he was uncharacteristically silent and later told Washington that he

---

16 Randall, 369.
17 Ibid., 369.

was too lame for such an assignment. Instead, he proposed the available West Point command which Washington reluctantly agreed to realizing the strategic importance of that fort. In late August, acting through his wife, Peggy, he learned that Clinton had approved paying him £20,000 for his defection, payment of all Arnold's debts and monies owed him in return for the surrender of West Point and three thousand men.[18] In less than two months Arnold weakened the garrison by one-half. He sold off supplies for his personal gain and redeployed men away from the fort and did all this under the guise of needing more men and material and building the stronger defense that Washington ordered.

Washington wrote to Arnold on August 16, 1780, that he would be traveling from his headquarters at Newburgh to meet with the French generals in Hartford and would be staying the night in Peekskill. He was to be accompanied by Knox and Lafayette and asked this to be kept secret. Arnold passed this information on to Clinton by courier, but his letter arrived too late for the British to act. Washington was also asking more information about the defenses at West Point, and Arnold relayed that he would answer them in person. However, the report he prepared was also sent to Major John Andre, head of Clinton's secret service in New York and Arnold's chief contact for over a year. Arnold reported to Washington that a British attack would not succeed, but he was not forthcoming with any strategic advice. Andre left New York on September 20 for a secret rendezvous with Arnold. He was delivered by ship up the Hudson but had to return by land when the ship was forced father down river. Arnold gave him a pass along with detailed papers of West Point for delivery to Clinton. It was the same British ship, *Vulture*, that Arnold was able to escape to later when the plot was discovered. On September 18, 1780, Arnold had personally led Washington and his staff across

---

18   Randall, 374.

the Hudson to Peekskill passing within range of the British ships anchored in the river, but his message had not reached the British in time. Arnold then sent another message to Clinton revealing that Washington was expected to spend the night of September 24, 1780 at West Point and could be easily captured along with the fortress. On the morning of September 25, the Arnolds were preparing a breakfast reception for Washington at their nearby home, Beverley, but Washington sent word that he would be late. Arnold was suddenly interrupted by a messenger from Colonel Jameson at New Castle who advised that he had found incriminating suspicious papers on a certain "John Anderson" and was sending them to Washington. Apparently, three young militiamen were absent without leave and set out robbing Loyalist travelers. They stopped "Anderson" and not finding any money, they ordered him to strip whereupon they discovered papers inside his stockings and immediately deduced him to be a spy. Arnold realized what had happened and ran upstairs to tell his duplicitous wife before Washington's expected arrival. He then excused himself to go over to West Point where he would later greet Washington. Washington did not stop for breakfast but wanted to first inspect the fortress. After two hours of inspection he was dismayed to see it in such disrepair. Just then, the messenger from Colonel Jameson arrived to hand Washington the suspicious papers. Some reports say Washington was so shocked that his hands trembled and he was rendered numb. Others say he was calm and simply ordered Hamilton and James McHenry to find Arnold. It is agreed that Washington did say: "Arnold has betrayed me. Who can I trust now."[19] Some critics say Washington was so stung that he failed to take the proper immediate steps of warning his troops of possible British assaults, which he finally did that evening.[20]

---

19   GW Papers at the Library of Congress
20   Flexner, 147.

However, Washington's first reaction was to capture Arnold to determine the extent of the plot. He was extremely upset with Jameson for first informing Arnold about the capture of Andre ("Anderson"). It was critical that the discovery should be kept as quiet as possible in order to apprehend Arnold. In Washington's mind this was the most serious crisis of the war. He put Nathanael Greene in command of West Point and called in his best officers and men to West Point to fend off a possible British attack led by Arnold. With the British forces in New York and on the Hudson together with the weakened condition of West Point, Washington knew his vulnerability. When matters subsided with no British activity, Washington ordered that Andre be interrogated and court-martialed. Although Andre acted bravely and evoked some sympathies among his staff, there was no alternative but execution. Washington asked Clinton for an exchange of Andre for Arnold, but Clinton declined, and Andre was hanged as a spy. Washington did not suspect Peggy Arnold's involvement and allowed her to return home to her parents in Philadelphia. Benedict Arnold fought for the British in Connecticut and Virginia. Washington tried to have him assassinated but without success. Peggy and Benedict Arnold eventually emigrated to England where they lived for the rest of their lives. The British never gave him an important command because they could never trust him. He died in 1801 almost a forgotten man, and Peggy died three years later. Washington's investigations had revealed that there was no widespread plot, but he had to sustain the recriminations of the radicals for having one of his most trusted generals turn against America and him personally. Recent historians have conjectured that Arnold may have been duped by his wife into his treachery. Peggy had apparently socialized earlier with Andre when the British occupied Philadelphia and continued to correspond with him after she married Benedict. Andre was in New York serving as one of General Clinton's principal aides responsible for spying and was in a perfect position to assume his role in the plot.

Marquis de Lafayette: 1757–1834

If George Washington could have had a son, he would have had all the characteristics of Gilbert de Motier, the Marquis de Lafayette. This young, idealistic, engaging and brave French aristocrat arrived in Washington's camp in August 1777, and from that day forward for the rest of their lives he and Washington formed the kind of deep friendship that only a father-son relationship can produce. Lafayette was not only a devoted officer and pupil of Washington, but he was a genuine hero of the American Revolution whose military exploits were combined with his diplomatic achievements as well. He played such a significant role that one wonders how the conflict could have succeeded without him. Every historian knows that the military and financial contributions of France were essential to the American Cause, and it was Lafayette who was chiefly responsible for bringing their support to the conflict.

Born into an aristocratic and military family, Lafayette came into the family fortune when he was only thirteen following his father's and then his mother's death. At the age of fourteen he entered the Royal Army. He married Marie Adrienne de Noailles in 1774, and, as she was related to King Louis XVI, he participated in the social life at Versailles. Although he was a warm and affectionate person, he was uncomfortable in those surroundings and preferred to be part of the military life. After his marriage he was promoted to captain, but France was changing to a peacetime footing making advancement and excitement less likely. Historians are somewhat perplexed by Lafayette's rather sudden interest in the liberal teachings of Rousseau and Voltaire, but the idealism of the American struggle must have intrigued him. As he followed reports of Washington's battles from 1775 to 1777 while the scaling down of the French army reduced him to a reserve status, his interest in America seemed to have increased. In July 1776, Silas Deane was named as the first representative to France, and one of his principal missions was to recruit experienced French military officers. Both Deane and Franklin conferred with the many Europeans who were seeking a commission in the American army and would sign up good prospects subject to the approval of Congress. One such recruit was Baron de Kalb, who then arranged for Lafayette to meet with Deane. On December 7, 1776, Deane agreed to appoint the nineteen-year-old Lafayette a major general thereby making him the youngest and the wealthiest highest ranking officer in the Continental Army. By that time, Deane had signed up seventeen French officers. Lafayette financed his own ship, *Victoire*, and along with de Kalb and others sailed for Charleston, arriving on June 13, 1777. After accepting the stipulations from Congress that he would receive neither pay nor a command, Lafayette was introduced to Washington in July in Philadelphia. It should be noted that because Washington was flooded with Europeans seeking fame and commissions including many without legitimate credentials, he was not enthusiastic about meeting yet another adventurer, especially one so young and inexperienced. After dinner, Washington invited Lafayette to further private discussions and the next day to join him in reviewing Philadelphia's defenses. In Lafayette Washington apparently saw an enthusiastic, modest and sincere pupil. His immediate acceptance of Lafayette was enhanced by letters from Deane and Franklin endorsing the young Frenchman. Further, Washington expressed his willingness to serve as his father and friend. In turn, Lafayette was honored to have such a mentor, and both men began to form a bond of affection and respect. Also, Lafayette's personality affected the officer staff, and he quickly became popular at headquarters.

Lafayette fought with Washington at Chad's Ford on the Brandywine in September 1777, where he was wounded after rallying the retreating Americans. His friend, de Kalb, wrote glowing accounts of his bravery back to the French War Department. After his leg healed in November, Lafayette fought with Greene at Gloucester, New Jersey, where he successfully took control of a small command. In recognition of his valor, Washington gave him command of three Virginia brigades in December. Lafayette revealed some secrets of his early success in a letter written to his father-in-law:

> I read, I study, I examine, I listen, I think, and out of all that I try to form an idea into which I put as much common sense as I can. I shall not speak much for fear of saying foolish things; I will risk still less for fear of doing them, for I am not disposed to abuse the confidence which they have deigned to show me. Such is the conduct which until now I have followed and will follow.[21]

Lafayette joined Washington's winter quarters at Valley Forge in December. During that winter several officers led by Horatio Gates and Thomas Conway tried to bring Lafayette to their side in an attempt to replace Washington as commander in chief. The so-called Conway Cabal was revealed to Washington, and after confronting Conway with his own correspondence to Gates, the entire effort collapsed. Lafayette assured Washington of his own loyalty. During this time, Gates as head of the newly created Board of War planned an invasion of Canada with Congressional approval. Unbelievably, Washington was not informed of the plan or their orders for Lafayette to command it. Lafayette reluctantly

21   Billias, 219. (Lafayette's Memoires)

accepted the post and went to Albany to review conditions in the Northern army. Washington assured Lafayette that the invasion would never take place because Congress would probably not furnish the necessary supplies, food, clothing or pay. When the plan was dropped by Congress, Lafayette rejoined Washington in Valley Forge in April 1778. When the Franco-American Treaty was announced on May 5, Washington and his entire army rejoiced, and Lafayette was then regarded as his country's principal spokesperson. Lafayette was soon sent on a reconnoiter with twenty-two hundred men toward Howe's troops in Philadelphia. Contrary to Washington's orders, he set up camp at Barren Hill and was soon surrounded by the British. A last minute warning enabled him to escape and return to Valley Forge. It was the only known incident where he disobeyed Washington, who later commented on his star pupil's skills. Anyone else would probably have been reprimanded.

On June 18, 1778, after the retiring Howe was replaced by Sir Henry Clinton, the British were ordered to leave Philadelphia and return to New York by land over New Jersey. They did this surprising move out of fear of an approaching powerful and superior French fleet under Admiral d'Estaing, which was sailing into Delaware Bay. This created an unexpected opportunity for Washington, who asked his staff for their recommendations. The question was whether to pursue the British with a general attack or to merely harass their rear and flanks. Lafayette, Greene and Wayne favored sending a large force to attack the rear, and if it went well, then a general attack should be made. When Washington offered the command to Lee, he rejected it on the grounds that it would fail. It should be remembered that Lee had a low opinion of the American forces which predated Valley Forge and his sixteen-month captivity. Washington then offered the command to Lafayette, and when he enlarged the force, Lee changed his mind and asked Lafayette as his senior, for the favor of relinquishing it back to him. Lafayette obliged and instead took command of one of the three divisions. Clinton anticipated such an attack and ordered a rearguard action against the advancing Americans near Monmouth Court House. Lee retreated, and when Washington arrived they exchanged harsh words, and he personally took charge and gave Lafayette the command of the second attack. Darkness intervened, allowing the British to return safely back to New York and denying Washington of a decisive victory. As a result of his defeatist retreat, Lee was court-martialed and suspended from the army for one year.

Lee tried to defend his actions and assailed his commander in chief through letters to Washington and the newspapers, only to become more isolated and rejected. He remained an embittered man until his death in 1782. Almost seventy years after his death, certain papers were uncovered suggesting that Lee may have tried to betray the Americans during his sixteen months of captivity in Philadelphia. Theories abound that he was only trying to mislead Howe and to save his own neck in the process. The British never trusted him, and therefore he was exchanged back to Valley Forge in April 1778.[22]

The British were strongly positioned in Newport, and in the spring of 1778, Washington sent General John Sullivan to command the three thousand American forces in Rhode Island. He then ordered Lafayette and Greene with another two thousand Continentals to support Sullivan. With promises of support from Admiral d'Estaing's fleet, they planned an early August attack on the British stronghold in Newport. A violent storm prevented the French from sailing out to Howe's approaching fleet thereby

---

22 Alden, 179.

denying a fight and causing d'Estaing to seek repairs in Boston. In spite of Sullivan's appeals and bitter disappointment, he launched an unsuccessful attack. Upon his return from Boston, Lafayette assisted Sullivan in his successful retreat and received high praise from Sullivan and Congress for his service. Lafayette was caught in the middle of the widespread criticism of the French and upholding their honor. He returned to headquarters in September and with Washington's approval he went home in January 1779, for a visit and consultations with the French government. Being warmly received by the King for his heroic services to the Americans, Lafayette used his contacts and influence to gain additional French aid. He worked diligently for another year and wrote Washington, "I hope I shall determine the government to greater sacrifices. Serving America is to my heart an inexpressible happiness."[23] In early 1780, Lafayette secured significant aid from the French government, which agreed to send twelve battalions of infantry under four major generals and supplies to Washington. The troops were to be under the command of Comte de Rochambeau, a fifty-five–year-old veteran of the French and Indian War and a major general for nineteen years; Lafayette was to command an American division. Because he was familiar with Washington's struggles with Congress, Lafayette insisted that the instructions given to Rochambeau explicitly state: "that the General, to whom his majesty entrusts the command of his troops, should always and in all cases be under the command of General Washington."[24] He also purchased at his own expense supplies for the troops he would later command in America.

Lafayette arrived back in Boston in April 1780, and Rochambeau arrived in Newport in July following the British withdrawal to defend New York from an expected French-

---

23 Independence Hall Association.
24 Ibid.

American attack. It was always Washington's desire to rout the British from their main headquarters in New York, and he had earlier planned for d'Estaing's and then later Rochambeau's necessary naval assistance to accomplish such a dramatic and hopefully decisive a battle. The latter's late arrival allowed the British to gain another squadron to reach New York beforehand, which thereby discouraged Washington's plans. Lafayette was equally disappointed when the French Admiral du Ternay insisted on his superiority at sea before any blockade of New York, and Rochambeau insisted on naval control in the New York harbor area. As a result, the attack was cancelled.

At this point in the conflict the American Cause looked bleak. The Continental Army had survived the worst winter in New England history when the Hudson River froze to a depth of eighteen feet. Taxes and prices were astronomical, the currency continued to depreciate, the army grew smaller and hungrier, and the Congress was poorly regarded. Charleston was under siege, Cornwallis had just beaten Gates at Camden, South Carolina, where de Kalb had been killed, and the British were taking control of Georgia and the Carolinas in their new strategy of defeating the colonies from the South up through Virginia to the North. In September 1780, Lafayette accompanied Washington, Knox, Hamilton and his staff to Hartford for a meeting with Rochambeau and du Ternay where it was decided to shift their focus to defending and liberating the southern colonies. On their way back at West Point they discovered the traitorous plot of Benedict Arnold and John Andre. Lafayette and thirteen other officers tried and convicted Andre of spying and sentenced him to hang. When du Ternay suddenly died in December and Rochambeau turned overly cautious, Lafayette was under increasing pressure to defend the honor of his country. He wrote

Vergennes in Paris for more men, ships and money. In February 1781, Washington sent Lafayette with twelve hundred Continentals to reinforce Steuben and keep the British under Arnold entrapped in Portsmouth, Virginia. He expected the French fleet to block any possible escape, but they were turned back by a superior British fleet and the the plan was thwarted. Meanwhile, Greene took charge in North Carolina following the dismissal of Gates, and Lafayette was sent to his aid. As the British advanced toward Richmond, Lafayette rushed to its defense where he was joined by Steuben. They forced the British to withdraw down the James River. Cornwallis was determined to take all of Virginia which he regarded as a critical supply and training base for the Americans. He gathered seventy-two hundred men to pursue Lafayette's twenty-five hundred mostly militia army only to experience the same old tactics that Lafayette learned from Washington of skirmish and retreat. After withdrawing from Richmond he headed to Fredericksburg where he was joined by Wayne's nine hundred men and General Daniel Morgan's and Colonel Campbell's riflemen. Cornwallis could not catch the Americans, and he even sent his veteran, General Banastre Tarleton, to capture Governor Thomas Jefferson who barely escaped from Monticello. As American reinforcements arrived Cornwallis decided to move toward Williamsburg to await further orders. Lafayette's strength increased to five thousand men so he turned to the offensive and chased Cornwallis. Washington wrote of Lafayette that "He possesses uncommon Military talents, is of a quick and sound judgment, persevering, and enterprising without rashness, and besides these, he is of a very conciliating temper and perfectly sober, which are qualities that rarely coincide in the same person."[25] In Williamsburg, Cornwallis received letters from Clinton ordering him to take a defensive position on the

---

25 GW Papers at the Library of Congress

coast and to send up part of his army to New York for a planned attack on Philadelphia. Then quite unexpectedly, Rochambeau learned that a large French fleet would reach America in July or August. Admiral Compte de Grasse was to carry troops and supplies first to the West Indies and then to the American coast. Washington hoped he would come to New York to be joined by Rochambeau and himself to finally and decisively drive the British off the continent.[26] Washington sent his plans to Lafayette, and the letter was intercepted by Clinton, who immediately directed Cornwallis to send more of his men to defend New York. Cornwallis moved on to Portsmouth with Lafayette on his heels. By July 6, 1781, they crossed the James after fending off attacks by Lafayette and Wayne. Clinton then changed his mind and ordered Cornwallis to occupy a port on the Chesapeake that would serve as a good naval station for the British fleet. Cornwallis therefore moved his men over to Yorktown on the York River. This was a logical choice because of its protected position and its deep water when compared to the shallow James River. There were several diversionary Franco-American skirmishes against New York, but Clinton held his ground with vastly superior forces. Washington did not know that Rochambeau had sent a message to de Grasse suggesting that Yorktown was an easier target than New York. In August de Grasse conveyed that he would be arriving off the coast of Virginia that month. Although Washington was disappointed, he nonetheless realized the opportunity of trapping Cornwallis at Yorktown. He ordered Lafayette to contain Cornwallis and immediately marched south with twenty-five hundred troops and Rochambeau's army. Clinton learned of the plan and while it was too late to aid Cornwallis by land, he did send a fleet to retrieve him. Remembering the several previous French disengagements, Washington worried of yet another failure to seize the moment.

---

26 Alden, 198.

On August 30, 1781, de Grasse arrived at the Chesapeake with thirty-four ships, thirty-one hundred marines and several thousand crew. The British fleet then arrived and engaged the French on September 5, 1781. Admirals Thomas Graces and Samuel Hood commanded twenty-four warships and six frigates, and de Grasse went out to Cape Henry to meet them in a brief and unorthodox battle whereby the French did not line up in the usual manner parallel to the British. deGrasse faced the enemy head on, and his superior guns wrecked the British in only two and one-half hours sending them back to New York. The siege of Yorktown began with Washington's eighty-eight hundred American troops and seventy-eight hundred French soldiers. Meanwhile, Admiral Barras arrived from Newport with siege guns. Knowing that de Grasse was ordered to leave in October, Washington began the battle on September 28. With well engineered trenches and overwhelming artillery, the Americans bombarded the British with little effective retaliation. Lieutenant Colonel Alexander Hamilton and Major General Lafayette stormed the British redoubts on October 14 and 15, and found the British had abandoned their outer fortifications. Cornwallis sent for help from Clinton, but it was too late. On October 16, Cornwallis tried to escape across the York over to Gloucester, but was met by French and American forces who repelled them back to Yorktown. On October 17, Cornwallis asked for a parley. Washington demanded an unconditional surrender which took place on October 19, 1781. Cornwallis feigned illness so he sent General Charles O'Hara instead. Washington responded by sending his General Benjamin Lincoln to accept their sword of surrender. This was a gesture to allow Lincoln revenge for his humiliation at Charleston. Cornwallis and his officers were released on parole, but his seven thousand men were imprisoned.[27]

---

27   Alden, 202.

After Yorktown, Lafayette was heartily thanks by Congress and arranged to return to France to confer with Franklin with the hope of attaining a loan and reinforcements for Rochambeau and another fleet. Before he left in December, Washington wrote to him:

> I owe it to your friendship and to my affectionate regard for you, my dear Marquis, not to let you leave this country without carrying with you fresh marks of my attachment to you, and new expressions of the high sense I entertain of your military conduct and other important services in the course of the last campaign, although the latter are too well known to need the testimony of my approbation.

Lafayette responded "Adieu, my dear General, I know your heart so well that I am sure that no distance can alter your attachment to me. With the same candour I assure that my love, respect, my gratitude for you, are above expression; that, at the moment of leaving you, I felt more than ever the strength of those friendly ties that forever bind me to you."[28] When he arrived back in Paris in January 1782, he was honored as a great hero. He and Franklin were successful in getting a new French loan and reinforcements for Rochambeau. England's war ministry fell, and there were signs that the British wanted peace. Lafayette worked diligently with the American Peace Commission composed of Franklin, Adams and Jay. England was forced into recognizing American sovereignty before negotiating a peace treaty that was drafted in December 1782. France signed a separate treaty on January 20, 1783.

Lafayette tried to emulate Washington and the American experiment for a republican France. He wanted to see a peaceful transfer of political power from the monarchy to the people, but events demonstrated some major differences between France and

---

28 Independence Hall Association.

America. He returned to America in August 1784, where he was received as a great hero. He visited Mount Vernon and worked to promote trade between the two countries. In 1790, Lafayette was at the pinnacle of popularity. He was appointed commander of the army in 1792 when war was declared on Austria, but with the rise of the Jacobins he fled to Belgium. He was captured by the Austrians who handed him over to the Prussians who held him until 1797. He was finally freed by Napoleon in 1797 and briefly retired from public service. The American Congress awarded him $200,000 for his unpaid services and gave him 11,500 acres in Louisiana. He sat in the Chamber of Deputies from 1818 to 1824 and then returned to America for a triumphal one-year tour given by the many grateful Americans who remembered him well. He died in 1834, and his grave in Paris was covered with soil from Bunker Hill.[29]

Anthony Wayne: 1745–1796

Scholars are unsure of exactly how General Wayne received the epithet "Mad Anthony" Wayne. Some ascribe it to one of his men who considered him "insane" in the sense that he was brave and courageous in attempting the impossible. Others ascribe it to Major John Andre, the co-conspirator of Benedict Arnold, who considered himself a poet and in his critical poem about Wayne, "The Cow Chace," one line refers to "mad Anthony's fierce eye." In any event, most agree that the nickname started some time in 1781, and it probably was connected in some way to his daring, almost reckless, military exploits.

Wayne was born in 1745 in East Town Township, Chester County, Pennsylvania, about five miles from Valley Forge. He received a good education and excelled in mathematics. While

---

29   Billias, 235.

working on his father's farm, Waynesborough, he studied surveying and at the age of twenty was commissioned by Benjamin Franklin to survey land he and his syndicate considered buying in Nova Scotia. He married Mary "Polly" Penrose in 1766 with whom they raised a daughter, Margaretta, and then a son, Isaac. Wayne developed a successful tannery and in 1774 inherited his father's fortune thereby assuring his financial security. He served in the Pennsylvania Legislature in 1774 and 1775 until the war broke out when he then raised a regiment and was appointed its Colonel in 1776. At this point in his life, he was regarded as handsome, vain and impulsive, but he was popular locally and was considered as a leader serving as Chairman of the Chester County Committee of Safety and heading the boycott on British goods proposed by the First Continental Congress.[30]

Washington first sent for him to New York in January 1776, but as Arnold's Canadian expedition faltered, he was sent to Trois Rivieres between Montreal and Quebec. Retreating from overwhelming British forces with a wound in his leg, Wayne miraculously led his Pennsylvanians to safety through rivers and swamps and down Lake Champlain. That fall he was made commandant at Ticonderoga which he termed "one confused jumble of stones, without order, beauty or profit."[31] Wayne was a strict disciplinarian, and amid much grumbling, discontent and threats of mutiny, he drew a pistol at the ringleader, slapped him across the face and sent him to Albany for court-martial. In February 1777, he was promoted to Brigadier General and joined Washington's army at Morristown. In June as Howe withdrew from his New Jersey posts, Wayne was sent to join Greene to harass them. He did this successfully and began serving as a division commander with Washington's main army. He was then

---

30   Billias, 261.
31   Ibid., 264.

stationed at Chad's Ford on the Brandywine to deter the British and Hessians from their march up to Philadelphia. While he was overcome by superior forces, his fine defense enabled Washington to escape. He then took his fifteen hundred men to Paoli where he waited to ambush Howe's left flank. But Major General Charles Grey silently slipped through the lines at night with flints removed and attacked the unsuspecting Americans with a fierce bayonet charge. The loss of 150 men came to be known as the "Paoli Massacre" and prompted Wayne to order his own court-martial because he had been warned beforehand of a surprise British maneuver. The Court of Inquiry found that Wayne "did every duty that could be expected from an active, brave and vigilant officer, under the orders he then had. The Court do acquit him with the highest honor."[32] Wayne was soon given the chance to vindicate that debacle in October 1777, at the Battle of Germantown. Washington had planned a complicated attack comprising four pincer columns which were to march at night and converge on the British lines from different directions. A heavy fog descended that night which caused confusion and prompted Wayne's men to fire on Adam Stephen's line, killing several Americans. Later, Wayne claimed they fired on "red coats", but the result was a defeat instead of the anticipated victory. Stephens claimed that the "red coats" were actually surrendering British troops, but he was later found guilty of drunkenness and dismissed from the army. Wayne believed an American victory at Germantown would have ended the war.

Wayne constantly urged Washington to take action, and some credit him with the suggestion of Valley Forge as the new headquarters because of its close proximity to the British in Philadelphia. There is some evidence that Wayne was not sure of Washington's abilities. He was aware of the growing

32 Independence Hall Association.

dissatisfactions of Generals Lee, Gates and Mifflin, and he disliked Washington's deference to his War Council. Reportedly, he wrote that "if our Worthy General will but follow his own good Judgment without listening too some Council."[33] On June 18, 1778, the British evacuated Philadelphia and began their long march across New Jersey to New York. The War Council was divided on what action to take, but Wayne was in favor of attack, and Washington took his advice. General Lee declined the command believing it too risky for the "inferior" American army. Washington then selected Lafayette, and when the forces were increased, Lee reconsidered and was granted the position. When Lee retreated at the height of battle, and Washington reprimanded him and took charge, it was Wayne who had to bear the greatest burden. He repulsed four attacks from the best British veterans and finally laid claim to the glory he so eagerly sought. Washington reported to Congress: "I cannot forbear mentioning Brigadier-General Wayne, whose good conduct and bravery through the whole action deserves particular commendation."[34] Congress rewarded Wayne with a gold medal. After the Battle of Monmouth, Wayne and General Charles Scott charged Lee with misconduct on the battlefield and later became witnesses for his successful prosecution.

Although Wayne was unhappily replaced as head of the Pennsylvania regiment by Major General Arthur St. Clair, he was named to command a new elite corps of Continental light infantry in June 1779. With two thousand soldiers Wayne was anxious to get into battle which he commenced in July against the strategic British stronghold on the Hudson Highlands known as Stony Point. He attempted this remarkable feat with empty weapons to preserve silence and relied on swift, surprise bayonet

---

33   Billias, 269.
34   Independence Hall Association.

charges similar to what General Grey inflicted on him at Paoli. Sustaining a bullet crease along his skull, he led his troops over the fortress walls and overran the fort in half an hour. He took over five hundred prisoners, fifteen cannon and valuable supplies, but more importantly for him he achieved his finest hour and established his own legend. Washington praised his victory believing it would inspire the American soldiers and build their self confidence.

Wayne briefly retired to his farm in December 1779, but Washington called him back in May 1780, to resume command of the Pennsylvania regiments. In addition to harassing British posts in the lower Hudson and New Jersey areas, he attacked the British blockhouse at Bergen, but it ended in a stalemate in which only a few boats and some cattle were destroyed. This was the event that prompted Major John Andre to compose his poem, "The Cow Chace," which ridiculed Wayne. In September 1780, when Benedict Arnold's plot was discovered, Wayne sped with his troops from Tappan to West Point, a distance of sixteen miles, in under four hours. Washington was amazed at such a feat and immediately put him in charge to defend against an expected British attack which to everyone's great relief did not occur. Throughout the war there was discontent over poor food, inadequate clothing and little or no pay. Wayne warned the Pennsylvania Executive Council that the British were aware of the situation and were actively using it to tempt defections. In addition, there were complaints about being kept in service beyond the contracted three years. All of these problems finally exploded on January 1, 1781, when a mutiny erupted in the Pennsylvania Eleventh Regiment. Mutineers wounded several officers and demanded to speak with their state officials. Wayne's attempt to stop them failed, but he followed them out as far as

Princeton in fear of their going over to the British side. They decided not to defect but insisted on dealing with Congress. A settlement was reached whereby they received all pay in arrears plus depreciation and adequate clothing. All soldiers who had served three years could be discharged, and by the end of the month 1,250 men left the Pennsylvania regiments. Wayne was ordered to rebuild his army but was faced with another mutiny in May over the less valuable Pennsylvania "money" that was disbursed. Although on a much smaller scale, Wayne was severe in dealing with the six main mutineers. Two were pardoned and four were executed by firing squad. By June, Wayne and his eight hundred men marched south to join Lafayette in Virginia where he was trying to hold back the advancing Cornwallis. In July, at Green Spring, near Jamestown, the Americans attempted a rearguard skirmish against the British who had just crossed the James River. Cornwallis surprised them by turning his whole army against them in a major full scale attack. Wayne responded by calling a bayonet charge, but Lafayette saw the risks of eight hundred men against six thousand British veterans and ordered a retreat. At the siege of Yorktown in October 1781, Wayne's Pennsylvanians were held in reserve but were in the trenches when hostilities stopped on October 17. After the surrender on the nineteenth, Wayne invited Cornwallis to dinner, but the British General had to decline because of so many requests from other American officers. Wayne rejoiced in the American victory and wrote a letter to Robert Morris, the "Financier of the Revolution": "Yet the resources of this country are great & if councils will call them forth we may produce a conviction to the world that we deserve to be free—for my own part, I am such, an enthusiast for independence, that I would hesitate to enter heaven thro' the means of a secondary cause unless I had made the utmost exertions to merit it."[35]

In November, Wayne and St. Clair were sent to support Greene in South Carolina arriving on January 4, 1782. Only there a short while, Wayne then went on to retrieve Savannah from the British. After dealing with the pro-British Indian tribes, he forced the British withdrawal from Savannah on July 11, 1782. Greene praised Wayne in his letter of July 14: "I am very happy to hear that the enemy have left Savannah, and congratulate you most heartily on the event. I have forwarded an account thereof to Congress and the commander in chief expressive of your singular merit & exertions during your command and doubt not that it will merit their entire approbation as it does mine."[36] An appreciative Georgia gave him a plantation not too distant from the one given to Nathanael Greene. After his return to South Carolina, Wayne concluded a treaty with the Creeks and Cherokees of Georgia. Greene granted him the honor of victoriously entering Charleston in December after the British evacuated. He then returned to Pennsylvania where he was promoted to Major General in early 1783. In 1784 and 1785 he served in the Chester County Assembly. He became a member of the Convention that ratified the Constitution and then returned to his Georgia plantation which he finally sold to repay his creditors. With American defeats by the Indians in the Northwest Territory, President Washington appointed Wayne as commander in chief of the United States Army to recapture and secure that area. He defeated the Indians at The Battle of Fallen Timbers in 1794 and was able to conclude The Treaty of Greenville in 1795 which opened the territory to future settlement. He died in Presque Isle (Erie) Pennsylvania on December 15, 1796 of poor health.

---

35 Independence Hall Association.
36 Ibid.

Perhaps the best summation of Anthony Wayne were the words of Washington when he was searching for a new commander in 1794. Of Wayne he said;

> More active and enterprising than Judicious & cautious. No economist it is feared: open to flattery—vain—easily imposed upon and liable to be drawn into scrapes. Too indulgent...to his officers and men—Whether sober—or a little addicted to the bottle, I know not....Under a full view of all circumstances, he appeared most eligible....has many good points as an officer, and it is to be hoped that time, reflection, good advice, and above all a due sense of the importance of the trust which is committed to him, will correct his foibles, or cast a shade over them.[37]

John Sullivan: 1740–1786

One of the lesser known Major Generals, Sullivan was a controversial person both in and out of the military. He was a difficult man and acquired such epithets as the "luckless Irishman" and the "fiery, fighting Irishman". Nonetheless, his military efforts were appreciated by Washington, Greene and Lafayette. He never achieved notable victories, but he always asked to be given commands in difficult situations.

John Sullivan came from a modest background of Irish immigrants who settled in New Hampshire. Fortunately, his father was a schoolteacher who gave him a good education which enabled John to read the law and set up a local practice at the age of eighteen. He married Lydia Worster in 1760 and moved to Durham, New Hampshire, for the rest of their lives. Known as an avid advocate for independence, he was sent to Philadelphia for the First Continental Congress in 1774 where he actively promoted the proposed economic sanctions against Great Britain. He first met Washington there as they both ardently supported

37 GW Papers at the Library of Congress.

such measures. He returned to Philadelphia for the Second Continental Congress in 1775 and from there went directly to Boston to serve as Brigadier General. Sullivan's career is cast in three phases. He exhibited courage and enthusiasm, but he lacked military experience. This accounted for his disastrous defeat and capture in Long Island where he allowed the one road not properly defended to be used by Howe to surround him. After his prisoner exchange, he partly redeemed himself at Trenton and Princeton and retained his self assurance and high opinion of himself. The next phase of his career was in late 1777 when he participated in the defeats at Staten Island, Brandywine and Germantown. The third phase was marked by more caution, and he performed admirably at Newport and in the Six Nations Indian War.

Sullivan's first military experience began in Boston where he advised Washington to wait until winter to attack the British pinned down in the city. He tried to rout the British from Bunker Hill in late December, but he failed. When the British finally evacuated in March 1776, Sullivan got into a dispute with the New Hampshire legislature over his right to appoint militia officers. This arose from his using officer appointments to re-enlistments from a fast-resigning militia. He was severely criticized which was the first of many controversies in which he was to become engaged throughout his life. Washington sent him from New York to Canada where the campaign was in serious difficulty. He had to replace the dying John Thomas, but the spreading smallpox and superior British forces finally caused the Americans to retreat to Crown Point in July 1776, thereby ending their effort to make Canada the "fourteenth colony." Congress then sent Horatio Gates to take charge of the Northern army. This infuriated Sullivan enough for him to travel to Philadelphia to offer his resignation. After many words and advice, Sullivan withheld his offer and returned to New York. Washington 's appraisal of Sullivan to Congress as they considered the Northern post reads:

> He is active, spirited, and Zealously attached to the Cause; that he does not want Abilities, many members of Congress, as well as myself, can testify. But he has his wants, and he has his foibles. The latter are manifested in a little tincture of vanity, and in an over desire of being popular, which now and then leads him into some embarrassments. His wants are common to us all; the want of experience to move upon a large Scale; for the limited, and contracted knowledge which any of us have in Military Matters stands in very little Stead; and is greatly overbalanced by sound judgment. And some knowledge of Men and Books; especially when accompanied by an enterprising genius, which I must do Genl. Sullivan the justice to say, I think he possesses. The Character I have drawn of Genl. Sullivan is just, according to my Ideas of him.[38]

Sullivan's bad luck started in earnest when Nathaneal Greene suddenly fell ill in August just as he was to take command of the forces to defend New York harbor from the Brooklyn Heights position. Washington gave Sullivan the post even though his adjutant, Joseph Reed, disagreed because Sullivan had no knowledge of the immediate area. When the British started to move their men from Staten Island to Long Island, Washington changed his mind and substituted Israel Putnam to take the command. Historians are still not certain about which general had what responsibility, but Sullivan did order regiments to all roads approaching their Brooklyn Heights entrenchments, but on the Jamaica pass he placed only five men. Howe learned of this apparent weakness and penetrated the lines at that point. However, even Washington had inspected all the American positions the prior evening and seemed satisfied with their placements. After Sullivan's surrender, the British could have

---

38   GW Papers at the Library of Congress.

easily driven the Americans off Long Island, but under cover of night and a "miraculous" morning fog, Washington was able to evacuate his army across the East River to Manhattan. During his captivity, Sullivan was besieged by Howe to carry a message to Congress offering a reconciliation. John Adams and other members of Congress dismissed the offer as a decoy to subvert their independence. Sullivan was exchanged in September and returned to Washington in New York.

Sullivan crossed the Delaware with Washington and took charge of the southern part of Trenton. He also fought at Princeton, so by the time the army settled at Morristown, he had gained the reputation as a courageous fighter. During that winter, he became ill with an ulcer that was probably irritated by his penchant for alcohol. When General St. Clair was appointed commander at Ticonderoga, Sullivan complained to Washington, who immediately accused him of being too suspicious of imaginary slights. After this, another incident brought cries of outrage from Sullivan, Greene and Knox when a French officer, Philippe du Coudray, was appointed a major general which prompted the infuriated Americans to threaten their resignations. The problem ended when du Coudray accidentally drowned. Sullivan was so anxious to gain a major victory that he prevailed upon Washington to command a raid on the British stronghold on Staten Island. The attack failed amid chaos and confusion, and as a result, Congress started to question Sullivan's abilities. In August 1777, Howe started his plan to take Philadelphia from the south, and Washington stationed his defense at Chad's Ford on the Brandywine River. He put Sullivan to his right flank at Brinton's Ford and advised him that there were no other likely crossing places to his northwest. When Howe faked a move at Chad's Ford, he sent Cornwallis north to cross above Brinton's

Ford in order to encircle Sullivan in a move similar to the attack on Long Island. Sullivan did not have the time to check on possible crossings above him but relied on Washington's information. Washington received reports of a possible flanking action but thought that if they were true 1) it would take a very long time to achieve, 2) it meant the British had divided their forces and 3) it would provide a great opportunity to attack Howe with superior forces. When further news arrived suggesting there was no British crossing, Washington hesitated his attack fearing a much stronger British force at Chad's Ford. Suddenly, Cornwallis was coming from the rear with seven thousand men and put the Americans to rout while Greene aided Sullivan in an orderly retreat. The Americans lost one thousand men, and Howe moved on towards Philadelphia. Congress became increasingly critical of Sullivan, but Washington defended his action based on the information he received. Congress was so upset at that point that they asked for Sullivan's recall, but Washington asked it to be delayed. The next line of defense was at Germantown where a complicated maneuver nearly succeeded but was foiled by a heavy fog and some confusion in its execution. Sullivan was again blamed for the first to retreat, but Washington came to his assistance, and he was cleared of any blame for Staten Island, Brandywine and Germantown.

While at Valley Forge, Sullivan continually asked Washington for an independent command. He finally got his wish when he was assigned to lead the Rhode Island forces in a joint operation with the French. The British were entrenched in Newport, but with the arrival of Comte d'Estaing's fleet on July 29, 1778, Sullivan planned a major assault against them. With veteran reinforcements and France's sixteen ships and four thousand troops, it appeared Sullivan could claim his sought after victory.

Suddenly, a large British fleet appeared so d'Estaing boarded his men and sailed out to engage the enemy. A violent storm broke out and inflicted so much damage to the ships that d'Estaing felt compelled to disengage and immediately sailed to Boston for repairs. Sullivan was furious but could not dissuade d'Estaing from leaving. He considered attacking Newport with only his land troops but decided to wait for the French to return. The British and Hessians did not wait but instead attacked Sullivan on the outskirts of town. He successfully held the enemy to a stalemate, but when he was advised of approaching British reinforcements, he executed a brilliant retreat without the loss of a single man. He was applauded for his decision, but from that day forward he openly criticized the French for deserting him and not fulfilling their promise. Lafayette was dismayed over the event and tried to uphold his country's honor, but the event did plant some deep concerns about reliance on the French. It was probably very much on Washington's mind when he changed plans and marched to Yorktown on the expectation of the arrival of Admiral de Grasse.

The Americans were also besieged by continual harassment and massacres at the hands of the pro-British Native American Indians, particularly from the six tribes of the Iroquois Nation composed of the Mohawks, Oneidas, Onondagas, Cayugas, Senecas and Tuscaroras. In the spring of 1779, Washington took advantage of the stalemate in the Revolutionary War and assigned Sullivan to retaliate against them. By August he and General James Clinton gathered four thousand men, twelve hundred pack horses and seven hundred beef cattle and engaged the Indians near Elmira, New York. They overwhelmed them, burned villages and crops and went on to Cuylerville, New York, and then Tioga. His campaign destroyed over forty villages and at least temporarily put an end to the Indian menace. Although Sullivan carried out his assignment successfully, he continually criticized the Board of War and made many enemies in doing so. He offered to resign in November 1779, and was surprised when Congress accepted his resignation thereby ending his military career. Washington wrote to him: "I flatter myself it is unnecessary for me to repeat to you, how high a place you hold in my esteem. The confidence you have experienced and the manner in which you have been employed on several important occasions testify the value I set upon your military qualifications and the regret I must feel that circumstances have deprived the army of your services."[39] Sullivan returned to his native New Hampshire and served in several political capacities. In 1789 he was a representative in the Continental Congress. In 1781 he was the state's attorney general and then its president for three terms. He supported ratification of the Federal Constitution, and in 1789, Washington appointed him a Federal District judge. His last years were marred by a nervous disorder and excessive drinking taking him to his death at age fifty-five in 1795. Although he never achieved fame for a decisive major battle victory, Washington always supported him because he believed Sullivan was a loyal and brave fighter and a true friend of the Cause.

Philip Schuyler: 1733–1804

It is not surprising that George Washington and Philip Schuyler became instant and lifelong friends. They both had many similar characteristics and prior experiences. The major differences were Schuyler's aristocratic birth, background and education. His mother was a Van Cortlandt, and he married a Van Rensslaer. However, both men were tall, strongly built and had a commanding stature. They both fought in the French and Indian

---

39   GW Papers at the Library of Congress.

War and gained battle experience in frontier warfare. They both owned and managed large estates, and they both served in their respective state assemblies. Schuyler had a gift for language, and his French and Mohawk Indian speaking abilities proved to be extremely valuable in later years.

Schuyler was born in Albany, New York, in 1733, making him one year younger than Washington. He was part of the Dutch aristocracy of wealth and high social standing. He served with the British who commissioned him a captain in 1755, and in 1756 he had orders from Colonel John Bradstreet to deliver supplies to Oswego which entailed travel by land and water to Lake Ontario. He resigned in 1757 but returned the following year to participate in the unsuccessful attack on Fort Ticonderoga. He then served again under Colonel Bradstreet in their capture of Fort Frontenac. His growing knowledge of logistics led him to serve under General Sir Jeffrey Amherst to forward supplies to forts along the frontier. When the war ended in 1763, Schuyler's father died leaving him heir to thousands of acres in the Mohawk and Hudson River areas. He soon became successful in many businesses in lumber, gristmills, sawmills, farming and trading. In 1768, he entered the Assembly and became known for his anti-British attitude against their interference in colonial commerce. Seven years later he introduced a measure calling for repeal of the taxes imposed by Britain as well as their use of the admiralty courts and their depriving Americans of trial by jury. Schuyler was appointed a delegate to the Second Continental Congress in May 1775, and when they asked New York for a military commander for that area, Schuyler was recommended. He was appointed a major general in June. Upon parting with Washington in New York, the new commander in chief ordered Schuyler, saying, "Your own good common sense must govern you in all matters not particularly pointed out as I do not wish to circumscribe you within narrow limits."[40] With only this as his instructions, Schuyler took charge of the Northern Department of the army. The general nature of this order led to significant complications in the future. The Americans were well aware of British intentions to use their two strongholds of Canada and New York City to sever New England from the other colonies. Schuyler realized that a crucial path in their strategy was to sail down Lake Champlain and up the Hudson, so he commenced building an American fleet. His business and organizational skills enabled him to accomplish the task. He then had to deal with the pro-British Iroquois Indians and invited them to meetings in Albany. They agreed to stay neutral in what they considered a "family" dispute, but this was achieved only through Schuyler's knowledge of the tribe's customs and language and the "carte blanche" instructions from a very concerned Congress over British strength in the north. They hoped to gain sympathy from Canadians who wanted independence from England and were making plans to invade Canada and make her a "fourteenth colony". Congress ordered Major General Schuyler and Brigadier General Richard Montgomery to take any part of Canada they considered necessary. At the same time, they ordered Benedict Arnold to cross Maine and meet up with Schuyler and Montgomery at Quebec. The British were based in St. John's, Montreal and Quebec. When Schuyler and Montgomery reached St. John's in September, Schuyler fell sick, returned to Ticonderoga, and Montgomery took command. The army was saved from starvation through Schuyler's prior preparations and his handling of food and supplies from his post in Ticonderoga. Montgomery took St. John's and Montreal but lost his life trying to take Quebec. British reinforcements and a decimated frozen army prevented Arnold from capturing Quebec, but Schuyler's

---

40 GW Papers at the Library of Congress.

continued supplies enabled them to survive and retreat back to New York. In spite of his valiant efforts, Schuyler fell victim to the sectional rivalries between the New England Yankees and the "Yorkers", and he was wrongly blamed for the unsuccessful Canadian venture. Congress sent out Brigadier General John Thomas to head the Northern army, but he died of smallpox and was replaced by Brigadier John Sullivan. In June 1776, Horatio Gates was appointed by Congress to command the retreating Northern army, and this touched off a bitter dispute between the American generals. Congress had to clarify the situation stating that Schuyler was to remain as head of the Northern Department. Meanwhile, the British under Sir Guy Carleton began their move down from Canada. Gates was in command at Ticonderoga, and Arnold was to build a fleet at Skenesborough. In October 1776, Carleton was engaged by Arnold at Valcour Island on Lake Champlain. Although Arnold's fleet was destroyed, his resistance was sufficient enough to delay the British to the point that they decided to withdraw to Canada to avoid the fast-approaching winter weather. However, it was Schuyler who had initiated and planned the need for naval power on Lake Champlain, and credit for the repulse of Carleton should go to him. That summer, Schuyler had ordered the American post at Crown Point to be evacuated claiming it was too weak. Unfortunately, Washington did not agree with the abandonment, so an indignant Schuyler submitted his resignation, but Congress did not accept it. The following spring New Englanders in Congress caused a reprimand against Schuyler for some trivial matters, but it temporarily cost him his command of the Northern army to Gates. Schuyler believed the Americans would have to take a stand at Ticonderoga against General Burgoyne advancing from Canada. He placed Major General Arthur St. Clair in command, but when he later inspected it he found it in poor condition. St. Clair was shocked when on July 3, he found Burgoyne and his seven thousand men and artillery facing him. Unbeknown to Schuyler, St. Clair ordered his three thousand men to withdraw without a fight. Because he was commander of the Northern army, Schuyler was severely criticized for the loss of Ticonderoga. Schuyler made continued efforts to slow the advancing Burgoyne by destroying bridges, placing trees along wagon roads, rolling boulders into river crossings and torching crops. He proved masterful in delaying tactics, but Congress became impatient and replaced him with Horatio Gates. Washington did not concur but stayed out of the fray over Schuyler, who had done so much to thwart Burgoyne. Two months after Schuyler's dismissal on August 19, 1777, Burgoyne was defeated at Saratoga, and while most of the credit went to Gates, it was Schuyler who deserves the credit for his brilliance, planning and courage.

On October 1, 1778, Schuyler's court martial charged him with a neglect of duty for being absent from Ticonderoga prior and during its fall. He presented many witnesses to his efforts at strengthening the Fort and was acquitted. He resigned the next spring. No longer in the army, Schuyler continued to render advice to Washington. His knowledge of the Iroquois enabled Sullivan to lead a successful campaign against the Mohawk tribes in 1779. He was a member of the New York delegation to Congress in 1779 and 1780.

Washington turned to Schuyler in 1782 for advice on dealing with the little-known effort by the British to lure Vermont into their province. Because the Continental Congress had labored so long on whether to bring Vermont into the Confederation, General Haldimand of the British army tried to negotiate with their leaders for them to join the empire. Washington was kept abreast of the situation and asked Schuyler to intercede on his behalf directly with Vermont President Thomas Chittenden. Schuyler advocated New York's approval of the Constitution and then served several terms in the New York State Senate and two terms in the United States Senate. He shared Washington's keen interest in building canals to foster commerce with the frontier, and in 1781 Washington became godfather to Schuyler's daughter. His wife, Catherine, and his son-in-law, Alexander Hamilton, both predeceased him. Again, like Washington, he freed all his slaves and provided for their support.[41] The Battle of Saratoga is considered by many historians as the turning point in the Revolutionary War, and because of his expert planning and courage in preparing for that conflict, Schuyler deserves a special place for his contribution to the American Cause.

Baron Friedrich von Steuben: 1730–1794

Whether it was fate or Providential, Baron von Steuben found himself in the right place at the right time. He appeared on the American scene at the precise moment of its nadir, and it is to the enormous credit of George Washington that he was given the opportunity to transform the defeated and rejected Continental Army into a disciplined and effective fighting force. He not only trained the lowest foot soldier, but he fashioned a unique American military code for command and control. He accomplished this during a wartime period of deprivation and dissention, and with Washington's and Congress's complete support and belief in his abilities, Baron von Steuben achieved great success.

Friedrich Wilhelm Augustus von Steuben was born in 1730 in Magdeburg, Germany into a military family. His first ten years were spent in Russia, and when he returned to Germany

---

41   Grizzard, 282.

he was educated by the Jesuits until he was seventeen, when he began his military career in the Prussian army. Little is known of his activities before he was assigned to the General Staff of Frederick the Great. It was that experience which later gave him the opportunity to serve on General Washington's staff for the training of the Continental Army. In 1763 with the rank of captain he was discharged for unknown reasons from the Prussian army. He traveled to Paris in 1777 and was introduced to Benjamin Franklin, who was looking to recruit experienced military officers. Franklin wrote him a letter of introduction to Washington, which apparently exaggerated von Steuben's service with the King of Prussia. He arrived in Portsmouth, New Hampshire, in September 1777, and eventually reached York, Pennsylvania, where Congress had set up its new capital after fleeing from Philadelphia. In February 1778, he volunteered to serve without pay, and by the end of the month he reported to Washington at Valley Forge. Because of the extreme sensitivity of the American officers to the appointment of foreigners to senior positions, the President of the Congress, Henry Laurens, sent Washington a letter of introduction, which diplomatically assured Steuben a favorable reception. It should be noted that Henry's son, John, was Washington's *aide-de-camp*, and both father and son were ardent and loyal admirers of Washington. John's covering report to Washington stated that Steuben did not desire any particular command but that he would serve as directed by Washington. He wanted to help the Americans in planning encampments and disciplining the troops and made no terms other than to gain the approval of his work.

Washington and both Laurenses realized the need for proper military training of the troops, and John went so far as to suggest Steuben as a possible Inspector General. This was at a time when Thomas Conway had just been appointed, on December 14, 1777, the first Inspector General and was causing dissension among the officers by speaking of Washington's incompetence. The Laurenses knew this and hoped Steuben could eventually replace that troublemaker. On March 12, 1778, Washington asked the Baron to serve as "acting Inspector General" after Conway was ordered to the Canadian expedition. The Baron went to work immediately in developing training maneuvers that were simple and flexible. He adjusted the European techniques to the American situation. He discarded the English system, which the Americans were practicing, because he did not believe in using drill sergeants without officer participation. He created a model company, which he drilled himself, and insisted that the officers should also be included. The model company received recognition and encouragement, and as soon as he wrote the lessons of the drills and maneuvers he handed it over to instructors. The next day he would start with another group and would write the lessons for them at the end of the day. He had Washington's approval. Because Steuben did not speak English, he memorized the words and ordered the soldiers to imitate him. He started his drills on March 19, 1778, and within two weeks he reported that his men "were perfect in their manual exercise; had acquired a military air; and knew how to march, to form columns, to deploy, and to execute some little maneuvers with admirable precision."[42] After one hundred men were trained he formed them into a company. He was a bit of a showman and had a loud, commanding voice, but the troops acquired self confidence and pride in their new skills, and the recognition they received on the Parade Grounds was infectious. The soldiers not only learned to march, but they were taught the use of arms and how to form a front line when facing the enemy. On March 24, Washington ordered the

---

42   Benninghoff, 112.

expansion of Steuben's model company to the entire army. There
was confusion, especially with the language difficulties, but soon
the Continental Army was marching and maneuvering in unison.
The Baron was astute enough to recognize the difference between
the American culture and the Europeans. In his own words "the
genius of this nation is not in the least to be compared to that
of the Prussians, Austrians or French. You say to your soldier,
'Do this, and he doeth it', but I am obliged to say, 'This is the
reason why you ought to do that; and then he does it'."[43] The day
would begin at 9:00 a.m. with the new instructions explained to
each regiment. This was followed by practice, and later in the
afternoon they would practice by brigades. Also, the Baron went
beyond the Parade Ground in that he adopted new sanitary codes
with the placement of latrines, garbage and anything to do with
proper health conditions. Sickness was immediately reduced,
and the soldiers soon acquired the kind of personal responsibility
he demanded. On April 1, 1778, John Laurens wrote his father
"Baron Steuben is making sensible progress with our soldiers.
The officers seem to have a high opinion of him, and discover a
docility from which we may auger the most happy effects. It would
enchant you to see the enlivened scene of our Campus Matius.
If Mr. Howe opens the campaign with his usual deliberation,
we shall be infinitely better prepared to meet him than we have
ever been."[44] While Washington was in command of the army, it
was the Baron who controlled the soldier's introduction to the
new Continental Army "command and control." He wrote the
first manuals in French, and they were translated and copied for
distribution to the regimental officers. His manual was codified
into the *1779 Regulations for Order and Discipline of the troops
of the United States*, known as the "Blue Book", and this served as

---

43   Benninghoff, 112.
44   Ibid., 114.

the forerunner for today's military operation's manual, *FM 100-5*. The genius of Washington was that he knew the necessity of having generals command and control the training of their troops, but he relegated the preparation of the training regulations to the Inspector General. If commanders failed in their responsibilities, the Baron was ordered to intervene and take control of training. Washington struck a careful balance between staff and line functions and thereby improved the army's chain of command. Baron von Steuben transformed the Continental Army at Valley Forge in six weeks, and for his outstanding work, Congress officially appointed him Inspector General with the rank and pay of a Major General on May 5, 1778.

During the winter of 1779-1780, Steuben represented Washington to Congress regarding the reorganization of the army. In 1780 he was stationed in Virginia to assist Nathanael Greene and supplied him with supplies and materials. In June 1781, he delivered 450 Continental soldiers to Lafayette, and after a brief illness he rejoined the army at

Yorktown. Washington gave him command of one of three divisions. He helped Washington with the demobilization of the army in 1783 and the construction of a national defense plan. Both Pennsylvania and New York made him a citizen, and in 1784 he was discharged with military honors. He settled in New York where he gained some prominence. However, he developed financial difficulties because he was never paid by Congress. This was rectified in June 1790, when he was given an annual pension of $2,500. Also, Alexander Hamilton helped him get a favorable mortgage on the sixteen thousand acres New York had granted him. He never married and died in 1794. He willed his land to his wartime aides William North and Benjamin Walker.

Benjamin Lincoln: 1733–1810

One of the more obscure heroes of the war, Major General Benjamin Lincoln played an important part in the battles of Saratoga and Yorktown and in the siege of Boston. His reputation was marred by his surrender of Charleston, but he earned the respect and confidence of Washington. His most notable contribution came after the war in western Massachusetts when in 1787, he prevented the forces of Captain Daniel Shays from capturing the arsenal at Springfield. The incident of Shays' Rebellion was brief but significant in that it convinced Washington and others of the need to convene a Constitutional Convention for the purpose of strengthening a weak and divided Continental government.

Lincoln was born in Hingham, Massachusetts, to a farmer who was a colonel in the Massachusetts militia. He followed in the tradition of his father and grandfather by becoming active in town politics and the local militia where he succeeded in becoming commander of his father's regiment. He also was appointed to Hingham's Committee of Safety, and in 1774, he was elected commissary by the Massachusetts Provincial Congress. As an active Whig he gradually replaced Tory officers in the militia with other Whigs appointed by the Governor. He mustered the Second Suffolk regiment on April 19, 1775 and marched to Cambridge but soon thereafter went alone to Watertown where he was made muster master of the army of Massachusetts. By July he was appointed President of the Provincial Congress, the senior executive position in the new rebel government. In 1776, the Council appointed him a major general under Artemus Ward, who headed the Continental troops in Massachusetts, and he saw his first combat in June 1776, with the breaking of the British blockade of Boston. As part of the new Continental Army, he commanded the right wing at the Battle of White Plains in

October 1776. In February 1777, he led his troops across the Hudson to join Washington's camp. In writing to Congress about Lincoln, Washington said: "I should not do him justice were I not to add that he is a Gentleman well worthy of Notice in the Military Line. He Commanded the Militia from Massachusetts last Summer… much to my satisfaction, having prov'd himself on all occasions an active, spirited, sensible man."[45] In spite of the negative attitudes of General Charles Lee and others, Congress appointed Lincoln a Major General in the Continental Army in February 1777.

After almost being captured by Cornwallis in Bound Brook, New Jersey, in April 1777, Washington sent him to command the militia in the Northern army at the time of the evacuation of Ticonderoga and rumors of General Schuyler's collaborating with the enemy. Washington was aware of Lincoln's popularity and respect of the Massachusetts militia, and he believed his integrity would bolster their morale. In July 1777, he camped at Manchester, Vermont, and organized the militia. Just after Stark's success at the Battle of Bennington, Lincoln secretly and independently cut off Burgoyne's communication lines with Canada. In October, he commanded the defensive works at the decisive Second Battle of Saratoga where a musket ball hit his right ankle. It was a serious wound that left him with one leg two inches shorter than the other. Washington recognized his bravery and wounds with a special medal. In September 1778, Lincoln was sent to command the militia in the Southern army principally to organize the troops. He arrived in Charleston in December just as the British landed in Georgia, but he received little help from the other colonial troops in slowing the British advance northward. He even complained to Washington about the lack of cooperation from the South Carolina government which would

45   GW Papers at the Library of Congress.

only obey orders from Congress in spite of imminent threats to their security. In March 1779, Lincoln lost a third of his men at Brier Creek in northern Georgia due to the mistakes of General Ashe. His opponent, British General Prevost, invaded South Carolina and found so much loyalist support there that he soon was negotiating with Governor Rutledge for South Carolina to remain neutral in the war. Lincoln was able to drive Prevost away and could possibly have captured him if he had received his promised reinforcements. He was so discouraged by army desertions and lack of local support that he asked for his retirement. The fact that the state persuaded him to stay reveals his popularity. His integrity overshadowed his military bearing, and he was strictly a Yankee in his mannerisms. He was overweight at 224 pounds, slow, temperate and frugal. His wounded leg caused him to limp, and this caused him to move slowly. However, he had the respect of his men because he had the innate ability to command without giving offense. He was unlike Southern officers in that he would literally get down and get his hands dirty with digging and laboring to build fortifications and defense works.

In September 1779, the French fleet under Admiral D'Estaing landed off Savannah. Lincoln joined with the French troops to recapture the city, but their plan was betrayed to the British. D'Estaing was wounded, Brigadier General Pulaski was killed, and the French fleet left the area because of the approaching weather. Lincoln retreated to Charleston where he prepared for its defense. He still hoped to gain the needed support of the local state militia, but in April 1780, Sir Henry Clinton arrived and forced Lincoln's surrender. Actually, it was the Carolinians who asked Lincoln to abandon Charleston without bloodshed, and when he did, the militia quickly took the oath of allegiance to King George. Worse still, those Carolinians who did not join

Lincoln captured one of his regiments and handed them over to the British. Even members of the city Council turned to work with Clinton claiming they were mislead by the northerners. However, this hatred was not ascribed to Lincoln, and he remained a trusted and respected officer. In June 1780, he was paroled in Philadelphia and later that month was awarded an honorary degree by Harvard. He was even proposed to be the governor of Massachusetts, but he had no political ambitions. He remained active in the military by helping to secure more troops in Massachusetts, and in June 1781, he assisted Washington in skirmishes around the New York City area. In August, he was asked by Washington to lead the troops southward to face Cornwallis at Yorktown, and during that siege he led the American right flank. He led the defeated British garrison through the allied lines to their surrender but treated the enemy with dignity and respect. While still at Yorktown, Lincoln was appointed by Congress as the first Secretary of War. He retained the support of other officers and looked after their interests rather than those of partisan politicians. He shared Washington's tendency to look to the future and that the immediate physical and economic hardships would benefit his children and future generations. He did not share Washington's disdain for the loyalists but instead tried to welcome them back to their homeland. In October 1783, Lincoln resigned from his Secretary position and returned to Hingham.

Three years later Governor Bowdoin appointed Lincoln as commander of the Massachusetts militia to deal with Shays' Rebellion in the western part of the state. At the age of fifty-three he marched his troops from Boston to the arsenal at Springfield. Shays asked Lincoln to halt all actions in favor of a formal hearing of his complaints. Lincoln ordered Shays to surrender but without success. He then split Shays' troops by chasing one unit across the western side of the Connecticut River and simultaneously moving against another unit up the river. He tried to convince Shays of his indefensible position and offered amnesty to some of his men. His efforts to avoid bloodshed were ignored so he attacked their headquarters in Petersham. Most of Shays' men fled to the safety of Vermont which was still an independent republic, but the governor agreed to disarm them. Lincoln urged a cautious and merciful resolution but was mindful that there were enough insurgents at large who could cause considerable civil unrest. As head of the General Court commission he freed most of the rebels, and by June 1787, he was allowed to resign the position.

Lincoln was loyal to Washington throughout his life and was appointed by the President as the first collector of the Port of Boston. He was so trusted by Washington that he sent Lincoln to negotiate peace with the Indian tribes in the South and then with the Western Indian tribes. He died at his Hingham home in May 1810.[46]

Retirement from the Military

The task is now accomplished; I now bid adieu to your Excellency, as the Chief Magistrate of your State; at the same time I bid a last farewell to the cares of office, and all the appointments of public life.

—General George Washington
Letter to the Executives of the States
June 21, 1783

In the fall of 1783, Congress moved from Philadelphia to Princeton for a brief time, and Washington held conferences with

46 Billias, 209.

them. In November he moved on to Newburgh to disband the army, and on November 25 he led a victorious march into New York City. On December 4 when the last British troop ship left the harbor he attended a farewell luncheon with his officers at Fraunces Tavern in lower Manhattan. Washington was reportedly silent and emotionally upset. He filled his wine glass and announced: "With a heart full of love and gratitude, now I take leave of you. I most devoutly wish that your later days may be as prosperous and happy as your former days have been glorious and honorable. I cannot come to each of you, but shall be obliged if each of you will take me by the hand." As each officer shook his hand he became tearful and excused himself from the room leaving twenty of his officers in tears. He hurried to join Martha for a four-week carriage ride back to Mount Vernon. He was fifty-one years old, and he as well as his military and political acquaintances thought they were never to see him again in public life. In fact, no one expected him to relinquish power, and his greatest adversary, George III commented that if Washington did give up his exalted position he would regard him as the greatest man of the eighteenth century.[47]

On his journey home Washington was greeted with receptions and banquets and fanfare in Philadelphia, Wilmington, Baltimore and Annapolis. His welcome as a hero overwhelmed him as he was never comfortable with praise. No doubt he appreciated the thanks of a grateful land, but his quiet and withdrawn nature made him uncomfortable with such lavish attention. At Annapolis Washington submitted his financial accounts for the eight years of the war. He did not include the yearly salary of $48,000 (today's $1.5 million) to which he was entitled but had agreed to forego. He did not include his loss of half his net worth from farm failures and currency depreciation. His expense account totaled

47   Randall, 402.

$414,000, but he submitted a bill of only $88,000, which included his personal expenses for operating his headquarters, staff and officer meals, bodyguards, secretaries, visitors, congressmen and foreign dignitaries. Congress paid him immediately.[48]

At Annapolis, Congressional delegates knew Washington was coming to meet with them, but they were not aware of Washington's planned resignation. Jefferson and Washington recognized the need for having a formal ceremony in this important step of returning power to the government. Both men were concerned with the future direction of the country under a Congress that at times seemed incapable of governing. Only seven states were present at Annapolis when Jefferson's detailed ceremony was performed. It was witnessed by two hundred women spectators, two hundred soldiers who fought under Washington, Maryland's four signers of the Declaration of Independence, two future presidents, four Revolutionary generals and several future cabinet members. On December 23, he prepared a written address in which he gave Providence and his fellow citizens credit for the victory. He then spoke:

> I consider it an indispensable duty to close this last solemn act of my official life by commending the interests of our dearest country to the protection of Almighty God, and of those who have superintendence of them to His holy keeping... Having now finished the work assigned me, I retire from the great theatre of action, and bidding affectionate farewell to this august body under whose orders I have so long acted, I here offer my commission, and take my leave of all the employments of public life.

Washington was not a great general but a great leader. He was more an administrator and diplomat than a military tactician. He is sometimes wrongly viewed as a military man rather than a volunteer citizen soldier-statesman, but he had no navy—when

---

48 Randall, 404.

England briefly lost control of the sea to Admiral de Grasse at Yorktown, they lost the war. Washington never had the complete support of Congress or the states, but his patience, perseverance, discipline and faith in the ultimate outcome made up for his lack of military training. Washington was a symbol that united the colonies against a common enemy, and that symbol gathered in strength. Criticized by some officers, he never could seriously be challenged because of his overwhelming popularity due in large measure to his selfless dedication and loyalty. His faith was infectious, and it never faltered.

CHAPTER 6
Washington's Retirement To Mount Vernon: 1783–1788

At length my Dear Marquis I am become a private citizen on the banks of the Potomac, & under the shadow of my own Vine & I my own Fig tree, free from the bustle of a camp & the busy scenes of public life...I am not only retired from all public employments, but I am retiring within myself; & shall be able to view the solitary walk, & tred the paths of private life with heartfelt satisfaction—Envious of none, I am determined to be pleased with all; & this my dear friend, being the order for my march, I will move gently down the stream of life, until I sleep with my fathers.

—George Washington
Letter to Marquis de Lafayette
February 1, 1784

Washington found the transition from public figure to private citizen a difficult step. Other than the work involved in rebuilding Mount Vernon, he searched for a sense of purpose. He seems to have been caught in the dilemma of wanting the tranquility of a squire's life to being concerned with his perceived instability of the new nation. He had lived such a long time in a demanding and Spartan manner that a lack of responsibility and a disciplined military order were foreign to him. He also became increasingly concerned with his mortality even though at fifty-one with a strong constitution he outlived the average age of men at that time. His family was short-lived and that gave him concern. He wrote to his favorite officers like Knox and Lafayette and even considered a trip to France to personally thank King Louis XVI for his assistance in the war. But Mount Vernon became his chief project with repairing and adding to the main house and planting new crops and breeding horses and sheep. He arose early at sunrise and after a light breakfast would then inspect his farms and constructions which comprised a twenty-four mile trip. His estate was composed of differing businesses, and he had to restore them to profitability. He was interrupted by the constant arrival of guests who would stay for dinner and the night even though they could be total strangers. His strong sense of hospitality learned from the *Rules of Civility* would dictate his obligations as a host. In August 1784, he was thrilled to receive Lafayette, who had named his son "George Washington Lafayette" and to whom Washington was godfather. In his letters home Lafayette commented that "Washington is even greater than he was during the Revolution. His simplicity is truly sublime. He is as completely involved with all the details of his lands and house as if he had always lived there."[1]

It had been many years since Washington visited his western lands, so on September 1, 1784, he journeyed west to the Ohio River territory where he had fought under General Braddock in the French and Indian War. He was accompanied by his nephew, Bushrod Washington, Dr. James Craik and his son and three servants. They started at five o'clock each morning and covered

---

1   Randall, 413.

thirty-six miles each day. In what is now West Virginia, he visited with his brother, Charles, who had settled in a place he named for himself, Charles Town. Moving on to the Cumberland Gap and then to Warm Springs, he finally reached that place where Braddock and two-thirds of his men were slaughtered in 1755. He proceeded through Indian country to his land where he called a meeting of the squatters to settle their far overdue accounts with him. With little success in getting paid, he took legal action to eject them from his property and eventually won his lawsuit two years later.

The significant outcome of his trip was his revival of the plan to bring the western settlers into closer ties with the eastern colonies. He was disappointed in the failure of each state to negotiate peace treaties with the various Native American Indian tribes in order to help with the anticipated settlement of the western lands. A plan had already been devised in 1754 to bridge the gap between the west and east by building a canal from the Potomac River to the Ohio River. The idea was first proposed by Charles Carter who was the member of the Virginia House of Burgesses who was responsible for managing the expenses for the military expedition to the Ohio River territory under the direction of Governor Dinwiddie. Carter requested that Washington should study the feasibility of clearing the Potomac sufficiently enough to open navigation. Washington reported his enthusiasm for the project but warned that many obstacles would have to be cleared, and the seventy-six foot drop in the Great Falls area would have to be dealt with. General Braddock also agreed with the concept and actually made some use of part of the Potomac in transporting artillery and supplies for his campaign in 1755. Braddock's death and the use of an alternate route to the west by General Forbes in 1758 created disinterest in the project. However, in 1762, a group of eleven Virginians and eleven Marylanders joined together to open the Potomac to small boat navigation as far as the Great Falls. Washington provided the group with copies of his 1754 notes, but again the project ceased with the King's Proclamation of 1763 which restricted the development of the western lands. This was terminated by 1770, and allowed Washington and Thomas Johnson, Jr., to form an enterprise to resuscitate the project. Their joint efforts resulted in Virginia's approval in 1772 to open the river. But Baltimore businessmen opposed the project and defeated a similar bill in Maryland. The war intervened, but soon thereafter Washington pursued the concept.[2] He had always believed in the future growth of America and that is why in the 1750s he purchased bounty land offered by the British for service in the French and Indian War. By 1783, he had acquired thirty-three thousand acres of good "bottom" land and had the vision to see their potential purpose and value. While still waiting for the completion of the Paris Peace Treaty, news was leaked that the British were going to cede the western territories between the Alleghenies and the Mississippi to the United States, and this started a major migration and a round of land speculation. Jefferson, Washington and other prominent Virginians became enthused about the possibility of developing Virginia into the commercial capital of the country if a waterway could be built from the Chesapeake to the Ohio River. In the fall of 1783, Jefferson was appointed by Congress to head a committee to determine the location of the new capital. Jefferson proposed an area in Virginia along the Potomac River. Others in New York State and Pennsylvania were also studying plans for canals into the interior which prompted the Virginians to move quickly and add the James River to their expansion plans which were to reach as far as Ohio. Virginia

---

2   Grizzard, 251-252.

was already the largest state in terms of land and population, but Jefferson wanted it also to be the commercial hub of the new nation. In early 1784, Jefferson wrote to James Madison that the project needed the leadership of a respected executive: "General Washington has the Potomac much at heart. The superintendence of it would be a noble amusement in his retirement and leave a monument of him as long as the waters should flow. I am of opinion he would accept of the direction as long as the money should be employed on the Potomac. The popularity of his name would carry it through the assembly."[3] In March 1784, Jefferson wrote to Washington to ask for his support of the project and on March 29, 1784, Washington agreed to head the project. In October 1784, Washington sent a petition to Governor Benjamin Harrison for incorporation papers and wrote to Thomas Johnson about his growing concern for the new republic: "The want of energy of the Federal government, the pulling of one state and party of states against another and the commotion amongst the Eastern people have sunk our national character much below par and has brought our politics and credit to the brink of precipice. A step or two farther must plunge us into a sea of troubles, perhaps anarchy and confusion."[4] Washington believed the waterway was not only commercially viable but was absolutely necessary for the economic and social strength of the country. He was more concerned than Congress over the continued occupation of seven key forts by the British on the western frontier. In December 1784, he wrote to the President of Congress, Richard Henry Lee, imploring Congress to study and survey the land, rivers and tributaries of the newly ceded western lands. But with Jefferson gone to Europe, Congress ignored Washington so he then pursued the Potomac project and the creation of the Potomac

3   Randall, 423.
4   GW Papers at the Library of Congress.

Company.[5] On March 25, 1785, Washington called a meeting of commissioners from Virginia and Maryland to Mount Vernon to discuss the project which he had proposed over a year earlier. He envisioned produce from the fertile west being marketed in an important seaport at Alexandria. He emphasized the need to develop the western lands as vital to a growing nation as well as the fact that European nations were trying to claim the loyalty of the thousands of settlers who were moving there. In May 1785, some of Virginia's and Maryland's wealthiest businessmen met in Annapolis to establish the Potomac Company. Washington believed America was vulnerable to the British in Canada and in forts along the Great Lakes, to the Indians who were loyal to them and to the Spanish in Florida and along the Mississippi. In addition, the British dominated the seas along the Atlantic Coast and suppressed American trade in the Caribbean. He saw the colonies competing with each other and despaired at their lack of cooperation and support for the Potomac project. His enormous prestige resulted in the simultaneous passage of bills in Virginia and Maryland to create the Potomac River Company which was to build a 190-mile canal. A grateful Virginia voted to give Washington fifty shares of the new company, but he directed the legislature to use the shares for a public project which later in the 1790s he contributed toward an endowment for a national university to be constructed in the new capital city. He knew he would be accused of having alternative motives for promoting the project, so he remained free of anything that appeared suspect. Washington served as the first president of the Potomac River Company and started works at Shenandoah Falls, Seneca Falls and Great Falls. The project reminded everyone that he still had the skills and energy to organize, lead and inspire. Washington remained president of the Potomac Company for four years

5   Randall, 425.

by which time seventy-foot long boats could haul produce and supplies to within twelve miles of Fort Cumberland. The waterway was functioning thirty-five years before the opening of the Erie Canal in upstate New York, and it opened the interior of the Ohio Valley to farmers and merchants where in earlier years Washington had fought and nearly lost his life.[6] The Potomac Waterway Project is an excellent example where Washington's leadership, vision and perseverance developed a project designed to benefit a fledgling nation.

The March conference at Mount Vernon discussed matters such as joint commercial and fishing rights in the Potomac and Chesapeake between Maryland and Virginia. Even a joint navy was proposed to protect the waterway because the federal government did not as yet have one. Most delegates were concerned with the inherent weakness of the Confederation government and sought to establish joint Virginia-Maryland regulations of state currencies, import duties and commerce. On May 18, 1786, Washington expressed his concern for the weakness of the Articles of Confederation and the need for a stronger central government in a letter he wrote to John Jay, "That it is necessary to revise and amend the Articles of Confederation, I entertain no doubt; but what may be the consequences of such an attempt is doubtful yet something must be done, or the fabric must fall, for it certainly is tottering."[7] These and other sentiments led the delegates to invite Pennsylvania and Delaware to attend their next meeting to be held in May 1786 at Annapolis. This became known as the Mount Vernon Compact, and according to James Madison it marked the very beginning of the process that led to the ultimate creation of the Constitution.[8] The Conference was delayed until September and <u>was intended</u> to review the strengths and weaknesses of

6   Randall, 431.
7   GW Papers at the Library of Congress.
8   Randall, 428.

the Articles of Confederation. Washington introduced other concerns such as the British continued occupation of forts in the New York and western territories. They, in turn, refused to leave until Americans repaid their debts to English merchants and Loyalists. The British also supplied goods and weapons to the frontier Indians which disturbed Washington in spite of the growing prosperity of America in general. Although Washington was known to be sensitive about his reputation, he was genuinely upset with the lack of power of Congress to address the new nation's needs and the reforms he regarded as necessary. He was seemingly more sensitive to the country's weaknesses, especially with the growing hostilities between England, France and Spain and their respective presence in North America. In September 1786, Governor Patrick Henry of Virginia invited fourteen delegates from five states to meet at Annapolis primarily to discuss ways to promote commerce among their respective states. The Annapolis Conference only included delegates from the middle Atlantic region who soon realized that they were too few to bring about the type of major changes deemed necessary. They issued a call to all the states to meet the following May in Philadelphia. Washington faced a dilemma because he believed his earlier promise to retire from all public office meant he could not be a Virginia delegate to Philadelphia. Moreover, he had already committed to attend the first national meeting of the Society of the Cincinnati also to be held in Philadelphia. He managed to feign sickness for the Cincinnati, but was still undecided about accepting the head delegate position for Virginia when an ugly incident occurred in western Massachusetts prompting him to quickly leave for Philadelphia.

Daniel Shays was a farmer and former captain in the Revolutionary army, who lived in western Massachusetts. Like other states, Massachusetts incurred sizeable debts from the war effort and also had their own currency and financial system. With the imposition of increased taxes, farmers were unable to pay their debts in the hard currency that was required, and as a result farms were seized and debtors thrown into jail. In late 1786, with Shays as their leader, mobs erupted, shut down the courts and chased sheriffs off properties. When the protestors numbered close to twelve hundred men they threatened to seize the United States arsenal in Springfield, which housed fifteen thousand stands of arms and ammunition. This was large enough to arm an army far larger than anything the government could produce. Congress sent Secretary of War, Henry Knox, to investigate the situation, and his reports revealed that the rebels believed that all property belonged to everyone because it was all saved from British domination. It was their intention to redistribute the property in Massachusetts. They also intended to drown their debts through the issuance of a sea of paper money. Richard Henry Lee, President of Congress, suggested to Washington that the disturbance might be calmed if he would go Massachusetts and use his influence to resolve the problem. Washington reportedly replied that "influence is no government", and with that comment we can see how deeply he felt about major reforms to the government. If Congress had the resources [money] and a standing army the incident would have been dealt with quickly. But lacking that, in January 1787, Governor James Bowdoin mustered the militia to defend the arsenal.[9] Then, Benjamin Lincoln and his state forces took command and drove an attacking column away from the arsenal.[10] He chased Shays and his men across the Connecticut River where they hid in the hills of the Republic of Vermont. It was a brief episode, but it alarmed Washington and Congress

---

9   Alden, 223.
10   Jones, 99.

and speeded the agreement in February 1787 to convene in Philadelphia. They knew that if the "tax rebellion" had spread there was no way it could be stopped, and this underlined the need for a stronger government to deal with this type of situation. Washington despaired whether the new nation could govern itself and wondered if the European critics would prove correct in their judgment that democracy would lead to anarchy. Shays' Rebellion quickly died out, but it accomplished the motivation to address the weaknesses of the Confederation government and the need to adopt adequate reforms. There were those who wanted mild reforms and feared a strong central government, but there were others who believed in the necessity of overhauling the entire Articles of Confederation. The latter included Washington and in particular those who viewed the new country in national rather than sectional terms. Everyone knew where Washington stood on this issue, but they also knew of his extreme reluctance to quit his retirement and become a public figure once again. Both Madison and Governor Edmund Randolph pressured him to attend believing that even his presence would add tremendous support for the convention. Mindful of his reputation, he initially did not care to get involved in the earlier discussions about such a convention. But the Shays incident prompted enough worry for him to question all that he had fought for. He fully realized the need to pull the country together before it fell apart from either internal strife or external interference. He also knew that once he headed the Virginia delegation, he would be asked to take a leading part in the deliberations. There really was only one other major candidate who could perform this role, and that was Benjamin Franklin, who was then eighty-one years old and unlikely to accept. There was no guarantee that the convention would be successful, and he realized he had far more to lose than gain in his legacy and reputation. Few might answer the call to attend, and their sectional differences might never allow for agreement. But by April 1787, he decided to take the personal risk because the nation's future was also at risk. In the words of James Madison, he decided "to forsake the honorable retreat to which he had retired and risk the reputation he had so deservedly acquired, manifested a zeal for the public interest that could, after so many and illustrious services, scarcely have been expected of him."[11]

The Society of the Cincinnati

Amongst the Romans the best and bravest of their Generals came from the Plough, contentedly returning when their work was over.

—John Trenchard, British political
philosopher of the seventeenth century

As the Continental Army was waiting for a conclusion to the War for Independence in 1783, Major General Henry Knox conceived the idea of establishing a philanthropic fraternity composed of veteran officers. Knox was elected vice president, and the Society voted Washington as president. It was to have no involvement with politics, but its structure did cause concern and criticism from such notables as Franklin and Jefferson. The Society was open to all American and foreign officers who served in the war, and the concept had wide support including Baron von Steuben, Captain Samuel Shaw of Massachusetts, Brigadier General Jedediah Huntington of Connecticut and Philip Van Cortlandt of New York as well as others. One of its purposes was to preserve some mark of their participation in the great fight

11 Flexner, 203.

for independence. They chose the name from the great Roman general, Cincinnatus, who left his farm to lead his countrymen in their fight against Aequi in 458 B.C., and upon his victory he then retired to his plough. The officers felt akin to him because they too had left their farms to fight the British and would then be returning to their civilian occupations. The Society wanted to establish a "home" to support other needy comrades who might require help in getting back to productive civilian lives. This in part was intended to fulfill a role that Congress had neglected with the hope that it would also provide an effective organization to lobby Congress to remedy their complaints over back pay and pensions. They were increasingly concerned over this issue because it was not addressed in wartime and there was a greater likelihood that it would become even less important to Congress in peacetime. The men had fought side-by-side for many years under severe conditions of privation, and they wanted to preserve the bond they had developed. They also wanted to preserve a record of their service for future generations and for this purpose they designed a medal fashioned on the Roman Empire's eagle motif.

But the public was wary of an organization comprised of former officers. Anything resembling a standing army or military presence was a sensitive colonial issue and subject to suspicion. The very nature of the Society struck many as too European and class-oriented and not in conformity with republican virtues in spite of its benevolent purposes. Washington was unsure of whether to lend his name to the Society and asked Jefferson for his opinion. While Jefferson supported its fraternal and charitable intentions, he was opposed to its foreign and particularly its hereditary elements whereby membership was passed down to the oldest male descendent. New Englanders regarded it as an elitist organization and counter to republican ideals. After gaining Jefferson's reactions, Washington responded to the Society in May 1784, that it should eliminate any reference to politics and hereditary requirements and exclude foreigners otherwise he would resign from it. Unfortunately, just as he was presenting his opinion, the French arrived with significant financial support of the organization and gifts from the king himself. For obvious political reasons, Washington could not pursue the issue and had to be satisfied with their removal of certain clauses like the hereditary one. But each state chapter of the Society had to act on any changes, so most of these same issues were undecided until long after Washington's death. He was torn between his approval of the fraternal and benevolent aspects of the Society that included the patriotic men who fought for the country's independence and the public's negative reaction to it. However much he wanted his revisions and threatened to resign, the Society kept electing him as their president. He tried to keep his distance from it because of its elitist appearances. He felt that criticisms and fears were excessive, and yet he did not want to offend the public trust. Opponents of creeping aristocracy used the Society as an illustration of social inequality. Jefferson continued to council Washington that the Society would injure his reputation. Washington could not understand why such a benevolent organization with the best of intentions should be regarded with such suspicions. To him, the Society was virtuous and honorable, but then it should be noted that Washington thought the war was fought for political and economic reasons and not for egalitarian social reasons.[12] Nonetheless, he did recognize that the public's attitude should prevail if that was how they regarded the Society, so he advocated its demise partly out of sympathy and partly as a pragmatic political move long before the

---

12   Ellis, *His Excellency: George Washington,* 275.

Constitutional Convention that created a presidential office. In the end, Washington reached a compromise by agreeing to lend his name to the organization if it adopted some of his proposals. The hereditary clause was removed, and other provisions were added that strengthened its charitable purposes.[13] Little did Washington or any of the founding fathers realize just how contentious some of these seemingly innocent ideologies were to become when nationalism, aristocratic monarchism and republicanism clashed in the next decade.

Washington and Freemasonry

In 1752, at the age of twenty, George Washington was initiated into the Masonic lodge at Fredericksburg, Virginia, and the following year he was duly elected a Master Mason. By that time, the Masons had evolved into a fraternal organization that was composed of members with similar ethical and moral standards. However, the Freemasons trace their origin to the laborers who erected King Solomon's temple around six thousand years ago. Its modern history dates from seventeenth-century Britain when it was a guild of stonemasons. By the early eighteenth century, it had changed into a more philosophical fraternity of leisure gentlemen who aspired to the emerging Enlightenment thinking of self-improvement and respect for ancient knowledge.[14] It then spread to Europe, and by the mid-1700s there were Masonic lodges in all thirteen American colonies. It is noteworthy to mention Washington's Masonic membership because of the symbolism that was to later characterize Washington's leadership with that of the biblical and legendary King Solomon.

---

13 Grizzard, 289.
14 Barbara J. Mitnick, ed., *George Washington: American Symbol* (New York: Hudson Hills Press, 1999) 71-73.

Solomon was the ancient civil and religious leader of Israel who, according to Masonic legend, appointed three levels of stonemasons to construct the holy temple. He and his two principal assistants were regarded as the Grand Masters. Artistic renderings of Solomon and Washington are replete with many architectural allegories and metaphors. Some portraits show a rough stone block on one side and a smooth finished stone block on the other symbolizing a transformation from a man with rough edges, emotional and irrational thought to one of usefulness in a stable society. Another image shows the Grand Master standing atop three steps which represent the successive degrees of learning required to become the Master. Tools of the stonemason's trade abound with a right angle, trowel, vaulted ceiling and tiled floor. The Master at the center stands under an illuminated letter *G* representing God and geometry, and pillars to each side represent the temple.

When Washington took the oath of office in New York on April 30, 1789, he was sworn in by Robert Livingston, who was Grand Master of a New York Lodge. He used a Bible that was owned by St. John's Lodge that is preserved to this day. At the time, Washington was a Master of the Alexandria Lodge and was the only president to serve simultaneously in both positions. At that time, Freemasonry was perceived as a society whose principal purpose was to teach the new republican ideals of virtue, learning and religious faith.[15] Because it served in somewhat of a civil religious function, Washington was regarded by some as a modern Solomon who held civil and quasi-religious positions. On September 18, 1793, Washington presided over laying the cornerstone to the United States Capitol. He wore a Masonic apron and placed an engraved silver plate on the cornerstone. It was

---

15 Barbara J. Mitnick, ed., *George Washington: American Symbol* (New York: Hudson Hills Press, 1999) 76.

engraved with "year of Masonry, 5793," thereby linking the event with the building of Solomon's temple. This link was particularly evident in 1866 when biographer Sidney Hayden described the earlier cornerstone laying of the Capitol, "[Washington] stood on that occasion before his brethren and the world as the representative of Solomon of old."[16] The Masonic connection between Solomon and Washington also implied a likening of America with ancient Israel. The Hebrews under Solomon built a temple to celebrate their thanks to Jehovah for providing them with their Promised Land. America was the new promised land for the early settlers and under Washington established a democracy and a Constitution to ensure their inalienable, God-given rights.[17] In a tribute to Washington in 1844, journalist Joseph R. Chandler wrote in Louisville's "The Freemason," that those who wanted to improve their lives should look to Washington:

The glory of the name of Washington is in the sound integrity of his character, the purity and excellence of his motives, and the honorable perseverance with which he pressed forward in his duties... Providence has laid before you the bright example of Washington, and made you acquainted with the straightforward path by which he ascended from your position to that upon which nothing less than an angel can look down.[18]

The Constitutional Convention of 1787

That a thorough reform of the present system is indispensable, none who have capacities to judge will deny and with hand and heart I hope the business will be essayed in a full Convention... I am anxious to know how this matter really is, as my wish is, that the Convention may adopt no temporizing expedient, but

---

16 Barbara J. Mitnick, ed., *George Washington: American Symbol* (New York: Hudson Hills Press, 1999) 76.
17 Ibid., 80.
18 Ibid., 78.

probe the defects of the Constitution to the bottom, and provide radical cures, whether they are agreed to or not. A conduct like this, will stamp wisdom and dignity on the proceedings, and will be looked to as a luminary, which sooner or later will shed its influence.

—George Washington
Letter to James Madison
March 31, 1787

Washington reached Philadelphia on May 13, 1787, and found that only Pennsylvania and Virginia were represented. He used the next ten days to meet with his Virginia delegation, and together they crafted a plan for a strong central government that provided for checks and balances that would require agreement among all branches of government before proposals were enacted into law. They borrowed from the writings of England's Blackstone and France's Montesquieu. Notable among the missing were Thomas Jefferson, who was serving as minister in Paris; John Adams, who was envoy in Great Britain; and Patrick Henry and Sam Adams, who saw no need to change the Constitution. The convention included delegates who were former war veterans, governors, lawyers, merchants, legislators and planters. When a quorum was finally reached on May 25, Washington was appointed to preside as president of the convention. With most of the business conducted in committee, he could step down and allow a president pro-tem to preside. The delegates agreed to one vote for each state. On the first day of deliberations Edmond Randolph proposed to completely supplant the Articles of Confederation. On the second day Gouverneur Morris proposed the formation of a national government with executive, legislative and judicial branches to replace the Articles. Washington did not participate in the discussions because he realized he could unduly influence the course of events. He did speak out once on a motion to reduce the size of each representative's constituency from an initial forty thousand to thirty thousand to which the delegates unanimously agreed. The proceedings were kept secret as agreed, and Washington was the only delegate to attend all the meetings. In meetings with his delegates, Washington recommended "radical cures" to the Articles and anticipated compromise. He was decidedly in favor of measures that would strengthen the Union and suppress individual state interests. He was for a single executive who was not elected by the legislature and therefore not dependent on it. He lost on his idea of a three-fourths majority to overrule the executive, but he was ready to accept "tolerable" compromises. It took only five days to agree to do away with the Articles of Confederation and establish a national government. It was also decided to have each state call its own convention to ratify the new constitution. The challenge would be to have all the states ratify the proposal in order to hold the Union together. Sectional cultural differences were great, and few delegates had ever traveled far from their home state. Those who had served in the war had a greater knowledge and feel of colonists from different states, and they knew how it took cooperation and unity to process the war. These men favored a more powerful central government. Washington made it his business to wine and dine with representatives from all over the country, and it was at such informal gatherings that he sought to heal differences and bring harmony through compromise. He already knew many of the delegates from his war years, and his contemporaries and historians acknowledge that his contributions and influence were great. Even those who had not met him before the convention were impressed with his prestige and ability to find common areas of agreement without offending those with differing points of view.

The critical issue at the heart of the debates was the power of the national government versus the power of the individual states. Other important issues concerned slavery, trade regulations, taxation and the fears of tyranny and anarchy. Washington favored government control on issues affecting the entire nation and local control strictly concerning individual states. The latter issue was of particular concern to Washington because of his wartime experience when individual states seemed to paralyze the Congress. Each state had one vote, and they were not about to give that up. This contentious issue was finally settled by a compromise that allowed the House of Representatives to be voted by population and the Senate was established by the states. Even the role of the chief executive was heavily debated because of the past experience with kings and monarchs. The President was to be elected separately by the people and could be re-elected without limit. The convention granted great powers to the presidency, but he could not interfere with the legislature except to be able to veto their bills. He could only be removed by Congress in the event of criminal acts or treason. Perhaps the highest tribute to Washington was that the delegates envisioned the office of the presidency to be filled by Washington, and it was because of their highest regard for him that they granted so much power to that office.

There is some evidence that Washington was not overly enthusiastic about the final document. He wrote to Patrick Henry who opposed the document: "I wish the Constitution which is offered had been made more perfect, but I sincerely believe it is the best that could be obtained at this time; and, as a constitutional door is open to amendment hereafter, the adoption of it under the present circumstances of the Union is in my opinion desirable."[19] On the issue of slavery, the delegates realized that its restrictions or prohibition would not permit the southern states to accept the new Constitution, so that contentious issue was set aside for future resolution. On September 17, 1787, forty-two delegates voted to approve the Constitution. Virginia Governor Edmund Randolph and Washington's friend and neighbor, George Mason, voted against it because they found it provided no protection for the individual and lacked a Bill of Rights. Thomas Jefferson wrote to Madison from Paris that had he been in Philadelphia he would have fought against the Constitution, but with Madison's assurance of a Bill of Rights amendment he would then support it.[20] Alexander Hamilton signed for New York but his single vote did not authorize him to commit for New York. Officially, delegates from eleven of the thirteen states approved the draft with only Rhode Island not in attendance and New York not sufficiently represented.[21] The next challenge was its ratification by at least nine of the states. Debates raged in each state's convention as well as in coffeehouses, taverns and newspapers, but the most noteworthy arguments in favor of the Constitution were the pamphlets written by James Madison, Alexander Hamilton and John Jay known as *The Federalist Papers*. Their principle theme was that the new Constitution provided a government of laws derived from the people and for the people and that it provided a series of checks and balances designed to prevent misuse of power. Opponents argued that the Constitution was written by lawyers, merchants, planters and the wealthy, who would use it to dominate the poor. They believed it would be used by the northerners to the detriment of the agricultural southerners. This was rebutted with the argument that such trustworthy leaders as

---

19   GW Papers at the Library of Congress.
20   Randall, 436.
21   Alden, 227.

Franklin and Washington favored the document and would never use their influence and power improperly. Also, it would provide America with the tools to defend and grow the nation and solidify the independence for which it fought.

Washington was anxious to have the document ratified, but he refrained from taking part in any of the debates. He was well aware that he was likely to be nominated for the presidency, and because of the prevalent fears about despots and tyrants, he stayed apart from interfering in any formal discussions lest he was regarded with suspicion. Nonetheless, his reputation was on the line for its passage, and he dreaded the possible anarchy that could result from its defeat. The first states to approve the Constitution were Delaware, Pennsylvania, and New Jersey, soon followed by Connecticut, Georgia, Massachusetts, Maryland and South Carolina. Only one more state was required for ratification, but by the summer of 1788, New Hampshire had not voted, Rhode Island was inclined to vote negative, and New York and North Carolina were expected to follow whichever way Virginia voted. In Virginia's convention in June, powerful Anti-Federalists like Patrick Henry, Benjamin Harrison, George Mason, Richard Henry Lee and Edmond Randolph spoke against it on the grounds that there was no Bill of Rights and that the North would dictate national policy on issues such as commerce, British war debts and slavery. Arguing for the Constitution was James Madison, who ultimately promised to work for a Bill of Rights and protect his fellow Virginians. Madison was credited with the eighty-nine to seventy-nine vote in favor of the Constitution. New Hampshire voted in favor and Hamilton persuaded New York to agree. North Carolina voted for it in 1789, and Rhode Island agreed in 1790 after the new government was already in operation. Washington had won his greatest victory in what some called the "second

American revolution." The new Constitution was far superior to the Articles of Confederation. It provided authority to impose levies and taxes; maintain an army and navy; regulate interstate and foreign commerce; make treaties; create new states equal in authority with the original states; govern territories and abolish trans-Atlantic slave trade after 1807. It also could not impose export taxes or create titled nobilities. It forbid states to issue their own currency or grant hereditary titles. It created a Congress to consist of a House of Representatives to be elected by the people with each state appointing two members to the Senate. It authorized an independent federal judiciary with judges appointed for life and an ultimate arbiter in a Supreme Court. A president was to be elected by an Electoral College composed of electors representing the districts of their respective states. The President could veto acts of Congress, command the army and navy, play a primary role in foreign affairs and make federal appointments subject to the approval of Congress. Most importantly, it provided for future amendments to address issues not covered. As for Washington's role in the Constitutional Convention, James Monroe best describes this historic event when he wrote to Jefferson in Paris: "Be assured, his [Washington] influence carried this government."[22]

Although the issue of individual rights was discussed during the convention, passage of such measures was not achieved because most delegates believed such provisions were unnecessary. They regarded them as "natural law" retained by the people, and government had only those powers specifically delegated to it. Washington was well aware of the sensitivity to this issue and suggested that certain rights such as freedom of religion, speech and the press should be added as soon as possible. Washington returned to Mount Vernon in September

22   Flexner, 211.

and remained there while the Continental Congress went through the process of transforming the new government. Everyone expected Washington to be elected as the first president, but he made no effort or comment on the subject because he did not want to be seen as campaigning for the office. However, he did contemplate what he might do as president. His first priority was to gain the support of the government by the people. This he would do through the virtue of reconciling regional differences and improving the economic prosperity of the nation. He was genuinely excited about this historic experiment and wanted to assure its success. He fully realized the importance of resolving the great burden of debt accumulated from the war, and though he did not have a specific plan, he knew it was imperative to establish financial credit in the world. He believed the country's vast resources could enable that goal, and he thought free enterprise and prosperity would result from good government.[23] He recognized that America was primarily an agricultural land, but unlike Jefferson, he saw no reason why it could not become a manufacturing economy as well. He wanted to keep the costs of government to a minimum and planned for a minimal standing army and no navy because of the defensive barriers provided by the vast Atlantic Ocean. He envisioned a strong and prosperous country far beyond that of his contemporaries, and this is what made him unique among his peers.

On February 4, 1789, the Electoral College unanimously elected Washington to be President, but due to technical factors requiring witnesses to the counting, delayed the official word until April 14. Washington was cautious and uncertain about accepting the position. He had to be convinced that his services were wanted. He related to his biographer, David Humphreys: "It is said that every man has his portion of ambition. I may have

23   Flexner, 214.

mine, I suppose, as well as the rest, but if I know my own heart my ambition would not lead me into public life. My only ambition is to do my duty in this world as well as I am capable of performing it and to merit the good opinion of all men."[24] Washington's deep sense of honor moved him to accept the presidency out of duty to his country. Washington confided to his friend wartime general, Henry Knox: "So unwilling am I, in the evening of a life nearly consumed in public cares to quit a peaceful abode for an ocean of difficulties without that competency of political skill, abilities and inclination which is necessary to manage the helm. Integrity and firmness is all I can promise. These, be the voyage long or short, never shall forsake me although I may be deserted by all men."[25] Similar to his self-deprecating remarks when accepting the appointment as commander in chief in 1775, he commented on the presidency with "so much is expected, so many untoward circumstances may intervene, in such a new and critical situation that I feel an insuperable diffidence in my own abilities."[26] The pressure on the new government to succeed would be enormous in that it was unprecedented and uncertain in a world that doubted its success. It was historic in that Europe and most of the world had accepted rule by monarchs and dictators throughout the ages and therefore thought people were not able to govern themselves.

A final impetus was the rumor that the anti-Federalists were advocating George Clinton of New York for the vice-presidency. Without declaring his own acceptance, Washington publicly announced that John Adams would be preferable as vice president. Before leaving for New York, Washington wanted to settle his financial debts, and with no cash to his name he tried to borrow £1,000. His credit was so poor he had to beg and borrow it from friends until he was inaugurated and could repay

---

24   GW Papers at the Library of Congress.
25   Ibid.
26   Ibid.

it from his presidential salary. His journey to New York was packed with receptions and banquets along the way. He was feted in Alexandria, Wilmington, Philadelphia, Trenton, Princeton, New Brunswick, Woodbridge and Elizabethtown. He then was escorted by barge to Wall Street in lower Manhattan. He was greeted there with cheering crowds as he rode his white horse in a parade interrupted with cannons firing in the harbor.

CHAPTER 7

President Washington's First Administration: 1789–1793

I thank a merciful God that He has given us the faith, the courage and the power from which to mold a victory. We have known the bitterness of defeat and the exultation of triumph, and from both we have learned there can be no turning back. We must go forward to preserve in peace what we won in war.

—General Douglas MacArthur
Surrender Ceremony, USS *Missouri*
September 2, 1945

On April 30, 1789, at Federal Hall, Washington solemnly swore to "faithfully execute the office of President of the United States and will, to the best of your [his] ability, preserve, protect and defend the Constitution of the United States." He then added his own words: "So help me God" and kissed the Bible. Both the title of "president" and the ceremony were approved by Washington, and at the age of fifty-seven he started on his journey to forge the workings of an executive office that have remained with us to this day. Washington's Inaugural Address was only twelve hundred words and contained only two specific recommendations because he expected national unity on the work that had to be done. First, he wanted Congress to correct the principal deficiencies of the Constitution regarding a Bill of Rights. Second, he declined a salary and instead asked that his compensation be limited to his expenses. Congress did pass the first ten amendments known as the Bill of Rights, but it still paid the president $25,000, which Washington later used as a credit against his expenses. It was not a memorable speech, but Washington never liked giving speeches. He did acknowledge the past blessings of the "Almighty Being" and asked the "Parent of the Human Race" for future guidance. The ceremony was followed by a thanksgiving service at St. Paul's Church which was a short distance from the City Hall on Wall Street. At that time there was no other elected official in any country in the Atlantic community, and Washington was well aware that he "walked on untrodden ground." He also knew that his actions would set precedence for future presidents.[1] People did not know how to address him, but it was soon decided to use "His Excellency" in ordinary discourse, and later this changed to "Mr. President" during the Jefferson administration. Washington was basically a shy person, and whether he was solemn and hid because of this or because he wanted the new government to appear serious and dignified no one is sure. In any event, he governed with a formal tone that some regarded as aristocratic. To allow others to gain access to him, he conducted weekly social receptions. Martha Washington also held receptions ("levees") for the ladies, which the president would attend. Even these functions later came to be regarded as too reminiscent of monarchial England and were discontinued by President Jefferson.

Congress immediately went to work on seeking ways to gain sufficient revenues to pay for war debts and the new government. Their first bill levied tariffs on imports and placed a tonnage tax

1   Jones, 109.

on all ships at American ports. Washington was not wholly in favor of every aspect of the bill, but in the interest of national unity at such an early stage, he signed it on July 4, 1789. He sincerely wished for a cooperative executive and legislative government and fully realized the various geographic and economic interests of the United States. To this end, he was granted three executive departments to help run the country; the State Department, the War Department and the Treasury Department. A fourth arm, the Attorney General, was to provide legal advice together with a system of federal courts under the jurisdiction of a Supreme Court. It was Washington's job to fill these positions, and he did this with considerations for individual qualifications as well as sectional interests. He first selected John Jay to lead the Supreme Court and Henry Knox to head the War Department. For State, Washington waited for Jefferson to return from Paris, and after several conferences convinced him to accept the new post which he assumed as late as March 1790. For Treasury, Washington considered his superintendent of finance during the war, Robert Morris, but he preferred to remain as a senator from Pennsylvania. This probably suited Washington as he was also very keen on his former aide, Alexander Hamilton. The final member of his official staff was Edmund Randolph as Attorney General. When it came to appointments, Washington preferred veterans who fought for the country's independence, but this was not always possible. He also preferred those who worked to ratify the constitution, but with all his appointments he sought to balance sectional interests realizing the political sensitivity of each one. Washington did not believe in nepotism and accordingly turned down his nephew, Bushrod Washington, for a federal district attorney position. The secretaries of the key departments were considered as his agents, and the name of "cabinet" did not come into use until 1793 when he started to meet with all his department heads on a more regular basis. Washington's agents were there to do whatever he asked of them. Washington kept track of all official business by reading every letter that went out under each secretary's signature as well as official letters that came into each secretary. This enabled Washington to have a total grasp on matters and to promote his design for a more communal government acting in everybody's best interests. He did not interfere with their work, but he did take responsibility for their actions. He met with his entire department heads only five times during his first administration and these were on policy matters. He met with each secretary individually on administrative issues. Washington wanted to have unity within his official family, but disagreements began to emerge on foreign policy when the French Revolution started to affect American interests. Also, he did not restrict himself to advice from his secretaries. Three of his closest advisors were John Adams, John Jay and James Madison. He also enquired through local communities about reactions to his government's policies and decisions. There was one major difference between the functions of Treasury and State, and that was the interaction with the President. Congress looked to Hamilton for fiscal reports and thereby tended to have a great deal of direct involvement with him. Also, finance was not one of Washington's strengths, so he was inclined to let Hamilton work independently with the Congress. Jefferson, on the other hand, was very much involved with foreign affairs, and this was a subject of great interest to Washington. Both men spent a great deal of time together discussing and resolving these issues. Washington liked and trusted Jefferson and relied on his personal experiences in Europe where he was minister to France from 1783 to 1789. While they agreed on many issues, they disagreed on the power of the House of Representatives regarding taxation. Jefferson thought such power would be abused, and he generally disliked a strong central government for the same reason.[2]

Washington could exercise his veto control over Congress on constitutional grounds or simply on policy matters. Washington's first veto was on constitutional grounds whereby representatives were chosen on the ratio of one to thirty thousand of population. Remaining numbers were then divided among the states starting with the most populous states and giving them more than one representative per thirty thousand. The smaller states were left with a disproportionate share, which they regarded as unfair. Washington was advised to accept the bill as written but asked Jefferson, Madison and Randolph to draft his veto. Within nine days the legislature amended the bill to allow representation per thirty-three thousand thereby showing their willingness to work with the executive. Later, Washington vetoed another bill on policy dealing with the discharge of certain troops, and the legislature again worked to accommodate the President's wishes. Another area of friction developed in August 1789 when Washington tried to follow the "advice and consent of the senate" clause of the constitution. He went directly to the Senate to discuss the subject of treaties with the American Indian tribes. When the senate tried to put the matter into committee, Washington was miffed and felt such a move defeated his purpose of going to the Congress. He stated he would never go there [to Congress] again on such matters, and thereby established the precedent of having the president negotiate future treaties.[3]

In Washington's first Annual Address to Congress in January 1790, he offered a long list of measures to be taken. Among these was the need to strengthen the military, increase manufacturing,

2   Alden, 240.
3   Jones, 118-119.

improve the roads and promote education. He reported on their first year's progress which saw government receiving revenue, the establishment and staffing of the various official departments, management of foreign affairs and the on-going discussions of resolving the remaining debt from the war. The United States was acquiring respect in the world, and England even sent their first minister to America in the person of George Hammond. Congress created a Bill of Rights to be voted on by the individual states, and the position of Postmaster General was approved. Having traveled throughout New England in the fall of 1789, Washington could report on conditions there in a positive light. Such trips also had the effect of promoting nationalism and loyalty in a very personal way because of his reputation as a wartime hero and leader. This was followed with a similar trip through the South in the spring of 1791. Also submitted in January 1790 was Hamilton's *First Report on the Public Credit*. The entire American indebtedness amounted to $80 million including foreign, state and congressional old debt, and Hamilton proposed a plan to pay it all through the issuance of new government bonds, which would be issued to the holders of the old debt. The plan had three different but related aspects: discrimination, funding and assumption. Madison's proposal of "discrimination" would offer the holder of certificates (the old debt) a discounted amount and the original holders of the same certificates the balance of the face amount. Congress deemed such a plan as unworkable and detrimental to the credit of the United States particularly to the vast number of European holders of the certificates. Washington liked the plan because it would have been fair to the soldiers who had sold their certificates at a discount for need of cash, but he made no public comment on it, and Congress voted against it. Funding involved the issuance of government bonds in exchange for the old certificates. This had the mutual advantages of lower taxes, which appealed to southerners, and the ability to trade as a type of currency, which appealed to financial circles, especially with the payment of interest to stimulate capital growth. Again, Washington made no comment, and Congress passed the measure without opposition. However, Hamilton's "Assumption Bill" gave no consideration to those who had previously sold their notes at a discount, and it really upset those in the South who were suspect of a strong central government and saw nothing in it for them except unfairness for having already paid off much of their debts. Virginia had settled most of is debts, but Massachusetts and South Carolina had not hoping that the new government would come to their aid. In fact, those two states threatened secession from the Union if they were not assisted.[4] Washington did not get into discussions about Assumption and had personal mixed feelings on the matter probably because of the impact on many of his former soldiers who had sold their certificates at a deep discount when the credit of the Continental Congress was at a low point. However, he did want to promote the power of the government and believed the country's credit was paramount. He had previously drawn up a plan for the new government to collect all taxes on the theory all the colonies fought for a common cause and that such a move would strengthen the government.[5] Virginia was the most upset over the Hamilton plan and had strong advocates in Madison and Jefferson. With insufficient votes in Congress for approval, Jefferson devised a scheme that would resolve the issue. Using the long-debated subject of the future capital of the United States, and knowing that the South wanted it located in their region while the North favored New York or Philadelphia, Jefferson proposed to Hamilton that for the South

---

4   Flexner, 236.
5   Jones, 123.

to support Assumption, then Hamilton would have to gather sufficient support in the North for the new capital to be located on the Potomac River.[6]

A compromise was reached whereby after one year in New York the capital would move to Philadelphia for ten years while a site in Virginia would be prepared for its eventual new home. Both sides agreed, and Congress passed the new measures and authorized Washington to select an appropriate location. In spite of his conduct in staying out of the debates on Hamilton's plans and the decision by Jefferson, Madison and Hamilton to relocate the capital, Washington sustained his first criticisms as president from those who thought he had mistreated the war's veterans on not supporting "discrimination" and for placing the new capital near his home at Mount Vernon. The commissioners who took charge of the project in 1791 decided to name the new Federal City in honor of the country's national hero. The entire area was named the District of Columbia. Northerners, particularly New Yorkers, were upset with the move and criticized Washington for favoring his hometown area of the Potomac where he had labored to bring commerce and industry. Whether he was partisan on the issue or not, Washington must have been pleased with the prospect of a more balanced economy for the country hoping that the South would emulate the commercial and industrial development in the North. In early 1792, with the project under the supervision of Pierre L'Enfant, progress was slowing, but Washington took a more personal interest in its success and supported a plan for one of the world's great capitals fit for the kind of nation he thought proper for the country he envisioned.

The first two years of Washington's administration saw the country prosper. Rhode Island adopted the Constitution on 1790,

---

6   Flexner, 236.

and Vermont and Kentucky were admitted as new states in 1791 and 1792 respectively. Settlers were moving west and south, and trade was flourishing. However, clouds were appearing in North-South relations with the agrarian south becoming more suspect of northern lawyers, bankers, merchants and speculators. Hamilton was at the center of this growing concern because of his financial plans. Not all of his proposals were approved by Congress, but he did obtain an excise tax on whiskey, which offended frontiersmen who not only drank it and sold it but also used it as a medium of barter and exchange. His most significant plan was the creation of the Bank of the United States. This was a quasi-public and private corporation designed to provide a national currency and a source of credit for loans to the new government. Southerners generally were agrarian and opposed financial schemes that allegedly benefited northern bankers and speculators. Washington could see the merit of such a bank, but he asked Jefferson, Madison and Randolph for their opinions. They raised the thorny issue of constitutionality and claimed that such an institution was not legal because it was not specifically authorized by the Constitution. Their argument was based on a "strict interpretation" of the Constitution, a complete reversal of their previous position as those who favored the "implied powers" of the Constitution. In fact, Madison was considered "the father of implied powers." Madison had written in the *Federalist* that "no axiom is more clearly established in law and reason that wherever the end is required, the means are authorized; wherever a general power to do a thing is given, every particular power for doing it is included"[7] Hamilton, on the other hand, cited the Constitution that did allow the government to issue currency, tax and borrow money. Further, he said that the proposed Bank was only a means of doing those things, and such means were "implied powers"

---

7   Flexner, 240.

granted by the Constitution. In fact, Hamilton responded with a fifteen-thousand word rebuttal built on the premise that Congress had the authority "to make all laws necessary and proper for the carrying into execution all the foregoing powers."[8] While Washington stayed above the debate, he did ask both sides to make their arguments, and only after studying them he made his executive decision based on reason and logic. Hamilton's case persuaded Washington to sign the bill into law, and while Jefferson and his allies accepted the measure, it added more fuel to the fire that was rapidly building between Hamilton and Jefferson. This soon led Jefferson to promote the creation of a new newspaper, the *National Gazette*, which was founded by Philip Freneau and which challenged the policies espoused in the *Gazette of the United States* edited by John Fenno, which supported the policies of Hamilton. Washington's hopes for a "communal" government were placed in jeopardy with the advent of publicly outspoken sectarian and philosophical points of view. Washington tried to stay above partisan politics because he disliked dissension and also because he believed the office of the president should not engage in party disagreements. Matters were fast-approaching a division into two political camps which were labeled "Federalist" and "anti-Federalist" or "Republican." However, there was far more to this divided political thinking than mere strict or implied powers. There was the intense personal dislike of the two antagonists who represented totally different family backgrounds, social standing, personal attributes and visions for the United States. They each reflected two totally different worlds which were coming into conflict: the agrarian and class world of England and colonial Virginia facing the emerging classless (or less class) commercial world of mercantilism and commerce. The irony is that Hamilton was regarded as a champion of the wealthy financial interests

---

8   Jones, 125.

with their attendant vices, and Jefferson was regarded as the advocate of the rural farmer with his simple and virtuous life. In fact, just the opposite was closer to the mark with Jefferson born to wealth and status while Hamilton was the illegitimate son from the West Indies who fought in the Revolution. Both men and their visions vied for Washington's approval, but the President's vision was even greater in that he saw both economic systems working together to bring the country unity and strength in the face of far more powerful forces abroad and at home. Washington did not have the financial or legal skills of his two brilliant secretaries, but he had the wisdom to see much farther into the future than either of them.

While the domestic situation showed good progress, there were serious problems with foreign relations. Spain claimed land on both sides of the Mississippi River and thereby denied use of the river to American traders. She also controlled land north of Florida and enlisted the Creeks to oppose American migration to Georgia and Alabama. Britain still controlled shipping in the Atlantic and Caribbean and stifled American navigation. Particularly alarming to Washington were the forts still occupied by the British on American land along the Canadian border and their practice of arming Indians in the Northwest Territory for attacks on American settlers. Above all, Washington did not want an armed conflict with Britain or Spain and instead tried to negotiate with them and buy sufficient time for future resolution of these issues.

Relations with Native American Indians

Responsibility for Indian affairs rested with the Secretary of War, Henry Knox. This was a matter that Washington took a personal interest in considering he was very familiar with Indian tribes from the French and Indian War as well as the Revolutionary War. Because of his own belief that the future of America was very dependent on the western territories, he wanted to develop good relations with the Native tribes and sought to bring them into the emerging American nation. Secretary Knox estimated there were a total of seventy-six thousand Native Americans living between the Alleghenies and the Mississippi, and Washington believed they were just as intent on their own independence as the colonists. He seems to have gained their confidence and respect judging from the letters and meetings with him. Washington was completely sympathetic to their requests for sufficient land to sustain them, and he and Knox developed plans for several independent lands which were to be treated as foreign nations outside the jurisdiction of any state. Both Washington and Knox acknowledged that the Indians had occupied the lands first and therefore should have use of it. They also agreed that the United States should have formal treaties with the various tribal nations and that their land should never be confiscated from them. They wanted American settlers to avoid these sanctuaries as they moved west. In 1790, Washington hosted the Creek chief, Alexander McGillivray, along with twenty-six other chiefs for weeks of elaborate celebrations and negotiations concluding with the Treaty of New York which established the boundaries of the Creek Nation. Sadly, Georgia did not honor the treaty and sold much of their designated land to speculators. Washington was not successful in making similar treaties in the Ohio River Valley, where most of the tribes were eliminated during the War for Independence. Also, when General St. Clair's regiment was slaughtered by several Ohio tribes in 1791, Congress was not supportive of Washington's efforts. Knox and Washington realized it would take a ring of forts from Lake Erie to the Gulf of Mexico to enforce any treaties, and this was clearly far too expensive and impractical. Failure to resolve the Native American issue was a deep disappointment to Washington.[9]

Considering a Second Term

Most all of these problems were only temporarily resolved while pioneers swarmed into the Northwest Territory and the Revolution in France became ugly and started to impact on America. The French monarchy was overthrown, and the new French Republic was looking to the United States for recognition and repayment of its loans to Revolutionary America. It was also miffed at the tonnage tax recently imposed on all foreign ships in American ports. Hamilton opposed any favors or repayments on the basis that American treaties had been made with the former government. Jefferson, ever the Francophile, pleaded for concessions in an effort to strengthen relations with France.

These issues weighed on Washington in early 1792 as he considered whether or not to seek a second term later that year. He realized that his sixty years were beginning to slow him down, and he believed the country was sufficiently stable to move on without him. He was not a politician, and he intensely disliked political infighting. Attacks on government policies were taken personally and upset him. Moreover, Washington was desperate to return home to Mount Vernon. He felt obliged to let the public know his intentions early enough so a smooth transition could occur. However, his closest advisers, Hamilton and Lear, urged him to run for a second term. He asked Madison and Jefferson for their opinion on the matter, and each of them begged for him to stay on in the belief that his presence and leadership would add more stability to the country.[10] When Washington asked Madison to draft him a farewell address, Madison complied but added

---

9   Ellis, *His Excellency: George Washington, 367-72.*
10   Alden, 250.

his own sentiments in his final paragraph, "Having thus, Sir, complied with your wishes, by proceeding on a supposition that the idea of retiring from public life is to be carried into execution, I must now gratify my own by hoping that a reconsideration of the measure in all its circumstances and consequences, will have produced an acquiescence in one more sacrifice, severe as it may be, to the desires and interests of your country."[11] While Jefferson praised Washington, he concurrently denounced the policies of Hamilton and his supporters. Washington tried desperately to have the two men reconcile their differences through "allowance" and "forebearance", but their animosity grew into a war of words published in the newspapers. Jefferson believed Hamilton was leading the country to a monarchy and was striping it of its liberty. Jefferson criticized Washington for his monarchial tendencies, but this was disingenuous considering how he soon begged Washington to stay in office for another term. Both Hamilton and Washington replied to their Republican critics that dissension and hostility could cause dissolution of the Union and thereby bring on a monarchy. Jefferson was so upset that he even stated his intention to retire at the end of Washington's first term in March 1793.[12] In spite of this, Jefferson and his Republicans pledged their support of Washington and pleaded for him to remain in office. They did, however, support New York's Governor, George Clinton, for vice president over the presiding John Adams. The disputes actually influenced Washington's decision to run for office again because he was genuinely concerned about the stability of the government. He was getting mixed signals in that the Republican press was critical of his policies (and therefore himself), but at the same time its leaders were urging him to remain. During this time, there was increased unrest in western Virginia and

---

11   Robert Rutland and Thomas Mason, eds., *The Papers of James Madison*, vol. 14 (Charlottesville: 1983), 319-321 (James Madison to George Washington).

12   Jones, 131.

Pennsylvania over the excise tax, and Washington feared that force might become necessary to bring law and order. No one was sure of Washington's decision to run, but when the Electoral College met in early December the matter was settled. When the results were announced in January 1793 both Washington and Adams were decidedly returned to office. Not one vote was cast against Washington, which gave him the satisfaction of knowing his presence was truly desired.

CHAPTER 8
President Washington's Second Administration: 1793–1797

Though in reviewing the incidents of my Administration, I am unconscious of intentional error—I am nevertheless too sensible of my defects not to think it probable that I may have committed many errors. Whatever they may be I fervently beseech the Almighty to avert or mitigate the evils to which they may tend. I shall also carry with me the hope that my Country will never cease to view them with indulgence; and that after forty five years of my life dedicated to its Service, with an upright zeal, the faults of incompetent abilities will be consigned to oblivion, as myself must soon be to the Mansions of rest.

—President George Washington
"Farewell Address," September 19, 1796

Knowing of Jefferson's stated intention of leaving office in March, Washington's first order of business was to persuade him to stay on at least until the end of the year. He did convince him to remain, and he tried to get him to appreciate the difficulties that his differences with Hamilton were causing within his administration. Washington resumed office with little joy and only a sense of duty to steer the country through the next four years. The major foreign disturbance was the Reign of Terror in France and the real possibility of being dragged into a war between France and England. He desperately wanted the country to remain neutral in any conflict. When England declared war on France in March 1793, Washington asked his Attorney General, Edmund Randolph, to issue a written proclamation declaring America's neutrality. Randolph was considered more bipartisan and an independent thinker so Washington used him rather than Jefferson who was openly favorable to the French. Washington did inform the French that the United States would recognize the new French Republic. The cabinet then discussed the problem of how to enforce the neutrality especially with the French practice of outfitting of privateering ships in American ports and the British lodging a strong protest with the administration. In April, France sent their minister, Edmund Genet, to America where he landed in Charleston, South Carolina. Genet stayed there for a month rallying support for the Republic, and then he met with Jefferson to call on Washington to present his credentials. While Jefferson was enthusiastic, Washington was withdrawn and cool possibly because of Genet's unusual and roundabout delay in coming to Philadelphia and also his desire to appear neutral. In any event, Genet was put off by his less than enthusiastic reception and proceeded to look for support directly with the American public which still regarded France as a close ally. He then violated protocol by outfitting a privateer and seizing an English ship, *Little Sarah*, to raid on British commerce. Jefferson finally became suspicious of "Citizen Genet" and warned him to cease and keep the stolen ship in port. Meanwhile, Washington was ill at Mount Vernon, and when he returned to Philadelphia in July, he learned that Genet had armed the ship and ordered it to sail. He was furious, particularly with Jefferson, and ordered a cabinet meeting where he expressed his outrage over allowing a French minister to defy the government. He demanded the recall of Genet. Also, this occurred while Freneau's press was continuing to attack Washington's government. It was one of the rare moments when Washington lost his temper and wondered out loud why he ever agreed to take the presidency again. Everyone knew he was directing his wrath at Jefferson because he employed Freneau in the State Department and supported his paper, and yet in several days he met with the cabinet expressing his desire that they be bipartisan.[1] When the French finally recalled Genet, he refused to return for fear of being executed. Washington offered him asylum, and he eventually married Governor George Clinton's daughter and settled in New York.

In the fall of 1793, Washington came to the realization that Genet had organized wide-spread opposition to his administration. So-called Democratic-Republican Societies had appeared expressing support for France and condemnation of Hamilton. When he returned to Philadelphia for his Annual Message to Congress, Washington explained in greater detail the reasons for Genet's ouster and the need to remain neutral, and to underline that policy he published the official correspondence of the French and British ambassadors. He also repeated his deep concern about the British forts on American soil which violated the 1783 Treaty of Paris. Jefferson resigned in December, and Edmund Randolph was appointed Secretary of State. British ships were reported to be intercepting American ships in the Caribbean and impressing its sailors into their navy. In retaliation, Congress proposed an embargo on all trade with England and demanded that all forts be evacuated and damages paid for the seized American ships. John Adams broke the tie vote and defeated the harsh measure, but through his efforts it was agreed to build four ships which

1   Randall, 486.

were to become the first United States Navy. Washington's level-headedness kept the warlike atmosphere under control. He sent James Monroe to Paris and John Jay to London in May 1794 with instructions for the English to evacuate the forts and pay for the seizure of ships. It is revealing that his advisers wanted Hamilton to go to London, but Washington knew that the public did not trust Hamilton so he chose Jay. Once again, Washington tried to be evenhanded in ameliorating the emerging political factions.

Throughout 1794 disturbances grew over the excise tax leveled on distillers of whiskey since 1790. Other taxes on snuff, loaf sugar and carriages were accepted, but on the frontier, where stills were owned and operated by very independent folks, open opposition finally erupted. Backwoodsmen did not like government intervention of any kind, but they especially disliked revenue collectors who came onto their property. In western Pennsylvania a gang of small backyard distillers attacked a tax collector and anyone who paid the tax. They killed a man and forced an army platoon to surrender. Democratic Societies tried to enlist the support of the Kentucky Society in a general rebellion. There was even talk of establishing a separate Allegheny nation and marching on Philadelphia. Washington was aware that such disturbances could occur anywhere when people opposed laws that they did not like. The challenge was to determine when these grievances were legitimate, and if they were not, how to deal with them. Washington knew the dangers of such disturbances and how they could spread, but he also knew that negotiated solutions were warranted before sterner measures were employed. To this end, he sent three commissioners to western Pennsylvania with commands for the insurgents to disburse and return to their homes. At the same time, he ordered 12,950 militiamen to prepare to march to that area in the event they were needed. Pennsylvania would not agree to such action alone, therefore forcing Washington to include militia from New Jersey, Maryland and Virginia. There was the added problem of how Pennsylvanians would react to other state militia in their territory and whether any of the militia would be Federalist or Republican sympathizers. Washington was fearful that any of these issues could incite further civil unrest or even war. As the local dialogue commenced, past fears of republican anarchy were raised, and, as in Shays' Rebellion, the rebelling leaders did not want to be seen as encouraging armed resistance to the law. The Pennsylvania Democratic Society voted in favor of upholding the law, and the situation was defused. Meanwhile, the date set for settlement had passed, so Washington called for the troops to assemble in Reading, Pennsylvania, and determined that he should take command. The insurrectionists never thought an army would be sent against them, and when they learned otherwise they became frightened. Local politicians believed the situation would right itself and did not want the army to proceed any farther. Washington was not convinced the rebellion was completely quenched, and even though he wanted no bloodshed, he thought the army's presence would have an effective psychological impact. He implored his soldiers to respect the rights of their fellow citizens and to only capture the instigators. Washington returned to Philadelphia and left the command to Governor Henry Lee of Virginia. The two men who were found guilty of the insurrection were later pardoned by Washington, and the army was disbanded. Washington was greatly relieved that contrary to world opinion the new country could govern itself.[2]

The Whiskey Rebellion marked a turning point in the relationship between Jefferson and Washington. The event illuminated the basic difference between the two men. Washington

2   Flexner, *Washington, The Indispensable Man*, 317-20.

was a doer, who believed in discipline and action. Jefferson was an idealist, who thought the Rebellion was a harmless expression of innocent discontent. Washington mobilized an army to protect civil law and government. Jefferson thought Washington overreacted and was merely a pawn of Hamilton and the Federalists. He looked on Washington as an old man who had reached senility and was not in control of his government.

Because the so-called "Democratic Societies" had supported the Whiskey Rebellion and were frequent critics of the administration in Freneau's *Gazette*, Washington was convinced that they were capable of destroying the country. In his Sixth Annual Address to Congress on November 19, 1794, Washington suggested that the people should examine the "certain self-created societies" to see if they were responsible for insurrections and were "careless of consequences." He was careful not to name names or political factions or recommend penalties or reprisals. In spite of strong support from the Republicans for the Democratic Societies, just a few criticisms from Washington about these types of activities caused their demise. Jefferson and other Republicans had warned Washington that he was treading on the delicate issue of free speech and thereby was opposing the democratic process itself. However, Washington regarded these groups as organized factions that did not represent individual citizens. He expected citizens to express their opinions through the ballot box or through town meetings which would bring their concerns to the federal government. He felt the organized societies were led by demagogues who had their own opinions, whereas government should not be a place of conflict but instead should be a place where divergent views were discussed and reconciled. He must have come to realize that his denunciation of the societies was a mistake because he never again uttered any criticisms that could be regarded as suppressing individual freedoms.

In 1794, there were close to one thousand British troops in eight forts in the western territories, and the British had seized hundreds of American ships on the grounds they were trading with their enemy, France. In April Jay was sent to London to resolve these problems. The Jay Treaty first reached Washington in November and was finally released to the public in March 1795. Before Washington had a chance to study it and discuss it with his advisors, a copy was leaked to the anti-Federalist press, which caused riots among the Francophiles and harsh criticism of Washington for allegedly trying to keep it secret. Actually, he wanted to study it until the Senate was scheduled to meet in June. The Treaty stipulated the British withdrawal of all their troops in the western forts, but it allowed only small American ships to trade in the British West Indies and gave the English the right to buy all the American cargoes they considered contraband. The Treaty offered favored nation status for American trade, and it did call for the withdrawal of all British forces from an area where their corroboration with the Indian tribes caused real dangers and problems for American settlers. It did not offer restitution for the seizure of American ships and impressments of sailors. Washington anguished over the document, and he was inclined to reject it. With British seizures continuing, Washington let it be known that these practices would have to stop before even considering the Treaty. In August, Washington met with Randolph to decline the Treaty, but his Secretary of War, Thomas Pickering, called Washington aside to show him some secret correspondence of Randolph that had been intercepted by the British. The compromising documents indicated that the French had offered Randolph a great amount of money for his influence in supporting French interests. Pickering suggested that Randolph was a traitor and that he had been the only cabinet officer to speak against the Jay Treaty. After studying the confiscated dispatches, Washington concluded that in fact Randolph was a traitor. Agonizing for a few days on what approach to take and not wanting to accuse Randolph without the benefit of an explanation, Washington confronted Randolph with the papers and asked for his comments. Randolph emphatically denied the indirect indictment or that he ever sought or received money from the French. He was so offended that he abruptly left the room and resigned shortly thereafter. This marked the departure of Washington's war aide, confidante, life-long friend and the only bipartisan member of his administration.

Washington did not like many of the Treaty's terms, but he saw the overriding benefit of some of the trade and political consequences. Most importantly, it bought more time for strengthening the country. He knew full well the antagonism it would cause, but he decided to sign the Treaty and accept the criticism. The Senate passed the measure for his signature with only one proviso—that the Provision Order affecting West Indian trade be eliminated. Washington agreed and withheld ratification until that Order was withdrawn. The British accepted the rescission, and the Treaty was enacted into law. Jay was hanged in effigy by the public, and Washington was vilified by the Republican press. In spite of receiving such harsh treatment and even being labeled a traitor and pro-British, Washington believed the Treaty would bring stability to the country and peace with England.

After two months had passed Randolph began his own defense by accusing Washington of being a hypocrite and assassin who was losing his mental capacity. He tried to vindicate himself by engaging in self-pity and asking for all documents to be released. Washington was too upset to fight him in the press, but he gave Randolph permission to publish all their correspondence believing that the public would understand his motives for his actions. Indeed, the public took offense at Randolph's unrelenting bitter attacks on their president, but they also heaped abuse on him for his tyrannical action, his age and infirmities, his poor dentures, his riding in carriages and his overdrawn accounts resulting from the expenses of the presidency. In the face of such overwhelming detractions, Washington delivered his Seventh Annual Address to Congress on December 8, 1795. He praised the Senate and House for the good condition of public affairs and the country's numerous blessings. He cited Anthony Wayne's triumphs over the warring northwestern Indian tribes, the *entente* with England, progress in the treaty with Spain concerning the Mississippi, and the removal of all discords that threatened the peace. To the utter amazement of the Congressional Francophiles, he never mentioned France or his critics on domestic affairs. He praised America's neutral stance in the world and expressed the strengths of an expanding population along with internal improvements: "is it too much to say that our country exhibits a spectacle of national happiness never before surpassed if ever before equaled?" Washington was able to do what he always did best: distill the noise and clamor to focus on the basics. He brought out the positive aspects of a growing, prosperous nation that was free and secure from foreign turmoil. He again proved to be a masterful leader who could grasp victory in the face of defeat.[3]

The Jay Treaty was a watershed event that prompted Congress to debate the entire issue of determining treaties. Jay had negotiated a commercial treaty that allegedly usurped the authority of both houses of the Congress. At that time, senators were voted by state

3   Flexner, *Washington, The Indispensable Man*, 342.

legislatures, so the House was the only real democratic branch of the government. The Senate had a Federalist majority, but the House was decidedly Republican, and it disliked the control of foreign affairs by the Senate, especially in relation to the Jay Treaty. Being upset with the Treaty, the House had authority over funding appropriations and was determined to undermine the Treaty by not voting the funds necessary for its implementation. Just as this issue was being debated in late February 1796, Spain opened the Mississippi to American trade and resolved its other territorial differences with the United States. Ironically, it was the Jay Treaty that prompted Spain to negotiate a treaty with America out of their fear of an alliance between England and America. At the same time, America was able to purchase a treaty with the Barbary Coast ending their harassment of American shipping in the Mediterranean. When the signed Jay Treaty arrived in Philadelphia in February, the House assumed Washington would wait for their consent. However, he decided to sign it into law immediately without consulting them, and they were annoyed enough to vote sixty-two to thirty-seven in favor of claiming their right to consent to all treaties and to see all the official papers accompanying the Jay Treaty. This posed a critical dilemma to Washington, who saw through to the real problem—not the Jay Treaty itself but rather the issue of the House wanting to increase its power by encroaching on the rights of the Senate. Attorney John Marshall advised Washington that he could create a gulf between himself and ordinary citizens—withholding papers could imply he had something to hide. Jefferson also knew the issue was a serious one that would affect the future of the Constitution. More practical issues would be the immediate impact on American trade if the House were allowed to overturn the signed Treaty and the real possibility of halting trade and thereby starting an economic depression. The House Republicans did not seem to be overly concerned with another possible conflict with England, but Washington continued to be cautious and greatly concerned. With all of the pressures coming to bear, Washington remained committed to his belief and the practice of not interfering with the legislative branch. He now stood his constitutional ground and would not allow the legislative body to interfere with the executive branch. He refused to hand over any documents to the House and thereby incurred the wrath of the Republicans. Not only Freneau, but Benjamin Franklin Bache in his *Aurora* castigated Washington as an enemy of democracy. He withstood the verbal attacks and refused to get into an open controversy. He regarded these "infamous scribblers" as intent on destroying the public's confidence in the government. As before, the attacks were so great that they created a public backlash against Congress and in favor of Washington. The episode marked the final break between Jefferson and Washington with July 1796 as the last exchange of letters between them. Jefferson's claim of being done with politics was totally disingenuous and Washington knew it. He was deeply hurt by all the affronts of his critics who did not appreciate his overriding policies of neutrality, peace, trade and compromise. His own words at that time were:

> While I was using my utmost exertions to establish a national character of our own, independent, as far as our obligations and justice would permit, of every nation of the earth; and wished, by steering a steady course, to preserve this country from the horrors of a desolating war, that I should be accused of being the enemy of one nation, and subject to the influence of another; and to prove it, that every act of my administration would be tortured, and the grossest and most insidious misrepresentations of them be made (by giving one side only of a subject, and that too in such exaggerated and indecent terms as could scarcely be applied

to a Nero, a notorious defaulter, or a common pickpocket). But enough... I have already gone further in the expression of my feelings than I intended.[4]

Washington's Farewell Address

As we have already noted, Washington always disliked political discord. The abuse he received following the Jay Treaty seems to have been the last straw in prompting him to retire. His first draft was an update on the address that Madison had prepared for him in his first administration. He added answers to his critics with some egotisms which were later deleted and which Hamilton felt would not serve as a lasting testimonial to his administration. It is unclear whether Hamilton asked to assist with the draft or whether Washington asked Hamilton to edit his own most recent draft. In any event, Hamilton followed Washington's instructions to remove the personal comments and add more advice on current problems. He asked Hamilton to draft a farewell address for him, and throughout the summer he edited several copies until he was satisfied that Hamilton had written Washington's own ideas and thoughts and none of Hamilton's. Washington never intended for it to be read. Instead, he arranged to have it printed in the *American Daily Advertiser* on September 19, 1796. As the country and the world began to grasp his message, they realized that indeed Washington would be retiring the following March. In the address Washington started by reminding the public that he did not seek the presidency nor did he want to serve a second term. He warned against attacks from domestic and foreign enemies. He accused political parties of fostering internal divisions by coming between the people and its government and encouraging the rule of minorities and demagogues. This was directed to both Republican and Federalist sympathizers. He stressed national

---

4   GW Papers at the Library of Congress.

256

unity and warned against domestic factionalism. He knew he had been accused of antidemocratic policies, but he recognized the need for parties to guard against their potential to create unrest and insurrection. He also commented on the need for religion as a source for public morality and that good national credit was essential for economic growth. The biggest part of his message concerned foreign affairs and particularly the need to maintain the policy of his Neutrality Proclamation. He advised not to become overly antagonistic or too attached to any one country: "The nation which indulges toward another an habitual hatred, or an habitual fondness, is in some degree a slave... it is a slave to its animosity or to its affection, either of which is sufficient to lead it astray from its duty and its interest."[5] He attacked those who served European policies. He stated that Europe had its own concerns and interests that differed from those of the United States: "why, by interweaving our destiny with that of any part of Europe, entangle our peace and prosperity in the toils of European ambition, rivalship, interest, humour, or caprice?"[6]

The country's reaction to the address was extremely positive. Some regarded it as the dying words of its greatest hero, while others revered it as a sacred document. Washington referred to it as "counsels from an old and affectionate friend [that] may be productive of some partial benefit, some occasional good; that they may now and then recur to moderate the fury of party spirit, to warn against the imposture of pretended patriotism."[7] Most of the states passed resolutions praising Washington and his counsel. However, Georgia, Kentucky and Tennessee were silent, and Virginia barely acknowledged it. Madison thought it was pro-British and anti-French. Jefferson dismissed it.

---

5   GW Papers at the Library of Congress.
6   Ibid.
7   Ibid.

When Washington was scheduled to give his Annual Message to Congress on December 7, 1796, everyone knew it would be his last. As was his usual custom, he praised the citizens for their many successes at self government. Regarding foreign relations, Washington was no longer bipartisan but instead chastised the French for their treatment of American shipping in the West Indies. He surprisingly excused the British for their tardiness in withdrawing their troops in the west owing to understandable reasons. On domestic affairs, he mentioned his continuing concern over keeping at peace with foreign nations and the need to build a strong navy and manufacture military supplies and weapons. He recommended government efforts to improve agriculture, and he even supported higher pay for government officials in order to attract the necessary talents. He thanked the "Supreme Ruler of the Universe" for guidance and wished his "Providential" care would continue to bless the people of the United States forever. When the message was finished Washington began his efforts to elect John Adams as the next president. Although he had not been close to Adams during his two administrations, he had come closer to his Federalist policies. Adams had been in favor of a political system closer to a monarchial government, which Washington disavowed. But by 1796, the two men's political views grew together with Adams being even a more independent American than Washington. The French continued to interfere with American politics. They actively supported Jefferson with agents in Pennsylvania and Kentucky. French Minister Adet sent threatening letters to Secretary of State Pickering just before the elections and just after they were already published in Bache's (and Jefferson's) Philadelphia *Aurora*. Adet attacked the Neutrality Proclamation and campaigned to defeat the Jay Treaty. He severely criticized Washington's administration and threatened to break diplomatic relations with France until the United States returned to an alliance with France.[8] Each elector had two votes with the winner needing half and the runner-up being selected as vice president. There were thirteen candidates of whom nine were Federalists. Adams defeated Jefferson by three votes in the Electoral College thereby making him the second president of the United States. As runner-up, Jefferson was elected vice president. On March 4, 1797, Adams was inaugurated, and after the ceremony, Washington gestured for his two successors to walk in front of him. Washington allegedly remarked to Adams that "Ay! I am fairly out and you fairly in! See which of us will be happiest."[9]

The most noteworthy aspect of Washington's retirement from office was the astounding fact that he voluntarily took this step. In spite of the political turmoil at that time, most historians agree that if he wanted to remain in office, Washington would have been reelected for a third term. He was one of the most powerful men on earth, and history records few, if any, other leaders who willingly relinquished such a position. Indeed, he was compared to the legendary Roman general, Cincinnatus, who returned to his farm after saving his country. Even his long-time adversary, King George III, remarked that by Washington's voluntary act of retiring as commander in chief and then as president "placed him in a light the most distinguished of any man living... [making him] the greatest character of the age."[10] Washington wanted to return to Mount Vernon and view the progress of his handiwork as a private citizen. He knew the nation faced grave dangers, but he believed that it was on a sufficiently strong foundation to withstand domestic and foreign attacks. Also, by taking this

8   Harrison Clark, *The Life of George Washington* (Washington, D. C.: Regnery Publishing, Inc., 1996) 338.
9   Jones, 176.
10   Brookhiser, 103.

step he bequeathed the tradition of having the presidential office outlive the occupant. Washington realized his health was failing and that both his body and mind were going weaker. He believed that he could easily die in office and wondered whether that would affect future terms of office that could be determined by longevity similar to a monarchy. In brief, he established the precedent that presidents are disposable.

CHAPTER 9

President Washington's Relationships With His Advisers

Let your Conversation be without Malice or Envy, for 'tis a Sign of a Tractable and Commendable Nature: And in all causes of Passion admit Reason to Govern.

—Ignatius Loyola, ca.1550
Rule 58—*Rules of Civility and Decent Behaviour in Company and Conversation*

Thomas Jefferson: 1743–1826

Washington and Jefferson met for the first time in 1769 as members of Virginia's House of Burgesses. Although their paths must have crossed many times over the next twenty years, particularly at the Second Continental Congress in 1775, their working relationship really started in 1790 when Jefferson accepted Washington's invitation to be his Secretary of State. As minister to France from 1784 to 1789, Jefferson was kept in touch with progress at the Constitutional Convention in 1788 by his Virginia friend and neighbor, James Madison. As the architect of the Constitution, Madison may have been influenced by Jefferson even though it is unlikely that Jefferson would have favored such a strong central government. It was only with the implementation of the new constitution that Jefferson's political philosophy began to diverge from Washington's. Actually, it was Hamilton's philosophy that differed so radically from Jefferson's, and it was Hamilton's influence on Washington that came to upset Jefferson. Washington liked and trusted Jefferson and believed his ministerial experience in France would serve the government well. No one appreciated the role France played in the Revolutionary War better than Washington. He even "adopted" the young Marquis de Lafayette as the son he never had and also became the godfather of Lafayette's own son and namesake, George Washington Motier de Lafayette. However, when the French Revolution of 1789 deteriorated into a mob-driven bloodbath and French ministers tried to bring America into their struggle with England, Washington became more circumspect. Meanwhile, Jefferson evolved into even more of a Francophile and seemed oblivious to the risk of becoming embroiled in a greater European conflict. No doubt that Washington better understood the dire consequences of another war with England and the fragility of America's military defense. Jefferson had no experience in warfare and believed that America's new-found liberty would be repeated in France and in all of Europe. The issue rapidly brought a division between the two men which had been building for several years. Even from the earliest days of Washington's administration, Jefferson was critical of the President's receptions (levees) and his Annual Message opening the new session of Congress. He disliked the declarations of days of thanksgiving, fasting and prayer or for that matter anything that resembled British practices. It should be remembered that Jefferson's first draft of the Declaration of Independence was much longer because it was filled with invectives against King

George III. Most of these were deleted by Franklin, but the document was still a stiff indictment of the British monarch. Jefferson later invented a term for his American pro-British adversaries—"Monocrat" which derives from "monarchist" and "aristocrat".

During his term as Secretary of State, Jefferson did share a common purpose with Washington, and that was to recognize that the first order of business was to stabilize the new government institutions and to consolidate the American interests in North America. Their shared focus was on domestic matters and to stay out of foreign conflicts. They both realized that America had great potential economic growth, but the new nation needed sufficient peaceful time to gather enough strength to face challenges from abroad. The disputes were more about how to best implement these basic principles as well as how to deal with the threats to her independence from the major super powers of Britain, France and Spain. It was no secret that Jefferson detested England and anything English. His feelings were emotional and deep and nearly caused another serious rift with England. In the Nootka Sound incident of 1790, when England and Spain argued over the Vancouver area the two countries came close to causing the entire northwest to erupt into war. Jefferson took a strong anti-British stand on the issue and almost brought America into a war. The 1783 Treaty of Paris ending the Revolutionary War was a continuing problem for years, and Jefferson was charged with resolving its implementation with George Hammond, the British minister. He proved not to be his usual diplomatic self and was not particularly successful in resolving the issues of discriminatory British trade practices or the removal of British troops from their western American forts. In 1793, he even recommended retaliatory tariffs against England, which would have been disastrous. He saw red when he dealt with England, and it is interesting to conjecture why his hatred ran so much deeper than that of Washington, who had suffered the trials of warfare at the hands of the British, with its dangers and risks, as Jefferson had not. However, Jefferson had more reason to hate the British during and after the war when they burned his crops and sacked Monticello and when King George III turned his back on him when he and Adams were presenting their papers at the Court of St. James after the war. As minister to France from 1784 to 1789, Jefferson read the British press and became incensed at the English arrogance towards America almost as if the war was never fought and lost by them. Jefferson's real issue was his fear of British military and economic strength, which they could, and to some extent did, use to control the colonies from their own development. He sensed that Britain could and would re-conquer the colonies, and his proof was their refusal to vacate the western forts. However, he never mentioned the enormous debts that he and other Virginia planters still owed to British and Scottish creditors. The debts were long overdue and were gathering compounded interest that only increased their burden under English authority.[1] Jefferson was openly a Francophile because of the role that France played in the war and the Franco-American Treaty they signed in 1778. When the French Revolution started in 1789 and the Reign of Terror brought down the monarchy, there was little support for new Jacobin rule, but Jefferson did convince Washington that the treaty was an agreement between nations and not governments. Jefferson's tenure in France for six years and his love of French wine, cuisine and architecture added to his already strong sympathies toward the country that helped America achieve its liberty and would also carry the torch of freedom throughout Europe. His last communiqué dated July

---

1   Joseph J. Ellis, *American Sphinx* (New York: Alfred A. Knopf, 1997) 125-126.

13, 1789, extolled the French for their glorious and bloodless revolution the day before the storming of the Bastille. But when this all changed and even when Edmund "Citizen" Genet blatantly interfered with Washington's administration, Jefferson still sided with France. We can only assume this was due to his fears of England. Jefferson actually went so far as to endorse the bloody excesses of the Jacobins when he wrote to his friend, William Short, in Paris: "Were there but an Adam and an Eve left in every country, and left free, it would be better than it is now."[2] While Jefferson's fears of subjugation by England are understandable, history has proved him wrong. Washington's vision was clearer, and his emotions were under control. The Jay Treaty created an Anglo-American Alliance that got rid of the British troops and provided the protection of the British fleet that allowed the new nation to trade and prosper. Jefferson was somewhat vindicated by the War of 1812, but over the longer course of the eighteenth century his projected decline of England was incorrect especially with the onset of the Victorian era and the British Empire.[3]

The first serious internal conflict occurred with Hamilton's proposed Assumption Bill whereby the Federal government would assume the total debts of all the states incurred in the war. Jefferson opposed the measure because Virginia had repaid most of its debts and the Bill did not compensate those who had earlier sold their notes at a discount. This largely affected soldiers who needed cash at an earlier time when the United States had poor credit. Washington favored the Bill because it was critical to quickly establish good international credit. Jefferson thought Washington was "selling out" his troops. The next issue that brought dissension was Hamilton's introduction of the Bank of the United States. The Bank was to provide a uniform currency

2   Joseph J. Ellis, *American Sphinx* (New York: Alfred A. Knopf, 1997) 127.
3   Ibid., 126.

and create a method to borrow much needed capital for the emerging government. Jefferson opposed it because it imitated the Bank of England and potentially favored financial speculators and bankers. Washington asked both sides for their respective rationales, and Hamilton's fifteen-thousand word response swayed him to accept it over Jefferson's strong objections. Washington used force to settle the Shays' Rebellion and the Whiskey Rebellion, but Jefferson opposed force as unnecessary. In 1793, French minister Genet interfered with Washington's stated policy of strict neutrality, but Jefferson was sympathetic with the Frenchman and quietly violated the President's policy. In one of his private letters of May 8, 1793, Jefferson wrote a friend in Paris: "I continue eternally attached to the principles of your revolution. I hope it will end in the establishment of some firm government, friendly to liberty & capable of maintaining it. If it does not, I feel that the zealous apostles of English despotism will increase the number of its disciples."[4] In another letter to the French interior minister, James Madison happily accepted honorary French citizenship and wished France to triumph over her enemies. This was done in blatant disregard of Washington's directives. Genet himself reported to Paris that the American people were disregarding Washington's policy of neutrality. Jefferson resigned in early 1793, but Washington persuaded him to stay on until year-end. In spite of his stated desire to stay out of politics, Jefferson began in earnest to organize resistance to Washington's policies by establishing open opposition to the Federalists from his Republican party. Relations between the two men deteriorated each passing month and finally hit rock bottom with the passage of the Jay Treaty in 1795.

In Jefferson's mind, the Jay Treaty represented his worse nightmare. He saw it as pro-British and thereby anti-French.

4   Thomas Jefferson Digital Archives at the University of Virginia Library, Number 484.

It assured England's naval and commercial superiority. It gave England the right to put tariffs on American goods, but it disallowed America to place tariffs on English goods. Although it promised to remove the British troops from American soil, it obligated the American repayment of British creditors. The last item was the *coup de grâce* for the Virginia planters and Jefferson in particular. In Jefferson's eyes, the Treaty violated everything he and America fought for and believed in, not to mention its anti-French implications. Most historians disagree with Jefferson's reaction. As noted earlier, the Treaty postponed a war America was not prepared for, and it gave her the protection of the British fleet for a long time. It sided with the emerging British Empire while France stagnated with its Napoleonic wars. Washington was not pleased with the Treaty and anguished over it. Also, it came at a time when tensions between Jefferson's Republicans and the Federalists were building, and perhaps if Jefferson had been closer to Washington he could have exercised some influence over him. Actually, the Treaty caused Jefferson to create one of his greatest blunders when he wrote a letter to his friend in Italy, Philip Mazzei, in April 1796: "It would give you a fever were I to name to you the apostates who have gone over to these heresies, men who were Samsons in the field and Solomons in the council, but who have had their head shaved by the harlot England."[5] Samson was assumed to be Washington. The letter was printed in the American press in 1797, but Jefferson claimed the translation did not accurately convey his meaning. Most historians believe it did as did Washington when he read it. Another incite into Jefferson's attitude toward Washington occurred in June 1796 when the Jefferson-supported Philadelphia *Aurora* published a secret memo that Washington had written to his cabinet in 1793 concerning the Neutrality Proclamation. Henry

5   Ellis, *American Sphinx*, 160.

Lee had implied to Washington that Jefferson was the newspaper informer, so Jefferson wrote to Washington on June 19 denying any involvement and attempted to discredit Lee for his behavior: "I learn that this last [Lee] has thought it worth his while to try to sow tares between you & me, by representing me as still engaged in the bustle of politics, & in turbulence & intrigue against the government."[6] Washington answered Jefferson on July 6 that he had never suspected Jefferson of giving cabinet secrets to the press and further:

> It would not be frank, candid, or friendly to conceal, that your conduct has been represented as derogatory from that opinion I had conceived you entertained of me. That to your particular friends and connexions you have described, and they have denounced me, as a person under a dangerous influence; and that, if I would listen more to some other opinions, all would be well... Until within the last year or two ago, I had no conception that Parties would, or even could, go the length I have been witness to; nor did I believe until lately, that it was within the bounds of probability, that, while I was using my utmost exertions to establish a national character of our own, independent, as far as our obligations and justice would permit, of every nation on earth.[7]

Washington replied to Lee that Jefferson's remarks appeared "enigmatical... or spoken ironically, and in that case they are too injurious to me, and have too little foundation in truth, to be ascribed to."[8] Considering this exchange occurred shortly before Jefferson's letter to Philip Mazzei, one has to wonder about Jefferson's true relationship with Washington. In any event it was the last exchange of letters between them.

With Jefferson and Madison leading the way, the Republicans tried one more ploy to defeat the Jay Treaty by trying to withhold

---

6   Thomas Jefferson Digital Archives at the University of Virginia Library, Number 9015.
7   GW Papers at the Library of Congress.
8   Ibid.

its necessary funding. All money bills were the prerogative of the House, and it was controlled by the Republicans. Jefferson did not anticipate support of the Treaty from the western representatives who were eager to see the British troops leave their territory and allow them greater access to develop the Mississippi Valley. The Federalists won the issue much to the dismay of Jefferson, Madison and Monroe. Jefferson wrote to Monroe in Paris and claimed Washington's enormous prestige won the day: "The Anglomen have in the end got their treaty through, and so far have triumphed over the cause of republicanism... they see that nothing can support them but the Colossus of the President's merits with the people, and the moment he retires, that his successor, if a Monocrat, will be overborne by the republican sense... In the meantime, patience."[9]

Alexander Hamilton: 1757–1804

Anyone who studies American history has to marvel about the extraordinary figures who appeared at that critical moment in the eighteenth century. Some believe that the military, legal and political men who came together from such diverse backgrounds represented the greatest assemblage of talents in all of American history. One of the most talented was Alexander Hamilton whose story is even more remarkable considering his humble background and foreign birth.

Born in Nevis in the West Indies to a Scottish merchant and a young divorcee, Alexander's mother died in 1768 leaving him virtually orphaned. Moving to St. Croix, he was educated by a Presbyterian minister, who noted the boy's intellect and his writing skills. He started working as a store clerk at the age of twelve but was eager to attain a higher education. His aunts on

---

9   Ellis, *American Sphinx*, 163.

St. Croix worked and saved enough funds to send him to New York in 1763 to attend King's College (Columbia). By the age of seventeen he already had acquired a knowledge of British and American government and actually was writing sophisticated pamphlets on these subjects. In 1775, he left college to organize a voluntary military company, and the next year he was commissioned a captain of the Provincial Company in the New York Artillery. Nathanael Greene noticed Hamilton's artillery skills, and he allegedly was the one who introduced him to George Washington. He was invited to serve on the staff of Lord Stirling, but he declined preferring active service which he saw at Long Island, Harlem Heights, White Plains, Trenton and Princeton. Washington was particularly impressed with Hamilton's conduct in supporting the Continental Army's retreat across New Jersey. At the age of twenty in 1777, Washington promoted Hamilton to Lieutenant Colonel and appointed him as his *aide-de-camp*. He served as Washington's secretary for four and a half years, and during this time he not only innovated military designs, but he also developed his political theories. Hamilton served at Valley Forge and escaped the attempted incrimination of Brigadier General Horatio Gates in the thwarted Conway Cabal. He did have a serious dispute with Washington in February 1781 which temporarily caused a rift between them. He continued with his duties, and in July of that year he gained Washington's support for an assignment at Yorktown where he served under Lafayette and commanded an assault on the British.

Soon after Yorktown, Hamilton returned to New York City to study law and was admitted to the bar. In 1782 he served in the Continental Congress for a year and then practiced law. In 1786 he was selected as a New York representative to the Annapolis Convention where discussions were held to improve and regulate commerce between the states. He recognized the need for political unity and drafted a report that called for a Constitutional Convention the following year in Philadelphia. In his work to adopt a new Constitution, Hamilton joined with Madison and Jay in writing most of *The Federalist*, a series of essays promoting the virtues of the newly proposed Constitution. He was a member of the New York convention that voted to approve the new document in 1788. Hamilton was an ardent Federalist who advocated a strong central government, and his close association with Washington made him an obvious choice for the Secretary of the Treasury position in the newly created administration in 1789. Although Washington was not knowledgeable in banking and finance, he appreciated the importance of establishing America's credit in the world and therefore placed that issue as his top priority. If placing competent people in the right place is a mark of leadership, then Washington performed admirably. Hamilton was the perfect choice for inventing and administering a comprehensive financial plan that dealt with the $80 million war debt, raising excise taxes and import tariffs to pay for the new government and creating a national bank to access the growing need for capital. Hamilton was familiar with the English system whereby the Treasury Lord served as the prime minister and therefore controlled Parliament and the cabinet. Hamilton regarded his role in government as something like a prime minister, especially with his direct relationship with both the president and the House of Representatives. Even though Hamilton faced bitter opposition to his strong federal government policies, he defended them against Jefferson's Republican anti-Federalists. Frequently, Washington was caught in the middle of these hotly contested measures, but he listened to both sides of the issues and based his decision on what he deemed was in the best long-term interests of the fledgling nation. The most difficult initial decisions concerned the Assumption Bill and creation of the Bank of the United States. Jefferson, Madison and Randolph simply argued that powers not delegated by the Constitution cannot be rightfully exercised. Hamilton's position was:

> It appears to the Secretary of the Treasury that this general principle is inherent in the very definition of government, and essential to every step of the progress to be made by that of the United States, namely: That every power vested in a government is in its nature sovereign, and includes, by force of the term, a right to employ all the means requisite and fairly applicable to the attainment of the ends of such power; and which are not precluded by restrictions and exceptions specified in the Constitution, or not immoral, or not contrary to the essential ends of political society.[10]

Hamilton's lengthy fifteen-thousand word response and carefully reasoned answers to Jefferson's and Madison's opposition were convincing arguments that persuaded Washington to sign them into law.

Hamilton resigned from office in January 1795 to pursue a more lucrative legal practice. Washington was sorry to see him leave, but his admiration is revealed in his letter saying:

> After so long an experience of your public services, I am naturally led, at this moment of departure from office, which it has always been my wish to prevent, to review them. In every relation, which you have borne to me, I have found that my confidence in your talents, exertions and integrity, has been well placed. I the more freely render this testimony of my approbation, because I speak from opportunities of information wch. cannot deceive me, and which furnish satisfactory proof of your title to public regard.[11]

---

10 Douglas Southall Freeman, Washington (New York: Simon & Schuster, 1995) 589. Reprinted with permission of Scribner, an imprint of Simon & Schuster Adult Publishing Group. Copyright 1968 by Charles Scribner's Sons.

11 GW Papers at the Library of Congress.

After leaving the cabinet, Hamilton became the spokesman for the Federalists in responding to Jefferson's and Madison's Republican philosophy. He therefore can be considered as one of the founders of the two-party political systems. Washington was fearful that such differing philosophies would split the country and render it vulnerable to European influence, intervention and possibly domination. However, by the end of his second administration, Washington became so frustrated with the increasing political squabbles that he abandoned his efforts at bipartisanship and openly adopted the strong central government policies of the Federalists. This shift led him even closer to Hamilton, who resumed his role as an adviser. In 1796, when Washington decided to retire, he asked Hamilton to review his previously prepared remarks for the public announcement. This indicates just how much he valued Hamilton's thoughts and candor. Hamilton edited and wrote the address, but it included only Washington's ideas.

In 1798, President John Adams was facing the real possibility of war with France over their continuing confiscation of American seamen and ships. With no standing army, or navy, he knew how vulnerable the country was so he asked Washington to assemble an army and be its commander. Washington agreed to do it but only on his terms, the major one being his authority to select his officers and aides. Although he knew it would be controversial, Washington chose Hamilton to be his principal and confidential aide and appointed him Major General in July 1798, a post he held for two years. Again, it is amazing to think of the physically declining, gray-haired Washington at the age of sixty-six donning a new uniform and mounting a horse to lead an army. War was averted, but it is another indication of Washington's reputation as well as Hamilton's abilities. Later, Hamilton was to become deeply involved in politics and the presidential election of 1800, but in December 1799, upon learning of Washington's death, he said: "I have been much indebted to the kindness of the General, and he was an Aegis very essential to me. But regrets are unavailing… If virtue can secure happiness in another world, he is happy. In this the seal is now set upon his glory."[12]

John Jay: 1745–1829

John Jay has always been known for the Treaty bearing his name which he negotiated with England in 1795, but he was another of those gifted minds that made many contributions to America's struggle for independence. Born in New York City into a wealthy merchant family, Jay received his education at King's College (Columbia) and in 1768 was admitted to the bar. His first civil function was secretary to the royal commission established in 1769 to settle the boundary dispute between New York and New Jersey. Jay was not in favor of independence from England, but once it was declared he rapidly came around to defend it. Because of his strong support for independence, he was selected as one of New York's delegates to the Continental Congress from 1774 to 1779 and served as president for the last two years. In 1776, he was appointed a colonel in the New York militia but did not serve owing to his critical work in writing the state constitution and his position as chief justice of New York. As Secretary for Foreign Affairs in the old congress, Jay was considered by Washington for the new post of Secretary of State. However, Jay had previously proposed closing the Mississippi to Americans as part of a peace treaty he was negotiating with Spain, and Washington feared the animosity to Jay by the western settlers would be too disruptive to the new government. Madison recommended Jefferson instead for the new position that combined foreign affairs with some

12   Grizzard, 143.

domestic responsibilities. It did not include Indian affairs, which were relegated to the Secretary of War inasmuch as there was no standing army and little else for that department to do.

One of Jay's first contacts with Washington was in 1779 when he wrote to him about Major General Horatio Gates. He believed the commander in chief should be apprised of Gates' "spurious ambition" just at the time of Washington's strained relations with his secret critic. Washington replied to Jay thanking him for his "confidence and friendship." Shortly thereafter, Jay was sent by Congress to Spain to propose an alliance with them, but Yorktown rendered the mission unnecessary.[13]

In 1782, Benjamin Franklin asked Jay for his assistance in negotiating a peace treaty with England. They were joined by John Adams and were charged with achieving only one goal: England's recognition of America's independence. They succeeded in gaining not only official independence but the ceding by Britain of all land east of the Mississippi River excluding Florida, the abandonment of British troops in the western territories and the right to commercial fishing in the North Atlantic. After helping Franklin with the Treaty of Paris, Jay stayed in Europe as secretary for foreign affairs and negotiated commercial differences with Morocco and Prussia.

In 1786 when Washington observed the obvious weakness of the Continental Congress he wrote an interesting letter to James McHenry in which he expressed his concern: "I have ever been a friend to adequate powers in Congress, without which, it is evident to me, we never shall establish a national character or be considered as on a respectable footing by the powers of Europe. We are either a united people under one head and for federal purposes, or we are thirteen independent sovereignties eternally

---

13   Grizzard, 160.

counteracting each other."[14] Subsequent to that, Jay wrote to Washington:

> Our affairs, seem to lead to some crisis, something that I cannot see or conjecture. I am uneasy and apprehensive, more so than during the war. Then we had a fixed object, and though the means and time of obtaining it were problematical, yet I did firmly believe that justice was with us. The case is now altered. We are going and doing wrong, and therefore I look forward to evils and calamities, but without being able to guess at the instrument, nature or measure of them.

In reply, Washington wrote:

> We have errors to correct. We probably have had too good an opinion of human nature in forming our confederation. Experience has taught us that men will not adopt and carry into execution measures the best calculated for their own good without the intervention of coercive power. I do not conceive we can exist long as a nation without lodging somewhere a power which will pervade the whole Union in as energetic a manner as the authority of the State governments extends over the several States. To be fearful of investing Congress, constituted as that body is, with ample authorities for national purposes appears to me the very climax of popular absurdity and madness. Could Congress exert them for the detriment of the people without injuring themselves in an equal or greater proportion? Are not their interests inseparably connected with those of their constituents?... we must take human nature as we find it. Perfection falls not to the share of mortals... Retired as I am from the world, I frankly acknowledge I cannot feel myself an unconcerned spectator. Yet, having happily assisted in the ship into port and having been fairly discharged, it is not my business to embark again on the sea of troubles.[15]

Because of his legal and diplomatic experience, Washington brought Jay into his first administration as the first chief justice of the United States Supreme Court, where he served until 1795.

14   GW Papers at the Library of Congress.
15   Ibid.

When the Congressional debate raged over the Assumption Bill, Hamilton urged the Supreme Court and the other federal departments to join him in support of the measure. Jay held that this matter was not in the Court's jurisdiction, and that it was there to solely rule on the constitutionality of the cases that were brought to it. Jay did not comment on the Assumption Bill. Jay presided over three other cases that established the principle of the Supreme Court's independence. In *Chisholm v. Georgia* the Court held that citizens from one state could sue citizens in another state. In *Georgia v. Brailford* the Court held that Britain's right to sue for reparations from an individual American's debt was dependent on the enforcement of treaties between the countries. In *Glass v. Sloop Betsy* where the ship's owners sued France for taking their ship as a prize, the Court ruled that a council representing a foreign government had no jurisdiction in the United States "without positive stipulation of a treaty."[16] Jay's management of the Supreme Court was commendable, and it not only established him as a highly reputable lawyer, but his stewardship was responsible for building a strong foundation for this new American institution.

In 1794, Washington appointed Jay as envoy to Great Britain for the purpose of negotiating a treaty to settle issues on debts, boundaries, trade, shipping and use of the Mississippi River. When the terms of the Treaty reached America in March 1795, Jay was accused of selling out to the British, and he was hanged in effigy throughout the colonies. Washington was extremely disappointed in its many commercial concessions to England and was inclined to reject it. Knowing that the Treaty had the positive elements regarding British troop withdrawals and British naval protection on the seas, Washington signed the Treaty in February 1796 with one condition which the British agreed to. In spite

16   *The Federalist*, biography of John Jay, 3, <www.leftjustified.com>.

of the severe criticisms he received, Washington supported Jay for his "judgment, candour, honor and discretion." The Senate ratified the Treaty much to the horrors of Jefferson, Madison and the Republican opposition. When Jay resigned from the Supreme Court in 1795 to become Governor of New York, Washington wrote to him: "In whatever line you may walk my best wishes will always accompany you; They will particularly do so on the theatre you are about to enter upon; which I sincerely wish may be as smooth, easy and happy, as it is honorable."[17] Jay did not want to leave the Court, and he was not even asked about the New York governorship. In fact, he was out of the country negotiating his Jay Treaty when New York unanimously elected him at the urging of Alexander Hamilton. Jay went on to serve a second term as Governor and achieved more notoriety for his elimination of party corruption. His many accomplishments included reform of the prison system, limiting the death penalty, abolishing flogging, abolishing imprisonment for debt and supporting and passing a bill to abolish slavery in New York. He was extremely popular in spite of the Jay Treaty and was even asked by President Adams to return as chief justice, which he declined because of poor health. He died at his home in Bedford, New York, on May 17, 1829.[18]

Henry Knox: 1750–1806

When Henry Knox arrived in Cambridge in June 1775, he and Washington became instant and life-long friends. When Washington rode from Newburgh to New York City for his farewell in 1783, it was Henry Knox who led the formation and was soon to replace Washington as commander in chief. In 1785, Knox succeeded Benjamin Lincoln as Secretary of War under the Continental Congress. With his vast experience in military

17 GW Papers at the Library of Congress.
18 Grizzard, 162.

artillery and engineering, and after serving Washington so effectively and loyally throughout the Revolutionary War, it is no wonder that Washington brought Knox into his administration as Secretary of War. In the years prior to this, it was Knox who kept Washington informed of events such as Shays' Rebellion in which he took an active part, and it was Knox who persuaded Washington to attend the Constitutional Convention. While serving in the Continental Congress, Knox had initiated plans for a national militia and also negotiated treaties with several Native American tribes.

Without a Secretary of State for its first year, all Indian affairs fell to the Secretary of War. As the first Secretary of War, Knox inherited an army of 840 men and a staff of five. By the end of his first year he had expanded the army to 1,216 noncommissioned officers. He really wanted a large enough army to be a permanent force to deal with the Indian problem. When he went to Congress just after two months in office to seek a treaty with the southern Indians, Washington decided to accompany him for the "advice and consent" of the Senate. When Senator Maclay opposed the larger army and suggested that the treaty be referred to committee, Washington was furious. He stated that such a move would "defeat every purpose of my coming here."[19] Maclay felt that Washington was there only to intimidate the Senate and supercede its powers. Washington said he brought Knox with him so the issue could be resolved quickly. The matter was postponed, and as Washington left the chamber he was alleged to have said that "he would be damned if he ever went there again." As a result of this first episode, no president in history has ever gone to the Senate for their advice and consent

---

19   GW Papers at the Library of Congress.

on a treaty. Instead, treaties are first negotiated by the executive and then sent to the Senate for ratification.[20]

Washington and Knox did not always agree. In 1793, when Citizen Genet was actively seeking public support against Washington's policy of neutrality and captured the British ship *Little Sarah* in Philadelphia, the crisis came to a head. The ship was outfitted with cannons and a pro-French American crew, and in spite of warnings to desist and not sail, Genet defied them and sailed out of port to begin its raids on British commerce. When Washington returned from Mount Vernon to find Jefferson's papers on Genet's conduct, he was outraged. Hamilton and Knox wanted to attack the *Little Sarah*, but Jefferson insisted that an attack would only provoke relations with France. Washington sent word to Paris asking for the recall of Genet, and while they awaited their official reply, discussions were held on how best to get rid of Genet. Hamilton and Knox wanted the official papers revealing Genet's activities to be published so the public would better understand what mischief he was up to, but Washington sided with Jefferson in reasoning that such revelations could only inflame the situation. Meanwhile, the Republican Democratic Societies were hurling more and more personal insults at Washington for his anti-French policies even to the point of suggesting that he be guillotined for his aristocratic crimes. Knox was fearful that civil unrest would ensue and implored Washington to respond. Even though he did not publish Genet's activities, he finally reacted to Knox by exploding in a pique of anger among his advisers. Jefferson recalled that Washington complained bitterly about the abuse he had sustained and "that he had never repented but once having slipped the moment of resigning his office, and that was every moment since, and that 'by God' he had rather be in his grave than in his present situation. That he had rather be on his

---

20   Randall, 461.

farm than to be made 'emperor of the world,' and yet that they were charging him with wanting to be a king."[21]

When Knox elected to retire as Secretary at the end of Washington's first term to attend to his personal financial situation, he submitted his report showing some small progress with the navy and better progress with the construction of coastal fortifications. His best achievement was in the growth of the army to 3,629 noncommissioned officers and privates. Although he did negotiate several treaties with various Indian tribes, Knox reported that these would be inadequate. He proposed:

> That a line of military posts... be established upon the frontiers within the Indian boundary and out of the jurisdiction of any State, provided consent can be obtained for the purpose from the Indian tribes and garrisoned with regular troops... If any murder or theft be committed upon any of the white Inhabitants by an Indian, his tribe shall be bound to deliver him to the nearest military post, in order to be tried and punished by Court Martial... All white persons who shall be assembled or embodied in arms on any lands belonging to Indians... for the purpose of warring against the Indians or of committing depredations upon any Indian town or persons or property, shall thereby become liable and subject to the rules and articles of War.[22]

When it was determined that such forts would require over fifty thousand soldiers stretching from Canada to the Gulf, the proposal was abandoned. Washington reluctantly accepted Knox's resignation on December 30, 1793 writing him

> I cannot suffer you, however to close your public service, without uniting with the satisfaction which must arise in your own mind from a conscious rectitude, my most perfect persuasion that you have deserved well of your Country. My personal knowledge of your exertions, while it authorizes me to hold this language,

---

21 Flexner, 295.
22 Clark, 290.

justifies the sincere friendship which I have ever borne for you, and which will accompany you in every situation of life, being with affectionate regards, always yours.[23]

Washington replaced Knox with Timothy Pickering who proved to be an effective Secretary. Immediately after assuming office in January 1794, the Senate ratified treaties with the Cherokees which had been negotiated by Henry Knox.

On March 3, 1797, the last day of Washington's presidency, he and Martha hosted a last dinner for the cabinet and ministers. Realizing this would be their last such meeting, Washington wrote to his old friends Governor Trumbull of Connecticut and Henry Knox that his only regret at leaving office was "parting with the few intimates whom I love."[24]

When President Adams asked Washington to organize an army in 1798 in anticipation of a possible war with France, Washington accepted on the condition that he could appoint his officers. He then selected Hamilton, Pinckney and Knox in that order. All three were Federalists because Washington did not want any Republican Francophiles. Pinckney accepted his position under Hamilton even though Hamilton was only a colonel in the war. Knox, on the other hand, had been a major general and was upset with his appointment. He wrote to Washington complaining of this arrangement and even had the support of Adams who did not trust Hamilton's ambitions and his possible ascent to commander in chief. Washington wrote to Adams stating that his decision was final and of Knox that "I can say with truth, there is no man in the United States with whom I have been in habits of greater intimacy; no one whom I have loved more sincerely, nor any for whom I have had a greater friendship."[25] Knox did

23 GW Papers at the Library of Congress.
24 Ibid.
25 Ibid.

not accept the appointment. Although Knox was disappointed, and the incident created a temporary rift between them, he and Washington renewed their friendship the following year. There is little question that Washington's personal preference for second in command would have been his good friend, Henry Knox. However, it is to Washington's credit that he made his decision after thoroughly analyzing the strengths and weaknesses of each candidate. Knox was the most senior officer in the war and being from New England he would have great support of that important area. But Knox had grown even fatter than his usual three hundred pounds and according to Washington he had become dull. Charles Cotesworth Pinckney was from South Carolina, the area most vulnerable to a French invasion, and the south had more French sympathizers than elsewhere. Also, Washington believed Pinckney to be an able and judicious officer with a good deal of influence in the southern states. Hamilton was the most junior officer of the three, but having been Washington's *aide-de-camp* in the war, his brilliant Secretary of the Treasury and someone who had a greater grasp of domestic and international affairs, Washington believed him to be the best choice. Most of the leading Federalists, including those in Massachusetts, wanted Hamilton to have a senior position. When Hamilton replied to Washington that he would step down if that was necessary for the public good, Washington did not comment but only insisted to Adams that he did not fear Hamilton's ambitious nature and would resign himself if his wishes were not followed. Some historians believe Washington had lost his pragmatic skills and exaggerated the question of military rank. Others believe Washington used sound judgment in making his decision.[26]

---

26   Flexner, 374.

Edmund Randolph: 1753–1813

In 1775, when Washington was organizing his Continental Army in Cambridge, he selected George Baylor and Edmund Randolph as his aides. They both were Virginians and had similar aristocratic backgrounds. Edmund was the nephew of Peyton Randolph, Governor of Virginia and the President of the First Continental Congress.

Following the agreement that was reached at the Annapolis Convention in the spring of 1786, the General Assembly of Virginia voted to call a general convention of all the states. They appointed a seven-man delegation to be headed by Washington even though he had not been asked and was not inclined to accept the call. Governor Edmund Randolph and James Madison urged Washington not to decline the position, but he wrote to them saying "it would be disingenuous not to express a wish that some other character, on whom greater reliance can be had, may be substituted in my place, the probability of my nonattendance being too great to continue my appointment."[27] Randolph decided to wait before appealing once again to Washington and wrote to him "perhaps, too, (and indeed I fear the event) every other consideration may seem of little weight, when compared with the crisis which may then hang over the United States."[28] Washington referred the matter to his aide, Humphreys, for advice while Madison followed with more urging realizing that Washington's presence at the convention would add considerable prestige to the deliberations. With the rebellion in Massachusetts and the general fear of unrest, Washington was deeply concerned about the growing instability of the country as well as the prospect of states flooding the markets with more paper currency. In February 1787, Congress voted to hold a convention of all the states in May

27 GW Papers at the Library of Congress.
28 Freeman, 536.

at Philadelphia to expressly revise the Articles of Confederation. Many political leaders were in favor of the convention and rapidly formed their delegations. However, many, including Washington, were fearful that it might not be well attended and that it would be difficult to have so many sectional interests agree to a new form of government. As time drew nearer, Washington wondered if his absence would make him appear disinterested. He had turned down a meeting in Philadelphia of the Society of the Cincinnati blaming poor health, but now he was faced with a chance to contribute something important to the survival of the Union. He wrote to Randolph that if none other could be found, he would agree to attend. He was troubled by the public's reaction to his re-involvement in politics when he had previously stated he would no longer do so. But with Randolph's influence and the conviction that he was truly wanted, he reluctantly left for the convention on May 9, 1787. While waiting for other delegates to arrive, he met with the other Virginia delegates and reviewed plans for the new government prepared by Randolph and Madison. When a quorum was reached in late May, Randolph presented his "Virginia Plan" which in essence would create a government of three branches, legislative, executive and judicial. The legislature was to be composed of two chambers, one of which was to be elected by the people and the other to be chosen by the elected branch from a list of nominees drawn by each of the state legislatures. The remaining details were discussed, debated and agreed to with unexpected speed and without major discord. By September, most items in the new Constitution were in place, but Randolph suddenly announced that he would not sign the measure unless it included a provision for another convention to vote on any possible amendments introduced from the various states. He was not alone as George Mason and Elbridge Gerry also declined to subscribe to the document. All the states voted against the Randolph motion for a second convention, and the Constitution was agreed subject to approval by each state. It is ironical that the enormous work of Randolph was in large measure approved, and yet he never agreed to sign the document. Historians generally agree that Washington did not add much, if anything, to the actual document nor did he exert much influence in the internal debates. However, it was outside the convention where Washington's enormous prestige came into play. His stamp of approval gave the public confidence in the new Constitution.[29]

When Washington formed his first group of advisers in 1789 (later referred to as the cabinet), the position of Attorney General was not considered a full-time employment and therefore was put on a retainer basis. The minor post was considered as a legal adviser to the president, so Washington appointed an agreeable friend who happened to be Jefferson's cousin and former law clerk, Edmund Randolph of Virginia. The selection of Randolph was a bit surprising considering he never signed the Constitution, and Washington favored those who fought in the war and who supported a strong central government. However, Randolph did fight vigorously for ratification of the Constitution in Virginia, and some believe this was sufficient in Washington's mind to justify his appointment. It appears that Washington did seek Randolph's advice on many occasions, but it is evident that he was not a staunch Federalist and often took Jefferson's position. It is not surprising that Randolph sided with Jefferson in opposing Hamilton's Bank of the United States on the grounds that it was not delegated to the government by the Constitution. As we have seen, Washington eventually signed the Bank Bill after reading Hamilton's lengthy argument for it. One of the next issues facing the new administration was the question of representation in the

---

29   Freeman, 548.

House. The law stated one representative for each thirty thousand population, but the Congress wanted to use the excess fractional quotient to add representatives. Jefferson and Randolph wanted Washington to veto the measure, and much to their surprise he agreed to do so because he was aware of the sensitivity of rural citizens to the influence of the big city northern states. This marked Washington's first veto, but it was quickly resolved when Congress enacted a new bill calling for representation based on one per thirty-three thousand population. It also underlined the sensitivity of Congress to working in a cooperative manner with the executive branch and especially with George Washington.

As the French Revolution turned savage with the execution of King Louis XVI and Marie Antoinette and France was at war with England, Washington was keenly aware of the need for maintaining a position of neutrality. Hamilton studied the 1778 Treaties of Alliance and Commerce with France in order to ascertain how America should treat the new Jacobin government. As the cabinet met in April 1793, it decided that a public policy statement should be issued to inform the citizens of proper neutral behavior. The more difficult question was how the new Minister of the French Republic should be received. Hamilton argued that the existing treaties were made with a monarchy and therefore should not be in effect for the new Republic. Jefferson and Randolph reasoned that treaties bound nations and not governments. As was his custom, Knox sided with Hamilton. Washington was caught in the middle of the fray, but this time Randolph came to the fore and suggested that more time should be taken to consider the matter. This marked the first major disruption in the Cabinet, and Randolph is credited with defusing the issue. In fact, Washington asked Randolph to craft a carefully worded document of neutrality that would mollify Jefferson and satisfy Hamilton. Randolph soon produced a draft that was agreed to be called the Proclamation of Neutrality, which Washington signed on April 22, 1793.[30] After months of violating his position in America by capturing and arming British ships, Washington and his Cabinet decided to take action in dealing with Minister Genet. At the same time, Genet and other American Francophiles fanned the flames of support for the new French republic in its efforts against the perceived common enemy, Great Britain. Washington was being severely maligned in the Republican press and was outraged not only by Genet's blatant violations but also by his orchestrated treachery in disrupting America's neutrality by inciting pro French feelings not to mention the capturing and arming of several British ships and setting them out to sea to maraud British shipping. Washington wanted to act decisively, but he waited for Randolph's return from Virginia to seek his advice. The issue of Genet's recall was a delicate one because if it was not handled diplomatically, relations between the two countries could spin out of control. Jefferson urged a soft approach on dealing directly with the Executive Council of France. Knox favored the immediate suspension of Genet's consular powers, but Hamilton and Randolph agreed to a proposal of notifying Genet of their demand for his recall. Washington adjourned the meeting and delayed his decision. Finally, after a month's time, Jefferson drafted a lengthy eight-thousand word reply to France in which he carefully distinguished between the behavior of Genet and the French Republic and stated the good will of the United States for the people of France. Washington's patience and sensitivity once again kept America on its even course of neutrality.[31]

In December 1793, when Jefferson decided to resign at the end of his term, Washington offered the Secretary of State position to

---

30 Freeman, 622.
31 Ibid., 637.

Randolph. He then filled the Attorney General post with Justice William Bradford of the Supreme Court of Pennsylvania. Having been Washington's trusted adviser who had frequently offered him confidential opinions, Randolph was a logical choice. In fact, because of the constant strained relations between Jefferson and Hamilton, Washington came to rely more and more on Randolph's opinions which often were in line with Washington's own views.

In 1795, when John Jay submitted his proposed treaty with Great Britain, Washington asked Randolph for his evaluation. He carefully listed its pro's and con's and came to the conclusion that the peace it offered was sufficient reason for consent. He then added a note about the "provision" clause which was a last-minute item allowing the British to haul in American ships headed for France into British ports and purchase the cargo they were carrying. Randolph stated that "the order for capturing provisions is too irreconcilable with a state of harmony, for the treaty to be put into motion during its existence... and the treaty ought to be absolutely broken up."[32] This created strong doubts in Washington's mind, so he decided to study Hamilton's assessment of the treaty. Concluding that the provision clause was legally drawn, Washington agreed to sign the treaty and advised Randolph not to come to Mount Vernon as planned. Shortly thereafter, Secretary of War Pickering sent an urgent message to Mount Vernon requesting Washington's immediate return to Philadelphia for a "special reason." When he arrived, Pickering explained how he had received from the British an intercepted message from the French minister, Fauchet, to Paris which indicated that Secretary of State Randolph had made "valuable disclosures" to Fauchet. It went on to say that Randolph was upset with Washington's handling of the western Pennsylvania insurrection and that Fauchet should bribe certain people in the

32   Clark, 305.

government to oppose Washington's policies. After Washington read the dispatch, he advised the three cabinet members, Pickering, Wolcott and Bradford, to keep the matter secret. When the cabinet met the following day on August 12, Randolph reiterated why the treaty should not be signed, but the other members advised Washington to sign it. Much to Randolph's surprise, the President said he would sign the treaty without any stipulation. Washington did not reveal the Fauchet dispatch to Randolph out of fear that the Treaty would be interrupted. He met with Randolph several times to be assured of the Treaty and to explain the urgency to have it ratified. He agonized over the matter but seems to have concluded that Randolph had been deeply implicated in treachery. On August 18, 1795, Washington signed the Treaty, and the next day he showed the Fauchet dispatch to Randolph in the presence of Pickering, Wolcott and Bradford having beforehand asked them to study Randolph's reaction to it. After some brief denials wherein he stated that he had never asked or received money from Fauchet, an indignant Randolph left the room and resigned the next day. His letter of resignation to Washington stated,

> My sensations, then, cannot be concealed when I find that confidence so immediately withdrawn without a word or distant hint being previously dropped to me! This, Sir, as I mentioned in your room, is a situation in which I cannot hold my present office, and therefore I hereby resign it. It will not, however, be concluded from hence that I mean to relinquish the inquiry, No, Sir, far from it. I will also meet any inquiry. And to prepare for it, if I learn this morning that there is a chance of overtaking Mr. Fauchet before he sails, I will go to him immediately.[33]

Meanwhile, he asked Washington to keep the matter secret until he had the opportunity to prove his innocence. Washington agreed and even gave him a copy of the letter. Randolph was able

---

33   Freeman, 678.

to meet with Fauchet and obtain a letter absolving him of any bribery. Randolph then wrote an aggrieved and unpleasant letter to Washington asking for more information. When Washington saw one of his earlier private letters to Randolph published in the Republican press violating Randolph's own request for secrecy, it only served to annoy and harden his attitude toward Randolph. Washington shared all of the correspondence on the matter with Pickering and Wolcott and sent his last letter on the subject to Randolph on October 21, 1795, stating,

> It is not difficult from the tenor of [your] letter to perceive what your objectives are. But that you may have no cause to complain of the withdrawing of any paper... I have directed that you should have the inspection of my letter of the twenty-second of July, agreeably to your request; and that you are at full liberty to publish, without reserve, any and every word I have ever uttered, to or in your presence, from whence you can derive any advantage in your vindication. I grant this permission inasmuch as the extract manifestly tends to impress on the public mind that something has passed between us which you should disclose with reluctance from motives of delicacy which respect me... I request that this letter may be inserted in the compilation you are now making as well to show my disposition to furnish you with every means I possess toward your vindication, as that I have no wish to conceal any act of my conduct from the public. That public will judge, when it comes to see your vindication, how far and how proper it has been for you to publish private and confidential communications which oftentimes have been written in a hurry, and sometimes without even copies being taken, And it will, I hope, appreciate my motives, even if it should condemn my prudence in allowing you the unlimited license herein contained.[34]

Randolph replied a few days later, but Washington's response was set aside. In December Randolph published a pamphlet entitled *A Vindication*, which was self-serving but did contain

---

34   GW Papers at the Library of Congress.

all the evidence supporting his case. Republicans were pleased in that it attacked the President's reputation. Federalists believed it was base and perhaps a confession of guilt. Newspapers ignored it, and Randolph never achieved his innocence from the general public. Washington did not attempt to respond to it and let the matter rest even though the affair ended a long-time friendship with his closest adviser.

John Adams: 1735–1826

Minister John Adams returned from Europe in June 1788 to a tumultuous welcome in Boston. Everyone knew Adams was going to be involved in the government, and there was widespread speculation on his being a senator or possibly chief justice of the Supreme Court. However, there was no talk of his being elected president because it was assumed that Washington would be chosen. While Adams was away there were many changes in the old guard either through death or retirement, and new men in their thirties such as James Madison, Alexander Hamilton and Fisher Ames were in leadership positions. It is said that when Washington had agreed to run for office that he informally mentioned that Adams would be a good choice for vice president. This made a lot of sense since Adams was a northerner from the important state of Massachusetts and would serve as a proper balance to the southerner Washington. In fact, he was personally quite different from Washington being known for his bluntness and intellectual orientation. However, like Washington, he envisioned a glorious future for the United States having stated at the Treaty of Paris negotiations in 1783 that the country one day would "form the greatest empire in the world."[35] Advisers around Washington were nonetheless concerned that Washington receive

---

35 David McCullough, *John Adams* (New York: Simon & Schuster, 2001) 395. Copyright by David McCullough. Reprinted by permission of Simon & Schuster Adult Publishing Group.

a significant margin of Electoral College votes to avoid a tie, and Hamilton is reported to have maneuvered some votes away from Adams just to make sure that this did not happen and to assure that Washington was not embarrassed. The vote in February 1789, totaled sixty-nine for Washington and in second place thirty-four for Adams. He supposedly was upset with his showing in spite of being well ahead of ten other candidates.[36]

Like Washington, Adams always regarded the greatest threat to the infant nation was possible disunion. By 1789, the country was prospering and the population had grown from 2.5 million in 1776 to 4 million. The Paris Treaty more than doubled the size of the country making it larger than Great Britain, France, Germany, Spain and Italy combined.[37] Adams was his usual doubtful self, worrying that he would not be up to his new position. Moreover, as president of the Senate, he would not be able to participate in the debates, and speaking was his greatest asset. He later admitted to his son, John Quincy, that the office of vice president was not fitted to his character. On taking his office, he praised the election of Washington, the adoption of the Constitution and the hope that he would perform his duties fairly: "But if from inexperience or inadvertency, anything should ever escape me inconsistent with propriety, I must entreat you, by putting it to its true cause and not to any want of respect, to pardon and excuse me... a trust of the greatest magnitude is committed to this legislature... and the eyes of the world are upon you."[38]

Because Adams wanted to bring dignity and respect to the new central government, he presided over the Senate's debate for over a month on an appropriate title for Washington. He even suggested "His Majesty the President", but the public and most of

36 David McCullough, *John Adams* (New York: Simon & Schuster, 2001) 395. Copyright by David McCullough. Reprinted by permission of Simon & Schuster Adult Publishing Group. 394.
37 Ibid., 395.
38 Ibid., 402.

the Congress did not concur. By May 14, 1789, the Senate voted Washington's title to be "The President of the United States." Unfortunately, Adams got off to a bad start and acquired a reputation for preferring monarchial trappings and titles that only hardened the infant anti-Federalist faction. He became unpopular and was the lightning rod for ridicule especially as no criticisms would be directed at Washington. Adams was particularly disliked in Virginia, and in spite of Washington's initial warm reception of Adams, he increasingly distanced himself from him. He was not a happy man, and with the relatively insignificant position of vice president, he felt isolated and ineffective. Some of his leading peers criticized him unmercifully. Jefferson wrote to Madison that Adams's behavior in the titles debate was ridiculous, and Franklin had called him absolutely mad. Adams did have integrity, and like Washington, he was besieged with requests for jobs in the new government. Likewise, he did not believe in patronage and rejected all such requests from friends and family. In spite of his difficult start, once he and his wife, Abigail, got settled into their house one mile north of Manhattan, life was pleasant and happy. After they attended one of the Washington receptions, Abigail recorded her impressions of the President:

> He is polite with dignity, affable without formality, distant without haughtiness, grave without austerity, modest, wise, and good. These are traits in his character which peculiarly fit him for the exalted station he holds, and God grant that he may hold it with the same applause and universal satisfaction for many, many years, as it is my firm opinion that no other man could rule over this great people and consolidate them into one mighty empire but he who is set over us.[39]

As for the Vice President, he seldom met with the President and reportedly he had no influence on him because Washington

---

39   David McCullough, *John Adams* (New York: Simon & Schuster, 2001) 395. Copyright by David McCullough. Reprinted by permission of Simon & Schuster Adult Publishing Group., 413.

never asked for his opinion. Adams had no input on the selection of secretaries. He did approve of all the appointments who were geographically represented and who had played a part in the Revolution. Adams marveled at Washington saying, "He seeks information from all quarters and judges more independently than any man I ever saw."[40] In May 1790, Washington became gravely ill from an influenza epidemic sweeping New York City. Several attending physicians declared that the President was dying and that his death was imminent. This shook the government to its core, and it particularly alarmed John Adams knowing that he would have to inherit all the unresolved problems of the fledgling country. Abigail Adams wrote, "his [Washington's] death would have had most disastrous consequences," and no one could imagine how the government could survive without him.[41] To everyone's great relief the President recovered in June.

Adams shared Washington's dislike of partisan politics and his concern about the potential damage that could result from political parties. Presiding over the Senate, he tried to maintain an apolitical position claiming he was not a party man. With growing criticism in the press and party dissension in Congress, Washington was ready to retire in 1793. The feud between Jefferson and Hamilton was particularly upsetting to Washington, but both men were united in the need for Washington to remain in office for a second term. As the unofficial leader of the Federalists, Hamilton befriended Adams and urged him to run for office again mostly out of fear of two other candidates, the New York Republicans Aaron Burr and Governor George Clinton. Washington was overwhelmingly elected to another term, and Adams received seventy-seven votes to fifty for Clinton, four for Jefferson and one for Burr. After the Republicans failed to oust Adams, they turned

---

40 David McCullough, *John Adams* (New York: Simon & Schuster, 2001) 395. Copyright by David McCullough. Reprinted by permission of Simon & Schuster Adult Publishing Group. 415.
41 Ibid., 423.

their attacks on Washington and Hamilton. Adams became alarmed at Jefferson's vehemence and partisanship and thought he had become a fanatic. When King Louis XVI was beheaded at the end of 1792, neither Washington nor Adams made any public comments. On the other hand, Jefferson who had recognized the King as a good man stated that "Monarchy and aristocracy must be annihilated, and the rights of the people firmly established."[42] Prior to that event when in London, Adams is reported to have warned, "Mankind will in time discover that unbridled majorities are as tyrannical and cruel as unlimited despots."[43] As early as 1779, Adams also was quoted as saying, "Let us above all things avoid as much as possible entangling ourselves with their [Europe's] ways and politics."[44] In the ensuing fiasco with "Citizen" Genet, Adams and Washington were of the same mind. In February 1793, Great Britain and Spain declared war on France, and the French tried desperately to bring America into the conflict. Adams was even more frightened than Washington of the wildly pro-French sympathizers in the States. But Jefferson remained a strong Francophile and actively supported and encouraged the democratic societies which castigated Washington's, and therefore Adams's, cautious attitude toward the French. When Jefferson finally resigned on December 31, 1793, it prompted Adams to write to Abigail, "his want of candor, his obstinate prejudices of both aversion and attachment, his real partiality in spite of all his pretensions, his low notions about many things, have so utterly reconciled me to his departure... that I will not weep."[45]

As Adams spent the summer of 1794 at home in Quincy, he anxiously read of the resolution of the Whiskey Rebellion in

---

42 David McCullough, *John Adams* (New York: Simon & Schuster, 2001) 395. Copyright by David McCullough. Reprinted by permission of Simon & Schuster Adult Publishing Group., 444.
43 Ibid., 444.
44 Ibid., 445.
45 Ibid., 448.

western Pennsylvania. In December both Hamilton and Knox announced their resignations thereby leaving only Edmund Randolph as the remaining member of the original cabinet. Meanwhile, he and Washington were patiently waiting for word from John Jay in England where a treaty was being negotiated to address the grievances with England. When news arrived in the spring of 1795, Washington and Adams realized that the terms of the treaty would cause a storm of protest. No one was pleased with it, but it would bring peace with England so Washington and Adams publicly supported its passage. Having dealt with the British while in England on the Treaty of Paris in 1783, Adams more than anybody appreciated how difficult the negotiations would be for Jay. Jefferson was outspoken in his criticism and even wrote from his mountaintop retreat to the French ambassador in Philadelphia that he was still a strong supporter of France. Adams believed that the flawed Treaty was still better than an imminent war with England. While Congress debated the Treaty that summer, Randolph resigned as Secretary of State over allegations of accepting French bribes for foreign policy favors, thereby marking the complete departure of all the brilliant original advisers. As the end of 1795 approached, Adams was increasingly sensitive to his future role in government. Adams debated his future with Abigail who knew full well that the next president would not have the same strong support that Washington commanded. The furor over the Jay Treaty was tearing the country apart, and Adams feared for its survival. When the Treaty was passed in May 1796, conditions improved and peace with Britain was assured. Adams left for home in early May and looked back on his accomplishments. He had served Washington faithfully and had successfully presided over the Senate. He assisted in passing the bill to relocate the new national capital, and he had protected Washington's authority as chief executive. He had cast thirty-one tie-breaking votes all in support of Washington's administration and, as history has proved, more than any other vice president in the history of the United States.[46] In the final months of Washington's second term both men met for one of their few serious discussions on their political philosophies. Afterward, Adams commented to his wife, Abigail, that "I found his opinions and sentiments are more exactly like mine than I ever knew before." At the end of his own presidency when referring to Washington, he said, "His example is complete, and it will teach wisdom and virtue to Magistrates, Citizens, and Me, not only in the present age, but in future generations."[47]

James Madison: 1751–1836

Although Madison was not a member of Washington's cabinet, he nonetheless was one of his closest and most talented advisers. A graduate of the College of New Jersey (Princeton), he was perhaps the brightest intellectual that Washington brought into his inner circle. Even though they met briefly in Philadelphia in 1781 just as Washington was leading his troops down to Yorktown to face Cornwallis, their relationship actually started in early 1778 when Madison joined the Virginia Council of State. Only twenty-six, he was the youngest member of Governor Patrick Henry's Council and nineteen years junior to General Washington. Just at that time, the demoralized Continental army was camped at Valley Forge, and Washington had written an urgent letter to Congress bluntly stating that unless adequate provisions were supplied, the army would have to dissolve. The letter was shown to Governor Henry who shared it with his advisers. Madison quickly learned the plight of Washington's situation, and because of Henry's close

46 David McCullough, *John Adams* (New York: Simon & Schuster, 2001) 395. Copyright by David McCullough. Reprinted by permission of Simon & Schuster Adult Publishing Group.., 460.
47 Grizzard, 2.

relationship and correspondence with Washington, Madison came to know and appreciate the General. However, he also learned about military administration and the importance of military and civilian cooperation. Governor Henry and his Council complied with Washington's many requests for food, supplies and recruits by sharing his letters with the public and encouraging their sacrifice for the war effort. From his seat on the Council in Williamsburg, "Madison, in fact, found himself entangled almost immediately with most of the major persistent problems of the revolution. His day-to-day work there gave him a practical grasp of these issues a mere observer, or even a legislator, would not likely attain."[48] Madison began to empathize with Washington's problems, and unbeknown to Washington, Madison came to regard him as his mentor. Just by reading Washington's correspondence, Madison learned a great deal about the importance of administrative and financial needs of an army. He regarded Washington as a patient and caring general and that the fate of the revolution rested in his hands. In December 1779, Madison was elected to the Continental Congress by the Virginia Assembly partly in response to Washington's plea for greater talent at the national level. Virginia also sent one of Washington's closest friends and fellow burgess, Joseph Jones, to the Congress. It was Jones together with Madison who had drawn up Virginia's Declaration of Rights in 1776, and Jones would become the catalyst to bring Washington closer to Madison.

It is important to note that there were significant political and philosophical differences between the founding fathers. These emerged toward the end of the war around 1781–1782 initially among the nationalists and years before the major split between the Federalists and Republicans. There were moderate nationalists like Washington and Madison, and there were extreme nationalists

---

48 Leibiger, 15.

like Hamilton and the Morrises. With first-hand experience of dealing with Congress during the war and seeing its weaknesses, the moderates wanted to strengthen the Confederation but were willing to wait until the war was actually won. The extremists wanted to erect a strong central government before the war ended. These differences came to a head during the Newburgh crisis in the winter of 1782–1783. Madison's major efforts to resolve the army pay problem, and Washington's masterful control of an explosive situation, brought the two men into a close alignment. Madison wrote on the Newburgh resolution, "The steps taken by the Genl. To avert the gathering storm & his professions of inflexible adherence to his duty to Congress & to his country, excited the most affectionate sentiments toward him... The conduct of Washington does equal honor to his prudence and to his virtue."[49] Immediately following Washington's address to his men, he wrote to Joseph Jones urging Congress to move quickly on the revenue issue before the officers lost their patience. He wrote,

> Do not, My dear Sir, suffer this appearance of tranquility to relax your endeavors to bring the requests of the Army to an issue. Believe me, the Officers are too much pressed by their present wants, and rendered too sore by the recollection of the past sufferings to be touched much longer upon the string of forbearance... The well wishers of their Country, will exert themselves to... give every satisfaction that justice requires, and the means which Congress possess, will enable them to do.[50]

Madison used the letter to pursue his revenue plan and in April 1783 he issued his anonymous *Address to the States*, which carefully explained the need for a reliable federal income to pay its debts and secure the Revolution. He included all of Washington's correspondence concerning events at Newburgh, and with these

49 Leibiger, 28.
50 GW Papers at the Library of Congress.

he was able to both pass the revenue plan and raise the stature and reputation of Washington who used the issue to send his own circular to the governors of each state. Washington did not know the author of Madison's Address, but he ardently supported it. His own circular was very similar to Madison's in that it emphasized the need to preserve and strengthen the Confederation or run the risk of dissolving into local confederacies which could make alliances with foreign powers and lose the liberty it was fighting for. Speaking of the Congress he said,

> The eyes of the whole World are turned upon them, this is the moment to establish or ruin their national Character forever, this is the favorable moment to give such a tone to our Federal Government, as will enable it to answer the ends of its institution, or this may be the ill-fated moment for relaxing the powers of the Union, annihilating the cement of the Confederation, and exposing us to become the sport of European politics, which may play one State against another... to serve their own interested purposes. For, according to the system of Policy the States shall adopt at this moment, they will stand or fall, and by their confirmation or lapse, it is yet to be decided, whether the Revolution must ultimately be considered as a blessing or a curse...not to the present age alone, for with our fate will the destiny of unborn Millions be involved.[51]

Even though Madison and Washington got the Assembly's approval of the revenue plan, it was eventually turned down by the New England states because of their dislike of military pensions. Urgency for it died when the preliminary Treaty of Paris arrived in April 1783. We should note that Washington and Madison agreed on reform of the government within the confines of republicanism. However, Washington wanted national interests vested in the Confederation to supersede those of the states. Madison wanted a federal revenue but did not contemplate

---

51   GW Papers at the Library of Congress.

general centralized power. He also envisioned gradual changes through amendments rather than Washington's idea of a general convention to give Congress all the powers it needed to preserve the Union. Madison eventually changed his mind in favor of a convention.

Both Washington and Madison retired to private life in 1783. However, they had already started a correspondence that was to continue for the rest of their lives. It was Madison who assumed the responsibility for expressing the gratitude of Virginia for Washington's service to his country by having the renowned sculptor, Jean Antoine Houdon, do a life-sized statue of Washington to be placed in Richmond. Madison's inscription reads, "The General Assembly of the Commonwealth of Virginia, have caused this statue to be erected as a monument of affection and gratitude to George Washington, who, uniting the endowments of the hero, the virtues of the patriot, and exerting both in establishing the liberties of his country, has rendered his name dear to his fellow-citizens, and given to the world an immortal example of true glory."[52]

Madison shared Washington's vision for improving navigation on the Potomac and James Rivers. As a member of the Virginia delegation, it was Madison who worked closely with Washington in gaining legislation for the Potomac project. Making that area accessible for commerce in the immediate area and to the western lands was a life-long goal of Washington. Madison gained Washington's respect and confidence which later proved to be critical when he persuaded a reluctant Washington to attend and lead the Virginia delegation to the Constitutional Convention.

When the issue of commerce and trade in the Chesapeake emerged in the mid-1780s, a convention was scheduled for

---

52   Leibiger, 34.

September 1786 to meet in Annapolis to discuss giving Congress control of commerce. Washington was a strong supporter of such a measure, and Virginia sent Madison as a delegate. It was a time of sectional rivalry and distrust, and the only states present were Virginia, North Carolina and the mid-Atlantic states. Before adjourning, they called for another convention for May of the following year to be held in Philadelphia for the express purpose of improving the Confederation. Madison was able to gather experienced delegates for Philadelphia and by circulating names of all the delegates he helped bring similar support from other states. Washington had no intention of attending, but on learning of the widespread acceptance of the meeting and Madison's extensive administrative skills, he probably left the door open for that possibility even though he had just declined another invitation to Philadelphia on the grounds of poor health. Without his approval, Madison nominated Washington anyway. The delegates included Patrick Henry, Edmund Randolph, John Blair, George Mason, George Wythe and Madison, and they all selected Washington to lead the delegation. Washington deferred to Madison who then convinced him that his presence was critical to giving the convention a sense of legitimacy. At the same time, the farmer's revolt in Massachusetts known as the Shays' Rebellion convinced Washington that the government needed reforms immediately. Madison was able to convene all the states except Rhode Island, and this alone was considered a great accomplishment.

Madison had prepared well for the convention by studying the past history of confederations. He learned how their lack of central power caused them to fragment. He believed that his own state of Virginia had increasing disputes with other states owing to the failure of the Confederation to preserve national interests. Just before the convention in May, he wrote his essay "Vices of the

Political System of the United States," which extolled the benefits of a large republic being able to protect the minority rights better than a small republic because it would be more difficult for a self-interested group to attain a majority.[53] Madison agreed with Washington on trying for sweeping changes that would shift some powers from the states to the national government without excluding local authority. Madison and Washington agreed on the separation of executive, legislative and judicial departments with checks and balances. They agreed on a wholly new national government to control commerce, raise revenue through taxes and enforce its laws through a judicial system. Also, they wanted it to be voted upon by all the people instead of by state legislators. They spent four months together collaborating on their work and gaining mutual respect. Their united efforts were able to defeat the objections of Randolph and Mason who opposed a strong central government with powerful executive and legislative branches.[54] The entire Virginia delegation is credited for the original blueprint known as the Virginia Plan which had been discussed before the convention. However, its ideas were those previously agreed to by Madison and Washington. When the convention finally opened on May 25, 1787, Washington was elected as president of the gathering, and on May 29 Edmund Randolph presented the Virginia Plan. Intense debates followed wherein the smaller states insisted on equal representation in the Senate rather than based on population. Deliberations started to breakdown in July, and Washington became despondent over the small-state versus large-state issue. Then the convention voted to eliminate the right of Congress to veto state laws. Then a second convention was proposed to allow each state to propose amendments. Finally, a motion was made to change the House representatives to one

---

53   Leibiger, 71.
54   Ibid., 73.

per thirty thousand population instead of per forty thousand population. This last measure was supported by Washington and gave enough assurances to the smaller states that the entire plan was accepted by all the delegates except Randolph and Mason of Virginia and Elbridge Gerry of Massachusetts. Records indicate that Washington and Madison voted together on almost all the one hundred votes that were taken. The convention brought the two men to respect each other's talents after working closely together for four months of meetings that lasted six days a week for five hours a day. It is not certain which one took the leading role, but it is generally agreed that Washington's leadership was in quietly achieving compromises while Madison's scholarship, logic, industry and debating skills earned him the reputation as the most knowledgeable and effective man at the convention. The two men continued to work diligently for ratification by sharing information and strategies and telling the public of their collaboration. Both men recognized some of the weaknesses in the Constitution, and there were several features they personally would have changed. But as Washington stated that it was "little short of a miracle, that the Delegates from so many different States... should unite in forming a system of national Government, so little liable to well founded objections." Madison likewise said, "it is impossible to consider the degree of concord which ultimately prevailed as less than a miracle."[55] Madison defended the new Constitution by explaining it for the public in twenty-nine essays that were part of the *Federalist* publications. Washington equally supported it with articles in the newspapers. When Madison told Washington of his reluctance to take part in the Virginia ratification debates, Washington urged him to attend because he was so knowledgeable about the document and could explain it so well. After Madison decided to attend and

---

55   Leibiger, 86.

face his anti-Federalist friends, Washington wrote to him, "The consciousness of having discharged that duty which we owe to our Country, is superior to all other considerations, and will place smaller matters in a secondary point of view."[56] The Virginia debates were particularly arduous because of the powerhouse opponents to the Constitution. These included Patrick Henry, Edmund Randolph, George Mason and even Thomas Jefferson who was in Paris as the Minister to France. The most critical issue to them was the absence of a bill of rights, and Henry quoted Jefferson's suggestion that the best way to gain these rights was for Virginia to reject the Constitution. Madison cleverly neutralized Henry when he quickly replied that if Jefferson's name could be introduced, then he could cite the words of another important patriot. Without mentioning his name, Madison mentioned that, "At the conclusion of the war, that man who had the most extensive acquaintance with the nature of the country, publicly testified his disapprobation of the present system, and suggested that some alteration was necessary to render it adequate to the security of our happiness."[57] Everyone knew he was speaking about Washington, and eventually Madison won Virginia's ratification. However, it was Washington's enormous prestige that made the difference. According to James Monroe in his report to Jefferson, "[Washington's] influence carried this government."[58]

With public and private pressure building during the last half of 1788 for Washington to declare his acceptance for consideration of the presidency, he only discussed the matter with his private secretary, Colonel David Humphreys. Madison wanted Washington to accept the position, but he felt it would be better not to add further pressure. When Washington decided to be considered, he secretly asked Madison to review the seventy-

56 GW Papers at the Library of Congress.
57 Leibiger, 95.
58 Ibid., 95.

three page inaugural address that had presumably been prepared by Humphreys. Madison reduced the address to four pages that took twelve minutes to deliver. It simply stated Washington's own feelings of inadequacy for the task and asked for continued blessings of the Almighty. His principal objective was to gain the support of those Anti-federalists who had opposed the Constitution, and therefore he emphasized the need for corrections in the form of a bill of rights which both Madison and Washington had already agreed to the previous year. While at Mount Vernon in February 1789, Madison and Washington discussed many major issues facing the country as well as possible candidates for appointment in the new government. After the official vote of the Electoral College on April 6, 1789, Washington called on Madison for every kind of advice ranging from procedure, etiquette, scheduling, specific appointments and protocol. In effect, Madison became Washington's prime minister and chief executive not only because Washington valued his advice but because there were no government officials in place to assume these duties. The entire country knew of Madison's closeness with the President, and both men were besieged with applications for office. Knox and Hamilton did not take office until September, and Jefferson only arrived the following March. For six months Madison and Washington ran the entire government and breathed life into the organization that was created under the Constitution. Washington was exceedingly concerned with setting precedents, and he frequently relied on Madison's advice even for such seemingly routine matters as whether communications between the president and Congress should be oral or in writing, or how to address the president, or the nature and frequency of public access to the president. Madison decided on nearly all of these issues, and fortunately Washington was in complete agreement with him. Also, Madison agreed on all of Washington's appointments of his department secretaries and had a personal hand in getting Jefferson to accept the post of Secretary of State. It is surprising that Washington did not name Madison as one of his secretaries, but it was rumored that he would have been Secretary of State if Jefferson had not accepted. All this time Madison was fully occupied as a Virginia Representative in the House, and yet Washington continued to seek his counsel. Edmund Randolph was actually selected by Madison for Attorney General, and most of the secretaries continued to ask Madison to communicate some private matters for them to the President. Madison even knew that Knox and Hamilton were to be appointed three months before they themselves knew. Jefferson was extremely reluctant to serve, but Washington's wishes and patience together with Madison's influence, persuaded Jefferson to take the position even as late as March 1790. According to Gouverneur Morris, Washington never had a very high opinion of Jefferson, but he did believe his experience abroad would make him an effective Secretary of State.[59] Washington was almost totally dependent on Madison for advice, counsel and resolving disputes in government before they became problems. Madison shared his own correspondence with Washington, and Washington reciprocated with official correspondence and documents. They wanted each other to know as much as possible about how the country and the Congress were reacting to the new government. Madison was asked to write Washington's first annual message to Congress in December 1789 and then his second annual message in 1790. When Madison took up the issue of additional safeguards for personal liberties in 1789 and 1790, he was not successful in persuading enough colleagues to agree with him. The Federalist-dominated Congress grew tired of Madison's efforts to appease the Anti-federalists.

59   Leibiger, 117.

Madison studied over two hundred changes to the Constitution that had originated at the various state ratifying conventions and distilled them down to basic freedoms of the press, of speech, of conscience, and tried to incorporate the principles of the Declaration of Independence into the Constitutions. He even tried to restrict state laws from infringing on individual liberties, but he failed to gain approval. Finally, he asked Washington for his support, even though the President did not like to interfere with the legislature's business. Washington was sympathetic to Madison's efforts and did supply him with a letter stating that "Upon the whole, they have my wishes for a favorable reception in both houses."[60] Madison shared the letter with Congress and barely got his amendments approved. Once again, the prestige of George Washington played a critical role in shaping one of the most important developments in America's constitutional history.

As the new secretaries settled into their posts and basic protocols were established, Washington no longer had to depend on Madison. Their very close working relationship began to wane even though they remained on good terms. The first really serious threat to their friendship came with Hamilton's financial program when he submitted his *Report on Public Credit* in January 1790. His objectives were to establish national credit by resolving the outstanding wartime debt and to build a banking structure that would foster economic growth. He wanted to raise America from strictly an agricultural economy dependent on England for manufactures and trade to an independent economic power equal to or even better than Great Britain. Madison recognized the need for sound public credit, but he believed that government funding of mercantile interests would bring corruption and tyranny similar to Great Britain's, and that would lead to a loss of the liberties

60 GW Papers at the Library of Congress.

which America had just won. Madison's idealism was similar to Jefferson's in that they both viewed an agricultural society as a virtuous, independent and happy one. They were content to remain indebted to British merchants and blamed mercantilists in England or America for their economic problems, seldom blaming their own practice of living beyond their means. Hamilton grew up in the West Indies and was therefore influenced by the benefits of a mercantile system. Madison feared that too strong a central government would threaten individual freedom, whereas Washington never felt that a strong central government would threaten republicanism. Madison wanted the Country to operate under a strict interpretation of the Constitution, while Hamilton believed the Constitution provided a guide and framework to develop a broader economy of trade, finance and industrialization. Washington was sympathetic to Madison, especially on the debt-discrimination issue, and he did not wholly agree with Hamilton's entire program, but he definitely wanted to get the Country onto a sound credit footing in the world and he knew the importance of attaining a strong manufacturing economy. In fact, his life-long interest in promoting the Potomac River Basin and a canal system reaching to the western lands was for the purpose of building a broader based economy for that region and one that was less dependent on agriculture.

For the first six months of 1790, the House debated Hamilton's plans for his debt assumption measures. Meanwhile, there were discussions on the future location of a national capital. Pennsylvanians wanted it to remain in Philadelphia, and Virginians wanted it in the south believing that their future influence in the government could be greater. Still in New York in June 1790, Jefferson invited Madison and Hamilton for dinner to discuss a possible solution to the funding issue, and it was

Madison who took the initiative that resulted in the Compromise of 1790. Madison proposed that he would garner enough votes for the assumption measures if Hamilton would gain New England's support for a permanent capital on the Potomac after a ten-year temporary location in Philadelphia. As their informal bargain developed, it was Washington who became the major factor in the decision. He reportedly met with Madison and Hamilton behind the scenes in working out the plan, but his reluctance to openly interfere with the matter was never fully disclosed. New Yorkers were upset enough about losing the capital that the newspaper drew the first cartoon criticizing an American president for "self-gratification."[61] Hamilton's Bank Bill creating a national bank marked another episode in the Washington-Madison relationship. Washington discussed the measure at length with Madison and was supportive of his objections. He even asked Madison to draw up a veto message before he asked Hamilton for his arguments in favor of the bill. Hamilton's fifteen-thousand word reply convinced Washington of its merits, and he signed it in spite of knowing how upset Madison and Jefferson would be. Although some politics intervened with the tabling of the capital issue, Washington's real predicament was the possible use of his veto power on an issue that was not necessarily unconstitutional. Even in his later years, Madison reflected on Washington's dilemma and admitted that a veto could have caused a serious crisis and a possible reversal of Washington by the Congress. As Hamilton began to get closer to Washington in 1791, he pushed Madison farther away. However, it is interesting that Madison did not blame Washington but instead directed his hostility to Hamilton. It was Madison's jealousy of Hamilton that caused his distancing from Washington as well as

---

61   Leibiger, 133.

their differing fears of America's vulnerability. Madison feared a strong central government, while Washington feared localism.[62]

The origin of Madison's eventual split with Washington occurred in the fall of 1791, just after his summer trip with Jefferson throughout New England. Madison had become concerned over the *Gazette of the United States*, which he believed espoused strong Federalist policies bordering on monarchism. He wanted to produce another newspaper which promoted republicanism, and he did this with some support from Jefferson. The new paper was to be the *National Gazette* to be published by his friend, Philip Freneau, who also worked for Jefferson in the State Department. Madison wrote articles that reflected some of his *Federalist Papers* essays and the growing threat of monarchism. Freneau was less moderate and soon became so blatant that his attacks on Washington embarrassed Madison. Washington was unaware of Madison's involvement with the *National Gazette* until August 1792 when he was considering his possible retirement the following year. Ironically, he had already asked Madison for his advice on retirement and had asked him to compose a farewell address. Also, Freneau's harsh criticisms of Hamilton affected Washington, who took any attack on his secretaries as an attack on him and his administration. Madison and Hamilton continued to vie for Washington's favor, and their adversity was further exacerbated when Washington sided with the Republican-backed Apportionment Bill and Madison's efforts to alter the gold and silver content in United States coins. Madison became convinced that Hamilton was trying to defeat republicanism, but he did not blame Washington. On the other hand, Washington did support Hamilton's financial policies, but he did not share Madison's agrarian orientation.

---

62   Leibiger, 137.

In May 1792, Washington sought Madison's advice on how he should announce his intended retirement. Madison argued strongly for Washington to remain for a second term and that the country needed him and would not regard another four years as an attempt for further power. Washington responded that his health and stamina were slipping and that party politics had infected his cabinet. He also abhorred the negative attacks on his administration that he interpreted as personal attacks on him which all suggested that it was time for him to depart. Madison used the rise of party politics as all the more reason for Washington to hold the Country together. Madison did not add that he wanted another four years to build republicanism sufficiently enough to beat the Federalists in the 1796 election. However, he thought Washington would remain neutral and never imagined that he would shift decidedly to the Federalist camp. By June Washington had made up his mind to retire and presented a preliminary draft to Madison for his editing. Madison wrote a simple non-partisan farewell valedictory and a separate retirement notice suggesting that they should be published in the newspapers by mid-September. Washington also received a letter from Jefferson in May urging him to stay for another term. The fact that Washington waited six weeks to answer Jefferson indicates that he did not have the same trust in him as he did for Madison. As Madison and Hamilton continued their public attacks on each other in the newspapers, and both men tried to enlist Washington's sympathies to the real political dangers to the Country, it became more obvious that Madison, not Jefferson, was the leading Anti-federalist. Washington tried to pacify his two closest advisers, but their antagonism only increased. Oddly enough, as hostility grew, Washington realized that he could not leave the country is such a divided state. In spite of his great reluctance, by October he decided to stay for the good of the country. After Washington's second inaugural, Madison tried to woo Washington by undermining Hamilton with a Congressional accusation of mishandling appropriated funds. When Hamilton responded with a complete accounting, the Republicans and Madison in particular were shamed. At the same time, Freneau started personal attacks against the President who by then had learned of Madison's connection to the *National Gazette*. By the spring of 1793, Washington no longer sought Madison's advice. The great friends and authors of so much wartime and peacetime work had ended their collaborations, and Washington had to look to his cabinet in a far different light than before. During his first administration, Washington considered his secretaries as advisers to assist in carrying out his wishes on a consensus basis. Now, he sought their opinions and weighed the pros and cons of their partisan positions.

The French Revolution had a strong impact on America and served to further divide Republicans and Federalists. Madison believed France was following America's example of discarding monarchy in favor of a democracy. Washington saw something quite different in that fanaticism in France was bordering on anarchy, and he was fearful that their behavior could spread to the United States. When France and England declared war on each other in 1793, the Federalists wanted a strict neutrality while Republicans wanted an undeclared neutrality that did not openly harm Franco-American treaties and relationships. Madison disagreed with Washington's Neutrality Proclamation in principle, and Jefferson believed it was an invasion on the rights of Congress. Both men did not publicly criticize Washington because they believed that Hamilton and Knox were to blame. Actually, Washington asked Madison for his advice beforehand, but Jefferson convinced Madison not to reply to him. Again, Freneau opened his attacks on the President in his *National Gazette*, and they were so vicious that Jefferson and Madison believed the Federalists deliberately wrote them in order to bring Washington to their side. Hamilton wrote in the *Gazette of the United States* supporting the Proclamation and introducing the word "neutrality", and he urged Madison to do the same. Madison declined on the lack of sufficient time, etc., but the real reason was he did not know if Washington really agreed with Hamilton's strong position and the word "neutrality." The essence of the entire issue came down to one of implied powers versus strict construction of the Constitution. Specifically, did the Constitution allow the executive to decide foreign policy and was the President simply stating the current legally peaceful conditions with France or was he stating a new policy of neutrality in the war between England and France. The question was then decided when the new French minister, Genet, blatantly opposed Washington's orders thereby bringing Federalist and Republican support to Washington.

When Jefferson announced his retirement in 1793, Washington turned to Madison as the most likely successor because as a republican southerner and authority on the Constitution, he would be the best candidate. Washington informally mentioned this to Jefferson hoping that he would persuade him to take the post. Madison never replied implying that Jefferson influenced his decision. History tells us that Madison was well aware of Jefferson's frustrations and disappointments with the position. He often complained of having to execute policies he was not in favor of as well as the long hours of work. Madison lost a great opportunity to regain his closeness to the President. He knew that Washington was even-handed in that he sided with Jefferson as often as he did with Hamilton. Washington was undoubtedly disappointed in Madison's decision in that it was Madison who convinced him to run for office again. Unlike Hamilton, who was always loyal to Washington, Madison abandoned the President at a critical time, and in so doing, he sealed his alienation from the chief executive and his possible influence on future events. He did not realize that with Edmund Randolph as Jefferson's replacement and William Bradford as Randolph's replacement, Washington would be left with little Republican advocates in his cabinet, and there would be ineffective opposition to such strong Federalists as Hamilton, Knox, Bradford and Randolph. It is no wonder that Washington began to side more with the Federalist position in spite of his desire to maintain a nonpartisan course. In spite of their increasingly different political philosophies, it was delegate Madison who spoke in the Virginia General Assembly just after Washington's death: "Death has robbed our country of its most distinguished ornament, and the world of one of its greatest benefactors. George Washington, the Hero of Liberty, the father of his Country, and the friend of man is no more. The General Assembly of his native state were ever the first to render him, living, the honors due to his virtues. They will not be the second, to pay to his memory the tribute of their tears."[63]

---

63 Grizzard, 210.

CHAPTER 10

Washington's Retirement and Final Days: 1797–1799

I anticipate with pleasing expectation that retreat, in which I promise myself to realize, without alloy, the sweet enjoyment of partaking, in the midst of my fellow Citizens, the benign influence of good Laws under a free Government—the ever favourite object of my heart, and the happy reward, as I trust, of our mutual cares, labours, and dangers.

—President George Washington
"Farewell Address," September 19, 1796

Soon after the inauguration of John Adams, the Washingtons left Philadelphia for Mount Vernon. There they took up a quiet but socially active life accompanied by the intrusion of many visitors who were simply curious to see the famous family. Included was his new ward and godson, George Washington Motier Lafayette, the sixteen-year-old son of Marquis de Lafayette who was held in an Austrian prison. Washington had financially supported the Lafayette family for several years and treated the young boy as a son until he rejoined his family upon release of the Marquis in 1797. Other than the constant hordes of visitors who Washington felt obliged to wine, dine and board, the Washingtons preferred a simple life and renewing some old friendships. However, Washington quickly grew restless from such inactivity and closely followed news from the capital. President Adams had inherited the strained relations with France, and the two allies were drifting farther apart. Relations with France were also the cause of increasingly bitter rivalries between Federalists and Republicans with the former referred to as the "British Party" and the latter as the "French Party." There were thirty thousand Frenchmen and fifty thousand Irishmen living in America, which added considerable fuel to the fire. At issue was the Jay Treaty which the French considered as a violation of the alliance of 1778 between France and America. The French regarded the Jay Treaty with annoyance because it relaxed tensions between their bitter enemy and America, and that jeopardized their objective of European domination. France brought the looming conflict to a head when the French Directory refused to receive the new American Minister, Thomas Pinckney, who was to replace the pro-French James Monroe. American indignation at this treatment prompted cries for war, but instead Adams initiated a commission to negotiate a peaceful resolution. Pinckney was joined by John Marshall and Elbridge Gerry who arrived in Paris on October 4, 1797. Washington followed these events very closely and even met with Marshall at Mount Vernon beforehand. Not a word was heard from the envoys for months, and the French continued their confiscation of American ships. In March the situation deteriorated rapidly when it was learned that foreign minister, Prince de Talleyrand, sent three representatives (subsequently named "X, Y and Z" by Adams) to the three American envoys in Paris to negotiate more favorable American policies toward France, demands for a $6 million loan and a $250,000 bribe for the opportunity just to meet with him.

When Washington received the news he thought it would unite Americans, but he was dismayed to see that there was still strong sympathy for France and criticism of the Adams administration. Adams was outraged and called to prepare a "new army" for a possible confrontation with France. When full disclosure of the shabby treatment by France was published in April 1778, the public changed its opinion of Adams and supported his call for retaliation. When Washington learned of the so-called XYZ Affair he wrote to Secretary of War, James McHenry, to offer his services in organizing the "new army." As the French continued to confiscate more American ships in the Caribbean, Congress authorized increasing the army to twelve regiments. Adams indicated that Washington would be chosen as the new commander. In his letter of June 22, 1778 Adams said, "In the very name of Washington there will be more efficacy... than in many an army."[1] Secretary of War McHenry also wrote asking Washington to be the new commander. Washington replied, "I see as you do that clouds are gathering and that a storm may ensue... [and however painful it would be] to quit the tranquil walks of retirement and enter the boundless field of responsibility and trouble... [and he would find it difficult] to remain an idle spectator under the plea of age or retirement."[2] Washington immediately ordered a new uniform and rode to Philadelphia to select his officers which was one of his conditions for accepting the post as well as his request that he not be called to active duty until he was needed. Adams commissioned Washington without officially accepting his previously stated conditions on the selection of officers. Also Washington wanted officers with Federalist beliefs rather than Republicans who he believed would be too sympathetic to France. Adams and Washington got into a

---

1   Freeman, 725.
2   GW Papers at the Library of Congress.

disagreement on whether Hamilton or Knox would be second in command. Washington believed Hamilton would be best because of his age, his military experience and his general knowledge of most government matters while his friend, Henry Knox, was just too old for a leading position. Knox was initially upset but soon wrote to Washington expressing his understanding and willingness to serve as his personal aide. Adams was leery of Hamilton's possible thirst for power, but Washington assured him that Hamilton's ambitions were not to be feared. When the anticipated French invasion did not materialize, Washington returned to Mount Vernon but still awaited progress reports from McHenry. Some believed that Adams merely wanted a show of force to the French in the hope of avoiding an armed conflict, but in any event, it seemed to work.[3]

The XYZ Affair had a stabilizing effect on the government. Congress was able to pass new legislation calling for a new army, a new navy, and a new tax to support the greater defense effort. The war of words with France did not go away. The Adams administration could no longer endure the harsh and possibly untruthful pro-French newspaper attacks which the Federalists believed would destabilize the government. In an effort to silence the outspoken press, Congress passed the Naturalization Bill which lengthened the residency requirement for citizenship from five to fourteen years and the Alien and Sedition Laws, which forbid unwarranted and unsubstantiated attacks on the government and armed the president with the power to deport aliens suspected of treasonable acts against the government in the event of war or threatened invasion. It also suppressed scandalous and false written, published or spoken statements against the government or anyone in the government. Washington agreed with the measures because they applied only to aliens, not

3   Clark, 383-97.

American citizens, who had no allegiance to the United States. He knew the new laws would provide the Republicans with lots of ammunition against the Federalists just when they needed it. Even Hamilton was not in favor of the measures knowing how they would help his adversaries. Kentucky and Virginia declared the laws unconstitutional. Actually, the laws resulted in the jailing of ten editors. Although they were unpopular, even Washington remained silent on the new laws because of his fears that continued divisiveness could result in domination by a foreign power. As confidence in the Adams administration waned, some Federalists led by Jonathan Trumbull of Connecticut tried to draft Washington for another term, but he emphatically suppressed the notion.

During this time, Washington was also deeply involved in the progress of the Federal City. Building had been slow due to inadequate private funds, but loans from Maryland and then Congress gave the project the needed impetus. Washington personally borrowed funds to build two residential dwellings as a personal investment. Since retiring, he needed income to provide living expenses, and he attempted to sell off parcels of land to produce the necessary cash for investments in dividend-producing assets. He visited the City in October several times and again in May 1799 when he saw his two houses completed. He also invested in the construction of a hotel in the City and met with those in charge of the rising capital which he envisioned as surpassing those of Europe.

Washington returned to Mount Vernon in November 1798 to concentrate on the work to be done on the plantation. Nonetheless, he corresponded at length with Secretary McHenry on the French situation. He was still waiting for instructions on recruitments, but no explanations for the delays were forthcoming. In January

1799, Washington received a letter from his friend in Paris, Joel Barlow, which stated that the entire affair with France was nothing more than a misunderstanding. He forwarded the letter to Adams who then proceeded to arrange an envoy to France, William Vans Murray, who had been American Minister at The Hague. Adams took it upon himself to send the envoy much to the horror of his own party who thought it was dishonorable and ill-advised. Adams overcame their opposition by appointing Chief Justice Oliver Ellsworth and Patrick Henry to join Murray. Meanwhile, with no outward appearance of any changes in French policy, Washington, Hamilton and Congress assumed that preparations for war should continue. However, there were still no progress reports from McHenry, so Washington wrote to him suggesting that he was to blame for such poor handling of the War Department. In fact, McHenry was not highly regarded in this and other Department matters, but Washington and McHenry soon resolved the issue and renewed their long friendship.

Most of Washington's time and efforts during 1799 were devoted to the plantation. He had prepared a long-term plan of simplification, part of which was bequeathing some two thousand acres to his nephew Lawrence Lewis, the son of his sister Betty. He also rented his mill and distillery to him and allowed him to settle on the land with his new bride. This was only a part of the lengthy will Washington had composed in July. While he seemed to enjoy good health, he frequently made remarks alluding to his demise. He always had acknowledged that his was a short-lived family, and he increasingly made reference to joining his ancestors soon and that his "glass had nearly run out." In September his younger brother Charles died, causing Washington to remark that although he himself was the first born of his father's second marriage, he was now the only one remaining of the four sons. He remained in close contact with McHenry for first-hand information on affairs of state, and in the fall Washington received a lengthy letter from him which was quite revealing. McHenry appealed to Washington for advice on the deteriorating Adams administration. He told of the rift between the President and his Cabinet over the mission to France and how Adams ignored his Secretaries. McHenry stated that,

> The evil does not lie in a change of secretaries... but in the mission which... is become an apple of discord to the Federalists that may so operate upon the ensuing election of President, as to put in jeopardy the fruits of all their past labors, by consigning to men devoted to French innovations and demoralizing principles, the reins of government. It is this dreaded consequence which afflicts and calls for all the wisdom of the Federalists... I see rocks and quicksands on all sides and the administration in the attitude of a sinking ship."[4]

Washington replied, "I believe it is better that I should remain mute than express any sentiment on the important matters which are related... The vessel is afloat, or very nearly so, and considering myself as a passenger only, I shall trust to the mariners whose duty it is to watch, to steer it into a safe port.[5]

Washington elected not to attend a meeting of the Potomac Company on December 10. Instead, he chose to work on his master plan for the plantation that involved a more efficient operation as well as crop rotation for the following four years. Early on December 12 he wrote to Hamilton about a military academy that he had frequently suggested to Congress but which he had no desire to organize owing to his lack of scientific expertise. By ten o'clock he started his usual round on horseback inspecting the fields and noting which areas needed work. It was a cold day with intermittent rain and snow, and he was out in the

4   Freeman, 747.
5   GW Papers at the Library of Congress.

elements for five hours. According to his secretary, Tobias Lear, Washington did not change from his damp clothing for dinner, which was not his usual custom. He went to bed appearing well, but on the following day he felt some soreness in his throat, which he attributed to an ordinary cold. When the snow stopped later in the day he went out in the cold sunset to mark certain trees he wanted removed. That evening the horseness in his throat grew more pronounced, but he maintained it was nothing but a cold that would soon go away. Lear later reported that otherwise Washington appeared and felt well. Late that night he suddenly became ill and awakened Martha. His breathing was labored so Lear sent for his lifelong companion, Doctor Craik. While waiting for Dr. Craik, Washington requested several bleedings, which were the customary treatment. When his condition did not improve, Martha sent for Doctor Gustavos Brown, who had previously been recommended in Dr. Craik's absence. Upon his arrival Dr. Craik diagnosed the illness as "inflammatory quinsy" and treated it with cantharides on the throat and sips of sage tea and vinegar but with little effect. Craik summoned Doctor Elisha Dick, and by three o'clock all three doctors were in a dilemma about additional treatments. Around 4:30 Washington asked for Martha and the will he had prepared realizing that the end was near. He then told Lear that he felt he was going because his breathing was failing. He instructed Lear to arrange his papers and accounts. He then thanked his doctors for their assistance and advised that they should just let him go quietly. At eight in the morning Washington murmured to Lear to have him "decently buried" and placed in the family vault two days after his death. When Lear responded that he understood his request, Washington uttered his last words, "'Tis well." Without a complaint of his pain or a sigh the great man was gone.

He has traveled on to the end of his journey, and carried with him an increasing weight of honour: he has deposited it safely where misfortune can not tarnish it; where malice can not blast it. Favoured of heaven, he departed without exhibiting the weakness of humanity; magnanimous in death, the darkness of the grave could not obscure his brightness.

—John Marshall
Chief Justice, United States Supreme Court

CHAPTER 11
Washington's Character

Let us descend the bluff on the banks of the Potomac to the little dell which George Washington in his last years selected for his tomb. There is no pomp here, just a small vault embedded in a hillside… bugles and drums may come here sometimes but they are out of place. Here lies greatness without ostentation, the dust of a man who denied the temptations of power as few other men in history have ever done. A man who desired from his fellow men not awe, not obedience, but love.

—James Thomas Flexner, biographer

Rather than imposing this author's or any historian's judgment of Washington's character on the reader, it is far more revealing to learn how his contemporaries assessed his behavior because they lived at a time when values were different from today. To gain this insight we can study the words of thousands of his countrymen who assessed Washington's character together with his many contributions. A significant source for such information would be the eulogies presented in 1800 across the country shortly after his death. Of the 241 eulogies made part of the *Early American Imprints*, historian Barry Schwartz has analyzed fifty-five of them suggesting that even after thirty-five of them the pattern became apparent.[1] While they reflect the thinking of the more educated class of that society, they do represent a broad enough spectrum of different believers and nonbelievers as well as varying political persuasions, that they offer valuable insights into how eighteenth century Americans regarded George Washington. Some historians view Washington in terms of classical heroes like Addison's Cato, Cincinnatus or Ceasar while others regard him in religious terms like the Old Testament's David or Moses. Still others believe he exemplified a mixture of both classical and religious virtues. Schwartz believes he personified the Whig political culture of the seventeenth and early eighteenth centuries dating from the English Civil War and owing to the writings of such British libertarians as Trenchard, Gordon, Locke, Hume, and Burgh, who had a great influence on America's revolutionaries.

The Whigs were very concerned with the use of power, which they regarded as an instrument used by the few for domination of the many. Power was the opposite of liberty, and it used aggressiveness in its expanding tendency to overrun the more passive nature of liberty. Power was brutal, but liberty was delicate and sensitive. Power had to be resisted, while liberty was to be defended. The images of power were tyrants and kings, while the image of liberty required a hero or model to whom people could look for leadership and inspiration. That leader would use power in a positive way and respect its limits. Viscount Bolingbroke's *Patriot King* was a concept that served to oppose abuses of the British government, and the American Whigs adopted those virtues to fit George Washington as their own patriot hero. American Whigs regarded their ideals as public virtue, disinterestedness, moderation, resoluteness, private virtue

---

1   James Thomas Flexner, *George Washington* (New York: Little Brown & Co., 1972 [originally published 1969]), vol. 4, 502.

and piety as the principal motivations of their heroes. In his *Creation of the American Republic*, historian Gordon Wood states that public virtue was the eighteenth century bulwark against political power. This was personified in one of America's greatest classical heroes, the Roman Cato, who gave his life for society's well-being. We have already noted that Washington's favorite play from his youth, Addison's *Cato*, was presented at Valley Forge for the benefit of his troops so they could be inspired by a man who gave his life for his country. Subordinating self-interest to the public good was the greatest Whig ideal. It was only through the dedication of selfless citizens that society could be protected from ambitious men. Unlike today's esteem for ambition and genius, the late eighteenth century extolled character, conservatism and diffidence. In his eulogy the Reverend John Fitch emphasized Washington's self-sacrifice and the fact that he did not seek a position of leadership but rather accepted it with reluctance. His devotion to the public good was made even greater because he was already well off and comfortable. John Mason's eulogy noted how Washington was well aware of his army's limitations against the most powerful army on earth. He realized that he could easily lose the war, and yet he "took the field selflessly." He put his life and his reputation on the line and at that point could only have possibly acquired some lesser place in history. He demonstrated no motives for personal gain since he had refused a salary as commander in chief. But, after he did win military fame, he again showed his public virtue by giving up his domestic ease and placing his reputation at risk by entering politics. He even declined to accept the praise due him by acknowledging the efforts of his officers and other leaders as well as God. Charles Atherton's eulogy tells us how Washington's services were "free will offerings at the altar of patriotism."

In eighteenth century American politics the most dangerous vice was ambition, and its offsetting virtue was disinterestedness. This was closely related to selflessness, and it meant that one's pursuit of social good should be accomplished without regard for the personal power it could bring. It was the opposite of ambition, and only those rulers who were disinterested could resist the lure of the selfish lust for power. Many of the eulogists of 1800 spoke of Washington's total lack of interest in securing or enlarging his power. This is substantiated by his voluntary resignation as commander in chief at Annapolis in 1783 to return to his hearth and family at Mount Vernon. He could have easily established a type of monarchy for himself, but in the words of eulogist Thomas Thacher he "quitted his high and exalted station with more pleasure than would have been received by the most sanguine votary of ambition and power." A masonic brother of Washington's claimed, "He who had conquered the proudest nation of Europe, by a nobler achievement, had now conquered himself, had vanquished the frailties and infirmities of nature."

When Washington declined the opportunity for a third term, he reestablished his greatness by not succumbing to human nature's lust for power when he clearly had the opportunity to do so. As eulogist John Mason said, "It was for him to set as great an example in the relinquishment, as in the acceptance of power." According to another eulogist, Fisher Ames, "Washington changed mankind's ideas of political greatness" through his disregard for himself, the absence of personal motives, his disinterestedness and the practice of moderation. This last trait was embodied in Whig philosophy in that extremes were considered bad. Moderation implied restraint and a proper balance between ambitious power for private gain and power for the public good. Washington's contemporaries viewed him with just such balance.

He not only had military and political talents, but with his high sense of moral values, he was able to properly balance these and other qualities that made him competent and virtuous as opposed to brilliant or fanatic. Many of the eulogists in the year 1800 cited Washington's other qualities, such as: mildness with firmness; passion with composure; private affection and public duty; grace and compassion with vigor and courage. He balanced these talents to perform his dual roles as dominating general and submissive citizen.[2]

Of vital concern to the eighteenth century gentleman was reputation. Above all else, reputation was one's most valuable asset, and we can see how it was one of Washington's greatest concerns. One's character went hand-in-hand with one's reputation, and it mattered how these were viewed by the public. When he reluctantly accepted his appointment as commander in chief, he felt he had no other option because his reputation demanded it. To refuse would have been dishonorable and would have had a negative impact on his reputation. This is evident in his letter to Martha where he told her it was "out of his power to refuse the appointment." By wearing his old military uniform at the Second Continental Congress in 1775, he obviously wanted to play a major position, and his duty to his country demanded it. When he reluctantly presided at the Constitutional Convention, he expressed concern that his reputation was at risk not knowing which, if any, states would attend and whether any agreements could be reached. Again, when asked to become president, Washington's sense of obligation to his country was pitted against his concern for the risk to his exalted reputation. Whereas one could judge that he was overly concerned with his reputation,

---

2   Barry Schwartz, "The Character of Washington: A Study in Republican Culture," *American Quarterly*, vol. 38, no. 2 (Summer 1986) 202-222. Copyright by The American Studies Associates. Reprinted with permission of The Johns Hopkins University Press.

we must remind ourselves that he always took that risk, and with each success his esteem increased.

One of Washington's greatest skills was his vision to see the "big picture" far beyond that of the other founders. Some call this wisdom, and it is evident in his decisions on how he prosecuted an "unwinable" war, how he recognized the need for a stronger central government, how he knew that national sound credit was vital, how he balanced his cabinet with northerners and southerners, how he suppressed anarchy in the Whiskey Rebellion, how he could see the long-term benefits of the controversial Jay Treaty and how he respected the need for national unity and civil authority. Washington had the wisdom to surround himself with far brighter and more educated minds than his own. People like Jefferson, Hamilton, Adams, Madison and Jay were stunning intellects. He tempered their views with his own sound judgment and tried to govern from having the benefit of often diverse and opposing ideas. As he balanced his own talents, so he also wanted balanced views in his administration. His ultimate strength lay in his self-control and his indomitable will. His military and political victories were the result of overcoming adversities by use of his self-control. He is credited with having been able to control events around him by first mastering himself. It should be remembered that America went through an abrupt and drastic change from the emotional cries for liberty in the 1770s to the need for restraint and self-government in the 1780s. No one was more aware of this than Washington, who saw what was happening in the French Revolution. He wanted to disprove what Europeans were saying about America—that man is incapable of governing himself. Shays' Rebellion and the Whiskey Rebellion were critical events to Washington because if they had gone unchecked there was a good chance that general anarchy would have followed. In a late eighteenth-century world of international wars between the super powers and revolution and anarchy in France, Washington governed with unswerving steadiness and remained unmovable by all the discord surrounding him. In his eulogy, Henry "Light Horse" Harry Lee said, "Washington traveled a fixed route, neither elated by success nor dismayed by failure, unaffected by the ragings upon which he threw his own heat and light... moving in his own orbit... he took his course, commiserating folly, disdaining vice, dismaying treason, and invigorating despondency." Leaders in Congress, as well as more experienced generals, urged him to face the British head-on, but he regarded such tactics as reckless. He must have had great apprehensions, but he never uttered them or gave the slightest hint of worry or concern. Eulogist Jeremiah Smith said of Washington, "he stood collected in himself, like a rock in a tempestuous sea, unmoved by the storms of popular fury that beat upon him... his was a spirit unbroken by adversity—a spirit, which not only enabled him to sustain the weight of cares, which devolved on him, but served to revive and animate his fainting troops." As commander in chief he defeated the enemy of liberty, and as president he saved the country from itself by protecting it from anarchy and foreign interference while the public heaped abuse on him for doing it.

In trying to assess Washington's motivations, contemporaries and historians looked to his conduct in personal life. Some must have wondered if he sought any personal gain, but no ambition, private vices or profit could ever be found. His behavior in his private life was totally consistent with his public life. According to Jeremiah Smith, Washington "believed that the foundation of national policy can be laid only in the pure and immutable principles of private morality." Everyone who knew Washington attested to his morality, and it was this bedrock virtue that Americans were asked to emulate. Those who observed his private life report that he was a virtuous husband and father (to Martha's children). He was generous to family, friends and strangers, and during the war while he was away from Mount Vernon he even instructed his caretakers to be hospitable to any poor supplicants. Eulogist David Ramsay related that Washington's "private character as well as his public one, will bear the strictest scrutiny. He was punctual in all his engagements—upright and honest in his dealings—temperate in his enjoyments—liberal and hospitable to an eminent degree—a lover of order—systematical and methodical in all his arrangements." Perhaps the most remembered words were those of Henry Lee in his eulogy before Congress when he referred to Washington as "First in war—first in peace—first in the hearts of his countrymen, he was second to none in the humble and enduring scenes of private life... his example was as edifying to all around him. As were the effects of that example lasting... the purity of his private character gave effulgence to his public virtues." Even in his death, Washington displayed the same virtues he had in life. In spite of suffering and pain while he struggled to breathe, he retained his Stoic nature and quietly submitted to his fate. He made sure all his papers were in order, and he expressed thanks and concern to his doctors in that they did their best but should not trouble any longer over him. He was acutely alert until the last moment when he felt his own pulse, closed his eyes and showed his remarkable self-control in passing away.

For the preachers and more religious citizens who eulogized him, Washington was identified not with the New Testament with its message of faith and love but rather with the Old Testament heroes like Solomon, David and especially Moses. For many years prior to the Revolution, colonists thought of America as the new Promised Land abounding in the "milk and honey" of so many natural resources. When King George interfered with their lives and imposed civil and military hegemony, it was relatively easy to equate this with Egypt's Pharaoh who suppressed the Hebrews and subjected them to tyranny. Washington was another Moses, sent by God to deliver the colonists from bondage. As Barry Schwartz tells us, this was not an analogy but rather an historical identity. The likenesses are striking in that both heroes were called from their peaceful surroundings to fight against vastly superior forces with very little chance of winning. Both were subjected to internal conflicts and severe criticisms, and both died just when they delivered their people to freedom. Moses bequeathed his advice in the Book of Deuteronomy while Washington left us the Constitution and his "Farewell Address." Both Moses and Washington were "disinterested" men without ambition for power, who were called from domestic life to save their people. Both men were pious and submissive to a higher authority. These themes are discussed at length by Robert P. Hay in his book *George Washington: American Moses*. Also, preacher Jedidiah Morse in his eulogy delivered in 1800, "A Prayer and Sermon on the Death of General Washington", developed the Moses comparisons with their similar virtues of self-control, dignity, calmness, civility, kindness and most importantly their selection by God who sanctified them in their faithfulness. Whether we in the twenty-first century choose to believe this or not is not important. What is important is that the attributes ascribed to Washington convey the image and significance presented by and to his contemporaries. The dominant attributes focus on his motivation and not so much on his deeds. Washington's virtues were the antithesis of those of other heroes like Napoleon, Catherine or Frederick, who changed their societies to their own purposes with little or no regard for the havoc they reaped. Washington exemplified the virtues of the eighteenth century Whigs by supporting their traditional values and maintaining the structure of their society. He projected a totally different heroism from his European counterparts by fighting a defensive war instead of an aggressive bloody conquest of geographic areas. Most importantly, he willingly and happily revoked the position of power that came to him after eight years of struggle and privation. It was his stunning reversal of fame and position that brought him the admiration of his countrymen and the world. It could be said that Washington's behavior fashioned the American ideal of their heroes. Since that time Americans have come to admire character, morality, humility, hard work, tenacity and resolve in the face of adversity.

One of the most insightful analyses of Washington's character appears in Marcus Cunliffe's 1958 biography; *George Washington: Man and Monument.* He tells us that Washington came from another world, another time and another place, and that to understand him we must appreciate that fact. If we try to humanize him by our current standards, we "run the risk of... losing the essential truth of his personality. He lived in a reticent era... and is better understood within a classical framework than as a man of modern times."[3] While many of the founding fathers ascribed to the virtues of the Roman republic, it was Washington who acted on them as if he himself was a Roman patriot. He embodied both Whig and Roman virtues which contributed to his image of aloofness, modesty and duty. Cunliffe believes that Washington knew he was no ordinary man, and during his times it was perfectly acceptable to be of a higher rank. We know how much Washington liked Addison's play *Cato*, which he saw in his

3   Barry Schwartz, "The Character of Washington: A Study in Republican Culture," *American Quarterly*, vol. 38, no. 2 (Summer 1986) 202-222. Copyright by The American Studies Associates. Reprinted with permission of The Johns Hopkins University Press. 209.

youth at Belvoir with the Fairfax family and many other times in his life. There is little doubt that Cato's valor and civic duty had a profound impact on Washington because he often quoted from it in his correspondence. It was the classical Roman virtue of disinterested patriot that probably prompted his unprecedented act of surrendering his commander in chief commission to Congress at Annapolis in December 1783. There is good reason to consider him as a second Cincinnatus, and Cunliffe reminds us that he "looked and behaved like a classical hero."[4] In his introduction to Cunliffe's book, historian Gordon Wood tells us that "Washington became the symbol of America; he proved in his own person the soundness of the country."[5]

But what about Washington the man? With all the studies of him for over two hundred years biographers and historians are still trying to capture the inner man. Many have judged him in terms of their own times, and perhaps that is why their portraits are so often lacking. Washington is not an easy person to bring to life in human terms because he was not only an eighteenth-century product, he was steeped in seventeenth-century Whig philosophy as well as in the classical culture of the Roman Empire. Historian Marcus Cunliffe refers to Washington as an English gentleman and an honorary Roman citizen. This is not surprising because there was a keen sense of Roman culture in eighteenth-century England witnessed by the plethora of Roman statuary placed in Westminster Abbey memorializing its heroes. We have previously noted Washington's attraction to Addison's *Cato*, which was first performed in London in 1712 and remained a very popular play throughout the 1700s. Even the patriot Nathan Hale borrowed from Addison just before he was hanged as a spy by the British

---

4   Marcus Cunliffe, *George Washington: Man and Monument* (Mount Vernon, Virginia: the Mount Vernon Ladies' Association, 1982 [originally published 1958]) viii. Copyright by Marcus Cunliffe. Used by permission of Dutton Signet, a division of Penguin Group (USA) Inc.
5   Ibid., viii.

in 1776 when he spoke his now-famous words, "I only regret that I have but one life to give for my country." This is taken almost verbatum from Cato's, "What pity is it that we can die but once to save our country."[6]

So many Roman virtues were learned by Americans who were well-educated in the classics. What is surprising is that Washington was not well educated and yet he learned and, more importantly, practiced such virtues as *gravitas* (seriousness), *pietas* (discipline and authority), *simplicitas* (lucidity), *integritas* (poise and serenity) and *gloria* (ambition for civic service).[7]

Duty was another key component, which included a broad spectrum of obligations to family and society. as a whole. Early biographers set Washington in an antique mold and had no hesitation of casting him as a second Cincinnatus who embodied those classic virtues and left the comfort of his private farm life to answer his country's call to defend it from foreign attack. Rome was a society not unlike eighteenth-century Virginia from which the family was a cohesive force that emanated affection, respect and loyalty. Duty and generosity were other classical traits that Washington exemplified in caring for his aging mother and his many brothers, cousins, nephews, nieces and stepchildren. While the Roman influence on Washington is obvious, the Roman state was not the model for the American colonies. Professor Cunliffe reminds us that America became a nation legally before it was one emotionally.[8] Washington's character was similar to many of his contemporaries, but it was wholly different from modern times. His Virginia was closer to Roman society than it was to England's. The founding fathers used Rome as a guide to building

---

6   Marcus Cunliffe, *George Washington: Man and Monument* (Mount Vernon, Virginia: the Mount Vernon Ladies' Association, 1982 [originally published 1958]) viii. Copyright by Marcus Cunliffe. Used by permission of Dutton Signet, a division of Penguin Group (USA) Inc. 130.
7   Ibid., 131.
8   Ibid., 133.

a republic. They saw America as a young country, and even though they were loyal British subjects at first, they wanted to get away from kings and monarchies and create something new. Their revolution was intended to be a reaffirmation of traditional values using the lessons of classical virtues. Perhaps more than anyone else, Washington actually believed it was possible to build a new republican nation, and he never faltered in that belief.[9]

One of the reasons for his fame was not his military or political skills but rather it was his character. He thought, looked and acted like a classical hero, and in so doing he joined the past with the present and the future. As commander in chief he listened to his officers. As President he consulted with his advisers and even tried to gauge the pulse of each part of the diverse and fractional country by taking the time and physical effort to travel throughout New England and the South. But when it came time to make decisions he relied on his vision and common sense. He made the tough decisions like the Jay Treaty and the Bank Act with classical and noble objectivity. He was admired for who he was and what he did. He was so admired that even as early as 1777, John Adams expressed concern for the "superstitious veneration" that the country paid to Washington. Other men such as Aaron Burr, Joseph Reed, Edmund Randolph, Timothy Pickering, Benjamin Rush and even Alexander Hamilton were critical of Washington because of his lesser intellectual qualities. They were probably jealous that someone with such little education could rise above them to the point of being idolized as a god. It was this excessive reverence that gave rise to the fear of monarchial tendencies that accompanied the new office of President. It should be remembered that Washington was the first president in the history of the world not just of the United

9   Marcus Cunliffe, *George Washington: Man and Monument* (Mount Vernon, Virginia: the Mount Vernon Ladies' Association, 1982 [originally published 1958]) viii. Copyright by Marcus Cunliffe. Used by permission of Dutton Signet, a division of Penguin Group (USA) Inc. 133.

States. We can be sympathetic to such fears, but knowing how Washington detested politics and longed for a return to domestic life at his beloved Mount Vernon, it is puzzling to understand the severe criticisms he received from the emerging democratic-republican party under the covert aegis of Thomas Jefferson.

Some critics wonder why he never offered to resign from the military when the war was proceeding so badly in 1777. This issue came to a head with the Horatio Gates and Thomas Conway Cabal at Valley Forge when rumblings and rumors were circulating in Congress about Washington's inabilities to win battles. His critics thought he wanted permanent power, but more sober minds prevailed. Washington always deferred to the Congress and knew the importance of maintaining civil control of the military. His sense of duty and patriotism convinced him that the cause of independence might collapse if he resigned. He had bound his sense of honor with the honor of America, and the two became one and the same. If he was at fault it was because his character allowed himself to symbolize America. His fate would also be the fate of the struggle for independence. As historian Marcus Cunliffe writes, "Having once come to epitomize America, he was trapped in public life as a self-perpetuating candidate. Nothing but death, illness or disgrace could save the commander in chief from re-emerging as the President."[10]

His critics were short-sighted, and instead of complaining about his unassailable position and the idolatry he received, they should have realized that America needed such a leader. He was their symbol of nationalism and in replacing King George he became Saint George in fighting the dragon of monarchial interference and domination. How fortunate that such a man

10 Marcus Cunliffe, *George Washington: Man and Monument* (Mount Vernon, Virginia: the Mount Vernon Ladies' Association, 1982 [originally published 1958]) viii. Copyright by Marcus Cunliffe. Used by permission of Dutton Signet, a division of Penguin Group (USA) Inc. 137.

enjoyed doing his duty, and at the same time he had no real interest in public life or exalted power.

When Washington entered the presidency he was the greatest hero ever to do so. He knew his reputation was at great risk, and he genuinely deplored leaving his domestic life. He knew that he was expected to be all things to all people, and he was intelligent enough to know that the expectations were impossible to fulfill. He had no guidelines for the position and fully appreciated that his every move and decision could establish precedence. By the end of his second term, the President was regarded as a mixture of a monarch, prime minister, party chief and father figure. Yet, he proved to be fallible and the object of abuse in spite of all his sacrifices in winning the war and keeping America from imploding with foreign and domestic strife.

After his retirement in 1797, the conflict with France became so grave that President Adams selected Washington as commander in chief without even discussing it with him. He was expected to raise an army and assume command at the age of sixty-six. Washington was not at all pleased with the summons saying he would go "with as much reluctance from my present peaceful abode, as I should do to the tomb of my ancestors."[11] Yet, he worked to fulfill the task from a sense of profound duty. Fortunately, the crisis passed when Adams appointed a peace commission to Paris.

Looking at Washington's personal life we know he was a refined member of eighteenth-century Virginia. He was fond of good food and wine. For amusement he enjoyed playing cards, fox hunting, horse racing and the theater. He had a dry sense of humor and excelled at dancing, where he was much admired by the ladies.

---

11   GW Papers at the Library of Congress.

He did have an emotional side, but it was well hidden behind his stoic façade. His most noticeable emotions were with his step children, his correspondence with Sally Fairfax and Eliza Powell, his relationship with several of his generals and in particular with his attachment to Lafayette, who he treated as a son. There is no doubt that he was brave, but he was not a dashing figure. He was not an intellectual, but he welcomed intellectuals as his advisers and was smart enough to listen and learn from them. He was unassuming and modest. While the British regarded him as a rebel, he never thought of himself as a revolutionary. He migrated from being a loyal British subject who fought for his country to a man who moved away from the European culture of monarchs and royal trappings. The process was not a sudden or seemingly difficult one of having to make the decision of choosing between two countries. It was a gradual one that evolved over a twenty-year period beginning around 1755. Washington was actually a plain and unassuming man, and this was particularly apparent in his final years when he dressed simply and warmly greeted strangers at Mount Vernon. Visitors remarked how genial he was, but he is known not to have had any very close personal friend. In assuming his roles as general and president, he managed to build a distance that prevented any close personal attachments to a contemporary friend. When he was commanding the Virginia militia early in his career, his officers admired and respected him, but "they looked up to him and not sideways at him."[12] Historians have attempted to humanize Washington by building such myths as the cherry tree and throwing a stone across the Rappahannock River. But such falsehoods meant to embellish his heroics only serve to move us away from the real man. Yes, Washington was a great hero, but his personality was shaped by Enlightenment and classical philosophies that came to the perfect man who was

12   Cunliffe, 128.

born at the perfect time. Call it Providence or mere coincidence, Washington was the "indispensable man."

Here was a man who did what he was asked to do, and whose very strength resided in a sobriety some took for fatal dullness; who in his own person proved the soundness of America. A good man, not a saint; a competent soldier, not a great one; an honest administrator, not a statesman of genius; a prudent conserver, not a brilliant reformer. But in sum an exceptional figure. He died knowing that America was intact, that he as much as any person had assisted in its formation. He had become so merged with America that he is one of the names on the land, the presence in the air. The man is the monument; the monument is America.

—Marcus Cunliffe
George Washington: Man and Monument[13]

---

13   Cunliffe, 145, 146, 147.

CHAPTER 12
Washington and Religion

Of all the dispositions and habits which lead to a political prosperity, religion and morality are indispensable supports.

—President George Washington,
"Farewell Address," September 19, 1796

Religious practices and beliefs played a very important part in the evolution of American political philosophies during the eighteenth century. The movement known as the Great Awakening changed the thinking of many Americans from their previously held views of established churches to a far more independent attitude preached by protestant ministers in the early 1700s. Not unlike the European Reformation of the fifteenth century, the Great Awakening taught that man could find God within himself. He could have a personal relationship with his Creator and not be dependent on organized churches. Man was no longer condemned to sin and hell and dependent on the church for salvation. It followed that man could achieve heaven through good works and also be on the same moral level as those with greater wealth or social standing. As the movement spread throughout the colonies, churchgoers switched from the established Anglican Church to Baptist and Presbyterian churches. The movement had a great impact in Pennsylvania where the Quaker belief in man's "divinity" had a special appeal. A good and responsible citizen was no longer confined to working through the church, but could achieve happiness and salvation by service to neighbors and country. It was a very small step to take from religious freedom and fervor to political freedom from British tyranny. As historian Bruce Chadwick states, "Democracy and evangelism would grow together."[1]

Eighteenth-century Americans aspired to a pious relationship with God, and they saw in Washington a man who deferred his accomplishments to the Creator. Because he never took credit himself alone and expressed thanks and subservience to God, the public was inclined to regard Washington as a pious man. This virtue gave further assurance that he was not an ambitious political figure seeking personal gain or power. Many times Washington extolled the need for public morality in order to achieve a just and happy society, and the basis for such morality was religion. Nonbelievers praised Washington's balanced view of religion and his religious piety. Some believers saw Washington as an instrument of God who was sent to save his country. Not unlike twentieth-century America, the eighteenth century witnessed a growth of secularism, and yet Washington was not reticent in public about acknowledging the blessings of Providence and the importance of attending religious services to seek His guidance. His membership in the Anglican Church and his regular attendance at Sunday services were important indicators of his belief in God, but his reluctance to take communion or publicly refer to Jesus Christ reflected his hesitancy to accept some basic Christian beliefs. Washington was baptized, married and buried in the Christian tradition, but he was never confirmed. He was a member of the Truro Parish Vestry from 1763 to 1784 and served as a church warden. These positions were primarily concerned

1   Chadwick, 110.

with community outreach programs. He attended services on a regular basis before and during the war until he was president at which time he went more frequently being aware of his example to the public. When he was in New York he attended St. Paul's and Trinity churches, and in Philadelphia he went to St. Peter's Church. At his headquarters in Morristown he attended the local Presbyterian Church. On one occasion when he was president, he was indirectly criticized from the pulpit for not taking communion, and he later remarked that he had never been a communicant, and if he were to become one he might be regarded as overly zealous because of his position as president. According to noted historian, Paul Boller, Washington did not take communion because he believed he was not spiritually ready for it, and he would feel a hypocrite if he were to change his practices. On the other hand, Martha Washington was a devoted communicant and Bible reader. However, Washington did like to have grace said at the dinner table.

Like so many other social aspects of his life, Washington learned some basic philosophies at an early age while visiting with his brother and the Fairfaxes at Belvoir where he was exposed to the fundamentals of Stoicism. Again, Paul Boller tells us that Washington adopted the classical virtues of the Deists, which were popular at that time. However, unlike true Deists who believed in a benign Creator who took little further notice in his creation, Washington only borrowed certain of the Deists beliefs. He seems to have had more experience with formal religion than such contemporaries as Jefferson, Franklin and Madison, and his frequent references to Providence, Great Ruler of Events, Author of all Good and Great Creator would indicate that he believed in a God who was very active in the course of human events. Indeed, he said it was this Supreme Ruler who interceded on behalf of America's fight for liberty, and we owed our thanks to Him. Also, we were to graciously accept the Divine Will, and while we could discover and work with Providence to the best of our reason and religion, we would nonetheless accept our destiny and fate. Evidence of these beliefs appears as early as the 1755 expedition with General Braddock in the French and Indian War. When Braddock was killed and Washington's two horses were shot from under him and his coat was riddled with four bullet holes, his diary tells us "of the living by the miraculous care of Providence, that protected me beyond all human expectation... but see the wondrous works of Providence!... the uncertainty of human things!"[2] In August 1778, when Washington had the British on the defensive in New York, he stated, "The hand of Providence has been so conspicuous in all this, that he must be worse than an infidel that lacks faith, and more than wicked, that has not gratitude enough to acknowledge his obligations, but, it will be time enough for me to turn preacher when my present appointment ceases; and therefore I shall add no more on the Doctrine of Providence."[3] In his farewell to his troops in November 1783, Washington declared "the singular interposition of Providence in our feeble condition were such, as could scarcely escape the attention of the most unobserving."[4]

Most historians focus their attention on Thomas Jefferson when it concerns the subject of religious freedom. His notoriety derives from the proposed religious freedom legislation in 1779 when he was Governor of Virginia and the opinions he expressed when he was president. Contrary to existing beliefs that he was non-religious, Jefferson was a member of the Christ Episcopal Church in the new Federal City in 1800, attended services regularly, financially supported the ministry, and actually

2   GW Papers at the Library of Congress.
3   Ibid.
4   Ibid.

opened Federal Buildings on Sundays to different faiths for their worship services.[5] Both Washington and Jefferson held somewhat similar views on Christianity in that they both believed in the teachings of Christ, but they dismissed anything to do with the supernatural or institutional aspects of religious practices. Jefferson had high praise for the teachings of Jesus and wrote two books about his philosophies, *The Life and Morals of Jesus* and *The Philosophy of Jesus*.[6] Whether both men's attitudes influenced each other is difficult to determine, but it does appear that Washington was an early believer in tolerance and religious freedom. In pre-revolutionary Virginia, the Anglican Church was the one legally established church and held a preferential place in society. Baptists and other sects suffered some persecution, and this must have been apparent to Washington. In 1751, Lawrence Washington represented the owners of fifty thousand acres who tried to sell the land to some Pennsylvania Germans, who did not want to pay the obligatory taxes to the Anglican Church. Lawrence was sympathetic to the Pennsylvanians and wrote to the owners, "It has been my opinion, and I hope ever will be, that restraints on conscience are cruel, in regard to those on whom they are imposed, and injurious to the country imposing them."[7] Young George was nineteen at that time and was very close to his mentor half-brother. It is quite likely that he developed his strong beliefs in religious freedom from Lawrence. Whatever the origin may be, there is ample evidence of Washington's position against religious intolerance. He personally expressed his views to Catholics, Universalists, Quakers, Presbyterians, Baptists and Jews. After Washington became president, he participated

5   James H. Hutson, "Thomas Jefferson's Letter to the Danbury Baptists: A Controversy Rejoined", *William & Mary Quarterly*, 3rd series, vol. LVI (October 4, 1999).
6   Noble E. Cunningham, *In Pursuit of Reason: The Life of Thomas Jefferson* (New York: Ballantine Books, 1988) 256.
7   Paul F. Boller, Jr., "George Washington and Religious Liberty", *William & Mary Quarterly*, 3rd series, vol. 17, no. 4 (October 1960) 488.

in twenty-two exchanges with the religious leaders of all the principal religions at that time.

An example of Washington's attitude toward religious tolerance is found as early as 1775 when he gave instructions to Colonel Benedict Arnold before his expedition to Canada which was predominantly Catholic:

> As the Contempt of the Religion of a Country by ridiculing any of its Ceremonies or affronting its Ministers or Votaries has ever been deeply resented, you are to be particularly careful to restrain every Officer and Soldier from such Imprudence and Folly and to punish every Instance of it. On the other Hand, as far as lays in your power, you are to protect and support the free Exercise of the Religion of the Country and the undisturbed Enjoyment and the rights of Conscience in religious Matters, with your utmost Influence and Authority... While we are contending for our own Liberty, we should be very cautious of violating the Rights of Conscience in others, ever considering that God alone is the Judge of the Hearts of Men, and to him only in this Case, they are answerable.[8]

Another example of Washington's attitude toward Catholics was in November 1775 at his headquarters in Cambridge. He learned that preparations were being made by his troops for celebrating Pope's Day which was popular in New England whereby the pope was hanged in effigy. He issued a stern statement to his men saying,

> As the Commander in Chief has been apprised of a design form'd for the observance of that ridiculous and childish custom of burning the Effigy of the pope—He cannot help expressing his surprise that there should be Officers and Soldiers in his army so void of common sense, as not to see the impropriety of such a step at this Juncture; at a time when we are soliciting... the friendship and alliance of the people of Canada, whom we ought

---

8   GW Papers at the Library of Congress.

to consider as Brethren embarked in the same Cause. The defence of the general Liberty of America: At such a juncture, and in such Circumstances, to be insulting their Religion, is so monstrous, as not to be suffered or excused.[9]

Catholic leaders praised Washington for his stand against a practice that ceased from that day forward.

As commander of the Rhode Island militia in May 1775, Nathanael Greene invited John Murray to be chaplain of the brigade. Murray was the founder of the American Universalists and was extremely popular among many New England clergymen except for the orthodox ministers who regarded him as an atheist for some of his more liberal teachings. Washington had barely arrived at camp when he was subjected to a great deal of pressure to remove Murray. On September 17, Washington announced that Murray was to be chaplain of the Rhode Island Regiments and was to be respected as such. He did this for several reasons: first, he wanted the troops to have the chaplains that they chose; second, he wanted an end to bigotry and intolerance; and lastly he did not want religious controversies in his army. To Washington, it was just plain common sense because he also needed as many men as possible, and he did not want religious disputes to upset or divide them.

Washington could have had a serious problem with the Quakers because of their pacifist stand on conscientious objection to war. This became acute when he retreated to Pennsylvania in 1777 and found that the Quakers were equally ambiguous about the Revolution itself. Many patriots, and perhaps Washington as well, suspected the Quakers of being Tory sympathizers, who were secretly helping the British. In spite of his wariness of them, Washington was courteous to the Quaker delegates who visited

---

9   GW Papers at the Library of Congress.

him and wined and dined them at his headquarters. When some Virginia Quakers were drafted into the army and marched two hundred miles to Washington's headquarters in Pennsylvania, he released them because he accepted their exemption from the draft laws. When the Pennsylvania government exiled some Quakers to Winchester, Virginia, some Pennsylvania Quakers tried to send them food and clothing but were only successful when Washington interceded on their behalf. Quaker writers and leaders praised Washington's respect of their beliefs. They felt he understood and appreciated them. In October 1789, the Philadelphia and New York Quakers sent a delegation to Washington to emphasize their support of the Constitution and the new Government as well as their desire for mutual respect and tolerance. They also wanted to end all doubts about their loyalty during the Revolution. Washington replied that the Government should protect everyone's right to worship God in accordance with their beliefs and that this was a citizen's right. He concluded that,

> Your principles and conduct are well known to me, and it is doing the People called Quakers, no more than justice to say, that (except their declining to share with others the burthen of the common defence) there is no denomination among us, who are more exemplary and useful citizens... I assure you very explicitly that in my opinion the conscientious scruples of all men should be treated with great delicacy and tenderness and it is my wish and desire that the laws may always be as extensively accommodated to them, as a due regard to the Protection and essential interests of the nation may justify and permit.[10]

According to historian, Paul Boller, the only time General Washington publicly joined religious liberties with civil liberties was in November 1782, when he was visiting the Dutch Reformed Church in Kingston, New York. In welcoming him, the church

10   GW Papers at the Library of Congress.

leaders stated that their religious rights were intertwined with their civil rights. Washington responded that he was "Convinced that our Religious Liberties were as essential as our Civil, my endeavors have never been wanting to encourage and promote the one, while I have been contending for the other."[11] Later that month he told two Dutch Reformed churches in New Jersey that he believed the protection of civil and religious liberties was "one" of the achievements of the Revolution.

When Washington disbanded the army in 1783, he wrote to the governors of each state saying:

> I now make it my earnest prayer that God… would incline the hearts of the citizens…to entertain a brotherly affection for one another, for their fellow citizens of the United States at large, and particularly for their brethren who have served in the field. And finally that He would most graciously be pleased to dispose us all to do justice, to love mercy, and to demean ourselves, with that charity, humility and pacific temper of mind, which were the characteristics of the Divine Author of our religion, and without an humble imitation of whose example in these things, we can never hope to be a happy nation.[12]

When Washington delivered his first inaugural address to Congress on April 30, 1789, his religious passages comprised one-third of the entire message. Although he never mentioned the word "God" he adhered to the deist custom of using "Providence" and the "Almighty." Excerpts from the deeply religious speech include:

> It would be peculiarly improper to omit in this first official act, my fervent supplications to that Almighty Being who rules over the Universe, who presides in the Councils of Nations and whose providential aids can supply every human defect, that his benediction may consecrate to the Liberties and happiness

11 GW Papers at the Library of Congress.
12 Ibid.

of the People of the United States, a Government instituted by themselves for these essential purposes... No People can be bound to acknowledge and adore the invisible hand which conducts the affairs of Men, more than those of the United States... Since we ought to be no less persuaded that the propitious smiles of Heaven, can never be expected on a Nation that disregards the eternal rules of order and right, which Heaven itself has ordained.[13]

During the Revolutionary War as well as during his presidency, Washington called for special days of prayer and thanksgiving which were originated by both Congresses and himself. These practices were continued by President Adams but were abandoned by President Jefferson who regarded them as too close to the Anglican practices and not in accordance with complete religious freedom.

In May 1789, less than one month in office as president, Washington received an address from the General Committee of Baptists in Virginia. They had been deliberating over the new Constitution and whether it provided enough safeguards for religious freedom especially in light of the severe discrimination they suffered prior to the Revolution. They now wanted to secure the proper amendments with the help of all Baptists and informed Washington of their position. They stated that their liberty of conscience was dearer to them than property or life, and while they supported the new Constitution, they were fearful of future religious discriminations. However, they took solace in the belief that "The plan [Constitution] must be good for it bears the signature of a tried, trusty friend... and... the administration will certainly prevent all oppression for a Washington will preside."[14] Washington thanked them for their efforts in the Revolution and answered their concern about religious freedom:

---

13 GW Papers at the Library of Congress.
14 Ibid.

> If I could have entertained the slightest apprehension that the Constitution might possibly endanger the religious rights of any ecclesiastical Society, certainly I would never have placed my signature to it... if I could now conceive that the general Government might ever be so administered as to render the liberty of conscience insecure, I beg you will be persuaded that no one would be more zealous than myself to establish effectual barriers against the horrors of spiritual tyranny, and every species of religious persecution—For you, doubtless, remember that I have often expressed my sentiments, that every man, conducting himself as a good citizen, and being accountable to God alone for his religious opinions, ought to be protected in worshipping the Deity according to the dictates of his own conscience.[15]

As he was traveling through New England in the fall of 1789, Washington was greeted by the Presbyterian clergy of northern Massachusetts and New Hampshire who praised his statements on religious tolerance. They also expressed appreciation for the passage of the clause prohibiting religious tests for holding office. However, they did profess some disappointment in the absence in the Constitution from any reference to God and Jesus Christ. Washington thanked them for their warm welcome and responded to their comments on God and the Constitution:

> And here, I am persuaded, you will permit me to observe that the path of true piety is so plain as to require but little political direction. To this consideration we ought to ascribe the absence of any regulation, respecting religion, from the Magna Charta of our country... To the guidance of the Ministers of the gospel, this important object is, perhaps, more properly committed— It will be your care to instruct the ignorant and to reclaim the devious—and, in the progress of morality and science, to which our government will give every furtherance, we may confidently expect the advancement of true religion, and the completion of our happiness.[16]

15 GW Papers at the Library of Congress.
16 Ibid.

In August 1790, Washington visited Newport, Rhode Island, which was home to one of the six Jewish congregations in the country. The total Jewish population was estimated at three thousand with other congregations in New York, Philadelphia, Savannah, Charleston and Richmond. They all pledged their support for the new Constitution and like the Catholics, they were thrilled with the abolition of religious tests. The Newport congregation praised the government for its stand on the "blessings of civil and religious liberty which we enjoy under an equal and benign administration." Washington replied in person saying that religious freedom was more than toleration—it was a right. In one of his most notable remarks on the subject he said:

> The Citizens of the United States of America have a right to applaud themselves for having given to Mankind examples of an enlarged and liberal policy; a policy worthy of imitation. All possess alike liberty of conscience and immunities of citizenship. It is now no more that toleration is spoken of, as if it was by the indulgence of one class of people, that another enjoyed the exercise of their inherent natural rights. For happily, the Government of the United States, which gives to bigotry no sanction, to persecution no assistance, requires only that they who live under its protection, should demean themselves as good citizens, in giving it on all occasions their effectual support.[17]

Throughout history Jewish scholars and historians have cited these words as among the most famous in the history of religious toleration.

As commander in chief and president, Washington played a leading role in promoting religious freedom and denigrating bigotry, intolerance and persecution. He used his positions of authority and his immense personal reputation to promote religious harmony in America and as a model for the rest of the world. In

---

17   GW Papers at the Library of Congress.

his first inaugural address we should note that Washington's first priority was his deference to the Almighty:

> In tendering this homage to the Great Author of every public and private good, I assure myself that it expresses your sentiments not less than my own; nor those of my fellow-citizens at large, less than either. No People can be bound to acknowledge and adore the invisible hand, which conducts the Affairs of men more than the People of the United States. Every step, by which they have advanced to the character of an independent nation, seems to have been distinguished by some token of providential agency. And in the important revolution just accomplished in the system of their United Government, the tranquil deliberations and voluntary consent of so many distinct communities, from which the event has resulted, cannot be compared with the means by which most Governments have been established, without some return of pious gratitude along with an humble anticipation of the future blessings which the past seem to presage.[18]

One of the first orders of business in the newly created government was to address amendments to the Constitution concerning individual rights. Madison drafted ten amendments protecting certain personal freedoms and property rights, the most important of which was the First Amendment which provided citizens with freedoms of religion, assembly, speech and the press. It forbid the Congress from making "any law respecting the establishment of a religion or prohibiting the free exercise thereof." Madison, Jefferson and Washington viewed this provision as a prohibition of the government to establish a national church of any denomination. Neither the Congress nor Washington envisioned that such a clause would be construed to prohibit anything religious taking place with federal approval or on federal property. In fact, such an anti-religious interpretation would have incensed Washington and, no doubt, others in

---

18   GW Papers at the Library of Congress.

Congress most of whom were deeply religious members of some established faith. This is evident in their decision on the day following the adoption of the First Amendment, September 25, 1789, when they passed a resolution establishing a day of national prayer and thanksgiving to be selected by Washington. The adopted resolution reads: "We acknowledge with grateful hearts the many signal favors of Almighty God, especially by affording them an opportunity peacefully to establish a constitutional government for their safety and happiness." When he appointed the national holiday of Thanksgiving, Washington said: "It is the duty of all nations to acknowledge the Providence of Almighty God, to obey His will, to be grateful for His mercy, to implore His protection and favour... that great and glorious Being who is the beneficent author of all the good that was, that is, or that ever will be, that we may then unite in rendering unto Him an sincere and humble thanks for His kind care and protection of the people."[19]

As we have previously noted, Washington was praised for his practice of religious toleration. When speaking of the swelling tide of immigration, he said: "If they are good workmen, they may be of Asia, Africa or Europe. They may be Mohamedans, Jews or Christians of any sect, or they may be atheists."[20] Ten years later President Jefferson, who was thought by some to be anti-religious, actually opened up several of the new Federal Office buildings every Sunday to various religious groups for services. He even persuaded the Congress to hire a Catholic priest to serve the Kaskasian Indians. Washington and many of the founders regarded religion as one of the strongest foundations for morality and a civil society. They would have been horrified

19 GW Papers at the Library of Congress.
20 Ibid.

by the thought of removing the free exercise of religion from the public place.

In his last message to Americans on religion and morality, Washington included these words in his Farewell Address:

> Of all the dispositions and habits which lead to political prosperity, Religion and morality are indispensable supports. In vain would that man claim the tribute of Patriotism, who should labour to subvert these great Pillars of human happiness, these firmest props of the duties of Men & citizens. The mere Politician, equally with the pious man ought to respect & to cherish them. A volume could not trace all their connections with private & public felicity. Let it simply be asked where is the security for property, for reputation, for life, if the sense of religious obligation desert the Oaths, which are the instruments of investigation in Courts of Justice? And let us with caution indulge the supposition, that morality can be maintained without religion. Whatever may be conceded to the influence of refined education on minds of peculiar structure— reason & experience both forbid us to expect that National morality can prevail in exclusion of religious principle.[21]

---

21   GW Papers at the Library of Congress.

CHAPTER 13

Washington and Slavery

Washington shared Franklin's views on slavery as a moral and political anachronism. What strikes us as a poignant failure of moral leadership appeared to Washington as a prudent exercise in political judgment... His highest public priority was the creation of a unified American nation... slavery was the one issue with the political potential to destroy the republican experiment in its infancy.

—Joseph J. Ellis
His Excellency: George Washington[1]

As the eighteenth century fades farther and farther into the past, and today's society views history by current standards and conditions, George Washington comes under severe criticism for having owned slaves and for not freeing them and for not speaking out publicly for the abolition of the institution of slavery. On the surface, this appears perplexing considering his own personal abolitionist beliefs and the eventual freeing of his slaves. Even his nobler and frequent moral behavior toward his slaves at Mount Vernon is criticized for being based on economic considerations. In spite of providing housing, food, clothing and medical care and taking a hands-on approach for the welfare of his slaves, he

---

1   Ellis, 350.

nonetheless is measured against social practices existing more than two hundred years later. We are certainly free to criticize, but we should do so with the benefit of understanding the world in which Washington lived, his personal and political conduct and the implications of his every decision. We should also learn how he viewed the entirely new concept of the presidency under the equally new experiment called liberal republicanism. We should know that he never strongly expressed his own convictions publicly on any issue least of all on such an explosive one like slavery. He conducted his presidency quite unlike those of later generations by maintaining silence in order not to interfere with the public's decisions as effected through their representative government. As John Adams stated in later years, "Washington had the gift of silence" and much of his wisdom was gained through listening and learning.[2]

George Washington abhorred the institution of slavery, and he devoted the last six years of his life to resolving his personal dilemma of slave ownership. When he finally determined how and when to free his slaves he did something that no other Founding Father or highly ranked American had ever done; namely, he personally provided an annuity for the housing, food, clothing, education and medical care for those slaves who remained at Mount Vernon as well as for their children. Critics of Washington denounce him for having owned slaves and for not freeing them sooner. However, this is more easily said in today's world than it was to do in the eighteenth-century Atlantic communities when economic, political and social customs were so deeply rooted. It took tremendous courage and financial resources to change centuries-old practices, and it took strong moral convictions to

2   Don Higginbotham, *George Washington Reconsidered* (Charlottesville: University Press of Virginia, 2001) 116.

do what Washington did. To understand this we have to learn the complexities of the issues that existed at that time.

Slavery was introduced to America in the mid-1600s primarily in the south where agriculture required manual labor. It had been practiced for thousands of years over most of the world and had long been sanctioned by Greeks, Romans, Europeans, Kings, Popes and Emperors. When John Washington arrived in Virginia in 1657, he acquired slaves to work on his Potomac River farm, and by the time of his grandson Augustine's death in 1743, the Washingtons owned a total of forty-eight slaves, who were then willed to his children. George inherited ten of these at the age of eleven and no doubt gave the matter very little thought. When George married Martha in 1759, he personally owned forty-nine slaves and assumed the management of Martha's inherited two hundred slaves from her deceased husband's estate. These became known as the "Dower Negroes", who were never legally owned by George but were able to work and intermarry with his slaves. Although Washington was reputed to have been a caring and fair-minded master, there is no recorded evidence of his personal attitude towards slavery until 1774, when he wrote to his former neighbors, the Fairfaxes, in London about the increasing British restrictions that "custom and use shall make us as tame and abject slaves as the blacks we rule over with such arbitrary sway."[3] As biographer James Flexner points out, Washington first acknowledges the dichotomy in the willingness to fight for the kind of rights they themselves were denying their slaves. By implication, Washington was expressing his belief that Negroes were being debased by their environment and not by their inherent nature. This implied that whites could also be debased, and therefore there was no real distinction between owners and slaves. It is unknown whether Washington formed these ideas

---

3   GW Papers at the Library of Congress.

alone or was influenced by Lord Chief Justice Mansfield of the King's Bench who in 1772 ruled that slavery was not supported by English law. Or Washington could have been influenced by his neighbor, George Mason, with whom he composed the Fairfax Resolves in 1774, which included a resolution to stop the "wicked, cruel and unnatural" slave trade. Actually, in 1772, as a member of the House of Burgesses, Washington supported a petition to the King that attacked the slave trade as a "great inhumanity that threatened the very existence of your Majesty's American dominions."[4] In any event, Washington's letter was a very significant step considering that slavery was as old as the human race and existed in most of the known world.

In July 1775, when Washington took command of the Continental Army in Cambridge, he was surprised to find it included a considerable number of free blacks. To the consternation of his generals, he recommended that they be excluded from the army because it would lose the cooperation of the colonies in the south. Black slaves and indentured servants belonging to the rebellious Americans then became political footballs when the British Governor in Williamsburg, Lord Dunmore, declared them free if they left their owners and joined the British army. In fact, seventeen of Washington's own slaves were part of the British fleet which bombarded Mount Vernon in 1781.[5] Dunmore's announcement stunned Washington enough to cause him to change his mind, and he agreed to re-enlist Negro veterans. However, he opposed recruiting slaves in return for their freedom on the grounds that the British would do the same and that this would benefit the British more than the Americans. Nonetheless, it is interesting that Washington's army was the only integrated army in the history of the United States until the

---

4   GW Papers at the Library of Congress.
5   Brookhiser, 178

Korean War in 1951. By 1778, Washington opposed segregation in the Rhode Island regiments and abolished the existence and any reference to a "black corps." In 1779, Congress was so alarmed at the military weakness of South Carolina that they authorized a regiment of three thousand slaves to augment the white recruits who were reluctant to leave their plantations for fear of possible revolts against them. South Carolina never organized the segregated corps.

Another early insight into Washington's disposition toward blacks occurred in 1775 in Cambridge when he received a poem written by the celebrated slave poetess, Phillis Wheatley. He responded by letter praising her talents and inviting her to his headquarters. His cordial salutation to her and his closing with "I am with great respect" were hardly the words of the typical Virginia slaveholder.[6]

While Washington led his army throughout the northern colonies he encountered varying local economies which were not dependent on slave labor. We should keep in mind that his first forty-three years were spent in Virginia, where slaves outnumbered whites and free labor dominated the agrarian economy. Historians agree that the war had an enormous impact on Washington's attitude toward slavery. He learned to respect the Negro soldier's abilities, and for the first time in his life he lived outside Virginia where he witnessed northern business and social lifestyles that included free blacks. There can be no doubt that these experiences influenced him on his path toward emancipation of his own slaves and the need to abolish the institution of slavery.

Washington did not leave the management of his slaves solely to white overseers but took a personal interest in their work.

---

6   Flexner, vol. 4, 116.

Their living conditions were stark, with only the rudimentary materials and tools, but he did provide food, clothing and medical attention. He closely observed their work habits and tried to match their skills with their tasks. He was not known to have interfered in their private lives and made no apparent effort to educate them. He did not sell slaves, but there was one incident when a "Runaway Rogue" named Tom caused so much trouble that Washington sent him back to the West Indies in exchange for food staples. Washington recognized and rewarded talent and actually appointed a black man named Davy to manage one of his four farms for many years. Even before the war Washington had adopted a more humane policy of never selling a slave without his consent, which supposedly never did happen. Also, he would never sell a slave that disrupted a family.[7] Many of Washington's slaves were African, and some even had their tribal markings. Reportedly, they were all treated fairly and very few tried to run away. In his book on slavery, Henry Wiencek includes a photo of a Washington newspaper ad seeking the return of four runaway slaves together with their specific features.[8] Those who gained Washington's trust were given a good deal of personal freedom and responsibility. The most notable was William "Billy" Lee who remained with Washington as his manservant for most of his life from the frontier war years through the Revolutionary War until his illness before the inauguration, when Washington arranged and paid for the best medical attention available in Philadelphia. Lee was even included in Washington's family portraits, and for his lifetime of loyal service Washington willed him an annuity and his freedom. When the capital was moved from New York to Philadelphia in 1790, Washington was unaware of Pennsylvania law which granted the freedom of adult slaves six months after

7   Brookhiser, 182.
8   Henry Wiencek, *An Imperfect God* (New York: Farrar, Straus and Giroux, 2003) 215f.

their owners became legal residents of the state. Attorney General Randolph decided to become a resident there in order to practice law, and he later reminded Washington of the unfamiliar law. Upon learning this, Washington instructed his secretary, Tobias Lear, to remove Martha's "Dower Negroes" back to Mount Vernon in fear of losing them. They belonged to her, and his first loyalty was to her. Also, as slaves were considered "property" he would have been legally responsible for compensating the Custis estate for their loss. When Washington thereby thwarted their possible freedom, he could easily be criticized by today's standards, but such behavior has to be taken within the context of those times. To have done otherwise would have violated his legal responsibilities as custodian and guardian. Offsetting this event was an unknown step taken by Washington that was only discovered in 1970 by biographer James Flexner. In a long-lost letter that he discovered we have learned that Washington quietly left his own black servants in Philadelphia when he retired from the presidency in 1797 knowing they would become free men.[9] This is disputed by historian Henry Wiencek who claims that Flexner mistook "servants" for "slaves" and that Washington did not free any slaves when he retired from the presidency in Philadelphia.[10]

However much he wanted to be "clear" of his own Negroes, he knew that such a move would force him to abandon his planter's world of agriculture. He actually researched the possibility of selling his slaves in 1779, but he refused on moral grounds to do anything that would break up families and have him become involved in the traffic of the "human species." Also, he longed for his beloved Mount Vernon and his study of and devotion to agriculture. After the war, Lafayette proposed a joint effort with

9   Flexner, vol. 4, 9.
10   Wiencek, 315.

367

his mentor to establish a plantation in French Guiana for freed Negroes. Washington expressed support for such a sanctuary, but nothing ever came of it. In 1785, Washington was approached by two British Methodists to petition for Virginia's emancipation of slaves. Again, Washington agreed to lend his support for the measure if it was considered by the General Assembly. The Virginia House of Delegates declined to even consider it, which gives us a good indication of just how deeply entrenched was the practice. At this time, there was no thought of a new Constitution or the type of government that emerged in 1788. If Washington had taken an active part in the Lafayette scheme or emancipation in general, there is little doubt that he never would have been chosen to lead the Constitutional Convention. It follows that he would never have been elected president. He was keenly aware that slavery was a divisive issue, but his principal focus was on holding the colonies together while so many domestic and international forces were tending to pull them apart. By 1786, Washington's attitude toward the institution of slavery is convincingly clear, but he repeatedly emphasized the need for a legal solution that would provide for an orderly transition to emancipation. When he opposed a Quaker effort to free a neighbor's slave who was inadvertently taken to Pennsylvania, he did so on legal grounds. Although criticized for his stand, he wrote to Robert Morris in Philadelphia that "there is not a man living who wishes more sincerely than I do, to see a plan adopted for the abolition of it [slavery]... there is only one proper and effectual mode by which it can be accomplished, and that is by Legislative authority; and this, as far as my suffrage will go, shall never be wanting."[11]

In the deliberations at the Constitutional Convention slavery was such an explosive issue that Georgia and South Carolina threatened to leave the Confederation if it was pursued. However,

11 GW Papers at the Library of Congress.

the best that could be achieved was a compromise on the slave trade that allowed it to continue for another twenty years and then permitted the government to intervene in its extinction in 1808. Washington knew this was just a step to avoid the issue, and he predicted that it would come to plague the country in the coming century. Although little could be done to abolish slavery on the national level, Washington was determined to put his own house in order. In the fall of 1793, he devised a plan to have his Mount Vernon farms leased to tenants who could then hire his slaves. This would enable the blacks to support themselves, and it would provide sufficient income for the Washingtons to live on at the Mansion House. In the plan he stipulated that the Negroes did not convey to the prospective lease holders. His concern was not only for their immediate welfare but for the needs of their children and the elderly who could not work. He believed he had an obligation to support them, but any such plan for emancipation required an enormous cash outlay for years to come. Having devoted most of his adult life to public service while operating a marginal farm, he was not in a strong enough financial position to carry out the self-imposed obligations to his slaves without selling them individually, and this he refused to do on moral principals. Like most other challenges he had faced, Washington was never satisfied with short-term quick fixes, but instead he looked for more lasting fundamental solutions that had future ramifications. The sudden, dramatic freeing of his slaves was not a simple matter either for him or the Negroes in his care. He wanted them to be free, but he also wanted them to be self-sufficient. Also, he did not have ownership of the 153 "Dower Negroes" who legally belonged to the Custis estate. The issue was further complicated by the intermarriage between many of the Mount Vernon slaves and the "Dower Negroes", which meant that it would have been impossible to treat them differently. From the standpoint of the slaves, they had very few skills, and for their entire lives they had little or no incentives to acquire them. Washington was genuinely concerned about their transition to self-reliance, and his farm tenant hiring plan was intended to cushion that transition. As for his personal living, he planned to remain at the Mount Vernon Mansion House where he would employ white and black servants and those who had sufficient skills to manage a household and not a productive farm. He knew his plan would take time to implement and realized it could not be carried out during his presidency because of the uproar it would cause among the republican southerners whom he was already confronting over international and central government issues. He kept the plan secret and only confided it to Arthur Young, the English editor of the prestigious *Annals of Agriculture*. He hoped to find qualified tenant farmers through Young and asked him to keep the matter quiet while they both considered its adoption.

During his presidency there was an incident involving one of Martha's servants, Ona Judge, who ran away to New Hampshire with her mulatto French lover. Martha was particularly upset because she had always treated her as family and was concerned for her welfare not knowing if she had been seduced and abducted. Historian Henry Wiencek sheds light on this incident whereby when Martha told her that she intended to bequeath her to one of her granddaughters, Ona assumed her chances for manumission were ended and therefore planned her escape.[12] Washington did make an effort to have her returned by corresponding with the local customs collector in Portsmouth. When he learned that her return could not be done discreetly, Washington dropped the matter. Several years after returning to Mount Vernon, the much-admired household cook, Hercules, vanished into freedom presumably

12 Wiencek, 321.

from the help of contacts he made while in Philadelphia. Certain of Washington's responsible servants were allowed considerable freedoms in Philadelphia, and they undoubtedly mixed with the "free blacks" in that state. They observed their freedoms and learned of methods to escape their bondage, particularly through the Quaker-led abolitionists.

When the 1793 tenant farmer plan confided to the British agriculturalist, Arthur Young, did not materialize by the end of his presidency in 1797, Washington devised another plan. He still owned large tracts of land in the Ohio and Kanawha River areas and thought their sale would produce sufficient cash to reinvest in income-producing securities. Such funds would provide the necessary income for Martha and him and would also allow him to care for the slaves he planned to free. Approximately twenty-three thousand acres were appraised for around $450,000, and he put them on the market. Unfortunately, he never received cash offers, and the one contract he signed included little cash up front and future payments he never received. By the summer of 1799, he decided that time would not allow him to complete his desired plan. Although he was in excellent health, he seems to have sensed that his "glass [was]… almost run." He was always aware that his ancestors and siblings were not long-lived, with none of them ever reaching beyond fifty years. At the age of sixty-seven he believed it was time to draw up a will, and after personally writing twenty-eight pages of instructions he signed it on July 9, 1799. It was only after his death on December 14, 1799, that he was able to fulfill his goal of freeing his slaves. But he did more than that, he provided for the welfare of his own 123 slaves and Martha's 153 slaves for the rest of their lives including that of their children.[13] His will contained fourteen separate items, and he placed instructions about his slaves high

13   Higginbotham, 116; Wiencek, 354

on the list at item two. He directed that all of the Mount Vernon slaves should be set free upon Martha's death—something she did one year later while still living. He wanted the older slaves and parentless children to be fed and clothed and taught to read and write. He also wanted them trained in some useful skills so they could become productive and self-reliant. He forbid any slave to be sold. Lastly, he established a trust fund for his estate to fulfill his wishes and even underlined in emphatic terms that his instructions regarding the welfare of his slaves should be carried out without "delay, neglect or evasion." Martha and his family faithfully followed his directions, and the last check to the surviving Washington and Custis slaves and their children was drawn from the fund in 1833.

CHAPTER 14
Washington's Relevancy Today

Evolution in man during recorded time has been social rather than biological: it has proceeded not by heritable variations in the species, but mostly by economic, political, intellectual, and moral innovation transmitted to individuals and generations by imitation, custom, or education. here the initiative individual— the 'great man,' the 'hero,' the 'genius'—regains his place as a formative force in history... he grows out of his time and land, and is the product and symbol of events as well as their agent and voice; without some situations requiring a new response his new ideas would be untimely and impracticable. When he is a hero of action, the demands of his position and the exaltation of crisis develop and inflate him to such magnitude and powers as would in normal times have remained normal and untapped. But he is not merely an effect. Events take place through him as well as around him; his ideas and decisions enter vitally into the course of history.

—Will and Ariel Durant
The Lessons of History[1]

---

1   Will and Ariel Durant, *The Lessons of History* (New York: Simon and Schuster, 1968) 34. Copyright 1968 by Will Durant and Ariel Durant. Copyright renewed by Monica Ariel Mihell and Will Durant Easton. Reprinted by permission of Simon & Schuster Adult Publishing Group.

Whether George Washington was a great military, political or social leader of his times may be researched and debated for years to come, but there is no dispute that he was one of the greatest leaders in the history of the United States. We should then study how a seemingly ordinary man became such an extraordinary leader. After all, he never had the kind of formal education that his peers enjoyed, and he never traveled outside colonial America for his entire life except for a very brief trip to the Caribbean to accompany his ailing half-brother Lawrence. He never had the legal or military training normally required to assume the enormous responsibilities he assumed. He never had the religious education that is usually associated with high moral values and convictions. In brief, he was a self-made man who possessed an abundance of many virtues including those of common sense, ambition and discipline to persevere in a vision he deemed as noble and necessary. Other founders may have shared a similar goal of personal freedom, but Washington emerged from life on a Tidewater farm to lead a small, heterogeneous agrarian society against the greatest of odds into an entirely new democratic and republican nation. Washington's determination and leadership under the constant threat of losing his life, possessions and sacred honor were strong enough to give birth to a country that became the most successful experiment in all of history.

One of the most celebrated business executives of modern times has been Jack Welch, retired chairman and chief executive of the General Electric Company. In a recent article he wrote for the *Wall Street Journal*, Mr. Welch shared his insight into the ingredients that make for outstanding leadership. To put Washington into today's context we should examine how he measures up to these standards:[2]

2   Jack Welch, editorial, *Wall Street Journal*, October 28, 2004.

Is he real:

- Does he make hard decisions?
- Does he hold unpopular positions?
- Does he stand tall for what he believes?
- Does he have self-confidence and conviction?
- Is he bold and decisive and able to act quickly?
- Does he reach people on an emotional level with words and actions that motivate them?
- Does he lead with authority and energize his followers?

Does he have vision:

- Can he see around corners?
- Can he anticipate the radically unexpected?
- Does he have the ability to see new challenges lurking just out of sight?
- Does he see a goal unseen by others?

Who does he choose for advisers:

- Does he surround himself with people smarter than himself?
- Do his advisers have the character to disagree with him and each other?
- Does he use sources from within and without?
- Does he challenge assumptions?

Does he get back on the horse:

- Does he learn from his mistakes?
- Does he revive from mistakes and resume with speed, conviction and confidence?
- Can he recover from a crisis?

If we look at Washington's military and political life we can see many examples of why he was so effective. From the siege of Boston to the retreat from Long Island and the attack on Trenton, we see hard decisions. Certainly, suppression of the Whiskey Rebellion and signing the Jay Treaty were unpopular positions. His decision to lead the fight for independence showed his willingness to stand tall for what he believed. His lightning move from Trenton to Princeton demonstrated an ability to strike quickly and boldly. His personal appeal to the retiring enlisted militia before Trenton and his words of encouragement at Newburgh touched all spectrums of his army from the common soldier to the highest officer. His putting himself at great risk at Princeton and Monmouth showed how he energized his followers. The British Proclamation of 1763 and the subsequent Intolerable Acts culminating with the Port of Boston closure and occupation all gave Washington a sense of the challenges that lay ahead. His investment in western lands and the sense of America's potential indicated a vision of the future that few contemporaries possessed. His calling for a convention to address the inadequate Articles of Confederation also showed a sense of the future. In forming a new government he surrounded himself with some of the most intelligent people available, realizing that he needed expert advice from those who had superior educations and skills. Further, he listened to them and valued their opinions. He put up with internal dissensions and tried to follow the best course without disrupting the fledgling nation. He could sense the fragility of the new republican experiment and kept his eye on the ultimate goal of stability and prosperity through peace. He was almost annihilated in New York and was defeated several times around Philadelphia. He regarded losses as temporary setbacks like the battle of Germantown, but he learned from his mistakes. He faced treachery at West Point and Valley Forge and constant loss of troop morale for most of the war. He listened to his officers and bowed to their advice when it was convincing. He recognized opportunities and was able to reverse his own plans such as Yorktown. He was responsible for an army that was inadequately fed or supplied by an ineffective Congress. He initiated the Constitutional Convention and presided over it with impartiality. He was maligned during his presidency for his stand against French intrigues and was accused at other times for behaving like a monarch. He stood his ground by signing the Jay Treaty knowing it would bring abuse and criticism. Yet, through all these setbacks, he never faltered in his convictions about the potential future of the United States. Even his anti-Federalist political foes urged him to run for a second term because they knew he represented the best chance for national survival. He sacrificed his personal desire to retire at the age of sixty-one to his beloved Mount Vernon and chose instead to keep working for national unity.

Still more criteria for effective leadership are discussed by noted author John C. Maxwell in his 1999 book on the subject, *The 21 Indispensable Qualities of a Leader*. Mr. Maxwell points out the important distinction between understanding leadership and being able to lead. The key to successful leadership is personal character, and this comes from inside each of us. His list of twenty-one attributes includes:[3]

<u>Character</u>: Perhaps Washington's greatest virtue as attested to by his subordinates, his peers and his superiors in all phases of his life. This was evident in his public service in the military and as president as well as in his private life. More than two hundred eulogies speak of his outstanding character.

---

3   John C. Maxwell, *The 21 Indispensable Qualities of a Leader* (Nashville, Tennessee: Thomas Nelson Publishers, 1999) 4-154. Reprinted by Permission. All rights reserved.

Charisma: Washington's stature and bearing were very much a factor in his reputation. He was generally serious in appearance and was always meticulously dressed. His countenance was graced with a pleasant and warm smile, but he learned from an early age to keep a distance from those around him which promoted a sense of authority. He gave the immediate impression of someone in charge, and his deportment confirmed that in fact he was.

Commitment: It is interesting to see how Washington changed from a loyal British subject to a revolutionary American. He accepted most of the British intrusions on his private life until the British hegemony became clear to him with the closing of the Port of Boston in 1774. He seems to have decided that a war for independence was inevitable long before his peers were willing or able to grasp the consequences of recent events. He offered to personally arm one thousand men to march to Boston well before his appointment as commander in chief, and as soon as he was charged with leading an army he never looked back. Through defeats and bitter disappointments he remained committed to the Cause for freedom.

Communication: There are two basic types of communication for a leader—from above downwards and from below upwards. Washington practiced both. As commander in chief he formed a War Council with which he met daily. He constantly asked his generals for their opinions, and once a decision was reached he used the chain of command to disseminate it. However, he also used a hands-on policy and would personally admonish troops through stern disciplinary directives. He would invite the officers of the day to dine with him so he could obtain feedback from the lower ranks. When morale was low at Trenton and Valley Forge he would speak plainly and directly to his men to inspire them with words that went directly to their souls. He visibly shared in their sufferings and despair by riding alone through their camps and encouraging their spirit to persist in the battle. He gave his men a goal of a brighter tomorrow and the prospect of freedom and future prosperity. Washington realized that the best way of defeating the British was to gain support at home with local townspeople and their state and local governments. He constantly visited legislators and governors and invited them into his quarters at Morristown. He asked them for advice and always thanked them in his own handwriting for measures they adopted to support the war. He was a master politician without claiming to be one. He would send them memos on the war's progress and would sometimes actually share military directives with them. He encouraged his officers to visit state capitols. As president, he listened to his advisers, and when greater differences started to appear in his second administration, he asked for further clarity on the subject and only then would he come to a decision. When he was first president, he took two unbelievable journeys, one through the north and the other nineteen hundred miles through the south realizing how important it was to not only learn more about the country he led but also to allow the American citizens to see first hand and feel a part of the new nation. These were not soft, cushy vacations but were bone-jarring horse and carriage trips over crude roads and trails not meant for a man in the sixtieth year of his life. Finally, as a communicator he gave us his Farewell Address to ponder for the rest of time.

Competence: Just before his daring attack on Trenton, Washington had lost 90 percent of his men through sickness, death and short-term discharges. Rural Americans were turning into loyalists, and some were enlisting with the British. This was partly due to incompetence by the mostly ill-trained militia which

Washington was acutely aware of. He knew he needed the morale boosters at Trenton and Princeton, but after defeats by the British throughout 1777, he knew he needed greater competence. Valley Forge provided the necessary six-month reprieve to build and train an army to reach that level of competence. As his army grew in skills acquired under the direction of von Steuben, the newly-found competence attracted sufficient recruits to successfully challenge their veteran enemy. Again, Washington took a hands-on approach to the entire project. He designed log huts, devised health codes and personally participated in most every aspect of the effort. He even designed uniform insignias and marks for ranks in establishing a chain of command. It was a daily routine of practice, practice and more practice. Improvements in drill and discipline increased the level of competence until he saw the degree of excellence he desired. As John Maxwell states "when considering competence, there are only three types of people: 1) those who can see what needs to happen, 2) those who can make it happen and 3) those who can make things happen when it really counts."[4] There is no doubt that Washington exemplified all three of these talents.

Courage: We have already read about Washington's courage, but it should be remembered that we are not only talking about military courage but political and moral courage as well. We should note that Washington's moral courage was demonstrated in his treatment of enemy prisoners. The British and the Germans were particularly brutal in their slaughter of Americans on Long Island and New York. The Hessian General Johann Rall was seen mercilessly killing Americans surrendering at Fort Washington. Yet, in spite of the harsh treatment meted out to his men, Washington ordered that his prisoners should be treated

---

4   John C. Maxwell, *The 21 Indispensable Qualities of a Leader* (Nashville, Tennessee: Thomas Nelson Publishers, 1999) 4-154. Reprinted by Permission. All rights reserved. 35.

humanely to show the world the kind of democratic society we were striving for. In fact, when the Hessian prisoners from Trenton were sent to the Lancaster area of Pennsylvania, they were amazed at their humanitarian treatment. Approximately one-fourth of them were so gratified that they elected to remain there after the war. Washington epitomized military, political and personal courage. He did not take the politically correct action. He led by vision, conviction and courage.

Discernment: This involves getting to the bottom of things, and it requires sifting through good information and bad information and having the intuition to determine which is accurate. Washington faced many instances where conflicting information and opinions made it difficult to arrive at a decision or solution to a problem. He certainly faced a dilemma at Valley Forge when he learned of Conway's letter and the rumor of dissatisfaction with his command. Rather than relying on rumor, he faced the problem head on by confronting Conway. The insubordination ended, and its resolution left Washington in an even stronger position. Another critical incident was the Newburgh Controversy that came perilously close to an uprising by the officers in early 1783 in demanding their promised salaries and pension. Washington was not certain of all the intrigues, but again he grasped the problem and hit it head on by taking charge of the situation. His memorable speech to his officers about growing gray and nearly blind in the service of his country was just the kind of message his unsettled officers needed to stop the insurgency in its tracks. Discernment is a combination of information and intuition, and Washington had both because he was a good listener and developed varying channels of information.

Focus: This requires priorities and concentration. During the war Washington had to learn to balance his focus on assuming a defensive strategy to one of taking offense risks when the opportunity presented itself. He was basically more inclined to an offensive strategy, but for the first three years he realized that he did not have the manpower, training or resources to take the offense against a vastly superior force. Even when the British decided to confine themselves to New York in the north while they tried to overrun the south, Washington was eager to attack the city. He listened to his officers and elected to remain outside the city defending New England from a possible British assault. He learned to focus on the need to stay in the field, realizing that holding large pieces of land was not important. Survival was more important than conquests. As president he focused on the need for unity and shaped his policies to achieve that goal. Both in war and in his presidencies he had to avoid the noise, static and pressures of differing opinions, and one of his great strengths was his ability to stay focused and to concentrate on his strengths and goals.

Generosity: Washington exhibited personal generosity with his humane treatment of enemy prisoners or allowing Benedict Arnold's wife to go unharmed in spite of her duplicity or even in granting Citizen Genet asylum in the United States after he had so brazenly tried to undermine the President. However, the greatest example of Washington's generosity surely was his devotion to his country. From entering the House of Burgesses in 1759 until his death in 1799, Washington was either in official or semi-official service to his country. Call it generosity or devotion, he was dedicated to the Cause of independence and the founding of a new nation. Not everyone agreed with his methods, such as suppression of the Whiskey Rebellion or creating the Bank of the United States or signing the Jay Treaty, but he had a vision for the future that few of his contemporaries had, including those who signed the Declaration of Independence. Financially, he was generous to his country for not accepting a salary for his war command. While away from Mount Vernon during the war he even directed his managers there to treat all supplicants generously. He paid for the education of his twenty-two nieces and nephews, and most all of his generosities were done on condition of anonymity. During and even after his presidency he welcomed, dined and housed hundreds of guests and perfect strangers mostly at his own expense. He was generous with the time he devoted to his family and in managing the Custis estate. Even in death, he was generous to the slaves he willed to be free in that he voluntarily assumed responsibility for their welfare and that of their children. In spite of the distance he maintained from others, Washington was a caring and generous person.

Initiative: Successful leaders know what they want and push themselves to attain it. Willpower is the essential ingredient, and if we know anything about Washington it was his indomitable will. Losing the war was out of the question for him, and losing the nation afterwards was equally unacceptable. He was determined to keep the sectional rivalries and political differences from splitting the nation. From his war experiences he knew the country needed a much stronger government, so he took the initiative in calling for a Constitutional Convention. Prior to the war, he took the initiative with George Mason in drafting the Fairfax Resolves which were a forerunner to the First Continental Congress. As president he adopted policies that were designed to keep the country at peace in spite of the republican cries for active support of foreign entanglements with France. In his administration, he made decisions that may have been mistakes, but he usually learned from his mistakes. Great leaders often do make mistakes, but in the words of President John F. Kennedy, "There are risks and costs to a program of action, but they are far less than the long-range risks and costs of comfortable inaction."[5]

Listening: As commander in chief in the war Washington listened to his generals, and while he did not always agree with them, he did follow their advice when it was convincing and the will of the majority. But he also listened to junior officers and heard the pleas from the trenches. He obeyed the wishes of Congress, but he drew the line when it came to military tactics and decisions. As president, Washington surrounded himself with great minds and depended on their collective wisdom and expertise. He recognized his own shortcomings, particularly in finance. At first, he regarded his advisers as secretaries to carry out his policies. As their differences grew, he called for more frequent meetings and solicited their opinions. In effect, he grew with the job and became an even better listener. Certainly when it came to writing his annual messages to Congress and his two farewell addresses, he relied on his closest advisers, James Madison and Alexander Hamilton. Although he did not always agree with them, he trusted them to transform his thoughts into more precise and eloquent prose and listened carefully to their suggestions. Washington's frequent silence enabled him to be a good listener.

Passion: Washington's desire and will combined to form a passion that outweighed his skills as a military tactician. Although he was never trained in the martial arts or the science of warfare, he is often viewed as a professional soldier. True, he did have experience under Braddock and Forbes and took command of the Virginia militia, but he really had no professional training when compared to the British or Germans. Sheer willpower and passion for his work enabled him to compensate for inadequate skills as

5   John C. Maxwell, *The 21 Indispensable Qualities of a Leader* (Nashville, Tennessee: Thomas Nelson Publishers, 1999) 4-154. Reprinted by Permission. All rights reserved. 70.

were demonstrated in his disastrous losses in Long Island and New York. But again, he learned from his mistakes and had the desire to improve. At the end of his first administration, he longed for retirement to Mount Vernon, but the passion of his mission to preserve the fledgling nation kept him at the helm for another term. As president during his second administration, in the face of increasing criticism from the republican press, Washington's desire to see the country through the potential disaster of another war kept the necessary peace. More importantly, he was able to impart that desire to his officers and troops.

Without Washington's enthusiasm for the ultimate Cause, it is doubtful that the war could have been won.

Positive Attitude: Washington was an optimist who believed in himself and the Cause for independence. One of the best illustrations was at Germantown where he was defeated, and yet he told Congress that it was only a setback. He saw something few others did. He saw that victory was in his sights and only poor weather had intervened. He saw the possibilities of his men. He saw improvement, and used his positive attitude in resolving to form an organized army at Valley Forge. He remained an optimist and did not allow a bad situation to demoralize him or his men. He could have easily fallen prey to self-pity considering the conditions of his ragged army and the recalcitrant Congress that repeatedly failed him and his troops. He must have instinctively known that he had to portray confidence in order to inspire his neglected and defeated army. He never wavered and ultimately prevailed by keeping a positive mental attitude.

As management consultant John Maxwell suggests, a mind must be "conditioned" to win, and it would appear that Washington's was so conditioned.

Problem Solving: When Washington was heading to New York for his first inauguration he said he felt like a prisoner going to his execution. In other words, he knew he would encounter problems. Judging from his reaction to the problems of party politics and outrageous criticisms hurled at him, he must have wondered why he allowed himself to be in that position, and he even expressed a preference for the peace and tranquility of his Mount Vernon farm to that of president. He had no precedent to guide him, and yet he took on the challenge. He could have ignored the early problems of the war debts or the anarchies of Shays' Rebellion and the Whiskey Rebellion. He could have buried his head in the sand with the Genet affair or the Edmund Randolph intrigue. Instead, he chose to accept these unforeseen challenges and face them straight on. Washington had that innate ability to identify the critical issues from merely the important ones, and he tried to solve them through negotiation and compromise. He saw the big picture and tried not to get mired in the smaller obstacles. He kept his eye on the long-term objectives and rejected short-term solutions that he regarded as temporary. One of the best illustrations of this was when General Knox asked Washington to just show up at Springfield and use his influence to quell Shays and his men. Washington replied that influence is no substitute for sound government and elected not to go. He let the militia clear out the insurgents.

Relationships: One of the extraordinary qualities of Washington was his aura of authority framed by his stature and serious countenance, and yet he exhibited great compassion for his men. He demanded excellence and never failed to compliment his troops. He gave them direction by leading them and giving them hope. This was particularly true at Trenton and Princeton and later at Valley Forge. Even when he was not directly involved like

South Carolina and most of the southern campaign, he praised Generals Greene and Lafayette. Before the treachery at West Point, Washington was sympathetic to Benedict Arnold in his controversy with Congress, and for his bravery he rewarded him with the ill-fated post at West Point. His quality of compassion was evident as early as the French and Indian War when his men gave him such a warm-hearted farewell. He obviously touched the minds and hearts of even the common soldier when he pursued their needs at Valley Forge. Again, at Newburgh he spoke of helping his officers to gain what was promised to them by an ineffective and lethargic Congress. In short, he put his men first, and that was how he gained their loyalty.

Responsibility: It could be said that Washington first showed his responsible nature when he offered to deliver Governor Dinwiddie's message to the French in 1753 at the age of twenty-one. He assumed a dangerous assignment not knowing how he would be treated by either the French or their Indian allies. When he went back again the next year with his regiment and came very close to being shot and then drowned, his bravery and responsibility became firmly established in Virginia and even abroad when his journals were published. Washington chose the military life for achieving a place in society, but he used self-discipline and a strong will for excellence to achieve his goal. His command of the British-American Virginia Regiment was noted for its precision, dress and horsemanship, and he raised its reputation to a very high level through ceaseless efforts. Washington had previously assumed a great responsibility by taking over the management of Mount Vernon in 1752 upon the death of his half-brother, Lawrence. Working tobacco farms in Virginia were notoriously unviable, but he was determined to avoid the financial pitfalls of his neighboring plantations. As a member of the House of Burgesses he led the Virginia delegates with the Fairfax Resolves and at the Williamsburg meetings with his support of the beleaguered Bostonians. He felt he was not experienced enough for command of the American army, but he willingly accepted that awesome responsibility. Some say he really wanted that position because he had worn his uniform there. Perhaps he did or perhaps he just wanted to play a major role in the conflict, but in either case he agreed to put his life and everything he owned on the line for a cause he believed in. As the war grew effort failed and morale ebbed with defeats, deaths and sickness, Washington always took responsibility. He was determined to finish the task, and whether it was for his reputation or his beliefs we do not know, but it was probably for both. And if he did not have the skills to get the job done, he read military books to learn from and implored his officers to do the same. And he hired some professionals like von Steuben and others to teach them new skills. He drove himself, and his men followed.

Security: If Washington was ever insecure in his positions as commander in chief or as president, he never revealed it to the public. His very nature as an authoritative person who tended to take control would not allow for insecurity. Also, he knew the importance of showing security in order to instill trust and confidence in others, whether it was for his soldiers, officers, advisers or Congressional superiors. Especially at Valley Forge when the so-called Conway Cabal tried to undermine his position as commander in chief, Washington had enough personal security to face the potential threat coming from critics within the army as well as from without in Congress. As President, he came under heavy verbal attacks from the French and the republican Americans for refusing to become embroiled in their increasingly bloody and anarchistic revolution. He was even termed a spy in the employ of the British and a "traitor" by editor Bache in his Francophile *Aurora* newspaper, but Washington had the personal strength of his security to withstand the outrageous attacks by simply stating that Bache, "has a celebrity in a certain way, for his calumnies are to be exceeded only by his impudence, and both stand unrivaled." When the accusations were found to be based on British forgeries, Washington made sure the documents were placed in the State Department archives.[6] Another instance of the security he possessed was his break with Thomas Jefferson in 1796. Washington had always trusted Jefferson and acknowledged his integrity in spite of their growing political differences. Jefferson kept his support of the *Aurora* and his criticisms of Washington quite secret. When Jefferson left the cabinet in 1793, both men tried to maintain their mutual respect for each other, and Washington always dismissed rumors of Jefferson's personal attacks. But by 1796, Washington was made aware of Jefferson's role in the Bache attacks, and when Jefferson learned he had, he wrote to assure him that he had no part in the matter. Washington responded with the final rejoinder that marked the end of their relationship,

> As you have mentioned the subject yourself, it would not be frank, candid, or friendly to conceal, that your conduct has been represented as derogatory from that opinion I had conceived you entertained to me... the accusations that could scarcely be applied to a Nero, a notorious defaulter; or even to a common pick-pocket... my answer invariably has been that I had never discovered anything in the conduct of Mr. Jefferson to raise suspicions, in my mind, of his sincerity.[7]

These are not the words of someone who is insecure in his position as president.

6   Ellis, *His Excellency*, 402.
7   GW Papers at the Library of Congress.

Self-Discipline: Washington must have developed an orderly disciplined routine early in life as a teenager. His ambition for self-improvement, self-reliance and social standing required a disciplined approach for success and no doubt accounted for his earning a surveyor's license at age seventeen. His first love was a military position, and his appointment as the officer in charge of Virginia's militia at age twenty-two was another indication of his bent towards a disciplined life. Certainly, as commander in chief he appreciated the need for discipline among his newly formed army, and as he was one to lead by example there is little doubt that he practiced self-discipline on a daily basis. But he also needed to live by priorities and staying focused on them in all aspects of his life. Running a complex plantation while leading an army or presiding over a government, all required enormous self-discipline. Historians marvel at how he accomplished all he did and still had the time and discipline to write over 135,000 letters, diaries, memos and directives, especially those during the war years. Just communicating with Congress would have been totally time-consuming, but he acquired the discipline early in life as a surveyor and frontier journalist which served him well in later years.

Servanthood: This virtue was best described by President John Kennedy in his inaugural address when he said, "Ask not what your country can do for you but rather what you can do for your country." Leadership requires a desire to serve without self-promotion and a sense of caring for those around you without regard to rank or position. The best example of Washington's attitude toward service was his acceptance of command without pay. Also, at Valley Forge he put the needs of his men at the top of his priorities, and they responded accordingly. As historian George Bancroft stated about the suffering men at Valley Forge, "love of country and attachment to their General sustained them under their unparalleled hardships; with any other leader, the army would have dissolved and vanished."[8] Washington's devotion to the American Cause for independence and liberty was the ultimate motivation for devoting more than forty years of his life to that purpose. He even exhibited that same desire for service to his country for the five years he served British America in the French and Indian War. Civic service was part of the Enlightenment that he inherited from his forefathers, and as we discussed in his character, he did this not for personal power but because of sense of duty. It could be said that his greatest service was not in the war, but rather in his unselfish and constant efforts to protect the country and cause he fought for. He shunned glorification and dismissed monarchial power. He sacrificed a life of personal ease even after he earned it to create a nation he loved.

Teachability: It is said that when he was commander in chief, Washington learned from his mistakes. This was definitely true after the disasters on Long Island and New York. From that point on, Washington did not allow the enemy to outflank him nor did he leave command to his subordinates, especially to junior officers as he did on Long Island. Also, he quickly learned that the Continental Army and the militia in particular were no match for the superior British veterans. He knew he had to organize a well-drilled army made up of enlistees with a longer-term commitment. He also learned that he had to fight a defensive war even though his preference and personal drive were strongly inclined toward an offensive one. In brief, Washington recognized his shortcomings and was willing to adopt new strategies. He was teachable and even welcomed the opportunity to learn from more experienced soldiers like von Steuben. By nature, he challenged

8   George Bancroft, *History of the United States* (Boston: 1878) vol. VI, 333.

himself as was evident in his volunteering as an aide to British General Forbes in the campaign to recapture Fort Duquense in the French and Indian War. He overcame his rejection as an officer and claimed to want the assignment merely for the experience of learning. Little did he realize that he would be fighting some of these same men seventeen years later in the Revolution.

Vision: According to John Maxwell, vision is the inward power that drives leaders who, in turn, inspire followers. It requires a desire for excellence that cannot be taught but comes from a person's past and from those around him. It is far-reaching and must serve others to be successful. Vision attracts and unites people who share in a leader's vision. A visionary is not content with mediocrity or the *status quo*. It is a burning desire to change things for the better, but it also requires assistance from others who share the dream and can rarely be done alone. Washington went into the War for Independence as a Virginian, but he emerged from it as an American who had a vision for the future of his country. He did not rest on his considerable laurels, but instead he worked to make the country strong enough to survive its inherent weaknesses and its serious challenges from abroad. He clearly had a vision of America's potential greatness, and it was a far-reaching vision that could see beyond the petty differences and political party strife. His concern over British soldiers in the western lands and French disruptions in American trade and politics was real. The emerging Democratic Republicans even with such intellectual leaders as Jefferson and Madison could not see what Washington saw. It took them another twenty years and the War of 1812 to face what Washington had feared and predicted. His critics did not understand the importance of peace in 1795 and the benefits of British naval protection that the Jay Treaty provided, not to mention the final withdrawal of their troops in the west. Most of his contemporaries envisioned thirteen separate states going forward, but Washington envisioned one nation. It was his vision that made him exceptional.

Throughout the course of this book certain key episodes are included in the life of Washington that provide illustrations of most of his attributes. Also included are some of his weaknesses and questionable actions. We have noted his temper, his tendency for control and his sensitivity to criticism. His poorest behavior was probably during the Forbes campaign when he questioned his superiors' judgment and was outspoken about their likely defeat. Also, he seems to have been ungrateful to his initial sponsor, Governor Dinwiddie, but this we can attribute to inadequate support while he was fighting in the wilderness and also his resentment in not obtaining a regular British army commission. Others criticize him for allegedly buying more than his fair share of the western land bounties that were offered to veterans of the French and Indian War. Washington defended his acquisitions as legal and that he took an active interest in them after others showed no interest. He put his life on the line for them and twice was nearly killed in the process. Also, when Parliament declared the Proclamation of 1763 nullifying all prior government deeds and contracts to the western lands, it was Washington who successfully overturned their actions. Washington never proclaimed to be an authority on many aspects of his military or political life, and in fact, his modesty and his lack of erudition as a public speaker contributed to his relative silence. He never claimed credit for his military victories or accomplishments as president but always thanked his Creator and the men around him for whatever successes he experienced. Whether the times created the man or whether Washington determined the times, one cannot help but admire him for his courage and sacrifices and his extraordinary leadership at such a critical moment in history. Surely, he was the one indispensable Founding Father who should be remembered for giving America the freedoms we enjoy today.

In 1932, Congress authorized the printing of one million copies of the famous Lansdowne Portrait by Gilbert Stuart of Washington to be distributed to public schools throughout America. It was to honor the two-hundred-year anniversary of Washington's birth. I very well remember the portrait hanging in my grade school and seeing it in other schools as well. We learned about Washington and American history in high school and college in the 1950s, but that seems to have changed. Today, we not only do not honor him, but he has been removed from the classroom altogether. Students, and sadly many teachers, have discontinued courses in American history owing in part to "political correctness" on the pretext that some of the early founders were slave holders or were "rich" or merely were dead Anglo-Saxon Americans. Much of this attitude can be ascribed to the "Baby Boomer" generation that matured in the nineteen sixties and seventies when Vietnam, race riots and Watergate made everything American look suspect to them. As the two major political parties moved farther to the right and left, many went so far as to proclaim belief in communism and Marxism. With the collapse of those ideologies, their American followers were lost, and according to Professor David Hackett Fischer many took refuge in academia where their anti-Americanism was preached to the young. American history was redefined in their terms or it was simply eliminated.[9] As a result, many young students take today's freedoms and luxuries as if they were ordained by government. They have no idea of where our democratic principles derive from and how or why our forefathers fought and died for what they believed. It is difficult to

9   David Hackett Fischer, *Washington's Crossing* (New York: Oxford University Press, 2004) 454.

imagine Congress today authorizing portraits of our founders for the public place. Two hundred years ago Americans were eager to have portraits of their heroes hung in their homes. America mourned the passing of George Washington for over a generation. In a speech delivered on February 15, 2005, historian David McCullough talked about today's appalling lack of enthusiastic and knowledgeable teaching of history. He cited the former Librarian of Congress, Daniel Boorstin, who stated that we must know our past if we want to successfully plan our future and that to do otherwise is like trying to plant cut flowers. McCullough then went on to say that we are now raising a generation of Americans who are historically illiterate largely through no fault of their own but because of the lack of trained and inspired teachers. He reminds us that we have all been shaped by those have gone before us including family, friends, teachers and even those we never met such as poets, painters, musicians and writers of great literature. Likewise, our laws and freedoms were all the work of others who went before us. We should not be ignorant of what they did for us. It is rude and the height of ingratitude for being indifferent to what others struggled and died for because they did it for us. These include not just our founding fathers but our own parents and grandparents as well.[10]

Fortunately, we recently have been blessed with a growing number of scholars who are now writing about American history and the men who sacrificed their lives for our ultimate benefit. History is coming alive through the recent writings of David McCullough, Joseph Ellis, Richard Brookhiser, David Hackett Fischer, Robert Jones, John Alden, John Ferling, Don Higginbotham, Richard Norton Smith, Stephen Ambrose, Willard Randall and others too numerous to mention here.

---

10 David McCullough, *American History and America's Future* (Phoenix, Arizona: Hillsdale College National Leadership Seminar, February 15, 2005) 1-7.

We have the extensive biographical works of James Flexner and Douglas Freeman as well as the many editors working on Washington's papers at the University of Virginia. Hopefully, students, parents, older Americans and immigrants to America will learn about how America achieved its greatness and will not succumb to the mistaken belief that we are or should be like other countries in the world. They will learn that America was founded as a covenant nation by men who truly believed that a Creator gave them certain inalienable rights to life, liberty and the pursuit of happiness. Unlike Europe and many countries of the world, America is not a contract nation with rights granted by a monarch or a civil government. It was founded by people with moral conviction and courage and not political correctness or populism. We should learn from Washington's experience, wisdom and common sense. His concern over political warfare is very relevant today as we witness an ever-widening rift between political parties. On political parties he said they were "fires not to be quenched but demand a uniform vigilance to prevent its bursting into a flame."[11]

Like President Eisenhower in 1961, Washington warned of overgrown military establishments, but at the same time he advised strong military preparedness. His warnings of "passionate attachments" to or against foreign countries and the brevity of friendships due to selfish interests are extremely pertinent today to those who want the United States to be more like Europe and who favor America's subjection to international institutions. We have strayed dangerously far from his advice on the necessity of moral values to maintain a peaceful and prosperous society. In spite of the overwhelming fear of "standing armies" based on the British occupation of Boston and later the colonies, Washington stressed the need for a national army and navy to protect our

11   GW Papers at the Library of Congress.

interests as his successors later discovered in the War of 1812 when the British burned our Capitol and many coastal cities. Washington understood the need for a strong banking system with reputable international credit. He would be appalled at the size of our national debt and our becoming a debtor nation rather than a creditor one. Washington was a visionary for domestic manufacturing and industry and the need to remain self-sufficient while many of his contemporaries dreamed of an idyllic agrarian society protected by the Atlantic Ocean. It is hard to imagine a politician of today emulating Washington by declining a salary and wanting to serve his country out of principle. Can we hope to see leaders emerge who place their country ahead of self or who try to solve problems instead of ignoring them for fear of being disliked or not being reelected? If nothing else, the life of Washington teaches us that one man can make a difference. That was true with Abraham Lincoln, Theodore Roosevelt, Franklin Roosevelt and Ronald Reagan. However, no one can equal the greatness of a man like Washington, who not only gave us America but turned the world upside down in the face of impossible obstacles and gave us the first lesson in a new experiment called democracy. Washington always focused on the future. All his plans and work were designed for a brighter tomorrow whether it was in the development of the western territories, agricultural advancements, canal building, laws and rights embodied in a Constitution, a banking system or even in providing the future security of the slaves he freed. He also envisioned a national university in the new capital and stressed the importance of education in a democratic society. Every succeeding generation since his time has tried to build a better life for the following generation, and this has been a constant strength of America. Today, we have enormous challenges with terrorism, personal and national debt, morality, health care, financial security and internal divisiveness. However, the problems our founders faced were just as great and perhaps even greater. We should learn from them and listen to their advice. Lastly, but most importantly, we should aspire to Washington's personal virtues which are timeless and which should serve as models for not only Americans but for all people of the world.

Liberty, when it begins to take root, is a plant of rapid growth.

—George Washington
President of the United States of America

Epilogue

We meet together upon those birthdays of our great men not only to review their lives, but to revive and cherish our own patriotism. What is it we admire about [George Washington] the soldier... that he has the power of losing his own life for the life of a larger cause; that he holds his personal suffering of no account; that he flings down in the rage of battle his all and says, "I will stand or fall with this cause."

George Washington as a statesman. What was it that sustained him during all those days, all those weeks, during all those months and years? It was the belief that they were founding a nation on the axiom that all men are created free and equal.

George Washington as a citizen. He thought of many possibilities, but looking out over his country, did he fear that there should rise up a crowd of men who held office not for their country's good, but for their own good? He would tell us that anything which makes for better civic service, which makes for a merit system, which makes for fitness of office, is the only thing which will tell against this wrong, and that this course is the wisest patriotism. He freed his own slaves in his will. His letters breathe a yearning for a better condition for the slaves, as the letters of all great men among us breathe a yearning for the better condition of the unskilled and underpaid. Let us say again that the lessons of great men are lost unless they reinforce upon our minds the highest demands which we make upon ourselves; that they are lost unless they drive our sluggish wills forward in the direction of their highest ideals.

—Jane Addams, first American woman to win the
Nobel Peace Prize, 1931

Appendix

Memorial Sites of George Washington

Popes Creek Plantation—Birthplace of George Washington
Route 301, sixty miles south of Mount Vernon
Westmorland County, Virginia

The first Washington site was purchased by John Augustine Washington in the 1670s. His grandson, Augustine, (George's father) built a house on the west side of the creek in the 1720s where George was born in 1732. Upon Augustine's death in 1743, the property was inherited by his second son, Augustine ("Austin"), who later passed it on to his son, William Augustine Washington in 1762. George and his family lived here for three years before moving on to Little Hunting Creek which was about sixty miles north on the Potomac River. William Augustine renamed the plantation Wakefield and was living there with his family until 1779 when a fire totally destroyed the house. He rebuilt another house one mile inland leaving Wakefield abandoned. In 1815, George Washington Parke Custis, the adopted grandson of Martha and George Washington, constructed a rudimentary stone pedestal marking George's birthplace. In 1858, a small site and burial ground were donated to the Commonwealth of Virginia. In 1879, 1881 and again in 1883, additional lands were given to the United States by Virginia, and a fifty-foot obelisk was constructed in 1896. In 1923, the Wakefield National Memorial Association was organized to rebuild the original house, and in 1932 all the buildings and 367 acres were given to the United States. It is now a shrine of the National Park Service under the U. S. Department of the Interior. An auditorium has been added which houses historic information about the Washington family.

Ferry Farm—Boyhood Home of George Washington
268 Kings Highway
Fredericksburg, Virginia

After George's first three years at Popes Creek and then three years at Little Hunting Creek (later to be renamed Mount Vernon), Augustine Washington moved his young family to Ferry Farm in 1738 reportedly to be closer to his iron mill. It was here that George lived his formative years where he acquired his love of horses, received his schooling and even took dancing lessons in nearby Fredericksburg. He loved to fish and was noted for his athletic skills, strength and endurance. When his father died in 1743, George took on the added responsibilities of working on the farm and sharing in the care of his three younger brothers and sister. In 1752, following his half-brother Lawrence's death and his widow's remarriage, George moved to Mount Vernon (which had been renamed by Lawrence). Today, there are no remaining buildings at Ferry Farm, but it is an active archeological site. There are self-guided tours, and it is open to the public all year except for Thanksgiving and most of Christmas week.

Mount Vernon—Home of George Washington from 1752 to 1799

A tract of 2.126 acres along the Potomac River was purchased by George Washington's great-grandfather in the 1670s. In 1735, Augustine Washington built a small house there and moved his growing family from Popes Creek Farm. George was three years old but only lived there for three years before moving thirty-six miles south to Ferry Farm. His older half brother, Lawrence, inherited the property upon his father's death in 1743 and renamed it Mount Vernon in honor of his military commander, Admiral Edward Vernon. When Lawrence died in 1752 the property passed to his wife, Ann, and when she remarried and her child by Lawrence died at the age of four, Mount Vernon was inherited by George. The plantation was vastly improved by George bringing the total acreage to eight thousand and adding wings and height to the original Mansion House. The property consisted of five main farms—Mansion, Union, Dogue Run, Muddy Hole and River. It also included three mills and some outlying acreage. George moved his bride, Martha and her two children, there in January 1759. He had just resigned from the Virginia military and devoted his efforts to improving the farms and learning politics in his new position as a member of the House of Burgesses which was located in Williamsburg. Washington abandoned the failing tobacco market and converted the farms to corn, rye and wheat and the production of flour. He experimented with crops and gardens and became a serious student of agriculture. He truly loved Mount Vernon where he spent the happiest years of his life from 1759 to 1775, 1784 to 1789 and 1796 to his death in 1799. Both George and Martha are buried there. He willed the property to his brother Jack's son, Bushrod. In 1858, Washington's great-grandnephew sold the house with five hundred acres to the Mount

Vernon Ladies' Association of the Union who have maintained it ever since. Recent improvements include an underground museum and several learning centers and official functions. It is open to the public all year.

Valley Forge National Historic Park
Pennsylvania Turnpike, Exit 326
Valley Forge, Pennsylvania

This site was chosen by General George Washington to camp for the winter of 1777–78. It was named for the iron forge that was built along the Valley Creek in the 1740s which was destroyed by the British in 1777 just before Washington's arrival. He selected the area for its strategic location not too distant from Congress in York and the British forces in Philadelphia and New York. It was here that Washington and Baron von Steuben transformed the American militia into a well-disciplined and trained Continental Army. An entire town was constructed with two thousand log huts to house the troops as well as trenches and bridges to defend the camp. Attractions include Washington's Headquarters, the memorial chapel, redoubts, statues of generals and a fine Welcome Center, which shows an eighteen-minute film every thirty minutes. There are picnic grounds and walking and driving tours that explain exactly what took place during this critically important encampment during the Revolutionary War.

General Washington's Headquarters
Morristown, New Jersey

Following the Christmas week battles at Trenton and Princeton, Washington moved his army to Morristown in January 1777 and again in the winter of 1779-1780. It was selected because of its strategic location in proximity to the British troops which were headquartered in New York City. His own headquarters were in the Ford Mansion which was a private residence offered to him for commanding the war. The area had good roads and communications and was also close to necessary resources. Unlike Valley Forge, it was in a community that supported the war effort. There are four separate areas scattered over seventeen hundred acres which include the Headquarters house and museum, the Fort Nonsense Unit, the Jockey Hollow Unit and the New Jersey Brigade section. The Jockey Hollow area includes the headquarters of General Arthur St. Clair, five reconstructed huts and close to twenty-seven miles of walking trails. The Ford Mansion offers a guided tour, but the Museum is closed for renovations and expansion until early 2007. The Jockey Hollow site is open daily and has self-guided tours. The entire complex is open all year.

The Washington Monument
15th Street & Constitution Avenue, SW
Washington, D.C.

While Washington was president Congress deliberated how to commemorate him for his heroic leadership during the war for independence as well as his leadership in defining the presidency. However, Washington himself urged Congress not to spend its precious funds on any such project but rather on more important things. Finally, in 1833 the Washington National Monument Society was formed by Congress, and it decided to build the largest monument in the world to honor the most important man in America's history. The Society stated that the monument's "dimensions and magnificence should be commensurate with the greatness and gratitude of the nation." In 1836, architect Robert Mills designed an obelisk which was to exemplify simplicity and grandeur in keeping with Washington's character and behavior. Construction began in 1848 but was halted due lack of funds and the Civil War. Finally, it was completed in 1884 at a total cost of $ 1,817,710. It is 555 feet tall and consists of 897 steps with a stairwell and an elevator to the top. There are 36,471 marble stones measuring approximately 4' x 2' x 1½' each. The interior walls contain 190 memorial carved stones from states, foreign countries, cities, societies and individuals inscribed with tributes to Washington. On the aluminum-clad granite pyramidian at the top which was added in 1913 is an inscription, *"Laus Deo,"* which means "Praise to God." The Monument stands amid 106 acres and offers guided tours and interpretive talks. During 2004, there were approximately five hundred thousand visitors.

The George Washington Masonic Memorial
101 Callahan Drive
Alexandria, Virginia

This 333-foot building was dedicated in 1932 as an expression of the Masonic fraternity's faith in civil and religious liberty and orderly government. It was constructed with voluntary contributions from members of the Masonic fraternity and is the only unified effort by all the Grand Lodges in the United States. It was built to honor George Washington, who was a brother and master of Lodge Number 22 in Alexandria. The building includes a library, theater and museum which displays many Washington relics as well as paintings, prints and historical documents. One can view the 1932 painting of Washington dressed in his Masonic apron as he lays the cornerstone of the U. S. Capitol in 1793. The building is open to the public daily.

The Genealogy of George Washington

FIRST GENERATION

John Washington   b. 1632   d. 1676 Arrives in America 1657

Anne Pope (d.1668)   m.1658

John receives half interest in land grant of five thousand acres from Lord Culpeper in 1674

Land is split equally with Nicholas Spencer in 1690 and called Little Hunting Creek

SECOND GENERATION (sons of John)

John Washington   b. 1661   d. 1698

Lawrence Washington   b. 1659   d. 1698

  Mildred Warner (1671-1701)   m. 1688

   Ann Wickliffe (d. 1704)   m.?

Lawrence inherits **Little Hunting Creek** from father in 1676

Daughter Mildred inherits **Little Hunting Creek** in 1698

THIRD GENERATION (son of Lawrence)

Augustine Washington (by Mildred Warner) b. 1694 d. 1743

    Jane Butler (1699-1729)　　m.1715

    Mary Ball (1708-1789)　　m.1731

Augustine buys **Little Hunting Creek** from sister

Mildred in 1726

FOURTH GENERATION (children of Augustine)

Butler Washington (by Jane Butler) b. 1716 d. 1716

Augustine Washington, Jr. (by Jane Butler) b. 1720 d. 1762

Jane Washington (by Jane Butler) b. 1722 d. 1735

Lawrence Washington (by Jane Butler) b. 1718 d.1752

    Ann Fairfax m.1743

Lawrence inherits **Little Hunting Creek**, builds house,

renames it **Mt. Vernon**

George inherits **Mt. Vernon** 1752 with life tenancy to

Ann and daughter Hannah who die in 1761 and 1754.

George leases it from 1752 -1761.

George Washington (by Mary Ball) b. 1732 d. 1799

    Martha Dandridge Custis (1731-1802)　　m.1759

    Martha "Patsy" Parke Custis (by Daniel Parke Custis)

    (1756–1773)

    John "Jacky" Parke Custis (by Daniel Parke Custis)

    (1754–1781)

    George inherits Mt. Vernon upon death of Ann's daughter

    (1754–1799)

Samuel Washington (by Mary Ball) b. 1734 d. 1781

    Anne Steptoe Allerton (1739–1777) m.

FIFTH GENERATION

(children of Samuel and Anne)

Lawrence Augustine Washington (1775–1824)

George Steptoe Washington (1773–1808)

Harriet Washington (1776–1822)

Ferdinand Washington (1767–1788)

John Augustine "Jack" Washington

(by Mary Ball) b. 1736   d. 1787

Hannah Bushrod (1738-1801) m. c. 1758

FIFTH GENERATION

(children of John and Hannah)

Corbin Washington b. 1765   d.1799

George Augustine Washington b. 1767 d. 1784

Jane Washington Washington b 1759 d. 1791

Bushrod Washington b. 1762 d. 1829

    Julia Anne Blackburn (1768-1829) m. 1785

    Bushrod inherits Mt. Vernon (1799–1829)

    No children

SIXTH GENERATION

(son of Corbin Washington)

John Washington 1792–1832

Jane Charlotte Blackburn   m. 1814

John inherits Mt. Vernon   1829–1832

Jane inherits Mt. Vernon   1832–1850

SEVENTH GENERATION

(son of John and Jane)

John Augustine Washington 1821–1861

Eleanor Love Seldon   m. 1843

Inherits **Mt. Vernon**   1850–1858

Mt. Vernon sold to MVLA   1858

Charles Washington (by Mary Ball) b. 1738   d. 1799

Mildred Thornton (1739–   ) m. 1757

FIFTH GENERATION

(son of Charles and Mildred)

George Augustine Washington   (1758–1793)

Frances Bassett (1767–1796)   m. 1785

SIXTH GENERATION

(children of George and Frances)

Lafayette Washington	(1787–1787)
Anna Maria Washington	(1788–1814)
Charles Augustine Washington	(1790–1790)
George Fayette Washington	(1790–1867)

Elizabeth "Betty" Washington (by Mary Ball) b. 1733   d. 1797

Fielding Lewis (1725–1782) m. 1750

FIFTH GENERATION

(children of Betty and Fielding)

Fielding Lewis	(1751–1803)
Augustine Lewis	(1752–1756)

Warner Lewis   (1755–1756)

George Lewis   (1757–1821)

Mary Lewis   (1759–1759)

Charles Lewis   (1760–1775)

Samuel Lewis   (1763–1774)

Betty Lewis   (1765–1830)

Lawrence Lewis   (1767–1839)

Robert Lewis   (1769–1829)

Howell Lewis   (1771–1822)

Augustine "Austin" Washington (by Jane Butler) b. 1720   d.1762

Anne Aylett (d. 1774)   m. c. 1746

FIFTH GENERATION

(children of Austin and Anne)

Elizabeth Washington (1750–1814)

Jane Washington (1756–1833)

Ann Washington (1752–1777)

George Washington (1758–1758)

William Augustine Washington (1747–1810)

Jane Washington (1759–1791) m. c.1779

SIXTH GENERATION

(children of William and Jane)

Augustine Washington   (1780–1798)

Hannah Bushrod Washington (1778–1797)

Anne Aylett Washington   (1783–   )

Bushrod Washington   (1785–   )

George Corbin Washington   (?)

Chronology of Events in the Life of George Washington

1602–1651: Lawrence Washington   Great-Great Grandfather
Age 49 yrs

1633–1677: John Washington   Great-Grandfather
Age 44 yrs

1635–1676: Lawrence Washington   Brother of John
Age 41 yrs

1659–1698: Lawrence Washington   Grandfather
Age 39 yrs

1694–1743: Augustine Washington   Father
Age 49 yrs

1718–1752: Lawrence Washington   Older Half-brother
Age 34 yrs

1720–1762: Augustine Washington, Jr.   Older Half-brother
Age 42 yrs

1732–1799: George Washington
Age 67 yrs

1732   Born Feb 11, 1731 (Old Julian Calendar) Popes Creek—
        Westmorland County
        (New Gregorian Calendar Feb 22, 1732). Schooling
        Fredericksburg / Death of Father / Career / Brother
        Lawrence / Navy / Col. Fairfax / Surveying / The Ohio
        Co. / Alexandria / Financial Independence / Mother

1743   Death of father Augustine.

1743   Marriage of half-brother Lawrence to Ann Fairfax.

1743   Lawrence inherits Little Hunting Creek and builds
        Mansion House and renames it Mount Vernon in honor
        of Admiral Edward Vernon.

1747   Leaves school to live at Mt. Vernon and learns
        surveying.

1749   Appointed Surveyor of Culpeper County.

1751   Visits Barbados with brother Lawrence in search of cure
        for tuberculosis. George contracts smallpox but recovers.

1752   Death of Lawrence. George named residual heir to Mt.
        Vernon and upon Ann's remarriage and her daughter's
        death in 1754, George inherits Mt. Vernon when Ann
        dies in 1761.

1752   Appointed Major in the Virginia militia.

1753   Volunteers to deliver Gov Dinwiddie's ultimatum to
        French at Ft. Le Boeuf.
        Writes journal of experience which is published in
        London and begins notoriety.

1754   One of two commanders sent by Gov. Dinwiddie to oust
        French at Ft. Duquesne (Pitt). Defeats French scouting
        party at Great Meadow where French Commander

Jumonville is killed. Washington is overwhelmed by 500 French and Indians at Ft. Necessity, but is allowed to leave because there is no declared war. Conflict marks true beginning of the French and Indian War (1756-1763). Soon after he suffers poor health and resigns from militia.

1755   Volunteers as *aide-de-camp* to Gen. Edward Braddock on mission to Ohio Valley. Braddock's army defeated and he is killed. Washington cited for bravery and is appointed Colonel and Commander of the Virginia Regiment.

1755-58 Trains Regiment into first-class unit/ Rejected twice for British Army Commission.

1758   Elected as Burgess for Frederick County.

Volunteers for service with Gen. John Forbes to oust French from Ft. Duquesne

Disagrees with Forbes/French abandon Ft/ British rename it Ft. Pitt (PM).

Again, suffers from ill health.

Washington meets widower Martha Dandridge Custis. Resigns from Virginia militia in November.

1759   Marries Martha on January 6 and moves into Mount Vernon which he proceeds to renovate. Becomes serious agriculturalist—uses Consignment System.

1761   Re-elected to House of Burgesses for Frederick County.

1762   Appointed a vestryman of Truro Parish in Fairfax County.

1763   Appointed warden of Pohick Church in Fairfax County.

1763   Parliament's Proclamation of 1763.

1765   Serves as Commissioner for settling the military accounts of Virginia.

1765   Elected to the House of Burgesses for Fairfax County (and re-elected in 1768, 1769, 1771, 1774).

1759-74 Washington participates and observes debates in the House on most of the key issues:

1759: The London Board of Trade orders the colonies to pay debts in sterling. War debts and scarcity of hard money force Burgesses to issue paper currency as legal tender. Colonies need a medium of exchange & ignore the Crown's order.

1763: Treaty of Paris ends the Seven Year War. England acquires Canada.

1763: Proclamation of 1763 drew a north-south boundary from Great Lakes to the Gulf and the Appalachians to the Mississippi River prohibiting settlers and speculators and voided all prior contracts of sales and deeds. It violated the Proclamation of 1762, which had allocated bounties of two hundred thousand acres of western lands to veterans of the French and Indian War. Washington protested and organized a reversal several years later when Parliament allowed English investors into the territory. Proclamation was to appease and win over Indians.

1763: The Lords of Trade in London reprimanded Burgesses for continuing the issuance of paper currency. Washington predicted that the issue would "set the whole country in flames."

1764: Parliament passes the Currency Act prohibiting the issuance of paper bills as legal tender thereby ignoring the plight of colonial debtors to repay English creditors.

1764: The Sugar Act increased customs revenues and protected British commerce with the colonies from foreign competition. Washington calls it a tax and warned that it would force Americans to reduce imports and hurt British manufacturers and crditors. Washington adopts a calm, self-assured manner and suppresses any emotional response and correctly predicts repeal of the Sugar Act.

1765: The Stamp Act required all legal documents, pamphlets, documents, etc., to contain official tax stamps in order to pay for British troops stationed in the colonies. Fairfax County (which was represented in Burgesses by Washington) led the movement to resist the Act. With Virginia's Stamp Act Resolves, the royal governor dissolved the Assembly and called for new elections. Washington called the Act an "unconstitutional method of taxation… a direful attack upon their liberties… an Act of Oppression." He again correctly predicted its repeal.

1766: Washington is named to the powerful Committee of Privileges and Elections which supervised admissions to House membership.

1766: Parliament passed the Declaratory Act which asserted its authority to raise revenues in the colonies. "The said colonies and plantations in America have been, are, and of right ought to be, subordinate unto, and dependent upon, the imperial crown and parliament of Great Britain." Washington says this is illegal.

1767: Parliament passed the Townshend Duties which placed taxes on tea, paper, glass and lead and forced the colonies to maintain a Board of Customs Commissioner for North America and to support British military defense and royally appointed civil official ls.

1767: Parliament suspended the New York Assembly for not adequately supplying the regular British army stationed there.

1768: Colonial militants in Boston, New York and Philadelphia adopted non-importation associations, and they urge other colonies to do the same.

1769: Washington is assigned to the newly created Committee for Religion which was designed to deal with the alarming decline in public virtue.

1769: Washington condemns the Townshend Duties and writes that Britain was deprecating American freedoms. He becomes the first politician to raise the issue of possible armed resistance but states that it should be avoided. He suggests that the non-importation of British goods should stir the colonies to build more manufacturing and economic self-determination. He consulted with his neighbor, George Mason, who then drafted a Virginia non-importation association for the boycott of British goods.

1769: The Crown sends Lord Botetourt as the new Governor of Virginia to quell the protests and opposition to the Townshend Duties by the House of Burgesses.

1769: Parliament threatens protestors in Massachusetts with transportation to London to be tried there for treason. They order General Gage to take a regiment to Boston to control the protests there.

1769: The House of Burgesses passes four resolves; 1) they had the sole right to impose taxes, 2) Virginians had the privilege to petition their Sovereign for redress of grievances, 3) all trials for criminals should take place in Virginia and 4) they assured King George of their loyalty to the Crown.

1770: Parliament repealed most of the Townshend Duties but retained the tax on tea for two reasons; 1) the East India Company was close to failing and was not required to remit the tax on tea thereby enabling them to gain a virtual monopoly and drive the colonial tea merchants out of business by undercutting their prices and 2) the tea tax remained as a symbol of British authority to raise taxes at any time.

1770: On March 5, a Boston mob confronts British soldiers who fire into the crowd and kill five colonists. John Adams successfully defends the nine British soldiers.

1773: Parliament passed the Quebec Act, which annexed part of western Pennsylvania above the Ohio River and east of the Mississippi River to the Province of Quebec. It was intended for the fur trade with the Indians but proved to be a menace to settlers in the surrounding areas.

1773: In December the Sons of Liberty opposed the tea tax and, dressed as Indians, they threw the newly arrived English tea into the harbor and refused to make restitution thereby enraging Parliament.

1774: Parliament passed the Boston Port Bill, which effectively closed Boston's port commerce until reparations for the Boston Tea Party were made.

1774: Burgesses showed their support for Boston by calling for a Day of Prayer.
Governor Dunmore dissolves Burgesses for introducing non-importation measures.

1774: Parliament alters the Massachusetts charter by reducing the authority of the Lower House and appointing some of its own delegates.

1774: Parliament protects some of its agents from criminal trials in Massachusetts and orders them to be transferred to England under the pretense of not getting a fair trial in the colony.

1774: Parliament passes the Quartering Act which allows their soldiers to be lodged in private homes in areas of unrest.

1774   Washington becomes a member and then chairman of the meeting in Alexandria that adopts the Fairfax County Resolves under the guidance of George Mason. The Resolves 1) call for non-importation of British goods, 2) support for Boston, 3) proposal for a Continental Congress, 4) proposal to end slave trade.

1774   Washington is elected to attend the First Continental Congress in Philadelphia which meets in September.

1775   Battles of Lexington and Concord on April 19.

1775   Washington selected as delegate to Second Continental
        Congress which convenes in Philadelphia on May 10.

1775   Ethan Allen and Benedict Arnold capture Fort
        Ticonderoga in early May without losing a man and take
        possession of British munitions and cannons. British
        send reinforcements to Boston with Generals William
        Howe, Henry Clinton and Admiral Richard Howe.

1775   Congress sends Olive Branch Petition to King George
        III on May 26.

1775   Battle of Bunker (Breed's) Hill June 15/16. British
        sustain heavy losses.

1775   Washington elected commander in chief of the
        Continental Army on June 16.

1775   Washington takes command of army at Cambridge,
        Massachusetts, on July 3. Issues general orders that all
        soldiers are troops of the United Provinces of North
        America and hopes "all distinctions of colonies will be
        laid aside; so the one and the same spirit may animate
        the whole, and the only contest be, who shall render, on
        this great and trying occasion, the most essential service
        to the Great and common cause in which we are all
        engaged."

1775   In August Washington establishes a naval force to battle
        the British off the New England coast and to prey on
        British supply ships.

1775   Washington issues his "Address to the Inhabitants of
        Canada" asking for their support. He sends Benedict
        Arnold with several hundred volunteers to deliver
        Address after their march through Maine wilderness

to Quebec. Arnold joins General Montgomery who has just taken Montreal. Their attack on Quebec is repulsed, Montgomery is killed and Arnold is wounded. Washington rewards Arnold with promotion to Brigadier General in January 1776.

1776   On January 1 Washington raises the "Grand Union" flag over Boston.

1776   Siege of Boston with Washington occupying Boston and British troops depart for Nova Scotia on March 27. No British troops remain in American colonies.

1776   In early April Washington leaves Boston for New York where Major Charles Lee had been sent to prepare for its defense. Washington is upset with loyalist New York, whose merchants and government officials have been supplying British ships and instructs the New York Committee of Safety to cease all communication with the enemy.

1776   On July 9 Washington leads an American Independence celebration in New York City where he reads the Declaration of Independence to his troops. British armada is on horizon with thirty-two thousand and twenty-nine thousand English and Hessian troops.

1776   On August 27 Howe's forces move from Staten Island headquarters to attack American forces on Long Island in war's first major battle. Americans are out-flanked and forced to retreat. General John Sullivan is captured. Under cover of unusual fog, Washington successfully evacuates all his troops to Manhattan by small fishing boats.

1776   On September 15 Howe invades Manhattan at Kip's Bay (Murray Hill) and routs the Connecticut militia. Washington is appalled and tries unsuccessfully to halt retreat. The next day, the same units defend Harlem Heights and receive Washington's praise.

1776   On October 13 Benedict Arnold wins a delaying victory off Crown Point on Lake Champlain and thereby thwarts Sir Guy Carleton from advancing to New York in the British attempt to sever the colonies and isolate New England.

1776   On October 23 Washington orders the retreat from New York City and moves up to White Plains where he is routed by General Howe on October 28. Washington moves on to New Castle and then across the Hudson to Fort Lee where he observes the slaughter over at Fort Washington.

1776   On November 16 General Nathanael Greene persuades Washington to defend Fort Washington in upper Manhattan, but its men are butchered by the Hessians under Colonel Johann Rall and the British force of thirteen thousand men take 2,818 prisoners.

1776   On December 11 Washington leads his army of twenty-four hundred men in retreat across the Delaware River just north of Trenton, New Jersey, into camp in Pennsylvania.

1776   American General Charles Lee is captured in Basking Ridge on December 13 and becomes an interesting figure in the future course of the war.

1776   On December 26 Congress gives Washington unlimited powers for six months to execute the war with complete freedom to act. He is permitted to raise troops and supplies from states directly, appoint officers, administer the army, and arrest inhabitants who refuse to accept Continental currency as payment or otherwise show themselves to be disloyal. Washington assures Congress he will act with honor.

1776   On Christmas Day Washington orders the readings to the troops of Thomas Paine's *The Crisis*, which had just been published in Philadelphia: "this is the time that tries men's souls." Christmas night, Washington leads his remaining army of twenty-four hundred men in a surprise attack on the Hessians near Trenton. Colonel Johann Rall is mortally wounded along with just under five hundred men. Over one thousand Germans are taken prisoner and sent to western Pennsylvania near Lancaster. Washington orders leniency on the grounds that they were only mercenaries and not a party to the conflict with Great Britain. Of the twenty-nine thousand Hessians hired by the British, around 25 percent decided to remain in America due to the good treatment they received and the opportunities they perceived here.

1777   On January 3 Washington followed the much-needed Trenton victory with another surprise against the British at Princeton and drives them to New Brunswick. Washington establishes winter quarters at Morristown. Spends next several months rebuilding army with new enlistments.

1777   In April, Cornwallis fails to lure Washington out from his Morristown Headquarters. In May, Washington moves his headquarters to Middlebrook—just south of

Morristown and is successful in forcing British out of New Jersey. British are unable to win locals' allegiance back to the Crown. By June, British move from New Brunswick to Amboy back to Staten Island. On June 27, the Marquis de Lafayette arrives in Philadelphia to offer his services. He is nineteen years old and is commissioned a Major General. Washington cautiously accepts him but admires his enthusiasm and courage and quickly forms a close "father-son" relationship, which later proves to be a critical aspect to the war when Lafayette intercedes in Paris to arrange French loans and the full support of the French government.

1777   In July, Washington moves his army to the Highlands of New York in the Hudson Valley where two forts on either side of the River are connected by an underwater thirty-five-ton , 850-link chain and hidden spiked logs protect water access to the interior. Washington orders Benedict Arnold to join General Schuyler and halt General Burgoyne's invasion of New York from Canada.

1777   General Howe sets sail on July 23 with fifteen thousand men to capture Philadelphia. Washington is baffled why they sail on a four hundred-mile sea voyage to land at Head of Elk (Elkton), Maryland, which is seventy miles south of Philadelphia when they were in New Brunswick only sixty miles away. He thought Howe was headed to Charleston but had time to impede Howe's advance and enable Congress to move from the capital to Lancaster and then on to York. First engagement was at Brandywine Creek near Wilmington in September. Washington was outnumbered—fifteen thousand to eleven thousand and lost one thousand men due to the same out-flanking maneuver Howe used on Long Island.

1777   In early October, Washington tries unsuccessfully to stop Howe just outside Philadelphia at Germantown, but loses another thousand. Battle is lost because of confusion, friendly fire and mistaken retreats. Washington calls it more "unfortunate than injurious." On October 19, British enter Philadelphia.

1777   On October 17, Burgoyne is defeated at Saratoga by Horatio Gates and Benedict Arnold. They take 5,871 British and Hessian prisoners who are detained near Charlottesville. The Convention Army is moved to Maryland and by war's end it dwindles to fifteen hundred men due to desertions and those who decide to settle in America. The American victory marked a significant change in Parliament (which attempted a peace negotiation but no recognition of independence) and in France which offered overt help in men and materials.

1777   December 16, Washington moves to Valley Forge to rebuild army and confer with Congress only ninety miles away in York. Discontent among several officers led by Horatio Gates and Thomas Conway results in surreptitious rumors and writing to Congress to replace Washington as commander in chief. Washington is supported by key members, including its president, Henry Laurens. Washington confronts Conway and thereby ends any threats to his position. The Conway Cabal has been generally overplayed by historians as any serious event.

1778   Valley Forge marks nadir of the war with inadequate men, training, supplies and food. Washington knows they cannot win without a well-trained disciplined army of regulars for longer-term commitments. Under Washington and the political support of Henry Laurens, conditions are improved. States are strongly urged to supply the army and accept continental currency. In February, Baron von Steuben arrives to train American troops. Congress publishes his military training manual. He and Washington supervise the training of a model company which in turn trains other companies. An Inner Circle of officers develops and "Command and Control" structure that provides for the organization of the army and the execution of orders. By the end of May, Washington is in command of a new well-trained army which he feels is much better able to cope with his adversaries—both English and German.

1778   On February 6, the Franco-American Treaty of Amity and Commerce is signed in Paris which promises financial and military aid and recognizes the independence of the U.S. The Treaty is ratified in May and by June, France and England are at war.

1778   In March, the British change their strategy by deciding to attack in the south where they hope to acquire many more loyalists. Howe resigns and is replaced by General Henry Clinton who vacates Philadelphia in June. In April the British send the Carlisle Commission to America to negotiate a settlement before the Franco-American Treaty is ratified. They repeal all the laws which were opposed by the colonies. Congress signs the Treaty, ignores the Commission and decides not to enter any negotiations that do not recognize their complete independence.

1778   As Clinton moves his army from Philadelphia across New Jersey to New York, Washington decides to attack their rear at the Battle of Monmouth Courthouse. Charles Lee, who had been in British captivity and later exchanged, is given command. He had not been part of the newly-trained army at Valley Forge and was unconvinced of their abilities. Washington wanted to inflict a major blow before Clinton could reach New York hoping to hasten the war's end. When he encountered hesitancy and retreat in the field at Monmouth, he regrouped his forces and relieved Lee of his command for disobeying orders. The battle is considered an American victory and ended in stalemate, but Washington was impressed with his men. He uses the militia to severely harass the flanks of the retreating British forces and eventually moves his entire army to White Plains.

1778   In the Pennsylvania-New York frontier north of the Susquehanna River the Onandagas, Cayugas, Senecas, and Mohawks of the Iroquois League ally with the British and invade the Wyoming Valley. The Oneidas and the Tuscororas ally with the Americans. Also in July, George Rogers Clark defeats the British and captures Kaskaskia near the Mississippi River. Clark convinces the French settlers and their Indian allies to support the Americans. The British manage to hold Fort Detroit.

1778   In July–August, Admiral Comte d'Estaing and his French fleet plan to join General John Sullivan in recapturing Newport, Rhode Island. The fleet is met by the British and a hurricane batters the ships forcing d'Estaing to abandon Sullivan and sail for repair to Boston and then on to the Caribbean to attack British islands. The event gives Washington much concern about French reliance.

1778   In November, Washington sends General McIntosh to command the western Ohio River Valley. He establishes several forts from which he attacks the British, Shawnee, Wyandot and Mingo allies operating from Fort Detroit. McIntosh is unsuccessful and is forced to abandon the forts in 1779.

1779   In January, the capital of Georgia, Augusta, falls to the British. General Benjamin Lincoln recaptures the city in February. Lincoln tries to defend British encroachments in Georgia and South Carolina for six months but is mainly fought to a standstill.

1779   In June, Spain declares war on Great Britain.

1779   In September and October, Washington attempts to organize a combined French and American attack on the British preferably in New York. In October, d'Estaing and the Americans fail to recapture Savannah. The French return to France to avoid the hurricane season leaving Washington in doubts once again.

1779   On December 26, British General Henry Clinton and Admiral Marriot Arbuthnot sail from New York and successfully invade Charleston with fourteen warships, ninety transports and eighty-five hundred troops.

1780   From January through June, the British and Hessians engage the Americans from New York throughout New Jersey in a series of skirmishes known as the Forage Wars. In April, Washington warns Congress of impending British moves in the south and in the Hudson River and advises that his ten thousand troops are insufficient especially with the twenty-eight hundred enlistees about to leave at the end of the month.

1780   On July 11, the new French squadron arrives in Newport under Lieutenant General Rochambeau. He quietly disagrees with Washington's suggestion of an attack on New York owing in part to the shallow New York harbor and the strong British defenses. He stays in Newport for another year and then moves closer to Washington's headquarters in Westchester in preparation for an attack on an undetermined location.

1780   September 25, Washington discovers the plot of Benedict Arnold to surrender the key fort at West Point to the British. His accomplice, Major John Andre, is captured by accident in possession of incriminating papers. Washington offers to exchange Andre for Arnold but the British decline. Andre is hanged as a spy. Evidence shows that part of the plot was to have Washington captured which probably would have quickly ended the war. Arnold is made a Brigadier General in the British army and given command of sixteen hundred regulars to invade Virginia.

1780   In April–May, British General Henry Clinton bombards Charleston and calls for General Benjamin Lincoln to surrender. Resistance lasts for one month before the local citizenry ask Lincoln to save the town from further destruction. American officers are confined to land and the enlisted men are held in the holds of prison ships in the harbor. In June Clinton returns to New York and directs Cornwallis to move inland and subdue the south.

1780   The loss of Charleston prompts Washington to reorganize the American army in the south under the command of Horatio Gates. He sends Maryland and Delaware Continental regiments under Baron de Kalb to augment the main force of Virginia and North Carolina militia. In August at the Battle of Camden, S.C. de Kalb is killed and Gates suffers one of the worst American defeats of the war with only seven hundred survivors from his force of four thousand men.

1780   In September, Cornwallis begins his invasion of North Carolina. In October, Cornwallis sends Major Ferguson ahead to warn the inhabitants of King's Mountain and threatens severe destruction. The local citizens are so aroused that they raise a force that defeats the British and thereby ends their hope of gaining loyalist support.

1780   In December, Washington replaces Gates with Nathanael Greene as commander of the American southern army. His officers include Brigadier General Daniel Morgan, Lieutenant Colonel William Washington (a cousin of George) and Lieutenant Colonel Henry Lee.

1781   On January 5, Benedict Arnold invades Richmond and threatens the capture of the fleeing Governor Thomas Jefferson and his government officials.

1781   On January 16–17, General Morgan and Lt. Colonel William Washington defeat British Lieutenant Banastre

Tarleton at Cowpens, South Carolina. From January through March, General Greene engages Cornwallis in a series of battles and skirmishes throughout South and North Carolina as the British attempt to move north. Greene employs tactics similar to Washington and only confronts him when his odds of success are best. He beats Cornwallis to Virginia and exhausts the British troops. Washington congratulates Greene for his astuteness in using retreating tactics.

1781   On January 1, the Pennsylvania Continentals mutiny for lack of supplies, necessities and pay. Washington sends the New Jersey Continentals to positions between the British on Staten Island and the mutineers. British General Clinton sends messengers to the Pennsylvania troops, but the mutineers turn them over to Congress which hangs them as British spies. Washington is dismayed at the prospect of mutiny and the possible harm to citizens and their property. He solves the problem by obtaining sufficient supplies for the troops.

1781   On January 20, the New Jersey Continentals mutiny, but Washington is less lenient because Congress was already working to resolve the grievances. He orders officer Robert Howe at West Point to suppress the mutiny and execute the ringleaders. Howe forms a court martial where two are shot and one is pardoned. Washington writes to the Congressional Committee "having punished guilt and supported authority, it now becomes proper to do justice" and urged them to seek redress for their grievances.

1781   In May, Washington and Rochambeau meet in Wethersfield, Connecticut, and together appeal to Admiral Comte de Grasse to sail north from the Caribbean to help with a combined Franco-American attack on the British.

1781   British Lieutenant Tarleton almost captures Governor Thomas Jefferson at Monticello.

1781   On July 6, Washington and Rochambeau meet at Dobb's Ferry, New York, to plan an assault on New York City. On August 14, Washington learns that the French fleet of thirty-four warships and thirty-two hundred troops will be arriving in the Chesapeake and will be available until October 19. Washington's hopes for an attack on New York are put aside even though the British are preparing for it. He then has to take the risk that the French fleet will arrive and join the campaign unlike two other earlier incidents when they abandoned the fight. Rochambeau convinces him of the plan so the Franco-American forces bypass New York and march straight for the Virginia peninsula. They then meet in Williamsburg with Lafayette and the other Americans who were defending the Richmond area. Cornwallis has avoided Richmond and heads to Yorktown where he plans to be evacuated by the British navy sent from New York. Clinton learns of the American plan too late and sends a fleet to intercept de Grasse, but it arrives after the French and is driven away from Cape Henry at the mouth of the Chesapeake

1781   On October 14, nine thousand Americans and eight thousand Frenchmen begin their bombardment of the

British. Cornwallis tries to escape across the York River to Gloucester but is turned back by American reinforcements placed there. On October 17, Cornwallis raises a white flag, and on October 19, the British surrender. The victory marks the last major battle of the war, but Washington is not convinced it is over fearing the British will send even greater numbers to defeat the Americans.

1782   Fighting continues in the Appalachian territory where the British and their Indian allies: the Wyandot, Ottawa, Ojibwa, Mingo and Delaware tribes inflict heavy casualties and force Daniel Boone and his Kentucky militia to retreat. George Rogers Clark takes command of the Kentuckians and leads them on an expedition against the British into the Ohio River Valley. Historians regard these battles as the last formal engagements of the war.

1782   On November 30, the Treaty of Paris is signed in London. It calls for 1) a full and complete recognition of America's independence and the withdrawal of all British troops including those in the western lands, 2) establishing the Mississippi River as the western boundary of the United States and the right to use the river, 3) re-establishing the Great Lakes as the northern boundary and 4) allowing Americans to secure fishing rights on the Newfoundland Grand Banks. Two issues remain unresolved; 1) reparations by Britain for the destruction of American property and 2) reparations by the U.S. for loyalist property that was seized by the rebels.

1783   In December 1782 American army officers at the
        Newburgh, N.Y. headquarters send a petition to
        Congress for immediate payment of long-overdue
        salaries and a request for lump-sum payments of
        pensions. When Congress rejects their petition, they
        organize a mutiny and threaten to march to Philadelphia.
        Washington is kept out of the loop, but when he learns
        of their plans he schedules a meeting to address the
        officers. On March 13, he asks his men to be patient and
        that he will continue to support their grievance. He then
        tries to read them a letter from Congress but hesitates
        and takes out his glasses and says, "Gentlemen, you
        must pardon me. I have grown gray in your service and
        now find myself growing blind." Many officers break
        down in tears and affirm their loyalty to Congress. The
        Newburgh Conspiracy is over and Washington writes
        to Congress on behalf of his officers. Recent historians
        reveal a more sinister plot in Philadelphia by political
        supporters of a strong national government who wanted
        to have the mutiny threaten the Congress into adopting
        greater centralized financial controls with independent
        revenue powers.

1783   On April 9, Sir Guy Carleton and Washington signed
        a cease-fire. On April 18, Washington announces the
        "cessation of hostilities between the United States
        of America and the King of Great Britain." He
        congratulates the army and everyone who participated
        in any way to the great drama "on the stage of human
        affairs… nothing now remains but for the actors of
        this mighty scene to preserve a perfect, unvarying,
        consistency of character through the very last act; to

disclose the drama with applause; and to retire from the military theatre with the same approbation of angels and men which have crowned all their former virtuous actions."

1783   While waiting for the war's end, General Henry Knox and many officers decide to establish a philanthropic fraternity of veteran officers to provide support to other needy comrades who may need help in re-entering civilian life. The Society of the Cincinnati is formed in part to fulfill a role that Congress had neglected and could also serve as an effective lobby to remedy back pay and pension grievances. The name derives from the famous Roman General Cincinnatus who left his farm in 458 B.C. to lead his countrymen to victory against the attacking Aequi. After the battle he returned home to his plough. The officers regard themselves and Washington in a similar situation and elect him as their first president. Later, when Jefferson learns of the hereditary nature of its membership, he suggests that Washington should not be associated with such a European monarchial position especially with its possibility of becoming a standing army, anathema to Jefferson and all anti-Federalist "Republicans."

1783   The Treaty of Paris is signed by the U.S. in September.

1783   In November, 32,224 American loyalists along with their personal property sail to Nova Scotia. Around the same time, 1,328 leave for Quebec and 1,458 sail to the Bahamas. In total, 6,284 Americans were killed in action and ten thousand died of disease. Eighty-five hundred American prisoners died from malnutrition and disease. Of the thirty-nine thousand British troops, ten thousand were killed and most of the fifteen thousand prisoners survived. Of the 29,867 Hessian mercenaries, five thousand deserted, 7,754 died, eighty-five hundred return home and eighty-five hundred elect to remain in the U.S. A total of 120,000 Americans served during the eight and a half years out of a total population of 3 million.

1783   On November 25, the last British soldiers disembark from New York and on December 4, they set sail for England after a successfully managed disengagement by Carleton that witnesses very little bloodshed or open hostilities.

1783   On November 30, a tearful Washington bids farewell to his officers in a reception at Fraunces' Tavern in downtown New York where he asks each of them to take his hand.

1783   On December 22, Washington resigns his military commission to Congress convening at Annapolis in what many historians regard as one of the most significant acts in history. Upon learning of his resignation, King George calls Washington "the greatest man on earth." He arrives back home at Mount Vernon by Christmas Day after been absent for close to eight and a half years.

1784   As early as 1754 when Virginia Burgess member, Charles Carter, proposed a Potomac River canal Washington had been an enthusiastic supporter of such a project. But the French and Indian War, the Revolution and local opposition prevented its development. He and Jefferson envisioned Virginia as a central commercial

hub of the country and promoted the economic
development of Virginia. They believed the means was a
waterway from the Chesapeake to the western lands via
the Potomac River. In early 1784, Jefferson proposes that
Washington should head the project and he agrees that it
is vital.

1785   In March he calls commissioners from Maryland and
Virginia to Mount Vernon to discuss his proposed canal
and joint commercial and fishing rights in the Potomac
and the Chesapeake. With Congress ignoring the project,
Washington calls wealthy businessmen to Alexandria
in May where they create the Potomac Company, and
he is elected its president. The Company is to build a
190-mile canal and during his four years as president,
work is begun at Shenandoah Falls, Seneca Falls and
Great Falls. It opens the interior of the Ohio Valley to
farmers and merchants. Seventy-foot long boats haul
produce to within twelve miles of Fort Cumberland,
and it is functioning thirty-five years before the opening
of the Erie Canal. The project is a good example of
Washington's leadership, vision and perseverance
designed to benefit a fledgling nation.

1786   The 1785 meeting at Mount Vernon becomes known as
the Mount Vernon Compact, and it invites Pennsylvania
and Delaware to the next meeting scheduled for May
1786 at Annapolis. James Madison say the Compact
marks the very beginning of the process that led to
the creation of the Constitution. The Conference is
delayed until September and includes a discussion
of the strengths and weaknesses of the Articles of
Confederation. Washington writes to John Jay in May:

"That it is necessary to revise and amend the Articles of Confederation, I entertain no doubt; but what may be the consequences of such an attempt is doubtful yet something must be done, or the fabric must fall, for it certainly is tottering."

1786   With only 5 states attending, the Annapolis Conference realizes they are too few to bring about the major changes deemed necessary, so they issue a call to all the states to meet in Philadelphia the following May.

1786   Massachusetts, like other states, incurred sizable war debts and had their own currency and financial system. As greater taxes were imposed, farmers were unable to pay in the hard currency required. Farms were seized and debtors were thrown into jail. On September 26, a former captain in the Revolutionary army and a farmer, Daniel Shays, leads a revolt to shut down the courts and chases sheriffs off properties. When his twelve hundred men threaten to seize the U.S. arsenal at Springfield, Congress sends Henry Knox to investigate. Richard Henry Lee, president of the Congress, suggests to Washington that he could calm the situation by using his influence. Washington replies that "influence is no government." After Benjamin Lincoln chases Shays and his men across the Connecticut River into the hills of the Republic of Vermont, the episode is over, but it alarms Washington because there are no Congressional moneys or army to deal with such lawlessness. Shays's Rebellion becomes a catalyst in motivating the need for reforms for a Constitution with a stronger national government.

1787   Washington is among those who believe the entire Articles of Confederation have to be overhauled. He is reluctant to attend the Constitutional Convention, but is finally persuaded that he should attend. Its first business is to elect him president of the Convention, and while he feels he should not participate in the many debates, he does privately express his opinion on the major issues. There is little doubt that his support for the measure assures its eventual adoption by the Convention on September 20, which sends it to the states for ratification by a minimum of nine states. Rhode Island is the only state not to send a delegate.

1788   On June 21, the New Hampshire vote makes the Constitution formally adopted.

1788   North Carolina ratifies the Constitution on November 21.

1788   Washington is elected Chancellor of William & Mary College

1789   On February 4, Washington is unanimously elected President of the United States.

1789   On April 30, Washington is inaugurated as president at Federal Hall in New York City and nervously delivers address (new tradition) co-written with James Madison.

1789   Appointments: Sec. Treasury—Alexander Hamilton

Sec. War—Henry Knox

Sec. State—Thomas Jefferson

Attorney Gen.—Edmund Randolph

Chief Justice of Supreme Court—John Jay

Postmaster Gen.—Samuel Osgood

1789 Washington's mother, Mary Ball Washington, dies August 25, in Fredericksburg.

1789 Congress submits Amendments—Bill of Rights appended to Constitution in 1791.

Bank of the U.S.

1789 In October & November Washington tours New England—except Rhode Island.

1790 In January, Hamilton introduces Assumption Bill that allows Federal Govt to assume the $80 million foreign, state and domestic debts by issuing U.S. Treasury Bonds at par to current holders. Favored by north, which has largest debt, but opposed by south, which has already arranged for repayment. Opposition led by James Madison, who fears the large national debt will cause greater taxation and increase Federal power over states. Approved in July 1790.

1790 On May 29, Rhode Island becomes the last state to ratify the Constitution. In August Washington visits the state.

1790 In December, Washington arrives in the new temporary national capital of Philadelphia, which was negotiated by Hamilton and Jefferson in exchange for the South's approval of the Assumption Bill and the promise that the North would agree to a permanent capital along the Potomac River.

1790 In December, Hamilton introduces a plan for a Bank of the U.S., which is designed to be the mechanism for funding the national debt under the Assumption Act and to establish national and international credit for the new nation. It is opposed by Patrick Henry and Thomas

Jefferson because they believe it supports monied interests, subordinates agricultural to commercial interests and is unconstitutional because a bank is not expressly permitted powers delegated to Congress. Hamilton argues that a bank is constitutional because Congress had the power to collect taxes and regulate trade. The argument marks the beginning of "strict constructionists" and the "theory of implied powers." Washington is undecided so asks for written opinions. He then decides in favor of the bank feeling he should support the cabinet official in charge of finance and also because he believes the fledgling country needed to create a sound credit system.

1791   In March, Congress passes the Whiskey Act, which raises revenue by an excise tax on distilled liquors and stills. It is strongly opposed by farmers in the backwoods who use surplus grain for distilling and Maryland, Virginia, and North Carolina pass resolutions protesting the Act.

1791   In March, Washington selects site for the proposed national capital.

1791   Washington tours the south from April to June.

1791   Jefferson and Madison tour New York and New England to organize anti-Federalist groups to oppose Washington's Federalist administration. Jefferson favors a "democratic" agrarian society while Hamilton supports a diversified industrial society with a strong central government. Washington remains neutral and tries to bring each side together through negotiation and compromise.

1791   Vermont enters the union as the fourteenth state.

1792   Twenty-four brokers meet at the Merchants Coffee
        House in lower Manhattan to establish the New York
        Stock Exchange.

1792   In October, Washington places the Cornerstone for the
        President's Palace later called the White House. The first
        public building in the new capital is projected to open in
        1800—which it does for John and Abigail Adams.

1792   Washington is re-elected with 132 electoral votes
        followed by Adams with seventy-seven votes. He is
        inaugurated on March 4, 1793 at Independence Hall in
        Philadelphia.

1792   Kentucky entered the union as the fifteenth state.

1793   French minister to the United States, Edouard
        Genet, arrives in Charleston and before presenting
        his credentials in Philadelphia, he commissions four
        privateering ships to raid British ships along the U.S.
        coast. He also initiates expeditions against Spanish
        and British territories. He is greeted warmly by most
        Americans—especially agrarian Republicans led by
        Secretary of State Jefferson.

1793   On April 22, Washington issued his Proclamation of
        Neutrality warning Americans to avoid involvement
        in the hostilities between France and England. Both
        Hamilton and Jefferson favor neutrality but Jefferson is
        partial to France while Hamilton sides with England.

1793   In June, "Citizen Genet" is ordered not to issue military
        commissions on American soil and to remove the four
        French privateers out of American waters. Genet breaks

his promise and arms another privateer going against Washington's orders and appeals directly to Americans for support. Washington's cabinet asks France to recall Genet because he has violated American neutrality, the Jacobins order his arrest. Genet asks for asylum and is pardoned by Washington. He later becomes an American citizen and marries New York Governor George Clinton's daughter.

1793   On September 18, Washington places the cornerstone on the Capitol building.

1793   On December 31, Thomas Jefferson resigns as Secretary of State and is replaced by Attorney General Edmund Randolph.

1794   In March Congress passes a bill banning slave trade with foreign countries.

1794   In March Congress authorizes the establishment of the U.S. Navy.

1794   In July, the Whiskey Rebellion breaks out in western Pennsylvania by farmers who oppose the excise tax on liquor and stills. They burn tax collectors' houses and tar and feather the revenue officers. Washington orders the insurgents to return home. When they do not he calls out the Virginia, Pennsylvania, New York and New Jersey militia (12,900 men) to put down the insurrection. By November, the insurgents return home. Two hundred are arrested, twenty-five tried for treason, two convicted but both pardoned by Washington even though he is criticized for such a heavy military response to the incident.

1794   Appointed in April as envoy to England to negotiate
a commercial treaty, John Jay returns in November
with Jay's Treaty. It requires the withdrawal of British
forces from the Northwest Territories in exchange for
American settlement of pre-Revolutionary War debts
owed to British citizens. British East Indian and West
Indian ports are opened to American vessels and puts
British trade with the United States on a most-favored-
nation basis. British impressments of American ship
crews are not addressed, but boundary disputes and
compensation for illegal maritime seizures are put into
a joint commission. The Treaty is not publicly disclosed
until March 1795 when it causes a national uproar for
being pro-British. The French are outraged as are the
North and South factions. Washington is disappointed
in the terms but the Senate narrowly passes it. The
Democratic Republicans try to defeat it in the House
by voting to withhold funds for its implementation,
but Washington uses his executive prerogative since
approval by both houses of Congress is not required
and signs the Treaty on August 14, 1795. His principal
reasons for supporting it are the removal of all British
troops from America and the protection it provides to
American commerce, which he believes are vital to
economic independence and stability. Washington is
vilified and called a traitor.

1795   In January Congress passed the Naturalization Act,
which requires a five-year residency in the United States
before citizenship is granted.

1795   In January, Hamilton resigns as Secretary of the Treasury and is succeeded by Oliver Wolcott, Jr. Hamilton remains a close adviser to Washington.

1795   Special envoy to Spain, Thomas Pinckney, signs the Treaty of San Lorenzo, resolving the southern and western boundaries between the United States and Spain at the thirty-first parallel and the Mississippi River and the use of port New Orleans for three years.

1796   In February, France informs the United States that the Jay Treaty annuls all previous French treaties and brings both countries to the brink of war.

1796   On June 1, Tennessee is admitted as the sixteenth state and elects Andrew Jackson as their first delegate to the House of Representatives.

1796   In September, Washington publishes his "Farewell Address" in the *Daily American Advertiser* (it is never delivered orally and was not intended to be). He declines a third term based on his age and the belief that America is now firmly established enough to move on without him. He warns against the divisiveness of political parties; he stresses the importance of a sound public credit system; he warns against permanent foreign alliances; he cautions against an all-powerful military establishment but the need for vigilance. The address is partly from the first farewell written in 1792 by James Madison but is primarily from his own mind with help from Alexander Hamilton.

1796   In November, France declares suspension of diplomatic relations with the United States.

1796   In December, John Adams is elected the next
        president with seventy-one electoral votes with
        Thomas Jefferson getting sixty-eight votes for the
        vice presidency. The vote gives rise to the influence
        of the Democratic Republican party primarily as a
        backlash to the Jay Treaty.

1797   On March 4, Adams is inaugurated and Washington
        retires to Mt. Vernon.

1797   In June, Secretary of State, Timothy Pickering, reports
        the capture by France of three hundred American
        vessels on the high seas. Congress passes a bill calling
        for an eighty thousand-man militia to get in readiness
        for war. In October, the American peace commission
        in Paris is approached by three agents of French
        foreign minister, Talleyrand, who suggests a loan of
        $240,000 to France and a bribe to Talleyrand as pre-
        conditions for negotiating a treaty. Known as the XYZ
        Affair, it results in an undeclared naval war between
        the two countries that lasts for two years. The details
        of the event were released in April 1798 and caused a
        sharp anti-French reaction.

1798   In June, Congress suspends commerce with France,
        and the Federalists pass legislation strengthening
        the government. It results in the Alien and Sedition
        Acts which silence any political opposition. The new
        Naturalization Act requires a residency of fourteen
        years to become eligible for citizenship. It is repealed in
        1802. The Alien Acts authorize the president to deport
        dangerous or treasonable aliens during peacetime. The
        Sedition Act declares any anti-government activity,

including the publication of any false, scandalous and malicious writing as a high misdemeanor punishable by fine and imprisonment

1798   Adams appoints Washington as commander in chief of the United States Army.

1799   On May 5, Talleyrand is notified of Adams' intent to reopen peace talks.

1799   In November, the French Directoire government is abolished by a *coup d'etat* that establishes Napoleon Bonaparte the ruler of France.

1799   George Washington dies at Mount Vernon on December 14 from a sudden attack of epiglottitis. Honors are paid to him across America, in England and by Napoleon, who proclaims a week of mourning in France. On December 26, General "Light Horse" Harry Lee delivers his eulogy to Congress describing Washington as "first in war, first in peace, first in the hearts of his countrymen."

Bibliography

Books

Alden, John R. *George Washington, A Biography*. Baton Rouge: Louisiana State University Press, 1984.

Bancroft, George. *History of the United States*, vol. VI. Boston: 1878.

Beliles, Mark A., and Stephen K. McDowell. *America's Providential History* (Charlottesville, Virginia: the Providence Foundation, 1989)

Benninghoff II, Hermann O. *Valley Forge: A Genesis for Command and Control, Continental Army Style*. Gettysburg, Pennsylvania: Thomas Publications, 2001.

Billias, George Athan. *George Washington's Generals and Opponents*. New York: First Da Capo Press, 1994.

Bodle, Wayne. *Valley Forge Winter: Civilians and Soldiers in War*, University Park: Pennsylvania State University Press, 2002.

Brookhiser, Richard. *Founding Father, Rediscovering George Washington*. New York: Simon and Schuster Inc., 1996.

Busch, Noel Fairchild. *Winter Quarters: George Washington and the Continental Army at Valley Forge.* New York: Liveright, 1974.

Chadwick, Bruce. *George Washington's War.* Naperville, Illinois: Sourcebooks, Inc., 2004.

Clark, Harrison. *All Cloudless Glory,* vol. 1. Washington, D.C.: Regnery Publishing, Inc., 1996.

Commanger, Henry Steele. *The Spirit of Seventy-Six.* New York: 1967.

Cunliffe, Marcus. *George Washington: Man and Monument.* Mount Vernon, Virginia: The Mount Vernon Ladies' Association, 1982; originally published 1958.

Cunningham, Jr., Noble E. *In Pursuit of Reason: The Life of Thomas Jefferson.* New York: Ballantine Books, 1988; originally published by Louisiana State University Press, 1987.

Durant, Will and Ariel. *The Lessons of History.* New York: Simon and Schuster, 1968.

Ellis, Joseph J. *American Sphinx.* New York: Alfred A. Knopf, 1997.

Ellis, Joseph J. *Founding Brothers.* New York: Random House Inc., 2000.

Ellis, Joseph J. *His Excellency: George Washington.* New York: Alfred A. Knopf, 2004.

Ferling, John E. *The First of Men: a Life of George Washington.* Knoxville: University of Tennessee Press, 1988.

Fischer, David Hackett. *Washington's Crossing.* New York: Oxford University Press, 2004.

Fitzpatrick, John C. *The Writings of George Washington*, vol. 10 (November 1777-February 1778); vol. 11 (March 1778-May 1778). Library of Congress.

Fleming, Thomas. *Liberty! The American Revolution*. New York: Viking Penguin, 1997.

Flexner, James Thomas. *Washington, The Indispensable Man*. New York: Little, Brown & Co., 1974; originally published 1969.

Flexner, James Thomas. *George Washington*, vols. 1-4. New York: Little, Brown & Co., 1972; originally published 1969.

Freeman, Douglas Southhall. *George Washington: A Biography*, vols. 1-7. New York: Charles Scribner's Sons, 1948.

Freeman, Douglas Southall. *George Washington: A Biography*. New York: Simon & Schuster, 1952.

Freeman, Douglas Southall. *Washington*. New York: Simon & Schuster, Touchstone Edition, 1995.

Grizzard, Jr., Frank E. *George Washington: A Biographical Companion*. Santa Barbara, California: ABC-CLIO, 2002.

Hall, Verna "The Character and Influence of One Man." *The Christian History of the American Revolution*. San Francisco: 1999.

Higginbotham, Don. *George Washington Reconsidered*. Charlottesville: University Press of Virginia, 2001.

Hoppin, Charles Arthur. *The Washington Ancestry*, vol. 1. Greenfield, Ohio: published privately for Edward Lee McClain, 1932.

Irving, Washington. *George Washington: a Biography*. New York: Da Capo Press, 1994.

Jackson, Douglas. *The Founding Fathers—George Washington—A Biography in His Own Words*. Newsweek Books based on *The Papers of George Washington*.

Johnson, Paul. *George Washington*. New York: HarperCollins Publishers, 2005.

Jones, Robert F. *George Washington: Ordinary Man, Extraordinary Leader*. New York: Fordham University Press, 2002.

Kaminsky, John P. and McCaughan, Jill Adair. *A Great and Good Man*. Madison, Wisconsin: Madison House Publishers, Inc., 1989.

Leibiger, Stuart. *Founding Friendship and the Creation of the American Republic*. Charlottesville: University Press of Virginia, 1999.

Longmore, Paul K. *The Invention of George Washington*. Charlottesville: University Press of Virginia, 1999.

Marshall, Peter and David Manuel. *The Light and the Glory*. Grand Rapids, Michigan: Fleming Revell, 1977.

Maxwell, John C. *The 21 Indispensable Qualities of a Leader*. Thomas Nelson Publishers, 1999.

McCullough, David. *John Adams*. New York: Simon & Schuster, 2001.

McCullough, David. *1776*. New York: Simon & Schuster, 2005.

McCullough, David. *American History and America's Future*. Phoenix, Arizona: Hillsdale College National Leadership Seminar, February 15, 2005. Permission of Imprimus.

McPherson, James M. *To the Best of My Ability*. New York: Dorling Kindersley Publishing, Inc., 2000.

Mitnick, Barbara J., ed. *George Washington: American Symbol*. New York: Hudson Hills Press, Inc., 1999.

Nickerson, Hoffman. *The Turning Point of the Revolution*. Boston: 1928

Papers of George Washington, vols. 12 and 13. Charlottesville: University of Virginia Press.

Randall, Willard Sterne. *George Washington: a Life*. New York: Henry Holt & Co., 1997.

Reed, John Ford. *Valley Forge, Crucible of Victory*. Monmouth Beach, New Jersey: Philip Freneau Press, 1969.

Smith, Richard Norton. *Patriarch*. New York: Houghton Mifflin Co., 1993.

Swiggert, Howard. *Forgotten Leaders of the Revolution*. New York: 1955.

Thacher, James. *A Military Journal During the American Revolutionary War*. Boston: 1827.

Torricelli, Robert and Andrew Carroll, eds. *In Our Own Words*. New York: Kodansha America, Inc., 1999.

Trussell, John B. B., Jr. *Birthplace of an Army: A Study of the Valley Forge Encampment*. Harrisburg: Pennsylvania Historical and Museum Commission, 1998.

Twohig, Dorothy. *George Washington's Diaries*. Charlottesville: University Press of Virginia, 1999.

Wiencek, Henry. *An Imperfect God*. New York: Farrar, Straus and Giroux, Inc., 2003.

Weintraub, Stanley. *General Washington's Christmas Farewell*. New York: Penguin Group, Inc., 2004.

Wills, George. *Cincinnatus: George Washington and the Enlightenment*. Garden City, New York: Doubleday, 1984.

Wood, Gordon S. *The Creation of the American Republic*. Chapel Hill: University of North Carolina Press, 1998; originally published 1969.

JOURNALS

Bodle, Wayne. "Generals and Gentlemen." *Pennsylvania History*, vol. 62, no. 1.

Boller, Paul. "George Washington and Religious Liberty." *William & Mary Quarterly*, 3rd series, vol. 17, no 4 (Oct. 1960).

Hutson, James H. "Thomas Jefferson's Letter to the Danbury Baptists: A Controversy Rejoined." *William & Mary Quarterly*, 3rd series, vol. LVI, no. 4 (October, 1999).

Schwartz, Barry. "The Character of Washington: A Study in Republican Culture." *American Quarterly*, vol. 38, no. 2 (Summer 1986).

Spaulding, Oliver L. "The Military Studies of George Washington." *American Historical Review*, vol. 29, no. 4 (July 1924).

Wall, Charles C. "Notes on the Early History of Mount Vernon." *William & Mary Quarterly*, vol. 2 (1945).

WEB SITES

1. The Papers of George Washington, <www.gwpapers.virginia.edu/project>.

2. George Washington Papers at the Library of Congress, <www.memory.loc.gov/ammem/gwhtml>.

3. <www.ushistory.org/valleyforge>.

4. *The Federalist*, Biography of John Jay, <www.leftjustified>.

5. <www.nps.gov/gewa/Page 15 graves>.

6. <www.google.com/search/Bushrod+Washington>.

7. <www.sulgravemanor.org.uk/history/Washington>.

8. Thomas Jefferson Digital Archives at the University of Virginia Library.

About The Author

A. Ward Burian first developed his interest in George Washington as a student of history at Dartmouth College. His business career started at the Federal Reserve Bank of New York and several New York banks before partnering the creation of a money market and bond-trading firm in Wall Street and London. He then co-partnered and managed a residential real estate brokerage in Connecticut. Mr. Burian's love of history brought him to Williamsburg where he is an associate member of the Omohundro Institute of Early American History and Culture, a volunteer for the Colonial Williamsburg Foundation, a volunteer researcher for the Jamestown-Yorktown Foundation and an instructor at the Christopher Wren Association, which was founded by the College of William & Mary. He also lectures about the life of George Washington at civic, social and educational organizations. This is his first book.

Printed in the United States
71876LV00004B/37-42